Feminism
and
World
Religions

*Arvind Sharma and
Katherine K. Young, Editors*

State University of New York Press

Published by
State University of New York Press, Albany

For information, address State University of New York Press,
State University Plaza, Albany, N.Y., 12246

Production by E. Moore
Marketing by Nancy Farrell

Library of Congress Cataloging-in-Publication Data

Feminism and world religions / Arvind Sharma and Katherine K. Young, editors.
     p.   cm. — (McGill studies in the history of religions)
   Includes bibliographical references and index.
   ISBN 0-7914-4023-0 (hardcover : alk. paper).—ISBN 0-7914-4024-9
(pbk. : alk. paper)
     1. Women and religion. 2. Feminism—Religious aspects.
3. Religions.   I. Sharma, Arvind.   II. Young, Katherine K., 1944–
.   III. Series.
BL458.F455   1998
2913.1′783442—dc21
                                                        98-10509
                                                        CIP

10 9 8 7 6 5 4 3

For

Barbara DeConcini

First Woman Executive Director
of
The American Academy of Religion

Any woman who tells the truth about herself is a feminist.

—Alice Munro

I define feminism as the belief that all human be-ings, beginning with women but not ending there, deserve the power to make dignified choices.

—Irshad Manji

Contents

Preface   *ix*
Arvind Sharma

Introduction   *1*
Katherine K. Young

1. Brimming with *Bhakti,* Embodiments of *Shakti*:
Devotees, Deities, Performers, Reformers, and Other Women
of Power in the Hindu Tradition   *25*
Vasudha Narayanan

2. Strategies for a Feminist Revalorization of Buddhism   *78*
Rita M. Gross

3. Confucianism and Feminism   *110*
Terry Woo

4. Feminism and/in Taoism   *148*
Karen Laughlin and Eva Wong

5. Feminism in Judaism   *179*
Ellen M. Umansky

6. Feminism in World Christianity   *214*
Rosemary Radford Ruether

7. Feminism in Islam   *248*
Riffat Hassan

Postscript   *279*
Katherine K. Young

Notes on Contributors   *313*

Name Index   *317*

Terms Index   *325*

Subject Index   *328*

Preface

Religions promise salvation or liberation to all human beings. But for too long the indivisibility of men and women as human beings has also entailed the invisibility of women. The phenomenon is not new. The mystical tradition of India posed the following questions in medieval times:

> If by circumcision one becomes a Muslim,
> Then how does one identify a Muslim woman?
>
> If a Brahmin can be recognized by his sacred thread,
> Then how does one recognize a Brahmin woman?

Although the phenomenon is not new, the response to it in our times, in the form of feminism, is certainly unprecedented. Religions have long thought in terms of what is *right;* this new development has forced them to come to terms with issues of *rights,* especially those of women. In this context, however, religions ought to be studied before they are condemned: Who is to say if the key that unlocks the cage might not lie hidden inside the cage?

This book represents an attempt to find the key. It is also an attempt both to reflect the current debate on feminism and world religions and to carry it a little further, or if need be, even to another level. In its pages leading woman scholars of their religious traditions: Vasudha Narayanan (Hinduism); Rita Gross (Buddhism); Terry Woo (Confucianism); Eva Wong and Karen Laughlin (Taoism); Ellen Umansky (Judaism); Rosemary R. Ruether (Christianity) and Riffat Hassan (Islam)—explore their own traditions, with imagination and sensitivity, for their amenability or otherwise to the demands feminism places on them. They examine the anatomies of their traditions to see if there is room for a change of heart, as it were, unless, of course, it was in the right place to begin with.

It is our hope that we have succeeded, as editors, in producing a good book on a tough subject, and that it will be welcomed with as much enthusiasm as the millennium—which it heralds.

—Arvind Sharma

Introduction

Katherine K. Young

My co-editor, Arvind Sharma, once said that "power might have no gender but gender has power." My thoughts on the topic of feminism and world religions began with these cryptic words. I quickly moved on to the topic of how the perspectives of female insiders within world religions are changing the way we all think about power, gender, and religion.

This introduction[1] consists of the following four sections: (1) preliminaries; (2) intellectual trends; (3) feminist borrowings and critiques; and (4) insiders and outsiders. In the postscript of this book, I will offer my own analysis of insiders and outsiders.

Preliminaries

Before launching into the topic of feminism and world religions, some comments on the following are in order: (1) definitions; (2) the purpose of this book; and (3) the authors of this book.

Definitions

It is difficult to offer basic definitions for some well-known terms. The word feminism, for example, can refer to the women's movement in general or any one theoretical position in particular. And the term *world religions* can include all religions of the world or only those that have had a major impact on the world. Like any discussion, therefore, this one must begin with some working definitions.

1

The basic aim of *feminism* is to identify the problems of women as a class and to promote their interests as a class. Terry Woo writes in this book that it provides "the impetus to critique and improve the disadvantaged status of women relative to men within a particular cultural situation."[2]

Feminism originated in a nineteenth-century debate about whether women should be confined to the private realm of home and family or be welcomed into the public realm of business and politics. The term *feminism* itself was coined by Alexandre Dumas in 1872 to describe the emerging movement for women's rights, especially the vote, and equality with men. Feminism, in other words, is all about power relations between the sexes. In addition, it is about female bonding to serve women's political goals. According to Vasudha Narayanan, in this book, "the bondage of women was alchemized to the bonding between women which then led to their empowerment." Over time, this renegotiation of power in the public realm was extended to all spheres—educational, social, political, economic, professional, and, of course, religious. Modern feminism has political roots. This fact is made obvious in two slogans of the women's movement: "the personal is political" and "sisterhood is powerful." Feminism is understood by some as a reform movement and by others as a revolutionary movement leading to the creation of a new world order—not unlike the "classless society" of Marxism.

With their entrance into the public realm, women have attacked fixed gender roles and the division of labor by sex. They have argued for full participation in the community through equal access (or parallel structures), legal changes (such as better divorce laws), and economic changes (more jobs, for example, and equal pay for equal work). In religious circles, feminists call for women's inclusion in liturgical or theological language, education, leadership, ritual, and symbolism. Like other feminists, they argue that this has a therapeutic dimension for women: they become more balanced as individuals by defining their own goals, thinking positively about their own lives, and finding in their own experiences the resources for healing themselves, others, or even "the planet."

But *women's studies* is something quite different. Karen Laughlin and Eva Wong note in their chapter that this focus on women as a class is embedded not only in the feminist concept of "sisterhood" but also in the academic field "focused on women as a specific category of analysis, united by common experiences or perhaps just by the fact of having for so long been excluded from dominant culture." Accordingly, women's studies is about restoring women to both the historical record—whenever the necessary information is available—and current academic research. Feminism and women's studies together constitute the "women's movement."

According to a conventional but by no means definitive list, the *world religions* include Hinduism, Buddhism, Confucianism, Taoism, Judaism, Christianity, and Islam.[3]

The Purpose of This Book

Feminism has had, and continues to have, an impact on the world religions, because it has criticized them for perpetuating male hegemony over women, or "patriarchy." But it has found inspiration, too, in these religions—especially those with female, androgynous, or abstract descriptions of the supreme. This book examines the interaction of feminism and world religions.

The Authors of This Book

All the authors of this book are women. All are insiders, moreover, in both the academic world and that of the religious communities they discuss. For some, this means that they have easy access to certain kinds of information. Moreover, it means that they know what kinds of interpretation are likely to be accepted by other insiders. This potentially enables them to come up with informed and nuanced discussions. In addition, of course, it allows them to set the historical record straight. For others, being insiders gives them credibility as political activists. They use their academic knowledge and academic methods to challenge tradition, demanding reform or revolution in the name of women.

Not surprisingly, the authors do not always agree with each other. Some write from the perspective of feminism; they want to change the nature of their religions. Others write from the perspective of women's studies; they want to document the religious orientations of women in their traditions, whether historical or contemporary, and the influence of feminism on these traditions. Still others write from perspectives that are critical of Western feminism. It is worth noting that the essays in this book cannot be divided along lines of West versus East or white versus "color."

Vasudha Narayanan discusses the renegotiation of power in Hinduism. She observes that equality and rights are unfamiliar concepts in a religion that has traditionally supported a hierarchical social system based on birth and occupation. Even so, some women have overcome the rules governing gender, class, and caste. They might become courtesans, for example, or find some other public role. Narayanan refers to female saints as well as musicians and dancers (reminding us that the arts are optional salvific paths according to the Nāṭya Śāstra). After describing the great female reformers who fought against discrimination, especially in connection with widows, she notes that modern women are inspired by these historic figures but do not imitate the extreme aspects of their lives. New developments in Hinduism include the right of women to study and chant the Vedas or to become gurus. Gender, class, and caste restrictions have all been removed from many descriptions of the path toward liberation (*mokṣa*). Most women no longer observe menstrual taboos, moreover, and the medium of one goddess in Tamil Nadu insists that all devotees—both male and female—wear red at the shrine, because "the color of blood under the skin of all human beings is red."

Rita Gross presents a feminist analysis of key Buddhist doctrines and a feminist reading of Buddhist history. She argues that there has been a deep contradiction between the theory and practice of Buddhism. For her, the "essence" of Buddhism—egolessness, emptiness, and Buddha nature—is beyond ascribed gender differences not to mention innate sexual ones. But Buddhism, like other religions, has "one long dismal record of misogyny and sexism" from the eight special rules[4] to the current domination by men of Buddhist institutions. She explains these as "accretions" (from Hinduism, for instance, or Confucianism) to the "essence" of Buddhism. Buddhism needs only to be reformed, she argues, in order to provide women with better religious education, full ordination and economic support for nuns, and more female teachers as role models. Gross calls for some changes, however, that would radically transform the very nature of Buddhism: (1) eliminating the eight special rules; (2) establishing a new, "post-patriarchal androgynous vision" relying heavily on the Vajrayāna view of the *yab-yum* image, which symbolizes the complementarity of male and female; (3) developing a spiritual path that integrates body, sexuality, and emotion; (4) providing better models for serious lay practice; (5) offering women more time for spiritual seeking by encouraging them to have fewer children and to choose slow-track careers; (6) placing less emphasis on solitary withdrawal; (7) adopting a more this-worldly orientation (cooking, gardening, and caring for children in a meditative manner within a spiritual discipline); and (8) extending the concept of community to promote wholeness, balance, and peace to create an egoless or enlightened androgynous being.

Terry Woo examines feminism in relation to Sinology and Confucianism. What troubles her is the stereotypical treatment of Confucianism by Western women—both colonial (missionary) and postcolonial (socialist). As an exegete and historian, she makes her own, more sympathetic, assessment of Confucianism. She discusses authors, philosophers, reformers, rulers, poets, farmers, and businessmen. Her aim is to discover their presuppositions or prejudices, their family relationships, their reactions to women in power, and so forth. In the process, she pays particular attention to the contexts in which they lived: unrest; relative peace; female rule and its aftermath; Taoist and Buddhist power; liberalism; and the Confucian revival. The result is a reassessment of feminist stereotypes. Dismissing some feminist criticisms of Confucius, she notes that he was a pragmatist who had to cope with social and political chaos. (In addition, she tackles problems in Confucius's own relations with women: his lack of female disciples; his endorsement, as a chief magistrate, of sexual segregation; and his maintenance of a rigid division of labor based on sex.) Woo notes many examples of support for women by Confucians throughout Chinese history: calls for reform, preservation of a sphere of influence for women, and recognition of women as important power brokers. She concludes that Western feminist caricatures of the Confucian tradition have been extreme, not superficial.

Karen Laughlin and Eva Wong revise the history of China, in effect, by incorporating that of women in China. They cover several topics: the confinement of women to traditional roles; diversity among women despite this confinement; and the subversion of traditional Chinese gender roles by Taoism. They find inspiration not only in the inherent equality of Taoist goals but also in Taoism's recognition that early stages of the spiritual path must take into account both biological and cultural differences between men and women. Taoism makes accommodations not only for menstruation and osteoporosis, for instance, but also for the fact that women must break patterns of respect and hierarchy (whereas men must learn how to respect women and treat them as equals). Apart from these differences, the Taoist path is the same for men and women.

Ellen Umansky provides a description of the private-public demarcation in traditional Judaism. Women's "natural" religious function, she observes, is in the home and involves the following: maintaining dietary regulations (*kashrut*); following rabbinic laws on the scheduling of, and ritual purification for, sexual relations (*niddah*); preparing their homes for the Sabbath by cleaning, baking *challah* in the ritually prescribed way, cooking festive meals, lighting the candles; and performing all or most of these duties on holy days and festivals such as the New Year and Passover. By contrast, men study religious texts and participate more regularly in public worship. Umansky then surveys the changes that are being introduced by feminists. Orthodox Jews have gone only as far as allowing parallel structures such as women's prayer groups (and some Orthodox men, she writes, resent even these). Other denominations have encouraged more religious education for girls and women: teaching them Hebrew so that they can read from the Torah, for example, and Aramaic so that they can study the Talmud and other rabbinic works. They have included women in the *minyan* (the quorum of ten necessary to distinguish public from private worship) and given women the right to receive *aliyot* (opportunities for contact with the Torah: opening or closing the Holy Ark containing it, holding it up before the congregation, and chanting passages from it—or blessing it before and after someone else does the chanting). Women have been encouraged to wear *tallitot* (prayer shawls); *tefillin* (small boxes containing biblical texts and worn on the head and arm during weekday prayers); and *kippot* (small caps that, in modernizing congregations, are replacing hats). Under feminist influence, non-Orthodox communities have instituted a ceremony for the naming of female infants (to parallel the circumcision ceremony for boys, which welcomes them into the community) and a *bat mitzvah* (to parallel the *bar mitzvah* for boys, which welcomes them into the adult community); hired women as cantors; and ordained women as rabbis. Finally, feminists have pressed for reforms to the *halakhah* (Jewish law) allowing women to become witnesses in religious courts, for example, or to initiate divorces. Umansky reports that some Jewish feminists are demanding even more radical changes, ones that would "bypass denominations altogether": modifying the liturgy's masculine imagery for God and abandoning the concepts of chosenness, male-female complementarity, and hierarchy. She notes that Jewish feminists criticize hierarchy based on race, ethnicity, class, or sexual orientation and ask everyone to work with God as a convenantal partner in healing the world (*tikkun olam*).

Rosemary Ruether challenges the notion that Christian feminism is a white, middle-class, North American movement of the 1960s. She identifies the roots of Christian feminism in the long history of Christianity itself, beginning with the New Testament and including reform movements in the late Middle Ages, the Renaissance, the Reformation, and the modern period (including liberalism, socialism, French feminism, and American post-Christian and anti-Christian theology). A geographical survey makes it clear, moreover, that Christian feminism is by no means confined to North America. Describing herself as a "feminist liberation theologian," Ruether draws parallels between Christian feminism and other liberation movements. She and others "see women's liberation in the context of an interstructured system of oppression of race, class, gender, and sexual orientation, both within nations and across the lines of an international system of neocolonialism." Ruether refers often to the fact that Christian women in the Middle East, Africa, Asia, and Latin America fight in addition for national liberation and political or economic justice. Unlike Woo, Ruether does not bemoan the influence of Western missionaries on Asia. On the contrary, she acknowledges beneficial influences such as Western education and Western political thought. Due to "contextualization," Christian feminism is becoming more diverse. but an underlying unity remains for several reasons: the common religious heritage; similar experiences of patriarchy; and leaders drawn from the professional class.

Riffat Hassan writes that the Islamic tradition can become true to its scripture, the *Qur'ān*, only through reform. For her, everything apart from scripture has been corrupted by misogynistic and other accretions. Muslim women must develop the exegetical expertise needed to interpret Islam's primary sources. Only after acquiring this can they mount an effective attack on misrepresentations that have been endorsed by men: "[U]nless, or until, the theological foundations of the misogynistic and androcentric tendencies which have become incorporated in Muslim countries are demolished, Muslim women continue to be brutalized and discriminated against despite improvement in statistics relating to women's education, employment, social and political rights, and so on." To illustrate the kind of approach required, Hassan attacks theological assumptions that give rise to sexual inequality—the assumption that women should think of their husbands as god (called *majazi khuda*, god in earthly form), say, or the assumption of *ird* (the honor of women based on maintenance of chastity) and the related practice of female circumcision. She concludes that these assumptions have no basis whatever in the *Qur'ān*, which is egalitarian. Some, in fact, constitute *shirk* (the act of associating anyone with God, which is often associated with polytheism). They were imported from extra-Islamic sources: Jewish and Christian (especially accounts of creation and the Fall in Genesis), Hindu (thinking of husbands as divine), Arab (killing women who voluntarily or involuntarily lose their chastity), and other (such as female infanticide or sexual segregation).

Intellectual Trends

"Every religious tradition," observes N. Ross Reat, "by its very existence and regardless of its claims to universality, divides the world into two sets: insiders of the tradition and outsiders to the tradition."[5] Because this book is written by insiders for outsiders, it is useful to consider the intellectual trends that have informed the transition to an insider perspective. The following will be discussed: (1) Romanticism; (2) phenomenology; (3) ecumenism; (4) Marxism; (5) the "Frankfurt school"; (6) hermeneutics; (7) deconstruction; (8) postmodern psychoanalysis; and (9) postcolonialism.

Romanticism

It could be argued that Romanticism is not an "intellectual" trend at all, because it focuses on either the non-rational or the irrational. It glorifies feeling at the expense of thinking. Nevertheless, it was strongly promoted by those who thought of themselves as intellectuals. And the intellectual history of Europe—its art, poetry, philosophy, and so on—cannot be discussed without reference to this movement. Romanticism, observes Paul Nathanson,[6] is usually said to have originated in the late eighteenth century as a revolt against rationalism. Its ultimate origin, however, can be traced back to the late medieval period. This is clear from the history of art. Earlier, art was intended primarily to reinforce doctrine (although sometimes, especially at the turn of the millennium, art did so by evoking intense fear). But late medieval art, especially after the Black Death, focused very heavy attention on *emotional identification;* worshipers were expected to feel the intense pain of Jesus and—especially—the intense sorrow of Mary. Eventually, the whole notion of Christian love (*agape*) was transformed. (This had originally been understood as a self-sacrificial act of the will—which is why it could be commanded—and had little or nothing to do with emotion or sentiment.) It would be impossible to understand Romanticism apart from its roots in medieval emotionalism.

In any case, Romanticism has never disappeared; its struggle against the Enlightenment continues to this day. Not surprisingly, continues Nathanson, Romanticism has been a potent source of ideologies on both the right (nationalism, for example, or racism) and the left.[7] To some extent, ideologies on both the right and left have insisted on their foundation in science: "racial science," "dialectical materialism," and so on. Nevertheless, every secular ideology has appealed strongly and even primarily to the emotions associated with identity—whether based on class, race, nation, or sex. A focus on emotions, in turn, contributes to the transition to the "insider's perspective." Until recently, though, the political importance of emotion has seldom been explicit; more about that in due course. For a variety of reasons, at any rate, Romanticism is stronger now than ever before—and not only in popular culture but in academic culture as well.

Phenomenology

The phenomenology of religion originated in the general philosophical movement called "phenomenology." Phenomenologists extended Edmund Husserl's dictum "to the things" (*zu den Sachen*).[8] They now included religious beliefs, myths, rituals, spiritual disciplines, and so forth. Mircea Eliade and others added *epoché* and empathy as ways of decreasing bias among researchers. The former has fostered self-awareness of presuppositions. The latter has fostered positive feelings toward insiders. Phenomenologists have long recognized that phenomena come into view only through the consciousness of observers. (The importance of consciousness shifts focus from what is out there to what appears "inside" the person.) They have long recognized in addition that perfect objectivity is impossible: new information becomes available, new methods uncover previously hidden dimensions, new analyses reveal mistakes in earlier ones, and so on. But they have always hoped that *epoché* and empathy—along with careful linguistic, textual and historical studies—can do justice to insider perspectives.

Ecumenism

Though not always identified as an "intellectual" movement, ecumenism eventually became strongly associated with intellectual trends in religious studies. By the late nineteenth century, people were coming to believe that members of the world's religious communities should have greater contact with each other. The aim, of course, was greater understanding. This was the purpose of a conference held in Chicago in 1893; at this World's Parliament of Religions, representatives of the world's religions met to explain their traditions to others. Gradually Christians began to hope that they could heal some of the rifts that still divided their own communities. This led, in some cases, to the merging of two or more churches.[9] By the 1950s, Christian theologians were calling for religious tolerance and understanding. At first, ecumenism was confined to relations among the various Christian churches. (Later, it was extended to include other religions as well). One expression of this movement was the World Council of Churches. Even churches that did not join, however, were heavily influenced. The Roman Catholic Church, for example, made ecumenism a major topic of its second Vatican Council. The method used by ecumenists was called "dialogue." It was strongly supported by some academics, too. Among the most important was Wilfred Cantwell Smith. He wanted to shift the focus of religious studies from ideas to people (distinguishing between "tradition" and "faith" on that basis).[10] Just as the language of "seeing" has dominated phenomenology, the language of "hearing" has dominated dialogue. Although Smith did not use the word "voices," he might have heralded its ubiquitous use today: "[A]s it becomes more widely recognized that the comparative religionist speaks in the *hearing* of those he describes, this will inescapably have its effect at least on how things are put and perhaps also on the kind of thing said. The point is that an author must write not only more courteously but more responsibly."[11] Smith took an even more significant step by arguing that "no statement about a religion is valid unless it can be acknowledged by that religion's believers."[12] The effect of all this has been to augment the importance of insiders. The latter are more than informants; they are also interpreters and judges of scholarship in their own right. As a result, the focus of religious studies shifted from traditional canons to contemporary expressions.

Marxism

Karl Marx and his disciples tried to show that capitalism was promoted by the ruling class in a conspiracy to perpetuate its power and wealth at the expense of the poor and powerless. This realization would motivate the latter to revolt, taking up arms if necessary, against the former. Inherent in this view[13] are (1) dualism ("oppressors" versus "oppressed," or the "bourgeoisie" versus the "proletariate"); (2) essentialism (the shared characteristics of a class); (3) collectivism (promoting class interests by subordinating the individual to the group); (4) utopianism (belief in the possibility of creating paradise, or the "classless society"); (5) revolutionary struggle to bring about the desired goal (defined as the classless society characterized by utopian equality[14]); and (6) using "fronts," including cooperation with religious groups, to infiltrate bourgeois institutions.

The "Frankfurt School"

Like Marx himself, theorists of this school argued that knowledge was historically and socially determined by those in power, and that it was used directly or indirectly as "false consciousness" to oppress people. Like Marx, moreover, they argued that the solution to social problems lay within history, not beyond it in some abstract or sacred realm. But Marxists emphasized agitation in the streets, and the critical theorists emphasized "education." The purpose of education, they said, was to reveal the hidden conditions of oppression—embedded in institutions and whatever passed for common sense—in order to liberate oppressed groups and transform society as a whole. These critical theorists coined the term the "social construction of knowledge," which has by now become so prevalent that few people actually think about its origin, much less question its accuracy or usefulness.

Although critical theory drew heavily from Marxism, it shifted Marx's emphasis on economics to "right knowledge" and from activism in the workplace to activism in the universities. For Marx, the proletarians were outsiders to power. For the critical theorists, all marginal groups were outsiders to power. Marxists of both the old and new schools, though, saw their goal as destruction of an all-powerful, or "hegemonic," class so that outsiders could gain the power of insiders. In connection with religion, like anything else, one worldview would be undermined to pave the way for another. The latter has usually been associated with postmodernism (a worldview acknowledging no absolutes, no objective truth, no intellectual unity), deconstruction (a method used to expose "textual" inconsistencies, especially those known as "phallocentric" or "Eurocentric"), feminism (activism to improve the economic and social circumstances of women as a class), and new political alliances (women and minorities in the name of "diversity," "pluralism," or "multivocality").

Hermeneutics

Paul Ricoeur argues that modern people are incapable of believing in their canonical texts (scripture and all other sources of tradition). The decentered self, for Ricoeur, is the product of both human finitude (nature) and secularization (characteristic of this particular historical moment). The only hope is for a "decentered" self to rediscover the "sacred" in literature and the other arts. Understanding the variety of "texts," he says, is like "play."[15] He claims that entering the many "worlds" of literary or other "texts" is the best way of destroying the idea that anyone can live at the centre of the universe. Ricoeur argues that "texts" can either reflect "structures of domination"—which are revealed by what he calls the "hermeneutics of suspicion"—or respond to the "voice" of the other. In this way, he shifts attention to the insiders of other religions and the arts.

Deconstruction

No "text," claims Jacques Derrida, is ever completely explicit; each retains "traces" (gaps, conflicts, ruptures) that betray its "complicity" with metaphysics. Like Ricoeur, his teacher, Derrida uses the word *play* to describe how words interact with each other so that meaning is never fixed. Like Ricoeur, he argues that each has a "surplus" of meaning. And like Ricoeur, who coined the term "hermeneutics of suspicion," Derrida argues that "texts" should always be read with the aim of destroying "logocentrism:" the assumption that its words and ideas point to an external reality. All of history is thus reduced to a series of ephemeral, but politically useful, "discourses." Applying this to "texts" of the Western canon—from those of the pre-Socratics to those of Heidegger— and inverting their Eurocentric meanings, Derrida tries to undermine the foundation of Western philosophy. After its "deconstruction," he believes, other religions and cultures will be considered more relevant by Westerners. By adding to or changing the canon, greater value and authority can be ascribed to those who had formerly been outsiders.

Postmodern Psychoanalysis

Michel Foucault, the founder of postmodern psychoanalysis, tried to deconstruct heterosexuality in the interest of sexual minorities. In *The History of Sexuality*,[16] he attacked Freud's theory of repression for diminishing the importance of power. For Foucault, the origin of sexuality lay in ruling ideologies. Until the mid-eighteenth century in the West, according to him, this was found in legal and moral discussions that defined sexuality in terms of licit or illicit behavior. Later on—in medical, psychological, and educational discussions— sexual desire was discussed in terms of normal or abnormal desires. Homosexuality was no longer an illicit form of behavior, for example, but a psychological disposition. This shift, observes Foucault, paralleled a more general one from central (heterosexual) to peripheral (lesbian, gay, or bisexual) orientations. This has given rise to an interest in the latter: the ways in which they are presented, the perceptions of the body that they imply, and the kinds of conduct they condone.

Postcolonialism

Applied to nationalism by Edward Said, deconstruction takes the form of postcolonialism. In *Orientalism*,[17] he discusses the West's creation of the "Orient." As its antithesis, the latter is part of both the West's self-definition and its misunderstanding of foreign cultures. This way of thinking, argues Said, is used to legitimate the West's political domination of the East. It gives rise, in turn, to notions of superiority and inferiority. Unlike the West, for example, the East is said to be static and incapable of development. Orientalism gives rise, in addition, to the projection of a collective identity onto what would otherwise be seen as many individual cultures. Said reserves his harshest criticism for colonialism. A Palestinian himself, he is especially hostile to "Zionist" rule over the Palestinians. It is at least partly due to his influence that immigrants to Western countries have come to think of themselves not merely as outsiders but as insiders as well in the sense of being allies of feminists. Of greatest importance here, though, is that Said rejects the deconstructive belief that only "texts" or "discourses" are worth thinking about. Proclaiming that "'solidarity before criticism' means the end of criticism,"[18] Said argues that criticism produces not only knowledge but also a foundation for intellectual and social change. In this sense, he wants to combine deconstruction and critical theory.

Feminist Borrowings and Critiques

Feminism has been influenced by all of these intellectual trends. In more ways than one, it is the product of its historical context. But it has made one major contribution. Feminism has detected in the work of many male thinkers a lack of attention to gender. Even Derrida, who has been useful to so many feminists, has not fared well. With this in mind, I now revisit the following topics: (1) Romanticism; (2) phenomenology; (3) ecumenism; (4) Marxism; (5) the "Frankfurt school"; (6) hermeneutics; (7) deconstruction; (8) postmodern psychoanalysis; and (9) postcolonialism.

Romanticism

Like the early Romantics, some feminists explicitly glorify emotion (which they associate with femaleness) at the expense of reason (which they associate with maleness).[19] They seldom expose its logical conclusion, of course: that women are unequal to men when it comes to intelligence. They focus instead on the idea that men and women are unequal when it comes to *emotion;* women, they claim, have some unique affinity for "nurturing" (giving emotional care). Moreover, they promote the common belief that merely expressing emotion—including rage—is cathartic and thus therapeutic. This is a revival of the Romantic rebellion against reason—one that is dressed up, ironically, in academic language supposedly based on reason.

Phenomenology

Feminists and phenomenologists are interested in many of the same things. Among the most important is resisting the superimposition of "values" (for feminists, these would be patriarchal ones) onto "things." Instead they let these things reveal themselves. Both philosophical phenomenologists and feminists refer to the "social construction" of knowledge. Both scrutinize the conditions for their knowledge of the world. Similarly, both are interested in the experience of the body, the "gaze," intuition, perspective, and engagement.[20] Despite the overlap, few feminists derive their thinking on these matters directly from phenomenology; some of it comes indirectly through the existential phenomenology of Jean-Paul Sartre and Simone de Beauvoir. A more direct line of continuity can be traced, however, from the phenomenologists of religion to female historians of religions.[21] They use *epoché* and empathy to affirm the importance of the insider perspectives in the study of religion. They then extend these methods to the understanding of female believers and to all women.

Ecumenism

Smith's notion of dialogue has been taken a step further by some feminists. To the extent that they consider feminism a worldview analogous to religion, they call for dialogue between the two. In this book, Laughlin and Wong explicitly call one section of their chapter "the Dialogue of Taoism and Feminism." After restoring the history of women to that of Taoism, they argue that dialogue between Taoism and feminism must begin with the fact that the former's spiritual goal is available to both men and women. For dialogue to take place, moreover, both parties must be self-critical, meet on common ground, and be open to change as a way of overcoming problems. The latter might include attachment to notions of power or lack of power, for instance, or to alienation from radical feminist wrath experienced by both men and by housewives "who could not reconcile their own position as wives and mothers with what they saw as extreme feminist rhetoric."

Woo tries to facilitate dialogue between feminists and Confucians. She begins by recognizing the great gulf between them. "Feminism is concerned with autonomy, freedom, equality, and social revolution. Confucius, on the other hand, regards the sexes together and is concerned with order, harmony, peace, and stability. The paradox is this: feminism also wants peace and stability: and Confucius too was asking for a complete social revolution from the greed, disloyalty, licentiousness, and violence of his times. But from Confucius's point of view, freedom cannot bring a peaceful society. Instead, freedom, with its complementary idea of rights, forms the antithesis of the Confucian sense of duty. In this way, Confucianism and feminism speak past each other, conveying parallel ways." Woo tries to prepare for dialogue, however, by creating a level playing field. To do this, she deconstructs Western stereotypes of China. At one point, she projects a currently popular Chinese stereotype onto Western feminists; that way, the latter can experience what the Chinese have experienced. Woo suggests that the failure of feminism can be measured in terms of either family instability or lack of care for the young, the old, and the poor. But she admits that these criticisms can be taken too far; they sometimes assume a particular kind of family as the standard, value harmony above all else, and attribute social problems solely to feminism. In point of fact, she observes, many additional economic and political factors have contributed to these problems. By claiming that both feminists and Confucians inherit prejudices, and by acknowledging that criticisms on both sides have at least some truth, Woo hopes to bridge the cultural gulf between Western feminists and Confucians. If Confucians were to take their own tradition seriously—equality, learning, sincerity, loyalty, reciprocity—but also reject traditional patrilineality and authoritarianism, they would come closer to feminist thinking. That would still leave a profound gulf between the modern West (which emphasizes individual autonomy) and Confucianism (which emphasizes not only the family but the complementarity of men and women). This makes Woo gravitate toward those Western feminists who emphasize "relationality" and complementarity, presumably because they are analogous to the Chinese family tradition.

Marxism

Most forms of feminism have been heavily influenced by Marxism, directly or indirectly. Only the names have been changed. Feminists tend to think of men as the class of "oppressors" and of women as the "oppressed." Like Marxists, feminists have adopted the technique of "consciousness raising" to reveal the true nature of "oppression" (that is, "the patriarchy"): a "superstructure" of lies perpetuated by those in power (men). Despite the popularity of "diversity," most feminists find it hard to let go of the idea that all women have at least some characteristics in common. For some feminists, these are the givens of biology; for others, they are byproducts of "male-dominated" culture. Like Marxism, moreover, feminism often has a collectivist orientation. The term "women's collective," in fact, is common in feminist circles. More important is the feminist appropriation of the legal school known as "communitarianism." Its focus on group rights and powers has been used effectively in the campaign for women's rights and powers. Unlike Marxists, few feminists actually use the word *revolution*. Nevertheless, there is often much more to their use of the word *reform* than meets the eye. Like Marxists, in fact, they really do hope to bring in a new world order, a new age, a new paradise (often under the aegis of a great goddess). Their language is not always explicitly eschatological. Like that of Marxists, though, it is always implicitly eschatological.

Betty Friedan was not influenced by Marxism. If she was influenced by any movement at all, it was the Civil Rights movement. It did not take long, however, for the latter to be transformed by the Black Power movement. And, at the same time, feminism began to reconsider its liberal and middle-class origins. What followed was heavily influenced by the radical student movements, especially those involved in protest against the Vietnam War. And *these* movements really were heavily influenced by Marxism—not the crude Marxism of earlier generations, of course, but the sophisticated Marxism that had by then been filtered through the Frankfurt school of critical theory. Among their leaders were women who later became academics.

Other countries have been heavily influenced by Western socialism with its Marxist roots. These socialist movements working for social change have fostered alliances among various marginalized groups. Narayanan draws attention to a long-standing alliance in the modern period in India between male and female activists dedicated to women's rights and those dedicated to the elimination of caste and poverty. The manifesto of Mahila Samta Sainik Dal, a militant feminist organization of college students in the state of Maharashtra, points out that "we . . . along with Dalits and Adivasis . . . make up 70-80 percent of the people. . . . We are battling for equality with the men in the war for human liberation." Dalit women (once called "outcastes"), who are at the lower end of the economic ladder, themselves say that they have had to fight on three fronts: sex, caste, and poverty.

The "Frankfurt School"

By the 1960s, Herbert Marcuse, in the tradition of the "Frankfurt School," argued that socialist feminists would be the vanguard of this new order through their fight for equality and the transformation of the deeply dualistic "structures" of society itself. But some of these feminists have trouble with male critical theorists such as Max Horkheimer, Theodore Adorno, and Marcuse. Marsha Hewitt,[22] for example, thinks that Marcuse was content to see the feminine as nothing but a form of Hegel's antithesis. The revolutionary potential of Marcuse was lost, she argues, because he associated the traditional qualities of women with biology; he romanticized and reified "gender difference into hypostatized categories in which no historical woman could possibly recognize herself, nor find political solutions adequate to address her situation."[23] In any case, the Frankfurt school has had an influence on virtually all forms of feminism (as it has on many other intellectual movements).

Hermeneutics

Many feminists in religious circles are attracted to the hermeneutics of Ricoeur. They like his suggestion of weaving together the fragments of identity into a narrative of integration and wholeness—that is, positive self-images. And they have certainly made use of his emphasis on metaphor (although Jewish and Christian exegetes have been referring to metaphors and allegories since the very early Middle Ages) to deconstruct the literal meanings of scripture in order to make way for change.

Deconstruction

That brings me to deconstruction itself. Feminists often find Derrida very useful indeed (although they seldom follow his logic to its conclusion, which would deconstruct their own work) because he can be used to legitimate their attempts to undermine and displace "patriarchy." Almost all "texts" in the Western canon were written by men, after all, and presumably reflect only their interests. Once all that is out of the way, women can move toward the center (even though Derrida denies, at least in theory, that there is a center), which gives them access to power.

Derrida has influenced other trends in feminism. Drawing from both his work and those of psychoanalysts, French feminists—such as Hélène Cixous, Luce Irigaray, and Julia Kristeva—have questioned the language and symbolism in which female experience is described. They attack the dualism that they believe is embedded in Western thought. This is a prelude, of course, to their larger project of dismantling philosophical, social, and political hierarchies. Heavily influenced by Derrida, moreover, some minority scholars and feminists have teamed up to create "subaltern studies." The goal of this alliance is to examine problems common to all marginal groups (those who have been outsiders in terms of intellectual and political power).

Derrida has contributed to the feminist discussion of "diversity,"[24] too. This is partly due to his attack on Eurocentrism. It is partly due as well to his claim in *Spurs* that "there is no such thing as the essence of woman because woman averts, she is averted of herself. Out of the depths, endless and unfathomable, she engulfs and distorts all vestige of essentiality, of identity, of property."[25] For some feminists this should destroy any naive belief in the category of "woman" and encourage a shift of focus to the multiple realities of women. Morny Joy writes that many feminists are attracted to postmodernism because they find in its focus on diversity and marginality "a sympathetic affiliation with their own revolt against the monolithic impositions of male-dominated systems of knowledge and power. Just as deconstruction displaces traditional ideas of truth, identity and subjectivity, so, such feminists argue, do contemporary feminists strive to formulate a new way of ordering their descriptions of the self and of the world in ways that are multiple, interconnected and non-oppositional."[26] All of this provides support for a major tenet of feminism: that women must "name" reality for themselves and proclaim their own "voices."[27] It was not until the late 1980s, however, that diverging tendencies among feminists themselves became obvious to everyone.

Some feminists, for instance, insist that women are equal to men, and others insist that women are superior to men. Karen Laughlin and Eva Wong mention several "waves" of feminism to indicate historical developments, the many outlooks and methods, and the recognition of racial, cultural, and class differences that influence theory and practice. Woo, like many other feminists, prefer to use the word *feminisms* instead of *feminism.*

It is worth noting that these diverging tendencies have caused both tensions and alliances. As for tensions, it is almost as if the feminist notion of "naming your own reality" has made feminism itself a contested idea. Who belongs within feminism? What does it stand for? And what are its roots? For some Western women, the word *feminism* conveys a white, middle-class orientation. African-American women, notes Ruether, have historically been the slaves or servants of white women. They have had to struggle side by side with African-American men against racism, although sexism has by no means been confined to the white community. To make this clear, they have chosen to call themselves "womanists" (a term coined by Alice Walker) and "women of color," not feminists.

The tensions and divisions created by postmodernism have threatened to erode the "solidarity of sisterhood." Nevertheless, different opinions are often not lamented as illustrations of conflict. On the contrary, they are praised as illustrations of "diversity," "pluralism," or "multivocality." When some feminist idea is attacked and no counterattack seems possible, the problem is often acknowledged only in connection with this or that brand of feminism (that is, someone else's).

Postmodern Psychoanalysis

Foucault's school of thought has encouraged many feminists to move away from the assumption that heterosexuality should be the norm. This has laid the foundation for a political alliance between many feminists (heterosexuals and lesbians) and gay men. Umansky, for instance, writes that feminism will replace the "normative male voice" with "divergent voices." It will form a new community cutting across the boundaries of race, ethnic group, class, and sexual orientation, a community in which "difference is honored and . . . [all] are accorded equal dignity and sense of worth."

Postcolonialism

Said's influence on feminism has been to foster an extension of the attack on male hegemony to include colonial hegemony. Minority feminists in both the West and the East have found his analysis useful in their demand for greater recognition as insiders. Other minority women often follow the lead of African-American women. Woo, for instance, prefers the term "woman of color" to "feminist." Narayanan prefers the term "womanist;" she observes that, from the perspective of Indian women, the Western feminist orientation toward "autonomy" is less desirable than their own orientation toward socialism. Because feminism was founded in the West, it carries a specifically Western flavor. "Many Hindu women consider the term feminism . . . inadequate," she observes, and worse, "misleading in the Hindu and Indian contexts." Western feminists judge early and medieval India by the standards of eighteenth-century America, for example, in connection with the ideal of universal access to education. (Of course, feminist anachronisms can be found in the West as well).

Insiders and Outsiders

Arvind Sharma has explored the interaction between insiders and out-siders.[28] For him, the word *insider* means simply a member of a religious tra-dition as distinguished from one who is not. He suggests that there are four combinations. These are not merely logical categories, moreover, but chrono-logical developments. In this section, I will explore the emergence of women as full insiders in the sense of speaking publicly about their religions and lead-ing debates and dialogues about the past, present, and future of their religions. This will be done by examining Sharma's four categories: (1)insider to insider; (2) outsider to outsider; (3) outsider to insider; and (4) insider to outsider. To these categories, however, I will add (5) insider to both outsiders and insiders. I will show also how female scholars, including those in this book, have un-derstood all five categories.

Insider to Insider

Most religious exchanges in the premodern period were between insid-ers within particular religious communities (although there were also debates between sects and occasionally between religions as well). These exchanges were about scripture, doctrine, law, and so forth. The authors of this book point out, however, that women have in some ways not been insiders within their own religions; on the contrary, they have often been ignored.

Hassan, for instance, writes that "through the centuries of Muslim his-tory, these sources [*Qur'ān* and the *Hadīth*] have been interpreted only by Mus-lim men who have arrogated to themselves the task of defining the ontological, theological, sociological, and eschatological status of Muslim women . . . While it is encouraging to know that women such as Khadījah and Ā'ishah (wives of the prophet Muhammad) and Rābi'ah al-Basrī (the outstanding woman Sūfī) figure significantly in early Islam, the fact remains that until the present time, traditional Islamic cultures remain overwhelmingly patriarchal, inhibiting the growth of scholarship among women particularly in the realm of religious thought." She argues that this has contributed in no small measure to the fact that Muslim women are virtually unaware of their religious rights and have been subject to physical, mental, and emotional confinement (although they are told repeatedly by men that they have more rights in Islam than women have in other religions).

Similarly, Gross observes that the Buddhist record *as selected and inter-preted* by insiders (and outsiders) has more information about men than about women and ascribes more honor to male heros than to female ones. Tibetan teachers typically argue that men and women are equal in Buddhism but that women have special responsibilities as mothers. They explain existing discrepancies by saying that these are due either to foreign influences or to women's lack of practice.

Outsider to Outsider

During the colonial period, Westerners began to write about non-Western religions in the countries under their rule. Their expositions were intended for other Westerners back home. This approach continued even after the colonial period, because of the institutes they had established for cultural, linguistic, and religious studies.

Laughlin and Wong note that early Western scholarship on Taoism focused on male leaders or deities, overlooking mythological or historical references to women. In this context, they mention a recent book. According to its author, there are only a few female Taoist immortals (although in point of fact there are many). Gross observes that Western scholars of Buddhism have studied and written mainly about Buddhist men, who describe their own situations.

Anthropological theories have been flawed for the same reason. Much of the fieldwork has been done by men—partly because they were given no access to women—and has focused on their academic interests. On this inadequate basis, scholars have based their theories of human nature, culture, prehistory, hunters, gatherers, horticulturalists and so on. Because of the androcentric bias of early scholarship, it is often argued that only women can write adequately about women; only women, presumably, can know a woman's experience.

Outsider to Insider

The establishment of outsider-to outsider scholarship in Western universities meant that a growing number of foreign and immigrant students were introduced to their own religions through Western scholarship. Salman Rushdie's education in Islam at Oxford is a celebrated case. He studied history and wrote about the prophet Muhammad in one of his major papers. Unlike other Muslims, Rushdie had no formal religious education. Nor did he grow up in the heart of a community of Muslims. "In so far as he delved into the tradition, then, it was via orientalism. Having been raised in a fairly secular atmosphere, deciding that he could not truly believe in God, and then studying Islam from the perspective of Western scholars: this would obviously result in a non-traditional attitude towards religion."[29] When outsiders learn about their own religion through Western eyes, they face the danger of perpetuating colonial biases or other errors resulting from ignorance of local languages, oral traditions, customs, and conventional understandings. Because Western scholarship dominated academic discussions, however, foreign students and immigrants were not the only ones to receive a potentially biased view of non-Western traditions. So did the citizens of former colonies. They read foreign publications by Westerners, which continued to flood the market after independence. But Western *women,* too, have participated in this outsider-to-insider orientation. That is why female minority scholars in the field of religious studies often attack Western feminist criticisms of their religions. Many of the colonial missionaries, after all, were women—that is *outsiders.*

Gross writes that the study of women in Buddhism "has almost always focused on questions *about* women in Buddhism, assuming that the questioner is an outsider analyzing information about a closed system in which she does not participate and which will not be affected by her analysis." Similarly, Woo analyzes the "orientalist" approach by Western women (missionaries and socialists), which has led to stereotypes of Chinese culture in general and of Chinese women (and men) in particular. She charges that Protestant missionaries were pioneer feminists in China. They attributed the problems of Chinese women such as foot binding and female infanticide to Confucius. They perpetuated stories of women being sold into slavery or suffering bad marriages under the tyrannical rule of mothers-in-law. Woo attributes these stereotypes to the belief in Western progress and democracy, which was seen in contrast to China's traditionalism and despotism. "And so it was that the plight of Chinese women, with the help of Christian feminist critique, became an outstanding standard for Chinese inferiority." Woo acknowledges that some of the really gross generalizations gradually gave way to more sympathetic accounts based on comparisons of the Confucian Analects and Christian Gospels and the goal of modernization in China. Nevertheless, socialists inherited and perpetuated the old stereotypes. In fact, these stereotypes have continued in Western feminist literature, which has ignored the testimony of Chinese women themselves.

Insider to Outsider

Despite the fact that women were once not participants in the public realm of religion, they were still insiders. Now that they have become scholars of religions as well, they speak with new authority about the insider's view. Woo says that her own role as an insider, as both a woman and as a Chinese, is to use her scholarly skills to set the record straight. She writes that "after a hundred and fifty years of a relatively one-sided affair, and at this time when the issue of race or charge of racism is threatening the integrity of feminism, an appreciation of *jen* and a better understanding of the history of Confucianism might offer a sense of cultural recovery for Chinese feminists and a better understanding and inspiration for non-Chinese feminists. This essay and the several mentioned here mark, I hope, the beginning of this new stage of development toward a less racist feminism or feminisms."

Insider to both Outsiders and Insiders

Women use Western scholarship when they speak not only to outsiders, especially in the West, but also to insiders—sometimes women, sometimes men— of their own religions. One form that this takes is criticism of their own religions. This has necessitated a new category.

Hassan writes as an insider (a Muslim woman) to outsiders (whoever reads this book, which is published in the West), but she notes that her analysis should be read by insiders as well. Unlike Woo, she says nothing about "women of color" or racism, although she might on other occasions. Her immediate aim is not to address outsiders. It is to address other Muslim women. That is due to the plight of women in Islamic countries that have passed "anti-woman laws." Because emancipated women threaten traditional society, according to Hassan, they are associated with promiscuity, family disintegration, drug addiction, and every other perceived evil of Western societies. Attributing evil to educated and working women is a way of keeping them at home; denying women opportunities in the public realm keeps them subordinate to men. Because of perceived retrogressive trends, Hassan makes grand criticisms of Islamic society (and, unlike Woo, does not worry about complexities and ambiguities). She thinks that the plight of most Muslim women is extremely grave, and she is not embarrassed to say so. In fact, she admits quite bluntly that Muslim women need to develop a feminist theology like those created by Christian and Jewish women in the West. Though inspired by Western feminism, both in its radical critique of society and in its approach to problem-solving, Hassan uses her knowledge of Islam to separate the true faith from its corrupt accretions.

Gross, too, criticizes Buddhism from a feminist perspective. And she, too, worries about conservative reactions to the women's movement. In Thailand, she observes, the Buddhist establishment has not welcomed the restoration of full ordination for nuns (because that is based on the Mahāyāna tradition, which is alien to the Theravāda Buddhism of Thailand). These fully ordained nuns are not allowed, therefore, to wear brown monastic robes; instead, they wear white garments of women whose status is between that of lay people and monastics. Because women have usually been outsiders to the public world of political power, feminists not only criticize this state of affairs but also develop ways of changing it.

The perspectives of insiders, whether those of women or other minority groups, are finally being recognized at the end of the millennium. This transition has been a long time in the making and has drawn on the great intellectual movements of the past few centuries—from the first extensive contact with remote cultures under the aegis of colonialism to the homogenization of cultures in the "global village." Shifts of power on the microcosmic level are related to those of the macrocosmic. One result has been the intertwining of two great themes—power and diversity—at individual, group, national, and international levels. This book on feminism and world religions explores both. In this sense, it is different from the first one in this series, *Women and World Religions,*[30] which was written over a decade ago.

Notes

1. I have quoted freely from the manuscripts of my colleagues working on this book. Because I was working with drafts, I have not furnished footnotes.

2. Terry Woo quoting Karen Offen, 1988, 132.

3. This list follows that of Huston Smith in *The Religions of Man* (New York: Harper, 1958). For an analysis of the term "world religions" in historical perspective, see Katherine K. Young, "World Religions: A Category in the Making?" in *Religion in History/La religion dans l'histoire,* ed. Michel Despland and Gerard Vallée (Waterloo, Ont.: Wilfrid Laurier University Press, 1992) 111–130. Although it has been used in a wide variety of ways, three adjectives since the 1950s have modified it: "living," "major," and "great." I argue that better criteria would be: (1) origination after state formation and (2) continued existence. This list would include, but by no means exhaust, the religions found on Huston Smith's list.

4. These require that nuns honor monks (and not admonish even those who are junior in status); that they be taught by monks (and not teach themselves); that they hold their formal ceremonies and their communal confessions in the presence of monks, and so forth.

5. N. Ross Reat, "Insiders and Outsiders in the Study of Religious Traditions," *Journal of the American Academy of Religion,* 51.3 (1983): 459.

6. I thank my colleague Paul Nathanson for this discussion of Romanticism.

7. Romanticism itself, however, cannot be blamed entirely for the horrors of twentieth-century Europe. These ideologies have depended in addition on the Enlightenment belief that perfect knowledge can be discerned—albeit through reason rather than revelation. If so, then the perfect society can be built within history. From this, some people believe, it follows that those who refuse to cooperate in building utopia should be eliminated, persecuted, or at least marginalized. Those who inaugurated France's Reign of Terror had learned this particular lesson from the Enlightenment. And they were merely the first of many.

8. H. Spiegelberg, *The Phenomenological Movement: A Historical Introduction,* vol.1 (The Hague:Martinus Nijhoff, 1965).

9. The following is an example. The United Church of Canada was formed in 1925 after the merger of Canadian Methodists, Presbyterians, and (some) Congregationalists.

10. Wilfred Cantwell Smith, "Comparative Religion: Whither—and Why?" in *The History of Religions: Essays in Methodology,* eds. Mircea Eliade and Joseph M. Kitagawa (Chicago: The University of Chicago Press, 1959).

11. Smith 43 (emphasis added). I would add that there is no inherent reason why hearing is better suited to the interpretation of people than seeing.

12. Smith, 42.

13. For a detailed discussion of these six characteristics, see Paul Nathanson and Katherine K. Young, *Beyond the Fall of Man: From Feminist Ideology to Intersexual Dialogue* (forthcoming).

14. This new notion of equality was itself derived from the Judeo-Christian notion of the Messianic Age or the Kingdom of God.

15. Paul Ricoeur, *Hermeneutics and the Human Sciences: Essays on Language, Action and Interpretation* (Cambridge: Cambridge University Press, 1981) 117.

16. Michel Foucault, *The History of Sexuality,* 3 vols. trans. Robert Hurley (New York: Pantheon Books, 1978).

17. Edward Said, *Orientalism* (New York: Pantheon Books, 1978).

18. Quoted by John Kucich, in *Modern American Critics Since 1955* in the *Dictionary of Literary Biography,* vol. 67 (Gale Research co., 1988) 67.

19. See Nathanson and Young (forthcoming).

20. Katherine K. Young, "Phenomenology of Religion" in *The Interface Between Women's Studies and Methodology in the Study of Religion,* Arvind Sharma (forthcoming).

21. Rita M. Gross, *Feminism and Religion: An Introduction* (Boston: Beacon Press, 1966) 10–16.

22. Marsha Hewitt, "'The Negative Power of the Feminine:' Herbert Marcuse, Mary Daly and Gynocentric Feminism" in *Gender, Genre and Religion: Feminist Reflections,* ed. Morny Joy and Eva K. Neumaier-Dargyay (Waterloo, Ont.: Wilfrid Laurier University Press, 1955) 258.

23. Hewitt, 263.

24. Jacques Derrida, "Différance," *Margins of Philosophy* (Chicago: University of Chicago Press, 1982).

25. Jacques Derrida, *Spurs: Nietzsche's Styles,* trans. B. Harlow (Chicago: University of Chicago Press, 1979) 51.

26. Morny Joy, "And What If Truth Were a Woman?" in *Gender, Genre and Religion: Feminist Reflections,* ed. Morny Joy and Eva K Neumaier-Dargyay (Waterloo, Canada: Wilfrid Laurier University Press, 1995) 278.

27. See Denise Riley, *"Am I That Name?":Feminism and the Category of "Woman"* (Minneapolis: University of Minnesota Press, 1988).

28. Arvind Sharma. "The Insider and the Outsider in the Study of Religion," *Eastern Anthropologist* 38 (1985): 331–33.

Chapter 1

Brimming with *Bhakti,* Embodiments of *Shakti:* Devotees, Deities, Performers, Reformers, and Other Women of Power in the Hindu Tradition[1]

Vasudha Narayanan

Bhakti is devotion, *shakti* is power. In *bhakti* there is both surrender and mutual love, in *shakti* there is vigor and energy; in both, there is potency. Both *bhakti* and *shakti* are major components in female religiosity in the many Hindu traditions. Paradoxically, in some Hindu theologies surrender and devotion lead to power. Western feminism is engaged in negotiating issues of submission and power as it seeks to level the terrains of opportunity. In this paper we will see how the concepts play out in the Hindu tradition. I will begin with problematizing the concepts of feminism, Hinduism, and the notion of equality in a traditionally hierarchical society. This will be followed by a typology of women who through literature, architecture, performing arts, and other ways, realized their full potential. Some built temples, some celebrated their *bhakti,* others realized they were divine and filled with *shakti.* Many of them serve as role models, empowering women in some Hindu castes and traditions. The paper will conclude with a discussion on the nature and texture of these forms of empowerment.

It is a formidable task to trace the diverse kinds of feminism through more than thirty-five hundred years of the different traditions that go to form what we call Hinduism. Feminism, as we know it in the West, is a word that was coined in 1872 by Alexandre Dumas the younger, to describe the emerging movement for women's rights. In general, the term has been used to designate the movement through which women seek to obtain equality with men in the religious, social, political, professional, educational, economic, and other spheres. The labor-intensive struggles of women to get this equality and create equal opportunities, of course, go several centuries if not millennia before the coinage of this word. As a phenomenon, however, we tend to use the term *feminism* with the movement that began in the United States, especially the northeastern part when the bondage of women was alchemized to the bonding between women, which then led to their empowerment. Specifically, the 1830s has been identified as a decade when:

> There surfaced publicly . . . an argument between two seemingly contra-dictory visions of women's relation to society: the ideology of domestic-ity, which gave women a limited and sex specific role to play, primarily in the home; and feminism, which attempted to remove sex specific lim-its on women's opportunities and capacities.[2]

The concept of feminism, therefore, as a movement that was founded in the context of specific cultural and political milieux carries a special Western flavor about it, and generally refers to a movement that seeks absolute and com-plete equality as far as is humanly possible in any given situation, at any given time. The seeking of the notion of equality within the explicitly hierarchical Hindu tradition is problematic, and I will have reason to revisit this issue sev-eral times in the course of this essay.

One may also note that the language of "rights" is also alien to the Hindu discourse. A fundamental word that comes up in several texts is dharma. Dharma refers to righteousness and duty, the duty of men, women, members of different *varnas* or the large, loosely organized social groups. There are debts to be paid to one's (male) ancestors, the gods; duties to oneself and to society. A conversation on "rights" is less admissible in texts than one on righteousness.

The word *Hindu* is also complex and it academically and legally covers many communities that may not even accept that name. *Hindu* as initially used by the Muslim traders and settlers of the Indian subcontinent is a geographic term which is drawn from the name *Sindhu,* the traditional name given to the River Indus. Specifically, the term seemed to have been used for the non-Mus-lim residents of India and it occurs in legal and political contexts where there is a distinction to be drawn between "Mussalman" and "Hindu."[3] The Hindu tradition does not have a single founder or holy book, although many modern, politically motivated movements tend to provide a more monolithic picture than warranted. Legally, in India, the term includes Buddhism, Jainism, and the Sikh traditions. The Hindu Succession Act of 1956 says the act applies to:

(a) any person who is Hindu by religion in any of its forms or developments, including a Virashaiva, a Lingayat, or a follower of the Brahmo, Prarthana, or Arya Samaj;

(b) to any person who is a Buddhist, Jain, or Sikh by religion; and
(c) to any other person who is not a Muslim, Christian, Parsi, or Jew by reli-
    gion, unless it is proved that any such person would not have been governed
    by the Hindu law or by any custom or usage as part of the law in respect of
    any of the matters dealt with herein if this Act had not been passed.

While this statement does not quite define who a Hindu is, it does extend the
legal understanding of the tradition to other religions that are theologically distinct from Hinduism. It is also problematic in applying the term as a religious
category; several sects and movements such as the Virashaiva, Swaminarayan,
the Ramakrishna Mission, and the like, which we traditionally identify as
Hindu, have at different times gone to court to argue that they do not come under that label.[4] We encounter hundreds of castes and communities encompassed
by the word Hinduism, and within many of these traditions one can expect to
find inequalities based on subsects, economic class, gender, and age. It has been
clearly shown in studies on American society and history that gender is just one
of the many issues in socially constructed hierarchies. Notions of masculinity
and femininity are relational constructs, in flux, and dependent on race, economic status, religion, and other factors in any given historical period. Rather
than see fixed roles for men and women, hierarchies and status issues may be
seen as emerging through shifting power bases.[5] Studies exploring the complexities of the interrelationship between gender, religion, society, and state
within the many Hindu traditions are just beginning to emerge.[6] Gender, thus,
becomes only one of the many issues within hierarchical studies in India.

In many communities, we also hear of special-case scenarios where traditional hierarchies are *reversed* and the last become the first; but the hierarchies, while reversed, are not abolished. Thus, when many devotional poets
sang in praise of a deity (seventh to tenth centuries C.E. in south India and fifteenth to seventeenth centuries in north India), women and lower-caste saints
were frequently held to be in high esteem, and in some cases deemed to be superior to the male "high" caste poets. While these reversal of hierarchies were
prevalent—and we shall see some of then in this chapter—the concept of equality is relatively new in the subcontinent. For instance, while respect for all religions is urged by King Asoka as early as the third century B.C.E., it is in this
century that the notion of *equality* of religions *(sarva dharma samadbhava)* has
gained currency. Hierarchy is so emphasized within the culture that there is no
generic greeting between "equals" in Indian languages. One blesses, or seeks
blessing, and although one may argue that much of the worshipful connotation
is no longer associated with it, the standard Hindu greeting of *namaste* literally
means "I bow down before you."

It is in these contexts of caste, class, and age hierarchies that we have to
consider questions of gender. Power is also not based on gender alone; age,

familial or social position may be equally important. Equality is then connected with passage of time, rather than being available in every given circumstance. Thus while a new daughter-in-law may have a relatively low status in a family, when she becomes a mother-in-law she may wield considerable power. In addition to these factors, we must note that the task of tracing issues of feminism within the Hindu traditions is compounded by structural differences due to historical and political contexts, geographic and linguistic boundaries, and community distinctions. Thus, there are commonly held perceptions that in certain areas (Kerala and parts of Tamilnadu) the position of women has traditionally been very high, and in some cases the communities have been matrilineal for centuries. But there are differences even within these geographic areas, and a high-caste Nambudiri Brahmin woman from Kerala had far fewer rights and very little freedom in the past, whereas, in the Nair community from the same area, the lines of inheritance both for property and name were matrilineal[7].

It has generally been accepted that the so-called higher-caste woman had a far more repressed lifestyle than that of the lower castes. Perceptions of Hindu women have been based primarily on the Sanskrit literature produced by Brahmin men and the practices imposed on high-caste women, and this has led to the commonly held stereotype that Hindu women have had very little freedom. For example, based on these texts, and the practices of the so-called higher-castes, it was deemed necessary to pass a law allowing widow remarriage within Hinduism in 1856, when actually, many of the castes within Hinduism had always been practicing forms of divorce and widow remarriage. Talking of widowhood, Kishwar writes:

> The phenomenon of child widowhood and ban on widow remarriage was almost exclusively confined to certain upper castes and classes. . . . [The] 1901 Census observes: " . . . the higher their [the castes'] social position, the lower is the age of betrothal and marriage."[8]

It has been estimated that in 1931 only 13.9 percent of Hindu castes did not allow widow remarriage. However, these groups, however small their percentage in terms of overall population, served as reference groups for society and were considered worthy of emulation for socially upward bound castes, and their influence in matters of women's freedom and rights has been insidious.[9]

The statements made in this essay, therefore, have to be understood as depicting issues that concern Hindu communities at certain places and at certain times, and as having exceptions. These arguments and observations are not to be used as blanket generalizations. We should also remember that while this essay seeks to trace discussion issues in broad strokes, everyone of the situations can and ought to be fine-tuned and seen in its socio-historical and political perspectives.

Apart from the many qualifying remarks made above, one will notice even after a cursory study of modern India that it is men who seem to have taken the initiative to "free" women. This situation in itself seems, at least at first glance, to make the Indian scene different from that of the feminist movement in the West. In her excellent overview of Hindu women in the history of modern India,[10] Nancy Falk has shown that many of the catalyzing agents to either improve the status of women or to include them in socio-political and religious movements have been Indian men. She quotes as examples the many religious institutions where men have nominated women as leaders. The leaders of the Shankaracharya orders have initiated women as ascetics. Ramakrishna, a famous nineteenth-century religious mystic, authorized his wife to administer mantras. Lala Devraj, an early twentieth-century Arya Samaj leader, educated young girls to recite Vedic mantras and perform Vedic fire rituals, which had hitherto been the province of twice-born men. Religious leaders like Aurobindo, Sivananda, Yogananda, Upasani Baba, and Muktananda have appointed women to succeed them—all without lobbying from women's movements.[11] Others like Ram Mohun Roy and Keshub Chunder Sen have promoted the cause of women's education. In her thoughtful concluding remarks, Falk assesses this phenomenon:

> The promotion of women for leadership roles has been intricately linked to a broader range of male projects, many of which have had decided political overtones. Women have been commandeered to advance the nation, to preserve the nation, to free the nation, to reconstruct the nation.[12]

Falk argues that all this has been done by appealing to the "high appealing pitch" to women's special properties—by saying that they are more spiritual, modest, tolerant, moral, devotional than men. Critics see these appeals to "special" womanly traits as having a detrimental effect on women's interests. The strategy of appealing to women's special traits results in reinforcing "the very qualities in women—such as self-restraint, tolerance, and modesty, that prevent women from protesting policies and decisions that they may experience as harmful."[13] It fails to radicalize women and tends to contain women's protests to arenas where they are least inconvenient to men and their organizations.

While men have encouraged, indeed, as Falk says, "commandeered" women into many roles and in many causes in the last two centuries (which is the focus of her essay), women have also endeavored to create many opportunities for themselves and for later generations. These opportunities are seen in the aspirations for liberation from the cycle of life and death on the one hand, and creating a more equitable life in this world on the other. In both these contexts we will see the spirit of feminism and the focus of this paper will be on women who created such spaces.

The word *feminism* has its detractors even among well known women activists in India and many of them explicitly reject the term *feminism*. Madhu Kishwar, the editor of *Manushi* (a journal about women and society), in an article "Why I do not Call Myself a Feminist," rejects the term for a number of reasons. She argues that the particular socio-historic context in which the movement arose in the West is specific to that culture. Feminism is known primarily through stereotypes in India and these stereotypes may be an unnecessary burden, for people would then impose their own understanding of feminism on any issue. The term also has a paucity of meaning for the Indian circumstances and culture; the agendas may be different in the subcontinent than in the West.[14] In one example, Ms. Kishwar shows how women's shelters in India may not have the same importance as they do in Western countries, which have the career-training opportunities and economic infrastructure that India may lack. Further, she says, the history of the movement in India has had the support of men, politicians, and the media. She also argues that the labeling distorts the present and the past; she recalls being attacked by a group of feminists at Delhi University when she presented the poetry of Hindu women in a positive way. They contended that these women poets had substituted slavery to the husband with slavery to God, and were inadequate sources of inspiration for women because they could not be called feminists. Kishwar continues:

> Expecting Mirabai to be feminist is as inappropriate as calling Gautam Buddha a Gandhian or Jesus Christ a civil libertarian.
>
> This approach in evaluating our past *is as inappropriate as the one that looks for feminists everywhere at all times* [italics added]. We need to understand the aspirations and nature of women's stirrings and protests in different epochs in the context of the dilemmas of their age, rather than impose our own aspirations on the past.[15]

Kishwar's counsel is to be taken seriously. One has to recognize at the outset of this paper that many Hindu women consider the term *feminism* as inadequate, and worse, misleading in the Hindu and Indian contexts. One may, for starters, pass over the term *feminism* in favor of another borrowed term, *womanism*. The women's movement within India even has names that parallel these categories; the feminist agenda is frequently called *autonomous* and the agenda where economic class and social caste struggles are brought in is called mixed.[16] Thus, a Dalit (a name preferred by communities that Western academia labels "untouchable" or "outcaste") woman who is at the lower end of the economic ladder has to fight on three fronts: gender, caste, and poverty. Many women movements in India work in all these spheres continuously. The manifesto of Mahila Samta Sainik Dal, a militant feminist organization of college students in the state of Maharashtra, says:

> It seems that men make all the decisions about how women should behave, how they should live. . . . Behind the idea that women should sacrifice everything for men is only self-interest. . . . In struggles that go on for whatever reason, women become victims in the end. . . . This hypocritical society has made us worship the men who have made us slaves. The strange system exists that the slaves are given the job of protecting the slavery. . . . Because of this we have to fight against the thoughts of Manu which treat women and shudras as inferior, against chaturvarnya [the fourfold caste system] which sticks the label of Karma on everything, against god who put women among the untouchables, *and against the ideology of natural inequality.*
>
> We are 28 crores [280,000,000] of slaves and along with Dalits and Adivasis we make up 70–80 percent of the people. . . . Those who rebel against slavery, the Dalits who aim for freedom, the Adivasis and the toilers, are our brothers. We are battling for equality with the men in the war for human liberation.[17]

The cry for equality is perhaps most strikingly stated in this manifesto, which links the struggles of women with those of Dalit and Adivasi (the groups which go under the administrative label of "scheduled tribes" in India) men and women. The toiling of women and the feminist agenda is only the tip of the hierarchical iceberg in India.

The discrimination against women within India, and within the Hindu tradition, is seen in many domains. The basis for these acts of malicious prejudice can arguably be seen in cultural norms, received ideologies, and texts of religious law, even though the influence of the latter, as we shall soon see, was not necessarily deep or far-reaching. Thus while there is considerable inequality in say, issues of education, access to health care and the like, and these inequalities directly rise because of the Hindu culture preference (on the whole) for male children, it would be beyond the scope of this paper to talk of all the women who have struggled for equal rights in all these areas. In many cases it is hard to draw a line between the religious/cultural and what the West terms secular. The term *feminism* therefore is used with caution in this essay, and as referring to women's struggles and aspirations in creating meaningful spaces by overcoming biases that obtain from gender, class, and caste issues. I will look at women's struggles for creating and making available, either directly or indirectly, opportunities that will enable themselves and others to live and die with a sense of fulfillment, in the large and loose areas that come under the rubric of *religion.*

These opportunities lie both in the realms of *dharma* (duty and righteousness in this life) and *moksha* (liberation from the cycle of life and death). They range from removing the barriers in educating widows to enabling women in the pursuit of salvation through singing and dancing. I have had to make choices; for instance, I focus on women who struggled to educate widows, thus going against prevailing religio-cultural norms that marginalized these women, rather than discuss women who struggle to save forests for economic and ecological reasons. While the struggle of both sets of women at different places and times may be laudable, the first can be seen more directly and crudely as a product of a prevailing religio-cultural climate than the latter in the Indian subcontinent. There are some issues that I have not addressed in this essay; prominent among these would be women and religious nationalism in India[18] and women and the Hindu family law.[19] In the areas that I do focus on, while I refer to many examples briefly, I have chosen to discuss only one or two women in any detail. These choices have been made with an eye on the relevance and importance of that person, as well as the areas of my familiarity. Within these boundaries, I have tended to highlight women who for various historical and occasionally arbitrary factors have remained relatively unknown in the West. These women have served as powerful role models for generations, empowering women. Falk and Gross address the concept of power and empowerment, and note that power and equality are not the same thing. Recognizing the importance of role models, they write, "When women have powerful or provocative myth-models with which they can identify, or when women *are* exemplary sacred sources, they feel powerful and they are powerful."[20]

Hindu women have both been empowered and subjugated by religious tradition over the centuries. The brahmanical Hindu tradition has been marked by its hegemonical sanctions against women and the so-called lower castes. And yet it may be argued that the Hindu tradition has continuously provided opportunities for women to do many things, and that the curtailment that they faced were paralleled by lack of similar opportunities for men. Thus men did not have the *option* to stay at home and nurture the young, men of certain castes did not have the option to pursue whatever careers they wanted. The opportunities for men and women were curtailed by their class, community, and caste. Women were not singled out for various forms of discrimination. In defense of this argument, one may even say that the concept of universal access to education by men and women of all classes is a seventeenth, indeed eighteenth-century ideal that arose in America, and therefore one cannot project this and other similar models on early or medieval India. This argument uses familiar rhetoric that it was not just women, but everyone (with the exception of the brahmin males) who lived with a curtailed sense of freedom.

In these arguments, we can go a step further and hear repeated references to certain women who were stars in the early Hindu tradition: there were women poets in the Vedas (few when compared to male poets, but nevertheless some), women poets in practically every century in different parts of India, women philosophers such as Gargi around the sixth century B.C.E. (who then becomes the token woman philosopher for ages), women patrons of temples; and so on. This line of reasoning implies that if women did not do something it was because they had no desire to do so. The opportunities existed and continue to exist. This argument would lead one to say that feminism as a movement is not necessary, just as the Equal Rights Amendment in the United Sates was deemed not to be necessary under a constitution that promises equality to all citizens. Variations of these arguments and apologia frequently come up in political speeches, temple discourses in the diaspora, and through parochial writings.

On the other extreme, there are voices that speak now for the millennia of oppression that women have undergone and are still undergoing. These voices range from those of Christian missionaries in the nineteenth century to dynamic magazines like *Manushi* in the last quarter of the twentieth century. Missionaries like Amy Carmichael (1867–1951) drew attention to the plight of young girls dedicated to the temple and left to a life of prostitution, and also denounced child marriages, whether to gods or men as an infamous custom.[21] *Manushi* educates women on various issues (inheritance, marriage laws) as they pertain to them and had an excellent feature on women poets, but many if not most of the articles alert the readers to the crimes and discriminatory political practices against women that have existed in the past and continue to thrive today. Many popular publications including magazine articles and books like Elisabeth Bumiller's *May You be the Mother of a Hundred Sons* point to the prevalence of female infanticide in some villages in India, amniocentesis which led to the aborting of female fetuses, and dowry deaths where newly married women are burnt because they did not bring in enough money from their natal homes. A feminist's work is cut out, it is said, and this is not in the luxury of seeking ordination as a minister or contemplating the sex of God, but in saving human lives from the tyranny of Hindu culture.

All these arguments provide bits of the complex patterns of the Hindu mosaic and I have to note that all these phenomena have been encompassed within Hindu traditions at various times and places. There have been women who were devotee-poets like Andal who *chose* to reject an earthly marriage, there have been queens like Sembiyan Mahadevi (tenth-century south Indian Chola queen) who made well considered decisions to endow money to and built enormous temple complexes. There have been women scholars and philosophers, but there have also been hundreds of thousands of women who were culturally trained to suffer in silence when alive and occasionally to dutifully accompany their husbands in death. One may draw an analogy (although it

would have many limitations, and some qualifications) and point out that
though Great Britain had powerful monarchs like Queen Elizabeth I, common
women in that country had limited rights to inheritance and certainly did not
get a chance to participate in the political process until this century. While historically we can count many powerful women in the Hindu tradition, it is
equally true that women in some Hindu communities have been and are treated
as commodities and that dowry deaths do take place. While acknowledging
these facts, and recognizing that burning brides who are said not to bring in
enough dowry are crimes committed only against women, we must also note
that the perpetuators of these crimes in many if not almost all cases are also
women. In almost all cases, the mother-in-law and sister-in-law of the newly
married woman are the instigators of the crime. While these are crimes against
only women, they are crimes of greed as are many other heinous crimes.

The path of this paper is to steer through these mazeways, pausing at
some moments of time and at some events to identify selectively, and by no
means exhaustively, those women who have worked and struggled to create opportunities for themselves, and sometimes for other women in the elastic realm
of religion. These women of strength are not always radical; they frequently
work within the softer parameters of the tradition to push the boundaries and
live a life of fulfillment. Some sought salvation, others worked for social reforms, creating opportunities for young widows who were abused in the name
of culture. This paper offers an initial typology of these women who questioned
the logic of patriarchal society, or who, without as much as questioning it, simply went on to do what they wanted to. These women would not recognize either the concept of feminism or worry about larger issues of equality, but
nevertheless made breakthroughs whether they explicitly intended to or not.

There are a few issues peculiar to the understanding of women's struggles within the Hindu tradition that are unique to this religion. I note these at
the outset to make clear why certain fields are included in the parameters of religious reform and protest. The first is the issue, or more properly, *the nonissue,
of sacred text.* While almost all Western books on the Hindu tradition speak extensively about the Vedas and scripture, and many scholars point out quite correctly that women are accorded a fairly low status in the Hindu texts that deal
with law and ethics (*dharma shastra*), what is not usually mentioned is that
these texts were not well known and utilized in many parts of Hindu India.
While some sections of the population, possibly some among the Brahmins
(who today form about three percent of the society) and a few other communities may have had nodding acquaintance with the *shastra,* but *custom and practice* were far more important than the dictates of these legal texts. There were
many legal texts and they were not in competition with each other; they were
written at different times in different parts of the country, but all of them were
superseded by local custom.[22]

To put it simply, it was the British who wanted to "create" a coherent set of legal tools for India, and therefore employed *male Brahmins* to translate what they believed to be important scriptures; through this process some texts began to receive the notoriety that they enjoy now. The laws of Manu (*Manu Smriti* or *Mānava Dharma Śāstra*) are a case in point; this text, while important in its own way, was but *one* of many legal texts, but received undue importance after this time. Even Ram Mohun Roy who fought against *sati* had to argue for the preeminence of *Manu Smriti*.[23] Texts like the *Nārada Smriti* which were liberal in their attitude toward women, did not make it to stardom.[24]

What the British did not know or care about when they promoted some texts (on the basis of their Brahmin consultants) was that the prescriptions in these *shastras* were not known or followed in many parts of India. Thus, while the *Manu Smriti* said that the *sudras* were the lowest category of social classes and that they should not own anything (and this was accepted by generations of scholars), many of the castes that came under the *sudra* umbrella in south India were wealthy and influential landowning communities.[25] While the Hindu tradition has used hyperbole in declaring the religious-legal texts to be an exposition of the Vedas, it did not mean that they actually *followed* all the rules. There is a sense of dissonance between scripture and practice in certain areas of dharma and the role of women and *sudras* sometimes falls in this category. Manu may have denied independence to women, but there were women of some castes and some economic classes who endowed money to temples in their own names and had these deeds inscribed on stone. It is important to note that there is no direct correlation that one can generalize on between these texts and women's status, rights, or behavior. I stress this fact because the spheres where women struggled to get opportunities in this century were not those from which they were traditionally barred or prohibited because of scriptural injunctions, but because of prevailing custom or practice that may have come into effect with the ripening of certain dominant ideologies at any given time. When women seek equality in religious realms within Hinduism, they do not always speak against these terrible texts; frequently they just ignore them, quote other texts which nullify the first or work in areas that are more meaningful in combating negative ideologies than texts.

While it is important to stress that law books may not have been considered to be law in many places, nevertheless, the pictures of the ideal, chaste woman, obedient to her husband, which came through the androcentric literature of the stories and legends found in the Hindu epics, the Ramayana and the Mahabharata, became part of the dominating ideology in the upper castes of society. These images, which until recently governed populist movies and mass media, included those of Sita who followed her husband to the forest and who in most of the epic, despite her husband's questioning of her fidelity, epitomized the complaisant wife. There were also other models like Sukanya who served her husband like God. Savitri saved her husband from death, and the story began to imply that if women were chaste and pure, their husbands would not die. In the process of such selfless service, these women also attained power to work miracles. Those women who were human beings (although many like Sita were considered to be divine) also received salvation. Many historical women reject the ideology that promotes the notion that service to and worship of the husband is the path to salvation that is open to women. They sought avenues that paralleled the ways in which men sought liberation from the cycle of life and death. Other women, at the beginning of the twentieth century, have questioned the logic of the ill treatment meted out to widows of the higher castes and have worked for their rights, or fought for the choice of singing and dancing in public.

The opportunities that some women created for themselves in the Hindu tradition also straddled domains which are not traditionally considered to be *religion* in Western cultures. For example, acting, music, and dance are considered to be some of the optional ways to salvation within Hinduism. The treatise on dance, the *Nāṭya Śāstra,* written by a legendary person called Bharata is considered to be Veda or scripture and dancing expressed the deepest longings of the soul for the deity. But for several centuries—until the mid-twentieth century—only men and courtesans performed in public. Although music and dance were theoretically considered to be sacred, the beauty of the music and the bodily movements were associated with physical sensuality and the performance of courtesans. It was considered inappropriate for women from "decent" families and the so-called higher castes to perform in public. It is in this century that some women have opened up these fields to all who choose to perform in public. Because of the close connection of performing arts and religion within the Hindu tradition, I have chosen to include the contribution of women who were instrumental in making them available to all people. The inclusion of the fields of music and dance underscore more than creating the opportunity for the entry of women into the realm of arts; it acknowledges the efforts of women who made it possible for others to *publicly* express their devotion and spiritual longing in ways that were not available to them earlier.

I will begin with a typology of women who have struggled to open doors for themselves, and in some cases, open doors and create meaningful opportunities for other women. I have included the former, even though the term *feminist* may be inappropriate and indeed incongruent with their aspirations and achievements. Nevertheless, their contributions have been immense in religious literature and music, and in the creation of religious institutions, their benefactions have been far too important to ignore. In this category would come the religious poets and patrons of temples in the medieval centuries. Despite their not actively working for other women's social rights, they were active seekers of religious liberation and actively raised religious consciousness in male dominated spheres.

A Typology of Women who Created Opportunities for Themselves and Others in Religious Domains

Devotional (bhakti) Poets and the Appropriation of their Devotion by Women in the Twentieth Century

A few women poets are named as authors of some of the hymns in the Vedas, the earliest scriptures of the Hindu tradition. Ghosha, Apala, and Lopamudra are some of these named women, but their social and religious impact remains unclear. Their voices, although clearly feminine (they seek husbands), do not carry any noticeable agenda. Ironically enough, although there were women who composed these Vedic hymns, by the time of the *dharma shastras* in the beginning of the first millennium C.E., women were equated with *śūdras* and it was considered reprehensible for them to even *listen* to the recitation of the Vedas. While these brahminical texts held that it was the recitation and study of the Vedas that led to salvation, the point was rendered moot with the emerging importance of two other factors in the Hindu tradition. The first was the advent of texts like the *Bhagavad Gita,* which said that through devotion, everyone was eligible for salvation. The second significant point I have to note is that by the end of the first millennium C.E. several local and vernacular texts competed for attention, with the claim made by devotees that these texts were the equivalent of the Sanskrit Veda. Texts like these, which include the poems of the woman devotee Andal, could be studied by everyone who desired to do so. The recitation of these texts was said to have salvific value. We also occasionally hear of women who did in fact study the Sanskrit Veda—the philosopher Mandana Misra's wife is said to have acted as a referee in a debate on Vedanta—and it seems clear that the proscription of women studying the Vedas was never quite taken seriously.

It was perhaps the rise of the devotional poems that firmly reinforced the accessibility of salvation to all human beings. Caste and gender inequalities were not abolished, in the devotional (*bhakti*) structures, but reversed. Devotees who composed and sang with passion were considered by some sections of the Hindu tradition (including by the so called "higher-caste" men) to be superior to those without this burning ardor. These devotees sought a spiritual experience and communion with God and did not comment much on the social scene. Should we then consider them as women who struggled for other women's rights? Madhu Kishwar, the editor of *Manushi* who dedicated the special tenth anniversary issue to women bhakta poets, says in her introduction:

> The *bhaktas'* poetry is not protest literature as the term is understood today. Nor does it carry an easily decipherable social message for other women. . . . Most of it is celebration of an individual choice. Nor does it

contain a call for an overall gender equality. To say this is not to view it as somehow inadequate. The idea of gender equality as a desirable and obtainable social and political ideal is a relatively new idea in human history, although in some societies it was occasionally envisaged much earlier in utopian writings. To look for its expression in contemporary terms by these women would be to do both the past and the present an injustice.[26]

Kishwar continues that to move Hindu/Indian society toward justice and freedom, one needs to understand the past, and the potentially liberating aspects of cultural traditions. The edition of *Manushi* that focuses on women poets is offered by way of education, to raise people's consciousness of their historical legacy.

Women poets of the *bhakti* movement that began in south India in the seventh century and spread through the rest of the country in the next millennium are revered by many communities within the Hindu tradition and worshipped in temples and homes. Their songs have been learned by heart and sung through the centuries. However, while many are known locally, there is not much pan-Indian awareness of all of them. I believe that they have to be highlighted because some of them have emerged in the twentieth century as role models, empowering women to seek and speak of a spiritual life.

Many of these women poets refused to get married. Andal-Goda, an eighth-century poet, forcefully sang:

> Sacred foods which are offerings to the sky-gods,
>   given by those skilled in the Vedas,
> become defiled when eaten by a fox
>   that strays from the forests
>   into the sacrificial ground.
> So too my soft breasts meant as offerings to the Lord
> will be violated even if you just *say*
> they are for the enjoyment of human beings.
> O god of love, just watch, I shall die.
>   —*Nācciyār Tirumoli* 1.5

South Indian women poets like Andal-Goda (8th cent.), Karaikkal Ammaiyar (7th cent.), and Akka Mahadevi (12th cent.) did not lead the ideal married life prescribed by the codes of law. Andal did not want to get married and consider her husband a God; she wanted God as her husband. Through her words and actions, Andal presents an alternative lifestyle to what Manu, the first-century lawgiver, perceived to be the role of women. She showed contempt at the idea of marrying a human being and instead gathered her friends and observed rites (*vratas*) to obtain the Lord, whom she saw as Vishnu.

Andal's songs are recited daily in domestic and temple liturgies of all Sri Vaishnavas. Andal's presence is powerfully felt in the community through her words and images; we see them in the many temples of Lord Vishnu and the Goddess Lakshmi not only in south India, but in temples in Atlanta, Malibu, Chicago, Pittsburgh. Obviously, Andal was not rejected by society; rather she and women like Mira (who was devoted to Krishna), and Karaikkal Ammaiyar, Akka Mahadevi, and Lalla (who expressed their love for Lord Shiva), are venerated by the traditions that appropriated them and regarded them as saints. Although this veneration is admirable, we shall soon see the ways in which later male biographers recast the character of women poets such that it did not *immediately* empower women in the social realm.

Most of the women poets—and several male poets as well—consider either the gods Shiva or Vishnu as their beloved one and seek a union with him. This union is spoken of in terms of a wedding or sometimes as an overwhelming mystical experience. What is interesting is that many male poets (contemporary with the women saints) also assume the persona of a woman, usually a girl in love, and seek union with God. While the female voice is one of many options that male poets adopt, a woman poet generally speaks in her own voice. However, this may not be as important as it may seem at first glance, because through both male and female voices several models of relationships are constructed between the subordinate human being and the powerful God. One may ask if these women—and men poets—were simply substituting one male authority figure for another. Certainly it is obvious that the overt framework of the poems is patriarchal, with the supreme Lord being the person with whom the poets seek a union. The symbolic structure of the poems suggests that that supreme one, the Lord, is the beloved and the husband. While this is true, several other factors have to be taken into account. The Lord is sought not only as a husband, but as an errant lover (who is scolded, berated, and teased and not just treated with formal respect), and at other times referred to as a father and as the mother. Nammalvar, a ninth-century male poet, portrays himself as a woman in love with Vishnu in about one-fourth of his poems, but he also calls the supreme Lord as "the mother who gave birth to me." Sometimes, the poet identifies himself as the mother of the incarnate deity and sings poems about the mischievous child. Even when the Lord is seen as a child, his superiority is not questioned. This supreme being is seen and addressed as male, as female, as beyond gender ("He is not a man, not a woman, not neither"—*Tiruvāymoli* of Nammalvar, 2.10.10). No relationship excludes others and the very unique nature of the divine-human relationship is such that no model of an earthly relationship completely describes it or exhausts it.

While there are devotional poems to the many goddesses of the Hindu tradition, we do not have available any works, interestingly enough, of the better known women poets. Male poets have shown their devotion to Minakshi (a form of Parvati in the city of Madurai) and have addressed her as a child, a mother, as the most supreme being, and other male lyricists/composers (Sanskrit: *vaggeyakara*) like Muthuswami Dikshitar have composed hundreds of hymns to several goddesses. In the nineteenth and twentieth centuries, many women have composed songs to gods and goddesses, but many of these women are not well known outside the regions where they lived.

Some women poets like Akka Mahadevi and Mira were married to human men but chose to honor their love for God over their love for their husbands.[27] A clear preference is shown for the lifestyle of piety that they desired and the domestic bonds forged. Akka Mahadevi bonds with the community of saints who worship Shiva and according to biographical tradition eventually reaches union with Shiva. In this realm of devotion, while the power of hierarchy is still felt, the brahmanical modes dictated by *dharma shastra* and epics and perpetuated by received ideology are undermined, and the criteria for hierarchy are changed. Male and female devotees seek to serve other devotees. What has changed is the brahminical and patriarchal authority of the sphere of *dharma* or earthly duty. Traditional hierarchies based on caste, age, and gender are now changed in the pursuit of *moksha* (liberation from the cycle of life and death) through devotion; devotees, notwithstanding caste or sex, are seen as higher souls. Even the traditional cultural norms regarding a woman's chastity do not seem to hold in the realm of devotion and liberation. An archetypal story that is found in traditional lore in the states of Tamilnadu and Gujarat focuses on a woman devotee who has no money to entertain visiting devotees. She therefore makes a bargain with the rich man in the village that she will sell her body to him in return for cash and merchandise to entertain her guests. When her husband returns, she informs him of her arrangement, and he accepts it.[28] Actions by women in the path of devotion—even if these actions include infidelity to the husband—have a different value in the *bhakti* tradition.

More common is to see women poets who abandon all sense of social "shame," jeopardize social approbation (Mira was called *bawari* or mad frequently) and aspire only to reach the Lord. Janabai's (1298–1350) poems are typical of this genre:

> Let me not be sad because I am born a woman
> In this world; many saints suffer this way. . . .
>
> Cast off all shame,
> and sell yourself
> in the market place

> then alone
> can you hope
> to reach the Lord. . . .
> The pallav of my sari
> falls away (A scandal!);
> yet will I enter
> the crowded marketplace
> without a thought.
> Jani says My Lord,
> I have become a slut
> to reach Your home.[29]

Male and female poets are at times mad with the love of God; but the actions of other devotees, while seeming to fly against the face of dharma, are really to be judged from the viewpoint of salvation.

What is the impact of these women poets on contemporary and later society? In this paper, I will look at some length on how Andal has been appropriated by some women today, and briefly talk of how Mate Mahadevi, a late twentieth-century woman ascetic, models herself after the paradigm of the twelfth-century woman poet Akka Mahadevi. While women poets were venerated (by male and female devotees), male "high"-caste biographers tended to isolate their cases and divinize them, thus emptying their lives of social value. By casting the women poets in divine roles, biographers removed them from their social role models and presented them as devotees who are spiritual models for *all* human beings. It would be impossible to generalize, but we can look at one case—that of Andal—to see the possibilities that have unfolded within the Hindu tradition. Andal is principally venerated by a community that worships Vishnu and Lakshmi (Sri Vaishnava) in south India. Every Sri Vaishnava bride is dressed like Andal and during wedding rituals, a particular set of songs in which Andal describes her dream in which she gets married to Lord Vishnu is recited. In one sense, the human bride is likened to Andal; but the theological explanation is that *all* human beings—the bride, the bridegroom, and the guests—ought to be like Andal, all devotees of the Lord. While this theme of Andal as a paradigmatic devotee is unquestioned, it seems to me that Sri Vaishnava community subscribes only to selective imitation of certain features of Andal's life. What is important to note here is that the community has avoided the issue of making Andal a social or *dharmic* role model, and has instead opted to make her a *theological model* or a model of one who seeks *moksha*; she then becomes a model for all human beings. Thus, the Sri Vaishnava community, does *not* encourage young girls to *socially* imitate Andal's life; that is, girls are not encouraged to be unmarried and dedicate their lives to the Lord. Andal's rejection of marriage and her subsequent union with the Lord is seen as a unique event and as suitable only for her.

This isolation of Andal's position is done by divinizing her character and by making her *more than human* in some ways, thus coopting her social role. She is portrayed in later literature as an incarnation of the Earth-Goddess, who sought a human life to experience an intimate and *physical* relationship with the Lord.[30] Local legends explain that as the consort-Goddess, Earth is constrained in her behavior and has to act with decorum and formally as the correct Hindu wife ought to (this is the Manu model); however, as a human lover, she is freed of her constraints and can let her heart rule her actions. In other words, the local legends recounted in the texts that recount the greatness of the place that she was born in (*sthala mahatmayam*) say that Andal is not constrained by the idea of a dharmic wife (as the Earth Goddess, consort of Vishnu would be). *She* approaches Vishnu herself, seeking a union and asks him to come to her. This union is consummated, physically, in a ritual in Srivilliputtur, the birthplace of Andal. Here, during the ten day celebrations in the month of Ati (July 15–Aug. 14), to mark Andal's birthday, on the seventh day, Vishnu is taken to her chambers and made to recline on her. The very *physical* nature of the union between Andal and the Lord is celebrated. The liberation of saints like Andal, therefore, is not a colorless *moksha* that is beyond human ken; rather, it is a full blooded union of the flesh and the spirit.

The local legends that describe Andal as the Earth Goddess strategically make two points. The first is divinizing of the human saint. This coopts the humanity and makes her a special figure who may behave in a manner that is not a viable alternative to a normal human being. Thus Andal's protests and rejection of a society that is dominated by earthly marriage are tamed and contained by the patriarchal biographers and framed as divine love from the celestial realm. The second point made is a more earthy, non-*dharma shastra* model of physical love seen through the ritual. Andal is said to come as a human lover, says the legend, because she is thus freed of the constraints of being a dutiful wife. In other words, in her original form as the Earth Goddess, she apparently has to behave as a dutiful restrained wife. The Manu model of this controlled wife is imposed even on the goddess. What is stated here is a curious position: *the Goddess does not empower the women, but instead the ideal, and dutiful behavior that is supposed to be followed by the brahminical woman is projected on the Goddess.* On the flip side of the coin, we see that this line of reasoning assumes, like the *Kama Sutra* did in earlier centuries, that the lover is free of these restrictions and can act in a manner that is congruent with love, and not one that seeks social approval. She may act with abandon, without the norms of earthly (dharmic, brahminical) society being applied to her. *In the realm of love, whether it be worldly, or spiritual, brahminical standards of "proper" womanly behavior are not to be held as normative.*

Andal's life then offers not just a theological model for all human beings, but a model of love that women may use in approaching God. Women see in her a person who attained salvation, not by worshiping her husband as God (as Manu would have it), but by approaching God directly and wanting a union with him. What Andal and other women poets did by living the way they did was to negotiate a space within a marriage-dominated society and made at least some sections of society make room for them. The typology of women we see in the *dharma shastras* are young unmarried girls, married women, and widows. Single women who either reject marriage, or who walk out on their husbands, are not recognized; by the power of their love and the consolidation of their aspirations, the women poets carve out a different space for themselves.

Andal's songs have been recited daily in domestic and temple liturgies and her lyrics have been set to *ragas* and performed on sacred and secular stages. Her songs, the *Tiruppāvai* ("Sacred Lady") and a set of verses from *Nācciyār Tirumoli* ("The Sacred Words of the Lady") in which she dreams that she is marrying Vishnu have been part of the repertoire for all classical Bharata Natyam dancers in the last thirty years. More important, Andal, Mira, and other women poets have become the focus of inspiration for many women's groups in India. Women like Usha Narayanan have choreographed large tracts of the saints' hymns in a style known as *araiyar sevai* (the "service of the cantors" style performed by traditional *male* performers in Sri Vaishnava temples) and have performed them on television. The public performance of this type of dancing is radical in itself within the conservative Sri Vaishnava circles. The *araiyar sevai* refers to the special dances performed by the male cantors who belong to a particular lineage within the precincts of the temple. The dances express the poet's love for God. For a woman to choreograph a religious dance in this style, which has been a monopoly of men, and perform it in public is unprecedented.

In the last few years, many groups of women in suburbs of Madras, a city in south India, have formed "circles" (*mandali*) to sing the poems of Andal and other Vaishnavaite Tamil saints. The groups I met have interesting names: Goda Mandali (the circle of Andal), Sreyas Mandali (the circle [leading] to the higher path), Ranganatha Paduka Mandali (the circle that venerates the sandals of Ranganatha [Vishnu]), Subhasri Mandali (the very auspicious circle) and Bhaktanjali (the worshipful circle of adoration). The groups meet once or twice a week, and also perform in music fests (like the Tamil Music Association festival in December) and temples. Sometimes, they raise money for the upkeep of various shrines through their singing In the last few years, the Goda Mandali (Goda's circle), located in T. Nagar, Madras, has used the medium of singing to reappropriate and participate in the passion of Andal-Goda.

Milton Singer and Venkateswaran wrote about the many *bhajana* groups (groups that sing semiclassical devotional songs of the medieval saints) in Madras about thirty years ago. Many of these were Brahmin based and the lead roles were frequently taken by men. In the last ten years or so many more *bhajana* groups have sprung up all over Madras and in many other cities as well; but these are not the eclectic, male-dominated groups that Singer wrote about. Rather, they are self-consciously sectarian, being either Sri Vaishnava or Saiva, and they are predominantly run by women.

"Goda Mandali" ("the circle, or group, of Goda") appropriately named after one of the earliest women poets dedicated to Vishnu, was first formed in 1970 and reorganized in 1982. The women of this group frequently sing for events connected with temples, and occasionally they sing for a secular audience. The piety of the Goda Mandali has also achieved considerable visibility through television and radio, leading to the formation of more circles, through which the passion of Andal lives again. All practice sessions and performances begin with a unique invocation. In the Sri Vaishnava community, recitation of the songs of the Tamil saints generally begins with the line "I take refuge with the sacred feet of Nammalvar and Emperumanar (Ramanuja, a male theologian of the twelfth century C.E.)." The Goda Mandali, however, begins with the line "I take refuge with the sacred feet of Nammalvar, Andal and Ramanuja; I take refuge with the sacred feet of Andal.") This special emphasis on Andal is unique to this circle of her companions in the Goda Mandali and some of the other women's groups. The Goda Mandali also has a unique *mangalam* or last song. In almost *all* classical south Indian (Carnatic) music concerts, the last "auspicious" song focuses (by tradition) on the male God, Rama, and either a song of Tyagaraja (eighteenth century) or Ramdas (seventeenth century) is sung. The Goda Mandali, however, sings a song praising the goddess Lakshmi in her manifestation in the temple of Srirangam.

The Goda Mandali is not an isolated example. Srinidhi Rangarajan, a physician and noted Bharata Natyam dancer, rearranged the verses of Andal's works to reflect her experience of a spiritually progressive sequence and choreographed it. This performance was held in December 1994 to inaugurate the Festival of Tiruppāvai. The Tiruppāvai is one of the two works of Andal and is recited, sung, and danced to by men and women in Tamilnadu. Following the performance of Dr. Rangarajan, students and teachers from a large school in Madras went around the streets in a lighted float, singing the verses of Andal. This float was subsequently taken out at dawn for several days in the month of Markali (December 15–January 13, a month that is considered to be sacred to Andal) through the city of Madras. These enterprises highlighting women's piety and public role in religious expression are becoming increasingly common; their popularity is attested to by the fact that the festival of the Tiruppāvai, with the dance by Dr. Rangarajan and the floats, were all sponsored by the Indian Bank, a leading commercial institution in India.

Another example of women who choose the figure of Andal and her works as empowering their religious activities is Mrs. Kothai Venkatachalapathy. Mrs. Kothai (her name is a variation of Andal's name, Goda) teaches the proper recitation of Andal's hymns and comments upon their meaning. She speaks of the emotional tensions of Andal and her teaching of the verses is interspersed with commentarial explanations. Women have not commented upon this devotional literature in public forums, at least in the last few centuries;[31] by doing so she is initiating a new role for other women and serves as a model.

How do these women relate to Andal? We have seen that in Sri Vaishnava theology, Andal is clearly a paradigmatic devotee and by identifying with or *imitating* her love, it may be possible to reach Vishnu. Bhattar, a twelfth-century theologian, is quoted as advising his male disciple that he ought to recite the entire *Tiruppāvai* every morning and experience its emotions. If it is not possible to recite at least one verse, he is advised to just think of the way they experienced the joy of the verses. In other words, the experiencing of the path taken by Andal, however vicariously, is highly recommended. Commentarial literature says that by the *practice* of some rituals, the cowherd girls got Krishna; by *imitation* of those rituals Andal reached Krishna. By making the words of Andal her words, the devotee is extolled to be like Andal, imitating her passion, emulating and appropriating her devotion. In other words, one seeks union with Vishnu through the words of Andal and by sharing her passion and her power. It is this feature of imitation and appropriation of emotion that is the basis of the Hindu theories of singing, acting, and dancing as ways to salvation, and I will discuss that issue a little later in this essay.

The women of Goda Mandali see Andal's words and the words of the other saints as portraying their own emotions and spiritual longing and giving them direct access to the Lord. Chitra Raghunathan, one of the members, says that singing with this group is the most fulfilling aspect of her religious life; in fact, she added, this is her only real religious life, this is her direct prayer. In temples, special groups (like the *adhyapakas* and *araiyars*, the traditional male cantors) have the religious and often the legal right to recite and pray; in household rituals a man may officiate; but through the singing and dancing, *the women communicate directly with the deity.* In this context, two factors are important: the companionship of the group, which is like the collective prayer of Andal and her friends, and secondly, the opportunity to sing the sacred words in private and *public* forums. The advent and growing popularity of these women's groups that sing the prayers in sacred and secular forums is leading to an increase in the feminization of ritual patterns in some Hindu communities.

Akka Mahadevi, a twelfth-century Kannada poet, was married to a king. Rejecting the lustful lifestyle he was trying to impose on her, as well as the luxuries of palace life, she wandered into the forests, claiming Lord Shiva to be her husband. Discarding all sense of ego and "I" hood, she also discarded her garments and concentrated only on union with her beloved. Akka Mahadevi now serves as the model for Mate Mahadevi ("The Great Mother Goddess") who was born in the state of Karnataka on March 13th, 1946.[32] Named

Ratnamma when she was born, she graduated from college with a degree in science. At this time she decided to become an ascetic. A devotee writes:

She is perhaps the first women in history who has ascended the pontifical seat of a Jagadguru ["world-teacher;" a title given to abbots of some traditional monasteries and lines of ascetics] so far reserved for men. . . . Undaunted by criticism from several quarters . . . is her ascent of a Jagadguru Pitha [seat of a monastic leader], founded by her revered Guru, Sri Lingananda Swamiji, as a challenge to show that a woman is as well qualified to become a Guru and entitled to sit on the pontifical seat of a Jagadguru as her right.[33]

Mate Mahadevi met her (male) teacher Lingananda Swamiji and received her first initiation ("ishta linga initiation") in 1965. Following this initiation she started composing and writing *vachanas* ("sayings") like those of Basava, the twelfth-century founder of the Lingayat community and contemporary of Akka Mahadevi, the woman poet. It was soon after this that "having a divine revelation of Akka Mahadevi's presence, her spiritual model, [that] she was transported with joy and charged with an irresistible energy and power. On 5th April 1966 she got her Jangama [ascetic] initiation."[34] When she was installed as the monastic leader (*jagadguru*), the *Samyukta Karnatak,* a daily newspaper, wrote in its editorial: "Today has started a new era in the fields of religion and society, with the installation of Her Holiness Mata Mahadevi as the first woman Jagadguru to a pontifical seat, which up till now was reserved for men."[35]

Akka Mahadevi, the twelfth-century poet, has served as a role model for and has been reappropriated by a twentieth-century seeker and reformer. But Mate Mahadevi has also proved to be a scholar and an institutional leader. As of 1973, Mate Mahadevi had already published twenty books on her own and had started an educational and religious institution called Jaganmata Akka Mahadevi Ashrama ("the Hermitage of the World-Mother Akka Mahadevi") at Dharwar, Karnataka, for training and guidance of "spiritual seekers, especially girls and women, dedicated to the cause of women's upliftment and propagation of religious ideals."[36] Her books include *Basava Tatva Darshana* in which she discusses the life and philosophy of the philosopher-reformer Basava in 860 pages. Mystic, writer, scholar, institutional leader, and reformer, she has been hailed as a "revolutionary religious leader, revitalizing religion" by *Prajavani Daily,* a local newspaper.[37]

In the two examples of women poets that I have discussed, those of Andal and Akka Mahadevi, I have focused less on their biographies and more on the ways in which women today are appropriating them. Andal, Akka Mahadevi, and other women saints live today through the songs, dances, reforms movements, and the spiritual quests of twentieth-century women. Appearing at times when according to the brahmanical texts and received ideologies, a woman could attain liberation by serving her husband as if he were God, Andal, Akka Mahadevi, Lalla, Mira, and others forged paths directly to the supreme being, and in the process, have continued to inspire thousands of women today.

Less well known than these poets and leaders but remarkable in their own right are the woman composers of lyrics and classical music. Almost all the well known composers of classical Carnatic music in the last five hundred years—Purandara, Annamacharya, Tyagaraja, Shyama Sastry, and Muthuswami Dikshitar—have been men. In the course of my research in south India I heard of many women composers in the field of classical Carnatic music. These women were usually not known outside their families. They were usually Brahmin women with knowledge of classical music ranging from cursory to excellent. Most of these works have never been published: the few books that were published were distributed privately. The notebooks I have examined from the early twentieth century had songs in Tamil and Telugu. While there are a handful of women composers (the exact count will not be known unless a systematic study is done, but I have heard of about a dozen composers) at least two are reasonably well known in the state of Tamilnadu.

By far the best known poet/composer is Mrs. Ambujam Krishna (1917–1989) whose works have been published and whose songs received considerable publicity. Her devotional songs, many of them addressed to the Lord Krishna, are regularly sung in classical music concerts and have also been choreographed. It seems felicitous that the name of her husband and the name of her chosen deity were the same: Krishna. A few hours after she had a mystic dream in which she saw an image of Krishna coming to her, her husband returned from Delhi, bringing with him the very image she saw in her dream. She remarked to her friend that evening: "He has come; *he* has also come."[38] While both Krishnas were important in her life, the warmth, delicacy, and beauty of her lyrics and music addressed to Lord Krishna is haunting and one sees the legacy of earlier *bhakti* poets in them.

The works of Sundaraja (the pen name of Parvati Srinivasan, 1925–1989) have also been published. Some of her songs—some addressed to a goddess—are regularly sung by well known Carnatic music exponents. Not as fortunate as these two women was Mrs. Seetha (1909–1974) of Basavangudi, Bangalore. A gifted poet, composer, and writer, her work was published in magazines. When she was about twelve, she was married to her maternal uncle. One day, when a money order came in the mail, as a payment for one of the published works, the (male) editor had enclosed a note addressed to her. The salutation, "My dear Madam," apparently enraged Mrs. Seetha's husband, who took a dim view of total strangers calling his wife "dear." He then forbade her from writing again.[39] She did continue, despite this command, both through her short marriage and through widowhood. Strong in her own quiet way, her songs of devotion preserved in handwritten notebooks are stirring in their tenderness and intensity.

Many of the women devotees/composers talk of songs "coming" to them; songs come in a flash, either through dreams or when sitting still. Entire verses pour forth and very little is done to change the lyrics later; the only work needed is to "tune" them—that is, see how the *raga* they envision it in fits in when actually sung. A full-scale study of these women composers—exploring the socio-political reasons they never sought or received any publicity, the themes of "divine inspiration" and revelation through dreams, comparison of the women's compositions with those of men, and studying these songs as expressions of religiosity—would be necessary before assessing their contributions.[40]

When Matrons Were Patrons: Women's Endowments to Temples

Whereas texts, including Manu, denied the right of financial agency, indeed any independence for women, we see that this prescription was not followed in some areas of India among women of some economic classes and social castes. Even a cursory study of inscriptions in south Indian temples reveals that several queens endowed money to and patronized rituals. The patronage extended by queens in the building of temples began as early as the sixth century C.E. when two queens built temples at Pattadakal (modern Karnataka).[41] These are, in fact, some of the earliest temples that we know of today in the subcontinent. These temples, however, were built in honor of the conquests that their husbands had undertaken. It is from the tenth century C.E. that we encounter queens who made donations that were not necessarily for increasing the glory of their husbands. Samavai (966 C.E.), a queen of the Pallava dynasty, in areas now covered by northern Tamilnadu and southern Andhra Pradesh; Sembiyan Mahadevi, the dowager Chola Queen (10th century C.E.); and Shantala Devi (12th century C.E.) were responsible for building several temples in south India. Samavai made the first major monetary endowment, and major land grant to the temple in Tirupati, which today is the richest temple in India. The inscriptions show that around the year 966 C.E. Samavai endowed within a short time two different parcels of land, one of ten acres and the other of 13 acres. She ordered that the revenues derived from these should finance the celebration of major festivals.[42] She also gave a large number of jewels to the temple and asked that these be used to adorn the image of the Lord. Samavai's endowments made possible several innovative features in worship and, as the inscriptions show, funded the celebration of many festivals in that temple.

Studies done by an art historian[43] show that Samavai was not an isolated example; Chola queens of the tenth century C.E. were enthusiastic patrons of temples and religious causes for the Shaivaite community of south India around the tenth century. Sembiyan Mahadevi and her daughters-in-law endowed money to temples along the Kaveri Delta. Shantala Devi, a queen belonging to the Jain religion, but who was married to a king who converted from Jainism to Hinduism, apparently planned and built temples at Shantigrama, Karnataka, and also the Channigaraya temple, an exquisitely beautiful Vishnu temple at Belur (modern Karnataka).[44] A reading of the published inscriptions of the Tirupati temple of even two centuries (fourteenth–fifteenth centuries) indicates that many women endowed money to the temple and participated in its activities. From the details of the inscriptions many seem to have been either of the royal families or nobility, thus having access to independent wealth, or courtesans. Donations by courtesans are seen in temples all over south India during the medieval period.[45] Through public records of their exemplary generosity, these women also serve as outstanding patrons of major religious institutions and rituals, in many parts of south India.

There is considerable evidence that women rulers were powerful in Bengal and patronized learning and literature. Temple endowments by women are also seen in Bengal and in the holy city of Benares.[46] Women's patronage of temples seems to have been confined to southern and eastern India in the medieval period; it is during this time that the Muslim dynasties (the Delhi sultanate began in 1206) were to being established in northern India. Politically it was a time of major political change in northern states and we do not have striking examples of women's patronage and benefactions in these areas.

Women in Performing Arts

In some cases, womanist goals are met by opening up activities and rituals that are confined to one caste or one sex to members of all castes and both sexes. The case of performing arts provides a striking example. As discussed in our section on women poets, singing, dancing, and acting were considered in certain circumstances to be ways to salvation. Rabindranath Tagore (1861–1941) writes in his *Religion of Man* about visiting a village, where:

> The villagers entertained me with an operatic performance the literature of which belonged to an obsolete religious sect that had wide influence. Though the religion itself is dead, its voice still continues preaching its philosophy to a people, who, in spite of their different culture are not tired of listening. It discussed according to its own doctrine the different elements, material and transcendental, that constitute human personality, comprehending the body, the self, and the soul. Then came a dialogue, during the course of which was related the incident of a person who wanted to make a journey to Brindaban, the Garden of Bliss, but was prevented by a watchman who startled him with an accusation of theft. The

thieving was proved when it was shown that inside his clothes he was secretly trying to smuggle into the garden the self, which only finds its fulfillment by its surrender. The culprit was caught with the incriminating bundle in his possession which barred for him his passage to the supreme goal. Under the tattered canopy, supported by bamboo poles . . . the village crowd, occasionally interrupted by the howls of jackals . . . attended with untired interest, till the small hours of the morning the performance of a drama that discussed the ultimate meaning of all things in a seemingly incongruous setting of dance, music, and humorous dialogue.[47]

Drama, dance, and music have been perceived to be vehicles of religious expression and conveyors of yearning in the Hindu tradition. Classical music and dance were considered to have been given by gods and goddesses to human beings. Even now, the Goddess Sarasvati is worshiped as the patron goddess of music and learning. Bharata's *Nātya Śāstra,* the treatise on classical dance, is considered to have the essence of the four Sanskrit Vedas and claims to be the fifth Veda. The performing arts therefore provide an alternative avenue to salvation, paralleling the way of knowledge seen in postVedic literature. While pure music and dance (as distinguished from music and dance with devotional content) is itself said to be of divine origin and understood to lead one to the divine, usually singing and dancing are connected with the *bhakti* or devotion contained in the lyrics being sung. Devotion to the deity is expressed through a number of *bhavas* or attitudes; these include the loving attitudes connected with service, maternal love, romantic love, and the like. The combination of the emotional lyrics sung with the abandon of devotion is said to be a path through which one can reach the divine goal of one's choice.

The ostensible reason for the "revelation" or composition of the treatise on dance is said to be that of making accessible the difficult statements of the Vedas to *all* human beings. However, it is interesting to note that at least after the fourteenth and fifteenth centuries, while we have documentation on male singers (of many castes) and dancers, the only women who sang and danced in public seem to have been courtesans. Even as late as the twelfth century, we see sculptures of women dancers adorning the niches of the Belur temple in Karnataka with which Queen Shantala Devi was connected. It is also said that one of the dancing figures within the temple is a figure of the queen herself. According to one account, her dance was admired by the king and the courtiers and "the king as desired by the courtiers gave her publicly the titles of "Natyasarasvati" [the Sarasvati or goddess of Dance] and "Sakala samaya rakshamani" (imperial protector of all faiths)."[48] The human body is celebrated in these sculptures and the later restrictions against women from "decent families" dancing in public may have come for many misogynistic reasons.

At the simplest level, we know that new forms of clothing and modesty about showing the body came into prominence around the thirteenth century even in south India. These new "fashions" as they were at the time were adopted by the court elite in the Vijayanagara empire, where the king and nobility imitated the clothing of the northern Muslim kings. Prior to this time, even kings and royal women delighted in showing their limbs and many parts of their bodies.[49] It is possible that with new attitudes toward the human body (attitudes that *reinforce* some of the negative statements made in some *dharma shastras* about a woman's uncontrollable sexual propensity), perspectives on the overtly sensual presentations involved in the performing arts also changed.

As we saw earlier, many devotional lyrics used the rapturous love metaphor in constructing the relationship between the human being and God. The singer or dancer displayed these sensual *bhavas* or expressions either with the face or with the entire body in the case of the dancer, and through voice modulation in the case of the singer. While the allegorical meaning of these poems clearly indicated the love to be spiritual, metaphors pertaining to the body were prominently used. Upper-class men would have thought this as inappropriate for women to display in public. Women did continue to dance and sing, but it seems to have been within the confines of the home, without a choice of whether they wanted to do this in public. It is possible that women did participate in devotional singing through the streets in some medieval traditions, especially those associated with the movement of Chaitanya. A striking example of public singing and dancing (though originally even these were contained within homes) is the *garbha* dance and worship in the state of Gujarat. *Garbha* or *garbhi* is "womb," the source of all creative energy; it is the mother goddess who is present in the lamp inside the clay pot that is called *garbha*. Women and young girls dance around the *garbha* all night, celebrating the goddess. However, it must be noted in recent years this splendid ritual has been taken over by men who have made it a commercial and economic enterprise, and act as promoters of large dance-fests.[50] Once again, as in the case of women poets, it seems that when the focus of discussion is *moksha* (liberation), rather then dharma (issues of righteousness) in this world, a greater freedom is seen in women's participation in public spaces. Androcentric norms on women's modesty or actions in public that were incumbent on some castes and classes are simply bypassed in cases where the tradition focuses on the salvific potential of all human beings.

In southern India, the dynamic creativity in the production and performance of classical song and dance seems to have been confined to male Brahmins and courtesans. The annals of the Tanjore court in the eighteenth and nineteenth centuries are filled with accounts of prominent male singers/musicians and courtesans.[51] Courtesans known as *devadasis* ("servants of God") performed these arts in temples and were also ritual specialists. There were also other courtesans, patronized by royalty and nobility. Courtesans were apparently the only women for many centuries—apart from royalty—to have access to scholarship and the arts of singing and dancing. They also held the right to inherit property and adopt children. Some well known courtesans were accomplished Sanskrit poets. Ramabhadramba, a courtesan-turned-queen of Raghunatha (c. 1600–1633), a king of the Tanjore, wrote a Sanskrit *mahākāvya* (epic poem) in honor of her husband. The poem identifies the king with Lord Rama and plays with his name as the incarnation of Lord Rama; but in his love-making, his wife compares him admiringly to Lord Krishna. His wife concludes the epic poem with the erotic frankness associated with the ritualized court poetry of the time and extols his sexual prowess as he goes through a typical night, making love to an "astounding series of women."[52]

Some of these courtesans have left their mark on society despite the repressive mores that were by now reinforced by Victorian sensibilities. Muddupalani (1730–1790), a courtesan in the Tanjore royal court of the Nayaka King Pratapasimha, was a scholar and poet. Inspired by the songs of the woman poet Andal, she composed a work called *Saptapadalu,* which purports to be a translation of Andal's *Tiruppavai* in the Telugu language.[53] Muddupalani's *Radhika Santwanam* (appeasing Radhika) is a collection of 584 poems, focusing on the advise on erotic love that Radha gives to her daughter, Ila Devi, and Krishna. The frank expression of sexuality seen in the text proved too heady a hundred years after its composition. In the late nineteenth century the published versions shied away from the elegance and erotica of the original manuscript. Venkatanarasu, a man who published the work in 1887, had not seen fit to print the prologue in which Muddupalani had traced her literary *parampara* or lineage through her grandmother and other women. Bangalore Nagaratnammal (1878–1952), another courtesan, studied the original manuscripts and found the published versions to be appallingly sanitized and censored. Her attempts to publish the original text were met with hostility from Veereshalingam, a male literary critic who denounced the erotic mood of the book and said it was unbecoming and unnatural for a woman to talk thus of sex. Muddupalani's work was written during the time of the Nayaka kings when male authors wrote explicitly on matters that involved sex; for instance, in *Raghunāthanāyakabhyu-dayamu* ("A day in the Life of Raghunatha") in Telugu, written by Vijayaraghava in honor of his father, he describes the king as sporting with the courtesan Citrarekha, and candidly writes in some detail about all the eighty-four positions of love that the lovers adopt through the endless night.[54] Knowing about these styles of writing, Bangalore Nagaratnammal questioned why it was proper for a man but improper for a woman to write thus. Notwithstanding this logic, the British government also thought that this book would endanger the morality of Indian subjects and despite several legal pleadings, banned its distribution.[55]

Bangalore Nagaratnammal was the daughter of a courtesan-singer in the royal court of Mysore. Coming from a community that was low in social status from certain brahmanical perspectives, it was nevertheless one that accorded young women the privilege of education of every kind. A celebrated singer and musician, Nagaratnammal was responsible for instituting a music-fest in honor of the (male) composer Tyagaraja (1767–1847) in the town of Tiruvaiyaru. This festival was instituted to encourage all singers—male, female, famous, and un-known—to participate equally, with equal time and opportunity for all to cele-brate the piety of Tyagaraja's music.[56] This was more than a music festival; the music itself was considered to be a form of worship, and was also accompanied by religious rituals, extolling the musical composer, and now, Bangalore Na-garatnammal. Nagaratnammal was apparently led by dreams to Tiruvaiyaru, a small village in Tamilnadu where the composer Tyagaraja had lived. She cleared the land where he had been buried, tirelessly collected funds to build a temple nearby, and then instituted the music festival. She befriended and en-couraged younger women to sing and perform, singing to celebrate the deity and give full expression to their talents and fervor. Bangalore Nagaratnammal is to be remembered for creating the public space for women and men to par-ticipate in a festival where one can sing the devotional lyrics of Tyagaraja and participate both in a choral and individual expression of reverence.

The Tyagaraja Utsava ("Festival of Tyagaraja") was and remains a grand vision and celebration, and has grow to be one of the best known music festivals in India and for Hindus in the diaspora. Tyagaraja Utsavas are celebrated with great éclat not just in Tiruvaiyaru, but in every major city in the United States and Canada with the most prominent one being in Cleveland, Ohio. The lead singers in many of these festivals in India and abroad are now women musicians. The establishing of this public, devotional forum for the display of talent—both that of men and women—is due to the efforts of Bangalore Nagarnatnammal.

While during the early part of Bangalore Nagaratnammal's life, Car-natic music was not sung in public by "high" caste women, they are now con-spicuous by their presence. The "Brahminization" of the performing arts and the opening up of classical dance and music to men and women of the "higher castes" is an important development in the twentieth century. While this is particularly true of Carnatic music, it is also true of the performing arts all over India.

Bharata Natyam, one of the classical dances of India, and probably its best known form outside the country, was originally known as *dasi attam,* or the dance of the servants [of the Lord]. It was in the province of *devadasi* or courtesan families for centuries. There were famous male choreographers of these dances in the royal courts of the nineteenth century: Chinniah, Ponniah, Sivanandam, and Vadivelu, more popularly known as the Tanjore Quartette, were famous composers, musicians and choreographers of the Tanjore court.

Even until the early part of the twentieth century, well known dancers came from established and talented courtesan families. It was only in this century that the pioneering efforts of Srimati Rukmini Devi Arundale resulted in making Bharata Natyam accessible to women of all castes.

Rukmini Devi Arundale (1904–1986), dancer, educator, nominee to be president of India in 1977, was born in a Brahmin family. Her parents belonged to the progressive Theosophist movement and were closely associated with Annie Besant. Rukmini Devi broke with orthodox tradition in many ways; when she was sixteen she married an Englishman. She was at the time learning ballet from Western teachers, and Bharata Natyam from Mylapore Gowri, an eminent dancer from a traditional family of courtesans. In 1935 she gave a public recital of dancing "in the midst of dissent and fury."[57] The storm of protest was evidently against the idea of a "high caste" woman giving a public dance performance. Rukmini Devi persisted in her efforts, and started "the Arena of Art" (Kalakshetra), an international academy of the arts in 1936. Classical music and many kinds of south Indian classical dance were taught here for all those who had desired to find fulfillment through these artistic forms. It is hard to imagine that Bharata Natyam, a field that is dominated by Brahmin women and girls today, was completely forbidden to them until late in this century. The pioneering efforts of Rukmini Devi Arundale resulted in opening these public arenas of religious expression.

The Shanti Niketan ("abode of peace") started by Rabindranath Tagore in Bengal in the beginning of this century also propagated the performing arts. However, in the domain of classical music in northern India, we encounter a situation not far removed from that of the south: women from respectable families were not allowed to sing in public. Even when they did learn music, certain styles and kinds of music considered to be "divine" were not taught to them. Sharbari Mukherjee writes:

> Traditionally, women have never been permitted to sing or learn *dhrupad* which is said to be the divine music meant for the gods, and was always associated with temple rituals. It was a male bastion strictly taught to the male members of the family or to son-in-law and the knowledge was sometimes handed down as dowry to those who married in to the family of some musicians of high status. But women were never practitioners.[58]

Dhrupad is a style and kind of composition that reached its height in the fifteenth century and developed from the ancient compositional type called *dhruva prabandha*.[59] Patronized by rulers like Akbar, the Mughal emperor, and Raja Mansingh Tomar of Gwalior, musicians like Tansen, Svami Haridas, and Baiju Bavra (legendary male exponents of this style) flourished. *Dhamar,* a variety of *prabandha* in a section of the *dhrupad,* describes the play of Lord

Krishna, especially the festival of colors. This style apparently has been the province of men only and it was only when a woman musician like Asghari Begum Sagarwali (born circa 1914) showed immense talent that her male teacher taught her the *dhrupad*.[60] Asghari Begum Sagarwali says:

> Dhrupad is the song of the gods. It enunciates the words "Narayan" and "Om" so while singing one is as though remembering god, which spontaneously infuses one with strength. My *ustad* [teacher] said: "I don't want you to feel deprived of anything or inferior to anyone, so I will teach you this also. This has not yet reached womankind, but I am giving you this also. Here, take it," and he taught me *dhrupad*.[61]

Asghari Begum also reiterates that while all men could sing, all women could not:

> Earlier, there were plenty of women instrumentalists. . . . In the days of court patronage women of musicians' families used to play as well as sing. Of course, housewives did not play or sing because women musicians were looked down upon. Men musicians were not looked down upon—the maharaja and his brothers used to sing and play.[62]

With the elimination of royal patronage from the rulers of the small kingdom after India got its independence in 1947, and difficulty in the availability of mass media for women in some parts of India soon after that, the tradition of women singers (even from the musician families) is said to have declined in northern India. Some people trace the derogatory status attached to women singers to the colonial times in India, when the British associated all forms of performance to *nautch* or vulgar dancing.[63] While attributing some of this decline to the loss of royal patronage—of which she herself was a victim—Begum Asghari also laments that the traditional forms of intensive learning, when a pupil lived with the teacher, learned and practiced music night and day, completely disappeared with the advent of Western forms of secular education.[64]

However, as in the case of south India, the negative associations seem to have gone back even further than in colonial times. It is only in this century that (a) music and dance as a public expression of religiosity and (b) forms of music and dance (*dhrupad, araiyar sevai*) that women were prohibited from learning and performing, because the art form was considered to be very sacred, have been made available to them. Despite the tremendous progress in some areas, as in the playing of accompanying percussion instruments such as the *mridangam* or *tabla,* women still face considerable discrimination from male lead performers. Very few of them, such as P. Santhakumari who plays the *thavil,* are regularly employed. The *thavil* is a special drum used for weddings and

auspicious occasions in the south, as well as for many temple rituals. P. Santhakumari is the only woman player of this instrument and is employed by a local temple. Special music fests for these women are held occasionally in Delhi
by the music organization Geetika founded by Shanno Khurana. In the introduction to the first such music fest, the announcer stated: "The Rigveda names
27 *vidushis* (learned women) who assisted in its composition. . . . This festival
too is a festival of *vidushis.* Today each of these *vidushis* is standing alone just
as courage always stands alone."[65]

The performing arts now serve as vehicles for further dynamic reform in
a way unparalleled within the Hindu tradition. The fight to render erotic/spiri-
tual longing in artistic form in public forums was a major landmark of this century. The performing arts are now used with skill by celebrated dancers like
Mallika Sarabhai and Chandralekha to express themes of anguish and strength
that pertain to women's issues. Mallika Sarabhai's new school of dance, dedicated to her mother is called "Natarani" or "queen of dance." This is a deliberate change from the name "Nataraja" or "king of dance," a popular name of Lord
Shiva, also known as the Lord of the Dance. Mallika Sarabhai has utilized the
forms of mime and dance to underscore some of the injustices done to women.
She initially set the feminist agenda through *Shakti: The Power of Women* and
has continued explorations of feminist issues through her recital "Sita's Daughters." *Shakti* is a solo performance in which Dr. Sarabhai portrays images of
women whose power has been negated or neutralized by male society.

"Sita's Daughters" starts with a focus on an episode from the *Rāmāyaṇa,*
an epic that is probably the best known story in the Hindu tradition. Prince
Rama, who is regarded as an incarnation of Lord Vishnu, is exiled to the forest
for fourteen years. Sita, his wife, follows him there and is kidnapped by Ravana, king of Lanka, who lusts after her. Rama searches for her, kills Ravana,
and rescues her after a long battle. At this point, there is no rapturous union of
the couple; rather, Rama coldly tells Sita that she is free to do what she wills.
Sita believes that her chastity and honor are being questioned and walks into a
freshly built fire. The god of fire miraculously hands her back to Rama, saying
that she is pure. After Rama and Sita are coronated in Ayodhya, Rama is told
that some subjects question the propriety of Sita's being held in Ravana's do-
minion for several months. Obviously, this had been against Sita's will; but it
seems a classic case of the blamed victim. Rama, ostensibly to preserve justice,
banishes the pregnant Sita without as much as seeing her. Several years later
when he meets his twin sons and Sita, he says he will accept her if she can give
him some "proof" that she is chaste. Sita proves this by an "act of truth." This
is an act by which a person swears that if something is true (for example, his
love for a particular person) a miracle will happen. Sita now swears and says
that if it true that she has always been faithful to Rama, mother earth will open
up and swallow her. Earth opens up and accepts Sita. Sita proves to Rama that
she is indeed chaste, but Rama does not get his wife back.

Dr. Sarabhai sees these instances of Rama's questioning and seeking of proof as a paradigmatic instance of injustice to women. This initial episode frames the later sequences when she portrays instances where religious culture (perhaps more aptly called brahminical values that had a hegemonic power) sanctions the instances of gender inequity. She also portrays the struggles of women in the northern Doon valley who work for ecological preservation and try to prevent trees from being cut down. This movement called "Chipko" is a protest against the developers who seek to level the land in the name of development without heed for longtime effects. Using very few props, Dr. Sarabhai focuses on women who refused to give in to pressures around them, women who did not accept, but who questioned and chafed. These women are called the "Sitas who refuse ever again to submit to the tests and trials of weak and doubting men."[66] Through "Sita's Daughters" we see Dr. Sarabhai on the cutting edge of the Hindu feminist agenda. Perhaps the agenda is best stated by Asghari Begum Sagarwali:

Let us [women] not be left with the feeling:. . . . Alas life has passed by and we have wasted it. Why spend life in cooking food? Cooking of food has to be done in any case, but women do nothing else. Little girls play games making believe to cook, in youth that game becomes their life, and in old age they play the same game for their grandchildren! Why not play this game of music which is so valuable? This festival of music for women will help women to come forward. Other women will hear the music and will think: "She plays the tabla! Why shouldn't I also learn to play?" In this way music will continue to live, will remain immortal in our Hindustan.[67]

Education of Widows

One of the most blatant areas of misogynism and discrimination within the Hindu tradition has been the prejudice shown against widows, especially against those of the higher classes and castes. This discrimination has been sanctioned and encouraged and perpetuated in the name of religion.[68] It was higher caste widows with no means, and who were left without progeny, who were generally physically and mentally abused. Others, like the Queen Sembiyan Mahadevi in the tenth century, went on to attain considerable fame through their philanthropic activities. While the higher caste widows were physically rendered ugly in some areas of India (their heads were shaven and they wore a rough white colored sari and no ornaments), it is generally held that the lower caste widows were allowed to remarry. With the increasing prevalence of child marriages, the trauma suffered by child widows has been one of the most callous aspects of the religious tradition.

In the nineteenth century, several social reformers in Maharashtra and some parts of northern India worked hard to relieve the lot of these women. Ramabai (1858–1922) a woman learned in traditional Hindu scriptures, was honored with the titles Pandita (learned lady) and Sarasvati (goddess of learning) in 1878. She married when she was twenty-two and was widowed within two years. She publicized the plight of widows through her writings. But unable to find a way of effecting social reform, she converted to Christianity in 1883. Ramabai Ranade (1862–1924) also worked tirelessly for the cause of widows as did Swarnakumari Devi (1856–1932)[69] from Bengal who started the Sakhi Samiti in 1887. This was an institution to help widows and destitute women. One of the women well known in Tamilnadu, but not in the rest of India, is "Sister" Subbalakshmi. She was a child widow herself, who worked hard for the education of other widows.

Subbalakshmi was born in 1886 into a brahmin family, which traced its ancestry to a long line of learned but not wealthy brahmins. Her father, however, had been educated in the Western system and eventually became a professor of agriculture. Subbulakshmi was her given name; it referred to the "auspicious" goddess Lakshmi. As was the custom in many parts of India, one's given name was one's official name; a father's name or husband's name did not become part of one's label in traditional India. It is only after the advent of colonialism that titles like Miss and Mrs., and the concept of a last name, which was patrilineal or caste oriented in scope, came into vogue. The name of one's traditional village from which one's ancestors hailed was sometimes tacked on to one's name in south India. Subbulakshmi's initial was Rishiyur, the village of her ancestors, and she had a middle initial of V to indicate her father's first name. This was the compromise made in Tamilnadu to accommodate the notion of surname demanded by the British. It is unfortunate that one of the few perks that Hindu women had in keeping their identity without making their father's or husband's names as part of their official label was removed, and disappeared in the last two centuries.[70]

Subbalakshmi was married when she was eleven. She did not know her husband, and as was the custom in those days, continued to live with her parents even after the wedding, without any contact with her husband or his family. When the young husband died soon thereafter, she did not feel bereaved, but knowing that she would soon face a life of discrimination and abuse, her parents and family grieved for her. Although her parents and the grandmother who lived with them were orthoprax, Subbalakshmi was encouraged to continue her formal education at school and a rigorous education at home. The first unusual and unorthodox act that her father did was to take the initiative to have his daughter learn the violin. Seeing grandmother's shock when he first brought home the violin, Subramania Iyer (Subbalakshmi's father) tried to mollify her by saying that it did not cost much. It was of course not the extravagance that scandalized the old lady. Monica Felton, Subbalakshmi's biographer, writes:

It was not, and he knew it, the extravagance of buying such a thing which shocked Grandmother. She had been far from pleased by the decision to give Subbalakshmi an education of a kind that was really only suitable for boys. She had disapproved actively when she had realized that the girl was not be shorn [of her hair] when she attained her age, or to lead the kind of life that was appropriate to a virgin widow. These things had been bad enough. The violin was really the last straw. Ladies might sometimes sing, though only in the privacy of their own homes. Even that was very unusual, and no lady would ever, in any circumstances whatever, learn to play a musical instrument. Music was for dancing girls, *devadasis,* as the temple prostitutes were called. Surely Subramania, who came from such a good family, could not really intend to engage a teacher and allow his widowed daughter, of all people, to take lessons?[71]

Subbalakshmi's parents taught her not only to play the violin, but also the *veena,* a traditional south Indian instrument. She was taught English, and by stages allowed to go to school. She procured the highest grades in her matriculation examinations (school finals) in the entire state, and eventually, went on to finish her undergraduate education, even when teased and hounded by the male students in the college. Encouraged by the example she had set, other parents from villages asked if their widowed daughters could live in the house of Subbalakshmi's family and study in the city of Madras. This was the humble beginnings for the Widows' Home. In 1912 Subbalakshmi received her LT (Licentiate in Teaching) degree. She and her widowed aunt who was a group leader in many discussions on philosophy and culture had also been catalysts in the formation of a women's group, which they named after Sarada, a name of Saraswati, the goddess of learning. The Sarada Ladies' union had members from all religious groups and were dedicated to women's education.

One of their first priorities was the establishment of a home for brahmin widows; to have a place for them to live under supervision, while they pursued their studies. Helped by the Sarada Ladies' Union's fund raising efforts, and Miss Lynch, a British teacher who eventually became the director of education in Madras presidency, Subbalakshmi, started a residence for young widows. These young girls generally had no education when they came in; Subbalakshmi's aunt and later an English women called Mrs. Briggs coached the widows and had them catch up with a regular school curriculum.

Subbalakshmi, who was affectionately known as "Sister," because she was everyone's sister, encouraged the learning of English and participation in a Western school curriculum. However, she also instilled in the young students a love for their mother tongue and traditional Indian dances, at a time when Indian culture was discouraged in schools. Although never associated officially with the nationalist cause, Sister Subbalakshmi's innocent though bold action when she was formally presented to the Prince of Wales in 1921 made her a sensation. Rather than accept his proffered hand, she pressed her own together in the Hindu salutation of *namaskar.* This was repeated thrice, and the prince, finally getting the point, returned the greeting with a similar one.

Sister Subbalakshmi's students showed a great deal of interest in continuing their studies. When one of them, Nallamuthu Ramamurthy, suggested in a prize-winning essay that a women's college was needed in Madras, the government decided to listen. Queen Mary's College was started in Madras in 1914, just before the First World War. It was located in front of the beach, in an old house that had been used as a dorm for sailors.

The efforts of Sister Subbalakshmi and others in creating this educational space for brahmin widows was initially met with hostility from brahmin families and later from the nonbrahmin community. While the sanctions against brahmin widows were the harshest and the home for them was urgent, eventually other homes for nonbrahmin women and Indian Christian women were started. Social segregation between the castes was rigid, and it was only in the small space of a school environment that they were temporarily lifted. Total integration would have led to the boycott of brahmin families and closing of educational opportunities for brahmin women.

Sister Subbalakshmi, now helped by many powerful women, including Lady Willingdon, the wife of the governor of Madras, managed to sensitively steer through some of these mazeways. Later, the schools were expanded to allow older women to join. By 1927, accepting a proposal by Sister Subbalakshmi, the Sarada Ladies' Union began a school called the Sarada Vidyalaya with twelve residents: five brahmins, six nonbrahmins, and one "untouchable." The institution grew, with the oldest student being thirty years, and some between twenty and thirty; most of them were still children. Some of the students were widows, some deserted by their husbands, and a few were single women who had never been married. In 1932, when she was transferred to Cuddalore, she started a school for untouchables, anticipating Mahatma Gandhi's reform movements.

Making educational opportunities available for all women in India was underway all over India by the end of the nineteenth century. Anandibai Karve, a child widow, was married to D. K. Karve, an eminent reformer and a promoter of women's education. D. K. Karve also started a widows' home and the SNDT university for women at Poona. However, Anandibai Karve, unlike Sister Subbalakshmi, was not involved "hands on" in the running of the widows' home, and did not touch the water the inmates drank and ate separately.[72] In later years when the home was moved to some distance, she was totally disassociated from it; she was a remarried widow, and it was thought necessary to keep up the image that the widows' home was not actively supporting remarriage.

Anandibai Joshi (1865–1887) was another person from the present state of Maharashtra to be a role model. She was a cousin of Pandita Ramabai, and the first woman physician of India in recent times.[73] After the loss of her infant daughter, she was convinced that if adequate medical care had been available, the child would have survived. Against all odds (she was a "high" caste woman) she and her husband struggled to get her a first rate medical education and she left for Philadelphia in 1883. She graduated in 1887, returned to India, and died soon thereafter; however, she served as a role model for hundreds of women who were soon to become physicians.

Not all attempts of reform were automatically as successful as those of Sister Subbalakshmi and Anandibai Joshi. In the biography of Sister Subbalakshmi, one reads that Dr. Muthulakshmi Reddy, a woman physician and prominent social worker, asked her to accept "dancing girls" into her widows' home. These dancing girls were the temple dancers or *devadasis* who had been dedicated to a deity when young and then led into a life of prostitution. Sister Subbalakshmi, after considering the issue, had to refuse; she had fought hard to get the permission of very orthodox parents to give their child widows to her so she could educate them; by inclusion of exprostitutes, however young, innocent, and victimized they were, the other girls would have been withdrawn and the goals that she had set herself of educating victimized widows would have been thwarted. Further, even though the rescued dancing girls were young, they already knew quite a bit about sex, and Subbalakshmi thought that their association with the child-virgin widows then would have been unwise.[74]

Dr. Muthulakshmi Reddy was eager to pass the bill outlawing the system of dedicating *devadasis* and withdrawing the economic and ritual rights they enjoyed by their connections with temples. The bill did pass, but without the infrastructure of education that had been supplied for the young widows, the *devadasis* who were ritual specialists, and who had enjoyed a certain prestige in their own right, lapsed into a life of illegal prostitution. We have already discussed the works—both literary and performing—of the skilled courtesans in the previous centuries. The climate of archmorality that came with colonialism and the projection of high-caste scruples on sexuality, along with the degradation and victimization of *devadasis* in some areas, had all combined to convey the impression that their lives consisted of rank immorality and debauchery. In 1927 the Madras Legislative Council passed a bill that put an end to the dedication of young girls to Hindu temples. In the following year, Dr. Reddy proposed an amendment to withdraw financial incentives that perpetuated the caste system.[75] At this point, the *devadasis* mobilized to defend themselves. Comparing themselves to Roman Catholic nuns and other religious specialists, they claimed that they were originally chaste temple servants; rather than moves to make their guild extinct, they asked the government's support in reforming and educating their community.

Although the self-perception of their past in which they portray themselves as chaste temple servants is questionable, it is true that even in the 1870s the "ordinary Hindu continued to regard these women as symbols of sexual vitality and auspiciousness who were an important and necessary element for domestic worship."[76] The _devadasis_ failed to convince the Madras legislature, which passed Dr. Muthulakshmi Reddy's bill in 1929; the Bombay legislature soon followed with a ban on dedication in 1934. While the reforms followed the tone of morality of the times and possibly saved some women from a life that they were forced into without choice, it must be recognized that through the legislation "an independent group of female ritual specialists were forced to give up both their autonomy and sacred profession. They lost the right to own property, adopt daughters, and pass that property on to their daughters."[77]

Reciters of the Vedas

The right of a woman to recite and study the Veda has been disputed in the Hindu tradition. In August 1994 Jagatguru Shankaracharya Kapileswaranand Saraswati is reported to have said that the recitation of Vedas by women will adversely affect their health and prevent them from having healthy babies.[78] While restrictions to study the Sanskrit Veda may have existed in some measure in many parts of India, around the fifteenth century we find Tirukkoneri Dasyai, a woman from south India, who wrote an exquisite commentary on the _Tiruvāymoḻi_ of Nammalvar, a poem that the Sri Vaishnava community acknowledged as being equivalent to the Sama Veda. Tirukkoneri Dasyai shows considerable familiarity with parts of the Sanskrit Veda and quotes the Taittiriya Upanishad and other works as proof texts for the Tamil work, proving that at least this women has more than a cursory knowledge of what was considered to be revelation in Sanskrit and in Tamil. While the Sri Vaishnava community considers about five commentaries on the _Tiruvāymoḻi_ (all written by men) to be extremely important and in fact only studies the poem through the prism of the commentaries, Tirukkoneri Dasyai's work is _not_ one of them and seems to have been unknown until the manuscript was found in this century. This is the only commentary on the Tiruvaymoḻi by a woman that is still extant; the commentaries revered by the tradition are all written by men.

While her knowledge of the Sanskrit Veda is amazing, and her commentary filled with scholarship, we do not know if Tirukkoneri Dasyai ever recited the Vedas and performed fire-sacrifices publicly. This has been done in the last one hundred years, initially through the efforts of the Arya Samaj leader Lala Devraj[79] and now through many women's groups in Maharashtra, India, and in south Africa. These _rshikas,_ women seers, learn to recite and conduct Vedic sacrifice, which has been performed only by brahmin men for several centuries.

There are two main groups learning to recite the Vedas and conduct rituals in Maharashtra.[80] The Kanya Kumari Sthan was founded by Upasani Baba in 1932 in Sakori in the Ahmadnagar district. It is dedicated to the religious training of women and provides a monastic environment for the young women ascetics. These women study the Vedas and perform seven major religious rituals (*yajna*) a year. This group influenced the founding of another organization in Pune. The second group, also started by a man in an organization called Udyan Mangal Karyalaya, includes women of all castes, and women who are housewives, to recite the Vedas and perform Vedic rituals. From women composers of Vedic hymns, it has taken a full thirty-five hundred years to come to women reciters of Vedic hymns.

Devotees and Deities: Women Gurus of Hinduism

Over the centuries there have been very few well known gurus or spiritual teachers who are appointed or selected to traditional spiritual lineages. There are quite a few well known ones now, many in the United States.[81] Sri Ma and Anandi Ma work out of California. Ma Yoga Shakti, an adept of yoga was apparently honored with the title Maha Mandaleswar (Lord of the Great Mandala) at the gathering of ascetics (*sannyasis*) at the festival of Kumbha Mela in 1974. This honor was also bestowed recently on Guru Ma Jyotishanand Bharati at the 1986 Kumbha Mela. Guru Ma, as she is affectionately known, is based in New York and is a devotee of Lord Hanuman, the monkey-devotee of Lord Rama in the *Ramayana*. Guru Ma was born in Rajasthan into a Jain family, and was later married. After the birth of two children, she gave up her married life and went in search of a teacher and the truth. She was initiated first in 1981 under a male guru, Acharya Viswanath Dev Sarma, under whom she also did her Ph.D. in astrology. In 1985, she took *sannyasa*—that is, was formally ordained as a renunciant—by Sri Ved Vyasanand Saraswati Maharaj. Guru Ma came to New York in 1978 and founded the Vedic Heritage in 1979. In 1984 this organization bought a 2.75 acre property in Long Island, and Guru Ma built a large temple for Hanuman. She uses a "prescription" of yoga, meditation, Indian classical dance, music, astrology, and spiritual discourses to "provide others with tools for leading a more productive and meaningful life."[82]

While her achievements are unquestionable and Guru Ma continues to inspire thousands of devotees through her lectures, singing, and advice, and none of this would have been possible without her courage to go out when she did and become a renunciant, she is still traditional on a number of issues.[83] She, like many other women leaders from India, would not consider herself as a feminist; in fact, she dismissed the distinction between men and women as not of consequence, and occurring only due to the grace and will of "Babaji" (Hanuman). Nevertheless, her views on menstruation are conservative, and she believes that women should not actively pray or read scripture during the time of their periods. If the name of God comes spontaneously to them or some prayers come to mind involuntarily, she says, nothing can be done about them; however, voluntary prayer is not recommended. She also stated that this was the case in many world religions. I will return to this issue of menstruation and purity a little later in this chapter.

Guru Ma has also decreed that she does not need any of her disciples to become a renunciant during her lifetime; she has appointed three successors, two men and a woman, to manage the mission after her lifetime. The woman nominee is married and lives in California; when the time is right for her to lead her section, she may become a *sannyasi* or renunciant.

Guru Ma celebrates her *bhakti* to Hanuman and to Shiv-Shakti (Shiva and Parvati). Her next project is to build a temple for Shiv-Shakti, the supreme couple. While the devotees of Guru Ma see her as a devotee, she herself, like many gurus, embodies through her surrender to the divine, the principle of *Shakti* or power. This is not explicitly stated in her case; it is, however, clearly articulated in the lives of famous gurus, Anandamayi Ma (1896–1982)[84] and Amritanandamayi Ma (b. 1953). Anandamayi Ma was married, but led a celibate life, and her husband became her devotee. After a number of spiritual experiences and practices, she heard an inner voice:

> One day I distinctly got the command: "From today you are not to bow down to anybody." I asked my invisible monitor: "Who are you?" The reply came: "Your *Sakti* (power)." I thought that there was a distinct *sakti* residing in me and guiding me by issuing commands from time to time. . . . After some time I again heard the voice within myself which told me: "Whom do you want to take obedience to? You are everything." At once I realized that the universe was all my own manifestation. Partial knowledge then gave place to the integral, and I found myself face to face with the One that appears as many.[85]

To many of her devotees, she appeared clearly as the goddess. Her disciple, Bhaiji, says that he saw "the figure of a divinely beautiful goddess, as genially bright as the sun at dawn, illuminating the whole interior of the room."[86] Another devotee saw her as the goddess Kali.

Armritanandamayi Ma (called Ammachi affectionately by her devotees) is also seen as "unconditional love" and as divine by her devotees. She was born in a fishing village on the shores of the Arabian Sea. Raised in a poor family, she rejected her marriage, and eventually came to identify herself with the goddess. She would walk on the beach feeling herself as one with the divine. She also advocates that women assume the virtues of detachment and courage; virtues that are traditionally considered as "male" in India.[87]

In both cases of Anandamayi Ma and Amritanandamayi Ma we see not devotees, but deities. The two are more than gurus; they are goddesses and have identified themselves as such through spiritual experiences. They are not embodiments of *bhakti,* but personify *shakti.* As embodiments of *bhakti,* women serve as role models; interestingly enough, as *shakti,* they are removed from humanity. Although Andal was filled with *bhakti* and not identified as *shakti,* we nevertheless see similar human/divine tensions in her hagiography. In both Anandamayi Ma's and Amritanandamayi Ma's cases we see that they are who they are without volition; when they have experiences saying that they are the supreme *shakti,* they do not question this; they accept the total reality of their experience. There is one more scenario where women are considered to be divine; after discussing the issue of possession, we will consider the case of how these women are empowered by the divine, or a goddess.

Recent research by Kathleen Erndl and Mary Hancock in different parts of India have highlighted the importance of goddess possession.[88] Erndl works in rural Kangra in the north with nonbrahmin, lower middle-class women. Hancock works in urban Madras, with brahmin smarta, middle-class families. In all cases discussed, the women were "possessed" (though "temporarily occupied" may be a better term) by a form of the goddess. In her vivid descriptions of Tara Devi, a rural housewife with four children, Erndl describes how the Mata ("Mother," here referring to a form of the goddess Jvala Mukhi) began to "play;" that is, temporarily use her body to make pronouncements, cure, exorcise evil, and so on, generally improving the welfare of the villagers and devotees. Tara Devi, herself filled with *bhakti* for the Mata, now becomes an embodiment of *shakti* or power in the eyes of her followers.

Erndl comments that if Tara Devi does seem to transgress "the expected gender norms for a woman of her caste, she does so in response to a divine call with which no one can argue."[89] Her power is acknowledged by the community and Erndl argues that Tara Devi and countless others have drawn on a mythic model, of very real female power to transform their personal identities. This transformation serves as sources of divine energy, empowering other women.[90]

Similar descriptions are seen in the cases of two brahmin smarta women reported by Mary Hancock. The two women she describes are possessed by the goddess Karumariamman, an independent village goddess, with generally a nonbrahmin following, but who is identified by the brahmin women with Shakti and Parvati, the consort of Shiva. The possession events are discreetly marked by brahmin flavor (use of milk as the predominant way of bathing the deity; vegetarian offerings, dialect, and so on), but there are few unconventional moments as well. The medium, a married woman whose husband is alive, wears her hair loose around her face, in emulation of the goddess. Normally, married women in Tamilnadu braid or tie their hair; disheveled or untied hair is either adopted by calendrical portrayals of the goddesses or by inauspicious women.

Sunithi, the medium, also in keeping with Karumariamman's general decrees, but unlike all other orthoprax smarta women, rejects all discrimination and rejection of women on the basis of menstruation or perceived bodily pollution. She also exudes an aura of tranquillity and domestic harmony, which was extremely important in attracting other brahmin smarta women to her flock. This projection is questioned at the end of the article that records that her daughter-in-law left the medium's son, spoke ill about the Goddess, and returned to her parents' home. These minor domestic infelicities aside, we may turn to the general question of empowerment through the Goddesses and deities in general.

The two dominant strains of philosophical speculation and experiencing reality within the Hindu tradition are through the modes of theism and nondualism. In the theistic mode, devotees are empowered by their devotion and by the deity. God and Goddesses create, love, nourish, rage, and destroy. Every one of them is the full, complete, ultimate reality in the eyes of the devotee. The gender of the ultimate has not been profusely debated within the many Hindu traditions because even the earliest texts provide a variety of prisms through which one can perceive the ultimate reality. The supreme being is a man (*purusha*) according to some hymns of the Vedas: this God is variously identified in later Hinduism as Vishnu, Shiva, or one of their many manifestations or incarnations. Some texts, especially the *puranas,* portray the supreme as one of the many Goddesses. Others speak of the supreme being as androgynous (*Ardhanāriśvara,* that is, as half-man, half-woman) in a literal and metaphoric way of conceptualizing the ineffable. Vishnu and Lakshmi are worshiped as the inseparable couple. The Upanishads and some later *bhakti* (especially those addressed to the lord as *nirguṇa* or without attributes) poems say that the supreme one is beyond gender, beyond all dualities, beyond number. It is neither male nor female.

One may add that the supreme is neither one nor many; numbers again are human conceptualizations and flimsy concepts such as monotheism or polytheism break at the limits of human understanding. This is not to relativize all divinities; devotees worship every God or Goddess whom they address their poems to as *the* supreme reality. Goddesses are one form of primal energy among many; a particular form like Karumariamman may be the *only* manifestation of the supreme for the devotee.

Both men and women have been devotees of the goddesses in India. While the Sanskrit hegemonic literature tries to contain the many goddesses in the roles of Lakshmi and Parvati, and makes allowances for Durga and Kali who are seen as distinct but sometimes as interconnected alter egos of Parvati in the eyes of the devotees, the reality calls for dozens of other *matas* and *am-*

mans, mothers of all forms and shapes in India. In Tamilnadu alone, there are the seven sisters, who although thought of as "village goddess" are as urban as they come. The list of the seven varies and most of these names—Nagatamma, Chelliamma, Ankalaparameswari—would not be recognized by the so called "high"-caste women down the street, let alone a pan-Indian Hindu audience. Names of Vaishno Devi and the seven sisters in northern India have a more regional recognition. All of them are powerful, individual beings, and do not admit to being boxed in and identified as a Kali or Durga. Many of them possess their devotees. While possession in the brahminical women whom Hancock describes is relatively rare, possession among the "scheduled" caste—that is, the untouchables—is very common. This is particularly seen in the Tamil month of Adi (July 15–August 14) and some goddesses demand a goat sacrifice, which is willingly given. All of them are powerful; variations of the term *shakti* are attached to all of them.

In general, the term *shakti* is not used for Lakshmi, the goddess of wealth, good fortune, and grace, except in some of the Tantric literature. Here, the experience of Lakshmi as *shakti* is primarily seen in tantric literature that was later accepted by some communities in a limited fashion. However, little pamphlets and manuals that women buy near the temple and that instruct them on the different ways of worship, now add the prayers to Lakshmi in pamphlets called *Sakti Nitya Parayanam* (daily/continuous prayers to Shakti) and *Devi Nitya Parayanam* (daily/continuous prayers to the Goddess). By Devi, the pamphlet means Sarasvati, Lakshmi, Kamakshi, Minakshi, the sacred basil leaf, Tulsi, and so on.[91] The many goddesses who are venerated and who possess are simply called goddess in this article; but it is in plurality that we find her ubiquitous presence. I do not mean to suggest by using the term *Goddess* in the upper case that I am assimilating all these goddesses to one Great Goddess; polytheism is a central experience in the many Hindu traditions; as central as the monism of the Upanishads, and to state otherwise would be reductionistic. When I refer to Shakti, it is to the power that is embodied and projected by all these goddesses.

Tara Devi, Sunithi, and some of the women gurus are filled with *bhakti* and through the mechanics of submission, they become the embodiments of *shakti* or power. This is a feature that is characteristic of theistic Hinduism and the practice of dharmic Hinduism. This model of submission leading to power is to be seen alongside the other model of Anandamayi and Amritanandamayi, who through their experience of a nondualistic reality still proclaim devotion or submission. To put it another way, if one is the supreme, there is no one to offer devotion to and no devotee to offer it. They are all encompassed in the ineffable nature of the supreme. The language of *bhakti* on the other hand is that of total surrender to the other with the goal being a union, which again is beyond words. The *bhakti* experience, while proclaiming surrender, paradoxically becomes the precursor of divine energy and power in the eyes of the beholder.

Thus, the name "Andal," the name given to the paradigmatic woman poet, literally means "she who rules." Mate Mahadevi, Goda Mandali, and all the dancers who surrender themselves to the divine, using the women poets and *bhaktas* as role models, seem to be empowered in the eyes of the onlooker, even if the language of power seems alien and contradictory to the language of devotion and love. This also is seen in the case of women mediums who are devotees of the goddesses. Although they would be quick in pointing out that it is not their devotion that makes the goddess dwell in them and issue proclamations through them, and that such acts occur through her random though welcome grace, the awe-stricken or respectful devotees of these human women see them as paradigmatic devotees.

Cases of total submission leading to miraculous powers is the language that legitimizes dharmic stories of faithful wives and testy husbands. It is the idiom of Sanskrit dharmic narrative to show how wives like Savitri, Sukanya, Arundati, and others who surrender to their husbands, get miraculous powers.[92] But this idiom is applied to religious *bhakti* also, to the negation of the dharmic ideals of proper married life. Among the cases of the women gurus and mediums, we encounter several models of marriage; some never marry (Amritanandamayi Ma), some marry but remain celibate (Anandamayi Ma), others bear children and continue to live with their husbands (Tara Devi, Sunithi), and still others bear children and then renounce them (Guru Ma Jyotishanand Bharati). A detailed flow chart about women poets has been drawn by A. K. Ramanujan.[93] The only common denominator is that the married life has been subsumed under or has totally eliminated the *bhakti* or *shakti* experience. There is room to be negotiated for all these forms of power and its negation within the Hindu traditions.

All bonds of dharmic regulations incumbent on women like chastity and modesty are lifted in the context of *moksha*. We saw *bhaktas* who sell their bodies to feed other devotees. Akka Mahadevi loses all sense of ego and "I-hood" and stops wearing clothes. Women gurus, even in the former eras when women in some areas veiled themselves, showed their faces to strange men and women. It is in the path to *moksha* that Hinduism has officially showed its removal of gender, class, and caste identifiable roles and regulations that it has generally considered to be incumbent on women.

Perceptions of menstruation have been some of the greatest unequalizers in Hindu literature and practice. Because women are considered to be polluted when menstruating, they have, especially in the upper classes and castes, been prohibited from full participation in religious activities. Even women gurus like Guru Ma, we saw, spoke in defense of seclusion during the time of menstruation. Again, the only realms where these taboos are sometimes in theory, and occasionally in practice, lifted, are those of *bhakti* and *shakti*. Draupadi, a powerful women in the epic *Mahabharata,* surrenders to Lord Krishna when she is menstruating. This is done because she is victimized in a situation in which no e husbands, can help her. This situation is used as a religious paradigm by some communities later, and theologians declare that it is *bhakti,* not the idea of bodily pollution, that is important in terms of *moksha.*[94]

While the pronouncements to this effect were laudable, they have seldom been practiced in brahminical communities. Recently, it is in the worship of the Goddess Karumariamman in Tamilnadu that the taboos on menstruating women have been completely lifted. We noticed this in the unorthodox pronouncement of Sunithi, the Brahmin medium who played hostess to this Goddess. Sunithi/the Goddess persona had said that menstruation is not a cause of defilement and allowed active participation of menstruating women in worship. I have also heard this of women devotees who go to the temple of this Goddess in the town of Melmaruvathur, near Madras city. Women worshiping in this shrine also use another marker of their equality with all men. All devotees worshiping at this temple wear red garb; while passing through the main road where this temple is located, I have seen entire chartered bus loads of devotees stop until all the *bhaktas* change to red. It is said that the Goddess had made a pronouncement several years earlier that in front of her, all human beings are equal. Distinctions of the skin, caste, community, and economic class do not apply, she said; the color of blood under the skin of all human beings is red. All *bhaktas* are to proclaim this simple truth when they approach her and dress in the color of human beings. Those with *bhakti* who so access the embodiment of power, become empowered, and become embodiments of *shakti* themselves. While all other Gods and Goddesses move restlessly in the spheres of *bhakti* and *shakti* and readjust the equations of equality, the Goddess Karumariamman for one comes out clearly as a feminist.

Notes and References

1. I am grateful to Professor Arvind Sharma, Professor Kathleen Erndl, and Mrs. Nutan Dave for taking time to discuss many issues in this paper. Please note that diacritics have been used sparingly, and primarily for names of texts.

2. Nancy F. Cott, *The Bonds of Womanhood: "Woman's Sphere" in New England, 1780–1835* (New Haven and London: Yale University Press, 1977) 5.

3. In this context, see Phillip Wagoner, "Sultan of Hindu Kings: Court Dress and the Islamicization of Hindu Culture at Vijayanagara," and Stewart Gordon, "Maratha Government Patronage of Local Muslim Saints and Educational Institutions, 1740–1780." Conference on "Shaping Indo-Muslim Identity in Pre-Modern India," organized by The Triangle South Asia Consortium and The Rockefeller Foundation, Duke University, April 1995. While both papers show the usage of the term *Hindu* as referring to the non-Mussulman inhabitants of India, evidence from Wagoner's paper suggests that this usage may be as early as the 13th century c.e. The standard work that

highlighted this issue is still Wilfred Cantwell Smith's *The Meaning and End of Religion* (San Francisco: Harper and Row, 1978) 63–66.

4. In this connection, see Robert D. Baird, "On Defining 'Hinduism' as a Religious and Legal Category," *Religion and Law in Independent India,* ed. Robert D. Baird, (New Delhi: Manohar, 1993), 41–58.

5. For a summary of these issues as pertaining to American history, see David Hackett, "Gender and Religion in American Culture 1880–1930" (forthcoming in *Religion and American Culture*). See also Jeff Hearn and David Morgan, eds., *Men, Masculinities and Social Theory* (London: Unwin Hymann, 1990) and Lynn Segal, *Slow Motion: Changing Masculinities, Changing Men* (New Brunswick, New Jersey: Rutgers University Press, 1990).

6. See the seminal studies of Katherine Young, especially "Hinduism" in *Women in World Religions* (Albany: SUNY Press, 1987), "Women in Hinduism" in *Today's Woman in World Religions,* edited by Arvind Sharma (Albany: SUNY Press, 1994), and "Srivaisnava Feminism: Intent or Effect?" In *Studies in Religion, 12/2, Spring 1983.* Interesting, provocative studies but debatable include Kumkum Sangari's, "Mirabai and the Spiritual Economy of Bhakti" (*Ecomonic and Political Weekly,* July 7, 1990, 1464–75 and July 14, 1990, 1537–52), Kumkum Sangari, "Consent, Agency and Rhetorics of Incitement" (*Economic and Political Weekly,* May 1, 1993, 867–82), Uma Chakravarti, "Conceptualising Brahmanical Patriarchy in Early India, Gender, Caste, Class and State" (*Economic and Political Weekly,* April 3, 1933, 579–85).

7. For a very readable account of the sexually restrictive norms that a Kerala Nambudiri Brahmin woman lived with, see the short stories of Lalitambika Antarjanam, especially, "The Admission of Guilt" in *Inner Spaces: New Writing by Women from Kerala* (New Delhi: Kali for Women, 1993), 1–12, and "Revenge Herself" in *The Inner Courtyard: Stories by Indian Women,* edited by Lakshmi Holmstrom (Calcutta: Rupa and Co, 1997) 1–13.

8. Madhu Kishwar, "The Daughters of Aryavarta," *Women in Colonial India: Essays on Survival, Work and State,* edited by J. Krishnamurty, (Delhi: Oxford University Press, 1989, 82. On similar conditions today in Bengal, see Ralph Nicholas, "Caste, Marriage and Divorce in Bengali Culture," *From the Margins of Hindu Marriage: Essays on Gender, Religion, and Culture,* edited by Lindsey Harlan and Paul B. Courtright (New York, NY: Oxford University Press, 1995), 156–57.

9. For a list of "High Castes" where widow remarriage was regularly practiced see " The Hindu Widow with special reference to Gujarat," by Vatsala Mehta, M.A. Thesis, Department of Sociology, University of Bombay, 1956. *Towards Equality: Report on the Committee of the Status of Women in India,* New Delhi: Government of India, Ministry of Education and Social Welfare, 1974, 77.

10. Nancy A. Falk, "*Shakti* Ascending: Hindu Women, Politics, and Religious Leadership during the Nineteenth and Twentieth Centuries," *Religion in Modern India,* edited by Robert D. Baird, third edition (New Delhi: Manohar, 1995), 298–334.

11. Falk, "*Shakti* Ascending" 300.

12. Falk, "*Shakti* Ascending" 324.

13. Ibid.

14. I remember my own sense of surprise when I realized that one of the areas women fought for in the West was to get the same pay as men for the same jobs. In my experience in India, except for manual labor, where there was rank discrimination against women, in most professional jobs, there had been standard levels of pay scales for men and women. I was equally unnerved by questions from my American friends about the prospects of Hindu women becoming priests and entering ministerial roles. There was no prominent equivalent to the ministerial role within the Hindu tradition, and most Hindu women had no aspirations to become a family "priest" who was a ritual specialist and did not have a particularly esteemed role except under certain ceremonial circumstances. The agenda in the Hindu traditions is quite different from the West.

15. Madhu Kishwar, "Why I do not call myself a Feminist," *Manushi,* no. 61 (Nov.-Dec. 1990), 5.

16. For a brief discussion of these issues, see Gabriele Dietrich, *Reflections on the Women's Movement in India: Religion, Ecology, Development* (Delhi: Horizon India Books, 1992), viii.

17. Quoted in Gail Omvedt, "Dalit Women: Point of No Return," *Manushi,* no. 1, January 1979, 31.

18. On this issue, see the discussion in Katherine Young's article "Women in Hinduism" especially the section on Uma Bharati (97–100). See also the entire issue of *Bulletin of Concerned Asian Scholars,* volume 25, number 4, October–December 1993, entitled "Women and Religious Nationalism in India."

19. See Madhu Kishwar, "Codified Hindu Law: Myth and Reality," *Economic and Political Weekly,* Aug. 13, 1994, 2145–61.

20. Nancy Auer Falk and Rita M. Gross, "Women's Power: Mythical Models and Sacred Sources," *Unspoken Worlds: Women's Religious Lives,* edited by Nancy Auer Falk and Rita M. Gross (Belmont, CA: Wadsworth, 1989), 233.

21. Kay Jordan, "The Feminist Scholar and the Problematic Case of Devadasi Reform in India." Paper presented at the Annual Meeting of the American Academy of Religion, New Orleans, November 1990.

22. For a general discussion of this concept, see Madhu Kishwar, "Codified Hindu Law: Myth and Reality," *Economic and Political Weekly,* Aug 13, 1994, 2145–61, especially, 2147–48. A Supreme Court decision in modern India that reinforced that custom was the case of *Krishna Singh* vs. *Mathura Ahir* (AIR 1980 SC 707).

23. Nancy A. Falk, "Men, Women and the Problem of Authority in 19th Century Hindu Movements," paper presented in the conference on "Gender and the Vedic Tradition," Columbia University, April 1995.

24. For a discussion of *Narada Smriti,* see Richard Lariviere, "Matrimonial Remedies for Women in Classical Hindu Law: Alternatives to Divorce," *Rules and Remedies in Classical Hindu Law,* edited by Julia Leslie, Leiden: E. J. Brill, 1991, 37–45.

25. The Vellallas, for instance, who were considered to be "sudras" from the brahminical viewpoint, were a landowning community in Tamilnadu, and perceived to be "high-caste Hindus." S. Manickam, *Slavery in the Tamil Country: A Historical Overview* (Madras: Christian Literature Society, 1982), 20. Burton Stein remarks of the Vellallas: "their ubiquity and prestige . . . has been a marked feature of agrarian society until the present time." Quoted in A. K. Ramanujan, *Hymns for the Drowning,* ix.

26. Madhu Kishwar, "Introduction," *Manushi: Tenth Anniversary Issue, Women Bhakta Poets,* nos. 50–52, 1989, 7.

27. For an interesting discussion, see A. K. Ramanujan, "On Women Saints," *Radha and the Divine Consorts of India,* edited by John Stratton Hawley and Donna Marie Wulff (Berkeley, CA: Berkeley Religious Studies Series, 1982), 316–24. For a discussion of Saiva women saints, see Sanjukta Gupta, "Women in the Saiva/Sakta Ethos," *Roles and Rituals for Hindu Women* (London: Pinter, 1991), 193–209.

28. The woman poet Toral apparently "pledged her body in return for groceries to feed pilgrims." However, Toral saves herself by teaching about devotion to the man who coveted her. Sonal Shukla, "Traditions of Teaching—Woman Sant Poets of Gujarat," *Manushi: Tenth Anniversary Issue: Women Bhakta Poets,* nos. 50–52, 1989, 69. A similar story is told of a Sri Vaisnava woman. See A. Govindacharya, *Life of Ramanujacharya* (Madras: S. Murthy and Co. 1906) 116–18.

29. Translated by Vilas Sarang, *Women Writing in India: 600 BC to the Present,* volume 1 (New York: Feminist Press, 1991), 83.

30. Sri Pe.Ka. Shanmukantan, *Srivilliputtur stala makātmiyam* (Madurai: Madurai Kūṭṭuravu Accakam Limited, 4th edition, 1972), 45.

31. In the last two decades women have begun commenting on both Sanskrit and vernacular religious literature in public, giving learned discourses. The role of a commentator and exponent of the Hindu religious narratives (the genre called *katha* or "story") has generally been appropriated by men. Thus, all the important "performers" of the Hindi version of the Ramayana, the Ramcaritmanas, are male. Since the 1970s, women exponents of the Bhagavad Gita and other religious texts are beginning to perform in public, both before live gatherings and on television.

32. I am indebted to Mr. N. G. Rajasekhar of Gainesville, Florida, for searching through his files and giving me several pamphlets on Mate Mahadevi's life and poems.

33. S. R. Gunjal, "Authoress: A Brief Sketch," Pamphlet dated 17 December 1973. There is no publication information but it is written by S. R. Gunjal, deputy librarian of the Karnatak University, Dharwar, Karnataka.

34. Gunjal, "Authoress."

35. *Samyukta Karnatak,* 21 April 1980.

36. Gunjal, "Authoress."

37. From a publicity pamphlet called "Here is What News Media Reports on Mataji," distributed in Pittsburgh in the mid 1970s.

38. Interview with Mrs. Krishna's daughter, Mrs. Radha Parthasarathy, herself a composer, on December 14, 1994.

39. Interview with her nephew's wife, Mrs. Ranganayaki Sampathkumaran of Koramangala, Bangalore, June 1995.

40. The composers whose works I have seen (apart from those mentioned in the text) are Mrs. Kanakavalli (1890–1945) and Mrs. Seetha (Bangalore 1909–1974). I have also spoken to Mrs. Raji Krishnan (Poughkeepsie, NY) and Mrs. Sundaravalli Narayanan (Jacksonville, Florida) and seen some of their compositions.

41. See *Royal Patrons and Great Temple Art,* edited by Vidya Dehejia (Bombay: Marg, 1988).

42. See *Tirupati Inscriptions,* vol. 1, Tirumalai-Tirupati Devasthanam Epigraphical Series. See also T. K. T. Viraraghavacharya, *History of Tirupati,* volume 3, (Tirupati: Tirumala Tirupati Devasthanams, 1982), 21–22, and S. Ramesan, *The Tirumala Temple* (Tirupati: Tirumala Tirupati Devasthanams, 1981), 57.

43. Vidya Dehejia, *Art of the Imperial Cholas* (New York: Columbia University Press, 1990).

44. B. Nagappachar, *The Belur Temple* (Saklaspur, Karnataka: Sri Krishna Power Press, 1960).

45. For a detailed study of the endowments made by courtesans and "servants of God" (*devadasis*) in temples, see Leslie Orr's dissertation, and "The Vaisnava Community at Srirangam." *Journal of Vaisnava Studies,* Vol 3, no. 3 1995, 109–136.

46. Donna Marie Wulff, "Images and Roles of Women in Bengali Vaisnava *Padavali Kirtan,"* *Women, Religion and Social Change,* edited by Yvonne Yazbeck Haddad and Ellison Banks Findly (Albany: State University of New York Press), 221–23.

47. Rabindranath Tagore, *The Religion of Man* (New York: Macmillan Company, 1931), 180–81.

48. B. Nagappachar, *The Belur Temple,* 7. Almost all the official guide books to the area point out the image inside the temple (marked as #40 now by the government

of India authorities and the Archeological Survey of India) as representing Shantala Devi. I am not familiar with the primary sources that make this identification. The restaurant in the official Indian Tourism Development Corporation Hotel at Hassan is called "Shantala." The general Indian stereotype of wifely virtue is to perceive a woman the server of food and it is interesting that of all places, a restaurant is named after this queen who contributed so much to the fine arts as well as architecture.

49. See Wagoner, "Sultan of Hindu Kings: Court Dress and the Islamicization of Hindu Culture at Vijayanagara."

50. These remarks are based on personal observation in Bombay and elsewhere. Also see *Manushi,* No. 38.

51. S. Seetha, *Tanjore as a Seat of Music,* Madras: University of Madras, 1981, 35, 98 and 122–226. In chapter 3, Dr. Seetha discusses the contributions of composers and musicians between the 17th and 19th centuries in the Tanjore area, and it is interesting to note that all sixty-two musicians/composers whom she focuses on are men. It is evident from other sources also (N. Rajagopalan's *A Garland,* which lists all the important musicians in south India) that prior to this century almost all musicians who were well known and who gained public approbation were men.

52. V. Narayana Rao and D. Shulman, "History, Biography and Poetry at the Tanjavur Nayaka Court," *Identity, Consciousness and the Past: The South Asian Scene,* edited by H. L. Seneviratne. Special issue of *Social Analysis: Journal of Cultural and Social Practice* (Adelaide, South Australia, 1989) 122.

53. S. Seetha, *Tanjore as a Seat of Music* (Madras: University of Madras, 1981), 98.

54. V. Narayana Rao and D. Shulman, "History, Biography and Poetry," 125.

55. For an account of this episode, see Susie Tharu and K. Lalita, eds., *Women Writing in India 600 BC to the Present* (New York: Feminist Press at the City University of New York, 1991) 1–8.

56. Adapted from a booklet containing the biography of Bangalore Nagaratnammal, written by her disciple, Banni Bai.

57. "Rukmini Devi Arundale," in N. Rajagopalan, *A Garland: Biographical Dictionary of Carnatic Composers and Musicians* (Bombay: Bharatiya Vidya Bhavan, 1990), 256.

58. Sharbari Mukherjee, "Women and Traditional Indian Music" in a brochure published by Geetika, a music organization for women. Quoted in Madhu and Ruth, " 'Bhairav se Sohni': Geetika's All-Women Classical Music Festival," *Manushi* vol. 3, no. 3 (March-May 1983), 7.

59. The information on *dhrupad* in this paragraph is based on conversations with Mrs. Nutan Dave of Gainesville, FL. It is augmented with materials from a book that she kindly gave me, B. Chaitanya Deva, *An Introduction to Indian Music* (Delhi: Ministry for Information and Broadcasting, Feb. 1973), 34–37. I am also grateful for conversations with Dr. Keskar, Gainesville, FL.

60. Asghari Begum Sagarwali is Muslim and learned music from another Muslim teacher, Ustad Zahoor Khan, but within the realm of music in India, religious distinctions have not created divisiveness. In south Indian classical music, Hindus dominate and in some spheres like the playing of the *nadaswaram,* Muslim men like Sheikh Chinna Maulana Sahab and women like Begum Mahabooba are stars. In northern India, however, both Hindus and Muslims have participated in the performance of classical music. I deal with this issue in my forthcoming article, "The Strains of Hindu-Muslim Relations: Babri Masjid, Music and Other Areas Where The Traditions Cleave."

61. Madhu [Kishwar] and Ruth [Vanita], "A Grand Old Lady of Music: An interview with Asghari Begum Sagarwali," *Manushi,* vol. 3, no. 3, March-May 1983, 8.

62. Madhu [Kishwar] and Ruth [Vanita], "A Grand Old Lady of Music: An interview with Asghari Begum Sagarwali," 10.

63. The reasons for the decline of women's involvement in classical music in northern India have been based on Rita Ganguly and Vidya Hydari, "From Mother to Daughter: Women in Classical Music," *Manushi,* no. 33, vol. 6, no. 3 (March-April 1986), 12–14. Ganguly and Hydari write "Since 1947 we have an independent government of our own, but these women singers continue to face problems and prejudices. Mass Media, for instance, are not easily available to these women for performance. In fact, one of the first moves of the Ministry of Information and Broadcasting after 1947 was to ban the singing of professional singing women. Even after the ban was lifted, famous singers like Anwari Bai and Kesar Bai Kerkar refused, as a symbol of protest to perform for AIR [All India Radio]."

64. Madhu [Kishwar] and Ruth [Vanita]. "A Grand Old Lady of Music: An Interview with Asghari Begum Sagarwali," 10.

65. Ruth and Vanita "Bhairav se Sohni," 7.

66. Publicity pamphlet for "Sita's Daughters" by Darpana Academy of Dance.

67. Madhu [Kishwar] and Ruth [Vanita], "A Grand Old Lady of Music: An interview with Asghari Begum Sagarwali," 10.

68. I have discussed this in my article, "Hindu perceptions of Auspiciousness, and Sexuality," *Women, Religion, and Sexuality: Studies on the Impact of Religious Teachings on Women,* edited by Jeanne Becher (Geneva: WCC Publications, 1990), 64-92.

69. Swarnakumari Devi was a famous poet, writer, and editor whose style was initially imitated by her younger brother Rabindranath Tagore who was considerably better known.

70. Madhu Kishwar, "Was Sita Mrs. Ram?" *Manushi* no. 39, vol. 7, no. 3, 11.

71. Monica Felton, *A Child Widow's Story* (New York: Harcourt, Brace and World, 1967), 32.

72. Jyotsna Kapur, "Putting Herself into the Picture: Women's Accounts of the Social Reform Campaign, Maharashtra," *Manushi,* no. 56 (Jan.-Feb. 1990), 36.

73. Krishna Lahiri, "A Romantic Martyr or Exemplar? The Life of Doctor Anandibai Joshi (1865–1887)," *Gender in World Religions* (Montreal: McGill University, Faculty of Religious Studies) vol. 4, 1993, 59–86.

74. Felton, *A Child Widow's Story,* 141–42.

75. Kay Jordan, "The Feminist Scholar and the Problematic Case of Devadasi Reform in India."

76. Jordan, "The Feminist Scholar," 17.

77. Jordan, "The Feminist Scholar," 22.

78. *India Today,* August 15, 1994, 26.

79. Falk, "Shakti Ascending," 299–300.

80. My information on the *rshikas* in Maharashtra is based on Mary McGee's research, "The Vedas in New Key: Portraits of Contemporary Brahmacarinis and Rishikas." Work in progress, presented at the first conference on Gender and the Vedic tradition, Columbia University, April 1994.

81. For an account of the well known ones, see Linda Johnsen, *Daughters of the Goddess* (Minneapolis: Yves International Publishers), 1994. See also Catherine Clementin-Ojha, "The Tradition of Female Gurus," *Manushi,* no. 31, vol. 6, no. 1 (November-December 1985), 2–7 for an account for women gurus in and near Benares.

82. *Journal of Vedic Heritage* vol. 16, November 1994- February 1995, 18. The account of her life was based on an interview with her, held in Ocala, FL, on June 4, 1995.

83. The following statements are based on the interview held on June 4, 1995.

84. On the life of Anandamayi Ma, see Elizabeth Lasell Hallstrom's doctoral dissertation, "My Mother, My God: Anandamayi Ma, (1896–1982)," Harvard University, 1995. A brief account on the empowering aspects of her life is found in Dr. Hallstrom's article, "Beyond the Extraordinary: The Hindu Woman Saint, Anandamayi Ma," paper presented at the national meeting of the American Academy of Religion, San Francisco, 1992.

85. Lipski, *The Life and Teaching of Sri Anandamayi Ma* (Delhi: Motilal Banarsidass,) 1977), 10–11.

86. Sri Jyotish Chandra Ray, *Mother as Revealed to Me* (Varanasi: Shree Shree Anandamayee Sangha, 1962), 9.

87. Linda Johnsen, *Daughers of the Goddess,* 93–102.

88. For excellent studies of women's empowerment through the process of being possessed by a goddess, see Kathleen Erndl, "The Goddess and Women's Empowerment: A Hindu Case Study," *Women in Goddess Traditions,* edited by Karen L. King (Minneapolis: Frotress Press, 1997), 17-38, and *From the Margins of Hindu Marriage,* edited by Lindsey Harlan and Paul Courtright (New York: Oxford University Press, 1995)

89. "The Goddess and Women's Empowerment: A Hindu Case Study."

90. For a different portrayal of empowering women through goddess symbolism and reappropriating the power of the goddess, see Lina Gupta, "Kali, the Savior," *After Patriarchy: Feminist Reconstructions of the World Religions,* edited by Paula M. Cooey, William R. Eakin, and Jay B. McDaniel, (Maryknoll, N.Y.: 1991), 15–38.

91. A typical booklet that I found with assorted prayers to the various goddesses which mentioned her was in my mother's collection and was called *Devi Nitya Parayanam* (Madras: P.T. Pani coompany, 1948).

92. On the working out of a similar scenario in modern Tamilnadu, see Margaret Egnor, "On the Meaning of Sakti to Women in Tamil Nadu," *The Powers of Tamil Women,* edited by Susan S. Wadley (Syracuse University, 1980), 1–34.

93. A. K. Ramanujan, "On Women Saints," 318–19.

94. Pillai Lokacharya, a 13th-century theologian of the Sri Vaishnava community in south India, actively argues to this effect in his *Srī Vacana Bhūṣaṇam,* sutra 29. Pillai Lokacarya, "Śrī Vacana Bhūṣaṇam" in *Srīmadvaravaramunigranthamālai,* (Kanchi: P. B. Annagaracharyar, 1966).

Chapter 2

Strategies for a Feminist Revalorization of Buddhism

Rita M. Gross

The task outlined in my title is a daunting project which has occupied much of my scholarly attention for the previous twelve years.[1] It has been the subject of my recently published book, *Buddhism after Patriarchy: A Feminist History, Analysis, and Reconstruction of Buddhism.* Therefore, in this chapter, I will be able only to survey the outlines of the project.

Defining Key Terms

We may begin by looking at the title itself. The word *strategies* perhaps suggests too deliberate and manipulative a stance—as if someone were enjoying intellectual games with the terms *feminist* and *Buddhist,* playing them off against each other. The process about which I am speaking is more organic than that, growing out of years of existential involvement with both Buddhism and feminism, and thus no mere game plan.

Questions about the traditional Buddhist appraisal of women and women's position in Buddhism have long received some attention from Western scholars of Buddhism, but that attention has been somewhat limited. It has almost always focused on questions *about* women in Buddhism, assuming that the questioner is an outsider analyzing information about a closed system in which she does not participate and which will not be affected by her analysis. Recently, that situation has begun to change, as Buddhist women, and some men, both Asians and Westerners, begin to analyze, as insiders, what resources their tradition has for a truly egalitarian Buddhism in which women are not treated as lesser Buddhists. By *strategies* I have in mind the conclusions and arguments that such scholar-practitioners concerned about feminist issues might present.

These strategies do owe something to feminist insights. They are not the usual responses suggested by Buddhists unsympathetic or unacquainted with feminism. On the one hand, a segment of the contemporary Buddhist world is quite unsympathetic to any hint of feminist revalorization of Buddhism. We see this reaction, for example, in Thailand, where women who have received full nuns' ordination through Mahayana ordination lineages are not allowed to wear brown monastic robes, but are forced to wear the white garments of the *mae chi*.[2] Thai Buddhism had not previously had any form of nuns' ordination and the Buddhist establishment is unwilling to see that situation change.

Other traditional Buddhists are not so unsympathetic to women's aspirations, even though they may not be conversant with feminist thought. The typical Tibetan teacher's response to questions about women in Buddhism is to state that Buddhist teachings do not distinguish between men and women, but that women have special responsibilities as mothers. If pushed farther, they usually say women's poor track record in Buddhism is due to "cultural factors" and that if women study and practice very diligently they will progress along the path in the same manner as men.

Such a stance is much less harsh, but hardly sufficient from a feminist point of view. Reproductive tasks are still seen as women's primary vocation and responsibility. More problematic, women's low levels of achievement are subtly blamed on women themselves, citing their lack of sufficient study and practice. The responsibility of Buddhist institutions and perhaps of Buddhist teachings for discouraging women from more serious involvement with Buddhism, which feminist analysis would investigate, is not taken into account.

Thus, *feminist strategies* will go well beyond the usual repertoire of Buddhist responses to questions about women and the *dharma*. Buddhist feminist strategies also contain a built-in assumption; Buddhism is not a closed, finished, and unchangeable system, but like any living religious symbol system, changes and incorporates nontraditional elements into itself. For an insider to a symbol system that takes impermanence as a basic fact of existence to assert otherwise would be rather inconsistent.

One could hope that the term *feminism* would be understood without lengthy definition, but I fear that such an assumption is not realistic, both because some members of the academic establishment still have not integrated the implications of feminism into their scholarly methods and because of disagreements among feminists. I find it helpful and clarifying to distinguish three levels of feminism, all the them relevant to a feminist revalorization of Buddhism. The most basic and least controversial definition of feminism concerns feminism *as academic method.* Conventional androcentric scholarship, which proceeds as if it were sufficient to study the religious lives and opinions of men alone, is severely criticized for its incompleteness by feminist methods. Put most simply, feminism as academic method involves the transition from androcentric, or one-sexed, to androgynous, or two-sexed models of humanity.[3] This aspect of feminism, which brings a revolution of consciousness that touches all aspects of scholarship, is most central to the historical considerations in a feminist revalorization of Buddhism. One cannot study about something adequately if only half the data are considered, which is what happens in conventional nonfeminist scholarship. And this is why many experts on Buddhism, whether insiders or outsiders, have only the vaguest notions about roles and images of women in Buddhism.

The second level of feminism concerns feminism *as a value system* and *as a social vision*. This aspect of feminism regards conventional sexism and patriarchy as immoral. It proposes alternate social arrangements that would be more humane to women, and also to men. The heart of a feminist revalorization of Buddhism lies with this level of feminism, which fuels the Buddhist feminist's discontent with current gender arrangements within Buddhism, gives her the courage and the tenacity to keep up the critique, and inspires much of the vision for postpatriarchal Buddhism.

The third definition of feminism is one I reserve especially for "insider's discourse" on the topic of Buddhism and feminism. Feminism articulates that, in Buddhist terms, *women really are in the human realm* among the six realms of sentient beings, not in some half-step realm between the animal and human realms, which is the impression one might get from some Buddhist debates about women.[4] This definition of feminism is so simple as to be embarrassing; yet it was one of my earliest answers to questions of what's wrong with the status quo and why we need feminism; it has not lost relevance or cogency over the years.

The term *revalorization* in the title also requires some discussion, for it contains two implications readily apparent to those conversant with feminist theology that might slip by others. If we have decided to invest time and energy to "revalorize" a religious symbol system, that implies a prior judgment that the system is not beyond repair, is not so hopelessly sexist and patriarchal that a nonsexist version of the same symbol system would bear virtually no resemblance to its patriarchal predecessor. Some weighty feminists would argue that no traditional religious symbol system is reparable. I will spare you the arguments they might make vis-à-vis Buddhism, for if they were right, this chapter and perhaps this entire book would be pointless.

Issues in a Feminist Revalorization of Buddhism

The decision of whether or not to put one's energies into revalorization also brings up the question of whether the institutions of the tradition are at all sensitive to the cogency of feminist reforms. Some feminists feel that, while it might be possible to revalorize a religious symbol system, those in positions of hierarchical power are so out of touch and so unsympathetic to women that reform within the system is hopeless. In that case, they argue, heartbreak and burnout are the only possible results of trying to work within the system. I am not totally convinced that they are not right vis-à-vis Buddhism. One can readily question whether the Asian Buddhist males who hold all the most authoritative positions in the Buddhist hierarchy are willing to take the challenges of feminism seriously, but some causes are choiceless for some people.

The term *revalorization* contains another hidden implication. Not only *can* the system be revalorized, it *must* be revalorized. Not only can the traditional symbol system and teachings of Buddhism accommodate the insights of feminism. Buddhism as received tradition is not perfect and complete as it is. It *needs* to be revalorized by feminist insights in order to overcome patriarchal inadequacies and excesses, and to be true to its own vision. This implication of the task of revalorization transforms the agenda from incorporating a troublesome external criticism into Buddhism to recognizing the incompleteness and inadequacy of male dominated forms of Buddhism. Once feminist criticisms and revalorizations become clear, male dominated forms of Buddhism must be judged as undharmic, perhaps even antidharmic.

The outlines of an actual feminist revalorization of Buddhism can be presented rather succinctly. To explain the arguments fully and to fill in all the details would take considerably more than a single book chapter. A feminist revalorization of Buddhism would involve study of the historical record regarding roles and images of women in Buddhism, analysis of the key concepts of the Buddhist worldview vis-à-vis gender and gender privilege, and reconstruction of both Buddhist thought and Buddhist institutions in the light of feminist values. History, analysis, and reconstruction, in a nutshell.

Those familiar with Christian feminist thought, which is considerably more developed than its Buddhist counterpart, will notice at once that these same three categories dominate Christian feminist theology. This similarity is not due to conscious imitation, but to major likenesses in the current manifestations of the religions and in the problems to be solved. Perhaps because Christian feminist thought is relatively well developed, Buddhist feminists do not have to take all the detours and dead-ends that have occurred in Christian feminist thought.

Issues for a Feminist History of Buddhism

The question of the historical record is in some ways the simplest and in others the most complex. The record is the record and cannot be changed by feminist dreams. But the record *as selected and interpreted* by both insiders and outsiders is quite another matter. The task of the feminist historian vis-à-vis the history of a religious tradition is best summed up, in my view, as the quest for a record that is both *accurate* and *usable*. To get that record, it may well be necessary to "redress omissions and recast interpretations,"[5] because of the quadruple androcentism encountered in the usual records. In the first place, the contemporary records kept by Buddhists often preserved much more information about men than about women. Second, within Buddhist traditions of memory and honor, male heroes receive far more attention than female heroes, giving any outsider the impression that they are more important. Third, partly reflecting these Buddhist habits, but also reflecting the androcentism of their own scholarly milieu, Western scholars of Buddhism have also, for the most part, studied and written about Buddhist men. Finally, contemporary Buddhists, both Asian and Western, continue to focus on the tales of male heroes, to the relative downplaying of tales of female heroes, and to be generally unaware of Buddhism's patriarchal past, its male-dominated institutions, or the problems inherent in such values and behaviors.

In the quest for an accurate record, one should be on the alert especially for two pitfalls that have occurred frequently in studies of women's history. On the one hand, it is easy to become depressed by the record, especially in its most androcentric form. Early in one's studies, it can seem that the history of a religious tradition is merely one long dismal record of misogyny and sexism. Anyone who knows Buddhist history at all knows that such an interpretation is easily possible. This phase in the development of women's history is appropriately called "the pit;" it is often followed by a period of "compensatory history." In this phase, one looks for all the great women, seen as very much like the great men, but buried by the androcentric record. There is something to this, for there are great, but often unknown, women in the history of every tradition. But there are problems with this approach too. Some would co-opt the existence of a few great women into a defense of the status quo and rest content with tokenism—a tactic I hear most often from Buddhists. "Why Rita, Buddhism doesn't have a problem about discrimination against women. Four of the eighty-four *mahasiddha*s were women!" Mainly, however, the quest for great women, by itself, retains the standards of androcentric history and gives us no clue as to "women's history."

The accurate record can, in my view, be summed up by a number of generalizations. First, in every period of Buddhist history, there are at least two views about women, neither of which ever fully wins out. Some texts record fairly negative views of women, even some outright misogyny, which is different from patriarchy or male dominance. Women are viewed as more materialistic, emotional, and sexual than men, less able to renounce desire, and generally less capable of making significant progress on the Buddhist path.

Not uncommonly, women's best hope was thought to be rebirth as a male, whether offered out of pity and compassion, given the difficulties of women's lives, or recommended out of scorn for women's limited abilities. But, in every period, others stated and argued that women were not inherently deficient or inferior to men in their ability to achieve the calm and insight required to attain Buddhism's highest goals. This opinion is attributed even to the historical Buddha, despite his reluctance to found the nuns' order and some rather nasty comments about women also attributed to him.

The second major generalization is that in the broad sweep of Buddhist history, from early Indian Buddhism to Mahayana to Vajrayana, the bias against women becomes less acceptable. The weightier texts, stories, and teachers argue that "the dharma is neither male nor female,"[6] and that to denigrate women "who are the symbol of wisdom and *Sunyata,* showing both"[7] is a serious root downfall. This pattern, I believe, may differ significantly from the pattern demonstrated by other major religions, though more study would be required to verify that impression.

Thirdly, on the whole, Buddhist attitudes toward women throughout history are not especially misogynistic, if misogyny is narrowly defined and not confused with male dominance, especially when Buddhism is compared with other major religions. However, androcentrism is almost unrelieved throughout Buddhist history. This androcentrism, more than any other facet of the Buddhist past, prevents us from finding any truly reliable models in the past, but feminists are used to living in "a world without models."[8]

Feminist history also looks for a usable past, suppressed in the androcentric records. Though during my study of these materials, I have discovered many interesting and important narratives about women that are not easily available, even in fairly scholarly sources, I do not believe that recovering this information about women is the most usable aspect of the past for a Buddhist feminist. It should be recovered and become part of the general Buddhist record, of course. But the most usable information that one gains from a deliberate study of the history of Buddhist opinions about women is that there has always been a "quasi-feminist" position in Buddhism, if one can bear the anachronism involved in using a modern term to name earlier attitudes. There has always been controversy about women's options and abilities, and there have always been important Buddhist thinkers who stated clearly that the practice of some Buddhists to discriminate against women is inappropriate and undharmic. This is useful and important information because so many Buddhists today are naive and complacent about that history. Either they assume that Buddhists have never seriously limited and denigrated women, or they assume that until a few Western women came into the picture, "feminist" questions never emerged in Buddhism. Those who follow either version of naivety then often try to make Buddhists who are sensitive to feminist issues feel defensive, telling them that Buddhists should be beyond such "non-Buddhist attitudes" and such ego-involvement.

In the long run, I believe that historical questions are not as important for Buddhist feminists as they have been for Christian feminists because history is neither exemplary nor normative for Buddhists to the extent that it can be for Christians. A great deal seems to be at stake for Christian feminists in accurate portraits of the Jesus movement and the earliest church.[9] But I do not believe Buddhists evaluate historical precedent as normative in the same way. Much more critical for Buddhists is an analysis of the key dharmic teachings, of the central concepts of the Buddhist worldview. What are their implications for questions of gender hierarchy and the relevance of gender? Is it possible that Buddhist history is quite at odds with Buddhist dharma regarding the treatment of women? Of the two common points of view regarding women and gender issues found throughout Buddhist history, I believe that the view that femaleness is an unfortunate condition and that men have an edge over women has been the more popular. It is also the less normative. Feminist analysis of key Buddhist concepts reveals definitively that the essential Buddhist worldview is free of gender bias and that many longstanding Buddhist practices are in direct contradiction with Buddhist teachings on this score.

"The Dharma is Neither Male nor Female": A Feminist Analysis of Major Buddhist Teachings

Perhaps the key element in the strategy for a feminist revalorization of any major world religion is to demonstrate that the core teachings of the tradition do not permit bias or discrimination on the basis of gender, and that they are essentially egalitarian in their implications, no matter how sexist some historical interpretations may have been. This kind of feminist analysis is relatively undeveloped in Buddhist thought, especially in comparison with Christian thought. Because of its importance and relative underdevelopment in Buddhist feminism, in this chapter, I will undertake an extensive feminist analysis of selected Buddhist doctrines as my major task.

In my view, Buddhists can make the case very strongly that the core teachings of Buddhism are not sexist because Buddhism lacks two major doctrines, which prove to be extremely difficult for feminists to reconstruct, that are found in most other major religions. Because of Buddhist nontheism, there is no gendered Absolute or Supreme Being valorizing the male sex among humans in the fashion that the deity of male monotheism has often be used to justify male dominance in Western religions. Additionally, Buddhism lacks a divinely revealed or eternally valid cosmic law code or lifestyle that defines gender roles and gender relationships. The Jewish or Muslim law codes, thought of as divinely given, regulate gender relations; the eternal Hindu codes of proper behavior (dharma in its Hindu meaning) prescribe gender behavior equally precisely; in East Asia, Confucian notions of proper gender hierarchy are thought to be part of the cosmic natural order. There is no equivalent to any of these in Buddhism. In fact, when Buddhist leaders sought guidelines for the interactions of lay people, they almost always relied on the Hindu or Confucian norms already present in the cultures in which Buddhism flourished. Thus, Buddhism has no intrinsically binding norms concerning gender hierarchy or the proper relationships between women and men.

Of teachings *present* in the Buddhist outlook and important to it, only the pan-Indian notion of *karma* can possibly be interpreted in such a manner as to condone gender privilege and gender hierarchy. This idea, rather than any doctrine specific to Buddhism, has always been used when a defense of gender privilege and gender hierarchy within Buddhism was sought.

Let us look briefly at the way in which teachings about karma, cause and effect, are popularly interpreted, since they are usually the stronghold of those justifying the status quo of male privilege and preference for males as teachers, hierarchs, and monastics. The usual explanation goes something like this. Everyone's current position is a result of karma from the past. Women have an inferior position in a patriarchal society, and furthermore, their biology and intellectuality are said to be deficient and perhaps disgusting by those with patriarchal values. Their inferior social position, biology, and spiritual-intellectual capacities result from negative karma, so they must gracefully bear these liabilities, which will probably produce the future karmic reward of a better (male) rebirth. This thinking is so entrenched that when I gave my first paper on Buddhism and feminism, in 1980 at a Buddhist-Christian encounter conference, certain Asian male Buddhists stated that feminism might be relevant for Christians, but it certainly wasn't for Buddhists, since Buddhism, by virtue of holding out the promise of male rebirth for "deserving women," had already recognized and solved the problem of male privilege.

Let us look more closely. Both the feminist and the traditional Buddhist agree that female existence, *under current patriarchal conditions,* is less than ideal. The traditional Buddhist solves that problem by eliminating *femaleness,* taken to an extreme in Amitābha's exclusively male Pure Land. The feminist, on the other hand, would eliminate the *conditions,* especially male privilege, that make femaleness a liability, recognizing that femaleness itself is only one variant of the human, not a deficient, state of being. Any "deficiencies" that might be perceived are not intrinsic to femaleness, but the result of causes and conditions of patriarchy and male privilege. Furthermore, at most all that traditional interpretations of the doctrine of karma could do in this case is *explain* the current situation; *it cannot be used to justify continued mistreatment.* To continue to oppress people because "it's your karma to be oppressed by me" is to create negative karma for oneself. Seen in this way, the doctrine of karma has serious implications for social policy, which is perhaps why Buddhists usually advised kings to be kind and just.

The teaching of karma is a pan-Indian notion adopted by Buddhism rather than a teaching or point of view specific to Buddhism. It is interesting that whenever Buddhists attempt to explain or justify male dominance and gender hierarchy, they appeal to this idea, or to Hindu and Confucian justifications for male dominance. None of the major or minor doctrines that articulate the specifically Buddhist outlook has ever, to my knowledge, been called into service to justify male dominance, probably because they provide no basis whatsoever for such a justification. Instead, these teachings are always stated in an abstract, nongendered form that would promote the impression that they are intended to address all human beings, even all sentient beings, as many Buddhist teachers try to explain when asked specifically about women's position in Buddhism. Feminist analysis of these central Buddhist teachings will demonstrate clearly that they contain no gender bias, that indeed, they speak to human experience, rather than out of male experience.

However, a feminist analysis of these central Buddhist teachings will also do more; it will demonstrate that any practices of gender hierarchy are completely at odds with Buddhist dharma—a much more powerful conclusion than simply to argue that Buddhist teachings are gender-neutral. If one can demonstrate that gender bias or male dominance are at odds with Buddhist teachings, as I believe feminist analysis will demonstrate, then a feminist revalorization of Buddhism is not merely the low priority agenda of a few feminists; it is a matter of some urgency for all Buddhists. Obviously, a great deal is at stake if the latter, rather than the former, assessment is correct.

When attempting to organize the multifarious teachings of Buddhism in its full development, one must adopt one of a number of competing schemas of classification. Because I am most familiar with the "three turnings" organizational schema, familiar to Tibetan Kagyu and Nyingma schools of Buddhism, I choose that classification system, both in this chapter and in *Buddhism After Patriarchy*. This choice is not meant to discount other schools of Buddhism and their ways of understanding the full unfolding of Buddhist dharma, nor is it part of a debate about the best way to understand Buddhism; it simply is the organizational framework I have chosen out of familiarity.

To speak of the "three turnings" is to draw upon the old metaphor of the Buddha turning the wheel of dharma when he preached his first sermon at Benares. That was the "first turning," which coincides with the historically earliest teachings of Buddhism and with the first phase of the path of spiritual development according to Tibetan Vajrayana perspectives on the Buddhist path.

The "second turning," undoubtedly mythical rather than historical, occurred with the Heart Sutra and other Perfection of Wisdom literature, texts presenting many important Mahayana teachings, including teachings about emptiness or *śūnyatā*. The third turning is even more mythical in its origins. It concerns other Mahayana doctrines, especially those of the Mind-Only school of Mahayana Buddhism, which is the doctrinal basis for Vajrayana Buddhism as well.[10] A full-scale feminist analysis of key Buddhist concepts would consider all the major doctrines of all three turnings. In this chapter, only some doctrines can be discussed in depth and others must be referred to in a more cursory fashion.

Among first turning teachings, teachings about egolessness are perhaps the strongest basis for a feminist revalorization of Buddhism. Upon close analysis, using analytic tools derived from both Buddhism and feminism, gender identity must be seen as an aspect of ego, not of egolessness. Therefore, clinging to gender identity or gender privilege is conducive to *saṁsāra*, not nirvana. Though many feminists unfamiliar with Buddhism often regard Buddhism's claims about the desirability of egolessness to be irrelevant to women, correctly understood, the Buddhist concept of egolessness undercuts male dominance. It cannot be used to encourage women to become or remain spineless doormats, dependent on and subservient to males.

Egolessness is one of the three basic traits of all sentient beings. It, along with suffering and impermanence, can be seen as the most basic Buddhist diagnosis of the human condition. Without exception, when analyzed realistically, all beings share this same fate; they suffer anxiety, they experience unending impermanence, and they lack a permanent soul-entity. Impermanence is the fulcrum from which the other two traits can most readily be understood and the easiest to grasp and concede, at least superficially. Surely everything changes. At some level, everyone can grasp that basic fact. But people resist change, which inevitably causes suffering and mental anguish. Furthermore, if everything is constantly changing and impermanent, how can we exempt our self, our ego, our identity from this general rule? We are fundamentally egoless, but that state of being is difficult to bear, so we constantly create styles of ego or self, which often cause us great problems. Furthermore, we almost constantly are subject to the illusion that our self must have some permanent core somewhere, so that the veil of ego becomes so thick that we cannot imagine being without it.

Two methods of demonstrating the truth of egolessness are important in Buddhism. The more familiar method is the analytical method, which looks deeply into the assumed self of conventional thinking. The self is broken down into its component parts, but no real essence is discovered underneath these component parts. "There is no unmoving mover behind the movement. It is only movement."[11] The synthetic method shows that there can be no essence that demarcates an individual as existing in reality, rather than merely at the level of conventional appearance, because all things are interdependent. As important, perhaps more important, than the theory of karma in explaining cause and effect, this concept of interdependent, co-arising *(pratityasamutpāda)* emphasizes that nothing exists independent of its matrix, but only in interdependence with it. Thus, there can be no self, as anything more than a convenient and useful label for a particular momentary configuration of events in this vast web of interdependence and relationality.

It is important, however, to undercut some common misconceptions about egolessness by stating what it is *not.* Egolessness is not a nihilistic condition nor the attainment of nonexistence, as opposed to existence. It is not a blank vacuous state of nonperception and nonthinking. It is not an indifferent state of not caring what happens to one's self or others, and it certainly has nothing to do with being so psychologically beaten and victimized that one acquiesces to whatever happens. It has nothing to do with being spineless and indifferent, with being a pushover for others' aggression. An egoless person is quite the opposite of a zombie. Rather, she is cheerful, calm, humorous, compassionate, empowered, and energized because she has dropped the burden of ego.

Nevertheless, in the Buddhist diagnosis, that fluid, open, nonfixated way of being is too much for ordinary people to maintain. Instead, the fluid, open, egoless, nonfixated state is replaced by panic, which results in oppositional duality—me and my perceptions, conceptions, or states of consciousness dependent on objects experienced as "other." Gradually, we build a habitual, familiar, and conventional style of reactions that is "ours," that allows us to cope in one way or another with all the stimuli and otherness that seems to be barraging us from all directions. We develop a sense of being an isolated entity confined in our subjectivity, of being or having an ego that we evaluate as more or less healthy, with which we are often dissatisfied. We also worry a great deal about protecting that ego, which is beginning to cause us a good deal of suffering. We cling to things that seem to be desirable; we fight off other things aggressively; and everything else we ignore.[12] Along the way, we have also somehow come to feel that this vague "sense of me-ness" deserves to be permanent and eternal. We have moved from experience of a psychological ego to belief in a soul.

The link between this psychological or metaphysical ego and ethical dilemmas is very close:

> According to the teachings of the Buddha, the idea of self is an imaginary, false belief which has no corresponding reality, and it produces harmful thoughts of "me" and "mine," selfish desires, craving, attachment, hatred, ill-will, conceit, pride, egoism, and other defilements and impurities and problems. It is the source of all the troubles in the world from personal conflicts to wars between nations. In short, to this false view can be traced all the evils in the world.[13]

It is difficult to summarize feminist thinking on these issues in a similarly succinct way, because feminism lacks a similar consensus on these issues. Nevertheless, when we bring these Buddhist ideas into feminist discussions of the same territory, which emphasize that egos are gendered, we should not be surprised if the results are potent for both systems. Except for the fact that Buddhism has not looked at gender as a component of ego—a major oversight that, when corrected, has very significant implications for Buddhism—the two systems are remarkably consonant, despite rather sharp differences of terminology. Regarding issues of gender and ego, Buddhism and feminism are more like each other than either is like Western patriarchal thought, in that both explore how dysfunctional habitual patterns of mind cause great suffering.

First, we should discuss several objections to these Buddhist ideas that one frequently hears from feminists. The classic apocryphal story concerns the puzzled feminists who have just listened to a Buddhist speaker discussing how ego is the source of all human problems and how by dismantling ego, we can achieve some freedom. They comment, "That sounds like a good religion—for men!" Some assume that the Buddhist situation is like the Christian situation, as analyzed by Valerie Saiving[14] and others. She points out that men, who tend to be self-aggrandizing, preach the need for self-effacement to congregations full of women who have already internalized that virtue and need more self-confidence. This frequent comment results from misunderstanding the Buddhist use of the term *ego,* and probably from Buddhist speakers who are not alert to their potential to confuse listeners by their use of the term.

In popular conventional Western usage, it is assumed that everyone has an ego, that you can't function without one, but that it is somehow measurable or quantifiable, and that some people have "too much ego" while others have a "weak ego." Often, women, who tend to define themselves through relationships more than do men, are thought to have "weak ego boundaries," which some see as a problem and others laud. But it is often claimed by feminists that Buddhist concepts of ego and egolessness would be more relevant for men than for women because many women "need more ego, a stronger self-concept, not less ego."

From the Buddhist point of view, someone who is intensely co-dependent and someone who is intensely macho or self-aggrandizing suffer equally from ego. Ego, as we have seen, is any style of habitual patterns and responses that clouds over the clarity and openness of basic human nature. Self-effacement is just a style of ego different from self-aggrandizement, but both equally cause suffering to self and others. "Ego" names the defense mechanisms, projections, and other tactics habitually used to cope with and ward off direct experience. All ordinary people have some ego-style, some style of grasping and fixation. The amount of ego really isn't quantifiable; someone who is forceful doesn't have "more ego" than someone who is shy and retiring.

Feminists, concerned with the kinds of problems women develop in patriarchal systems, might not immediately see the relevance of this more inclusive and generic discussion of ego. However, it is helpful to see clearly that people with "weak egos," in Western terms, don't really need to build up a "strong ego," in Western terms, before they can get on to the basic task of becoming healthy, no longer needing to cover over the openness and fluidity of basic enlightened human nature. One can go directly from the unhealthy and often overweak or co-dependent ego styles that characterize women in patriarchy to the health of egolessness.

The feminist contribution to discussions of ego and egolessness, as defined by Buddhism, is to demonstrate, incontrovertibly and powerfully, the extent to which gender-fixation is part of ego, and therefore, damaging and destructive. As already mentioned several times, this aspect of ego has been totally overlooked by Buddhism, but bringing together these two methods of understanding ego is quite provocative. In feminist analysis, one's ego includes and is conditioned by gender identity. Feminist discussions of gender thus provide a major critique of conventional Buddhism.

Ego has often been called a pigeonholing device by Buddhists. It allows one to objectify phenomena and distance one's self from the immediacy, brilliance, and vividness of experience. Certainly one of the most pervasive and powerful pigeonholing devices of all is gender. "That's a man. I can expect these behaviors. I should behave in this way." "That's a woman. She can't do these things. She will demonstrate these traits and characteristics. Her function in life is to do the following." Such subconscious gossip is almost continuous. And in terms of Buddhist analysis, there's no place to put it except in the category of "ego," as well as the category of *saṁsāra*. One certainly couldn't place it within the mode of egoless, enlightened being in the world!

Nevertheless, much of the Buddhist institutional world is constituted by patterns of ego that rely on gender to pigeonhole the world. Stereotypically, males are thought to be more "spiritual" and able to develop calmness and tranquility, even though male anatomy itself seems to war against these qualities. In every realm, religious or secular, men have precedence and dominance over women, as is evidenced by the eight special rules subjugating nuns to monks. The preference for maleness extends even to the next life. All these practices of gender privilege and gender hierarchy encourage clinging to male ego; they do not encourage egolessness. Strangely, quite un-Buddhist attitudes—pride (in being male), scorn for other beings, clinging to and fixation upon being male— are condoned and encouraged by this situation. Thus, Buddhist institutions promote one of the more painful and pervasive manifestations of ego—an untenable situation, to say the least. It has always seemed strange to me that a tradition so keenly aware of the perils and pitfalls of ego has not been equally keen in its recognition that gender-privilege is one of the more destructive manifestations of ego.

If gender, or at least using gender to confer privilege, is one of the deep-seated tricks of ego, how would one correlate gender with egolessness? Would someone who does not use gender to pigeonhole the world not know whether she was male or female? Would he be unable to determine the sex of someone whom she encounters? I doubt it! But he would not use sex as a basis to organize the world or the *sangha;* she would not use people's sex to limit her expectations of them; most of all, she would not limit or categorize herself based on sex. If we may make the distinction between sex as a biological given and gender as an ego-filled and ego-ridden social construct based on sex, the enlightened or egoless person would be aware of sex but would have transcended the need to rely on gender-constructs. Such a person would become androgynous, perhaps even in physical appearance, as is the case with some old adepts who have practiced the egoless life for a long time.

Using the analytic categories of feminism and the insight born of the feminist understanding that gender is an aspect of ego, we can generate a powerful critique of conventional Buddhist habits and stereotypes. Seeing gender-fixation and gender privilege as an aspect of ego makes Buddhist patriarchy inadmissable *on Buddhist grounds.* This critique is much more powerful to a Buddhist, for we have shown that gender privilege is not compatible with Buddhism on Buddhism's terms, not just on feminism's terms. A Buddhist patriarch could ignore feminism with ease, and probably would. He should pay more attention to Buddhist demonstrations that patriarchy is contrary to Buddhism, that in fact it fosters one of the most basic samsaric traps discovered by Buddhist spiritual practice, that it fosters ego rather than egolessness.

Other teachings characteristic of the first turning and of the earliest layer of Buddhist thought, such as the basic ethical guideline of nonharming or the basic meditation techniques of mindfulness and awareness, could with equal facility be utilized in a feminist reconstruction of Buddhism. However, having chosen the method of fuller demonstration of feminist analysis of a few Buddhist doctrines over cursory discussion of the range of Buddhist teachings, I will now move on to discuss second-turning teachings.

Among second-turning teachings, the doctrine of emptiness has been the most widely utilized in feminist interpretations of Buddhism. In fact, the feminist interpretation of this doctrine did not need to wait for feminism, for the classic Buddhist arguments against automatic gender hierarchy, made almost two millennia ago, argue that since all categories are empty of intrinsic meaning, females cannot be automatically discounted but could understand and manifest the highest goals of Buddhism. In Mahayana Buddhist texts, women or young girls are frequently portrayed as highly developed Bodhisattvas whose understanding confounds and amazes their patriarchal detractors.

Because these stories are relatively well known and their feminist implications have been discussed by a number of commentators,[15] I will focus on a different set of second-turning teachings whose feminist implications have been less frequently discussed. In these stories about women who demonstrate the emptiness of categories such as "femaleness," another theme also stands out. They discover or rouse the thought of enlightenment, or *bodhicitta,* which is the basis for their spiritual accomplishments. For a Mahayanist, no other experience is more central than the discovery of *bodhicitta,* which is celebrated joyously in Mahayana texts and constantly aroused in Mahayana liturgies. Once this experience is firmly established, one is on the bodhisattva path toward the full enlightenment of a Buddha. In this experience, one intuits self-existing spontaneous compassion in the core of one's being. This compassion is not dutiful nor based on fear and need. It is utterly uncompelled and unstrategized and, therefore, completely genuine. Not based on hope of rewards and returned favors, such genuine compassion is accompanied by feelings of joy and freedom because one feels that one has recovered one's true nature, previously obscured by ego and attachment. This experience is so inspiring that one is motivated to pursue enlightenment, not merely for one's self, but for all beings, which is the essence of the famous bodhisattva vow. Often understood as a "future Buddha," a bodhisattva develops altruism, deep and widespread concern for others, to the point that self-interest is no longer the motivating force behind actions. Compassion takes its place.

In the three-yana perspective, such an awakening is the inevitable consequence of proper self-cultivation through meditation and contemplation, since they result in developing a healthy, sane sense of self relatively free of ego and negative habitual tendencies. This is because, in the Buddhist perspective, human nature, beneath the constructions of ego, is basically good.[16] Though it has been much less explicitly noted, experiencing that basic good nature also means experiencing one's sane, enlightened self as fundamentally relational rather than essentially autonomous. When *bodhicitta* is experienced and allegiance to it is expressed through the bodhisattva vow, one is affirming one's connections with others as fundamental and basic. They become the reference point of one's life, not in a co-dependent, but in a compassionate, way. One sees one's life as fundamentally and inextricably interlinked with all other lives. One cares about them. In this caring, emotions are cultivated and trained, not repressed or endured. It is assumed that properly developed and cultivated emotions are as fundamental to a sane, healthy person as is a trained and cultivated intellect, and that both are equally trainable and tameable. Furthermore, the person who acknowledges and treasures this interconnectedness, and who contemplates and develops the emotions that enable one to contribute well and wisely to the relational matrix of life, is the lauded and valued person.[17] A person who has these qualities is considered to be mature and developed. They are the whole point of spiritual discipline.

The Mahayana ideal of the bodhisattva path is strikingly consonant with much recent feminist ethical thinking. Carol Gilligan is best known for articulating the view that women tend to see life as fundamentally relational and, as a result, solve ethical problems differently from men.[18] The role of the emotions in being and knowing is also evaluated positively by many feminists, who criticize the conventional intellectual tradition for its dichotomizing of intellect and emotions, and its denigration of the emotions. The possibilities opened up and clarified by suggestions are among the most provocative, profound, and relevant of the contributions yet made by feminist thinking. Clearly, the ethics of feminism and of Mahayana Buddhism have more in common with each other than either has with the ethic of individual autonomy and self-sufficiency favored by the dominant androcentric culture. But what of the similarity between feminist and Mahayana Buddhist ethics?

For myself, I am comforted and inspired by the profound sympathy between Mahayana ethics and what I regard as some of the most important insights of feminism. My own criticisms, as usual, center much more on the gap between Buddhist ideals and the way in which Buddhism is manifested in the world. Women can and should feel affirmed in their mode of being, relating, and caring by the Mahayana emphasis on the centrality of such experiences to genuine spirituality. Feminists could well take the fact that Mahayana Buddhism gives such prominence to these emotions and experiences as outside confirmation of their conclusions and as a resource for continued development of these themes. The fact that Buddhism has such a well-developed repertoire of meditative and contemplative techniques for helping people develop their relational, compassionate selves[19] should not be overlooked by feminists, who have the same goal.

Sometimes, however, feminists see a potential pitfall with this ethic as a relevant ethic for women. They say that the message of the centrality of compassion is a message women have heard all too often and all too well in patriarchal culture. Internalizing this ethic, women are given, and take, most of the responsibility for nurturing others, without much compensation, or much change of being nurtured themselves. These critics would say that women need much more to learn to take care of themselves than to hear another religion telling them to take care of everyone else. This criticism shares something with the criticism discussed earlier that women need more, not less ego; in neither case do the critics understand Buddhism very well.

This criticism can be countered by two refutations. On the one hand, many feminists themselves would counter that patriarchal culture needs to be feminized by coming to value relationship appropriately. The problem of women as unnurtured nurturers is not solved by having women also become autonomous and isolated, like men, but rather by feminizing men and culture as a whole. Women should not give up what is sane and healthy about their modes of being and knowing, simply because it is not rewarded and affirmed by the general culture. The more important refutation, however, would recognize that many women do care in unwise and unhealthy ways. They need something besides another authority telling them to care more and be more compassionate. That, however, is not the Buddhist message.

As we have seen, for Buddhism, the development of compassion is not the first message or agenda for spiritual development. The first step is nonharming, which includes learning to overcome self-destructive ego patterns, such as loving too much[20] or caring unwisely, in unhealthy ways. Caring, by itself, is not enough. One needs to learn to care with the detached and all-encompassing compassion of a bodhisattva; in order to be able to do that, one first needs to learn nonharming and to develop some understanding of egolessness and emptiness. Caring, without the proper preparation of self-development, and not accompanied by clarity and wisdom, is often very destructive, of both self and other.

The term *compassion* is absolutely central in the traditional understanding of Mahayana ethics. However, the emphasis on "relationality" may not be so central to the traditional Buddhist understanding of compassion. In my own case, I have become much more aware of how interlinked are the practice of compassion and the primacy of relationality since my own life experiences and feminist thinking have forced this awareness upon me. But I was not taught by Buddhists to value relationality, at least not using that terminology. Now I see the two—relationship and compassion—as inextricable in Buddhist materials. Once I did not, and thought of compassion more as an attribute that I might possess than as the fruition of my utter interrelatedness with the world. I do not know if the fault lay with the inadequacy of my former understanding of Buddhist materials or if feminist thinking has added a nuance to Buddhist understandings of compassion that was slighted earlier. My suspicions favor the later hypothesis.

Finally, I wish to link feminist ethics and the bodhisattva path much more definitively with the need for Buddhism to develop its prophetic dimension.[21] Even more than the ethic of nonharming, the bodhisattva ethic of compassion and universal concern for all beings cries out for the development of a social ethic that includes prophetic social criticism and vision. Buddhism is sometimes accused of not having a social ethic. That is not really the case, since both first turning teachings and the bodhisattva path contain many guidelines for human interactions. What Buddhism has lacked is the will to direct significant amounts of communal energy into social concerns and reconstructions. But when one takes on universal liberation, rather than individual liberation alone, as one does when one takes the bodhisattva vow, the time has come to go beyond individual rectitude to the communal efforts that effect large-scale social changes. When one realizes how unliberating, how oppressive, economically, politically, psychologically, and spiritually, are some of the dominant forms of social organization and authority, it is hard to imagine being serious about liberation or the bodhisattva path without being involved in social action at some level. The ethics and vision of the bodhisattva path strike me as the most relevant arena into which to introduce such prophetic discourse in Buddhism.

To apply these comments more specifically to gender issues, it is difficult indeed to reconcile patriarchal religious institutions with the serious practice of the bodhisattva path. Yet it has been done repeatedly. Historically, nuns were subjugated to monks and their order was allowed to disappear in many parts of the Buddhist world. Women have repeatedly been actively discouraged from taking up serious spiritual discipline and were taught to look down upon their specific form of the precious human body. No religion, of course, could be utterly free of individuals who did not live up to its vision. But I have always been puzzled by the generations of Buddhists who have taken the bodhisattva vow with utmost sincerity and yet have also practiced, promoted, and justified gender hierarchy and gender privilege in Buddhism. The gap between the vision and the practice of Buddhism nowhere seems wider. Someone who has taken the bodhisattva vow should not promote gender inequality, whether by direct action or by passively accepting the status quo.

Third turning teachings and their extensions into Vajrayana Buddhism probably provide the most cogent resources for Buddhist feminism in all of Buddhist thought. *Tathāgatagarbha* theory, the cornerstone of the third turning, is especially relevant for feminist Buddhist thought. The term *tathāgatagarbha*[22] is often translated as Buddha-nature, though this is not a literal translation. More literal translations, which are often avoided, would be "Tathāgata-womb" or "Tathāgata-embryo." *Tathāgata* is a title for Buddha and *garbha* connotes both "womb" and "embryo." Therefore, this term posits an embryo of Buddhahood or a womb containing Buddhahood. The obvious positive feminine and uterine symbolism of the term should not be overlooked, though that feminine symbolism may explain why scholars have preferred the more bland and neuter "Buddha-nature." This term is used to refer to indwelling Buddhahood, which is the inherent potential of all sentient beings, in some interpretations, of all that is, including the physical universe.

Several things should be understood about this Buddha-embryo. Despite the positive "full" style of language used about Buddha-nature, it is not a self or soul, according to those who propose this language. Those inclined to see the second turning teachings, couched in a much more negative style of language, as the highest truth have often made this criticism about some of the interpretations of *tathāgatagarbha*.[23] Rather than being a self, soul, or essence, it is that which one discovers in the experience of egolessness, when *śūnyatā* is thoroughly intuited. According to these teachings, one discovers that one is Buddha and has always been so, though that wisdom was veiled and obscured previously. When the veils and obscurations are removed, what remains is intrinsic, indwelling, innate Buddhahood.

However, even before the veils are removed, Buddhahood is still there as seed. All the metaphors—seed, embryo, womb—suggest both growth potential and something obscured by or hidden in its container, but fully intact nevertheless. That is why the literal translations of Buddha-embryo, or womb containing Buddha, are so much more evocative than "Buddha-nature." These translations also acknowledge that, in this case, the Buddhist tradition has explicitly compared the process of developing enlightened qualities with the processes of pregnancy and gestation, which are especially drawn from women's experience.

Using modern terminology, this trait has also been called "the enlightened gene," which indicates that it is something intrinsic and fundamental to one's make-up, not an adventitious extra. Furthermore, this one element, this one "gene" among the many in one's make-up, is enlightened. Because this enlightened gene is already there, unborn, unceasing, and nondwelling, not subject to causes and conditions, one can become Buddha completely. Were it not there, one could never become Buddha, no matter how hard one tried. Compared to this most basic and fundamental trait of everything that is, all other traits are superficial and irrelevant.

And, finally, this Buddha-embryo is generic and common, not personal. It is not to be conflated in any way with personal identity and has no individuality. Certainly it has no gender and is not different in women than in men. Such a statement would be incomprehensible, and has never, to my knowledge, been made in any Buddhist text, important or minor. In fact, the opposite point is always made. Even if a being falls into extremely low forms of existence through evil deeds and negative karma, nevertheless, inherent, indwelling Buddha-nature continues to characterize that being as its basic nature.

Tathāgatagarbha theory has always struck me as providing a remarkably strong basis for feminist interpretations and criticisms of Buddhism. Perhaps it is no coincidence that Queen Śrīmālādevī, a mature woman who does not change her female sex to prove her competence as a teacher—as do some other women in Mahayana stories of the highly developed female—is a teacher of *tathāgatagarbha* theory. First, we should recognize this theory's more obvious, and perhaps superficial, implications regarding gender issues. When the actual meaning of the term is taken into account, the biological processes of gestation and pregnancy are valorized as the most apt metaphor for the existence and effects of indwelling inherent Buddhahood. It is self-contradictory to valorize these processes symbolically but at the same time to diminish and denigrate those among human beings who are most intimately involved with them.[24]

More critically, *tathāgatagarbha* theory implies that since all beings are fundamentally characterized by Buddha-nature, women and men, equally, are fundamentally Buddha, beneath adventitious secondary and superficial gender traits. This doctrine would be extremely difficult to use in any attempt to justify gender hierarchy. When brought it bear on gender issues, the only compelling conclusion is that *tathāgatagarbha* theory is gender neutral and gender blind. All *beings* are characterized by the enlightened gene. It is not stronger or more vigorous and dominant in men, weaker and more recessive in women.

That all sentient beings, certainly all men and women, equally have inherent potential for enlightenment provides an extremely strong criticism of existing Buddhist institutions. If women and men have the same basic endowment, the same potential for enlightenment, then their vastly different achievements, as recorded throughout Buddhist history, can only be due to inadequate institutions, to institutions that promote, encourage, and expect men to achieve higher levels of insight and realization. Some might try to justify the status quo by arguing that it is a woman's karma to live with religious institutions that discriminate against her, that do not provide her inherent Buddha-embryo with the same nourishment that is given to one growing in a male body.

That attempted explanation, by way of women's less fortunate karma, is simply another manifestation of the inadequate institutions and lowered expectations limiting women. The "explanation" is itself one building block within the self-perpetuating, socially created patriarchal institutions that attempt to justify continued oppression of women, not a genuine explanation that stands apart from the system that is being explained.

Also important is the way in which second and third turning teachings work together, building upon one another with both negative and positive arguments against gender privilege and for egalitarian gender arrangements. On the one hand, because all phenomena are empty and lack inherent existence, intrinsic maleness and femaleness cannot be found. Therefore women and men should not be stereotyped. On the other hand, the intrinsic nature of all people, without regard for gender, is their potential for Buddhahood. Therefore, it is not appropriate to place institutional obstacles, such as formal subordination, lower expectations, or discouragement from the life of study and practice, in the path of either gender. Unfortunately, Buddhist texts have not emphasized, or even noted, how these key Mahayana concepts, especially in conjunction with each other, undercut the current Buddhist norms and practices regarding gender. Furthermore, taken together, the concepts of emptiness and Buddha-nature provide a very firm basis to argue that gender equality is a normative, rather than an optional position, for Buddhists. If gender equality is normative, then actively working to undercut gender hierarchy and privilege is a required ethical norm for all Buddhists, not merely a marginal position for a few feminists. It becomes a matter, not merely that bodhisattvas should not perpetuate gender inequities, but that, as part of their bodhisattva activity, they should promote the vision of a Buddhist world that is not based on gender privilege and gender oppression.

When these teachings were extended into the Vajrayana interpretations of suchness, primordial purity, and nondualism, they gave rise to the symbolic and anthropomorphic richness of the Vajrayana concepts of feminine and masculine principles, which I believe are our best resource for a Buddhist understanding and practice regarding gender that is neither hierarchal nor sex-neutral. In this context, however, we can only hint at all the possible analyses of these rich doctrines.

Vajrayana Buddhism advocates that the most adequate language about "things as they are" is nondualistic,[25] rather than monistic or dualistic. That is to say, disparate phenomena neither collapse into an overarching unity into which their specific qualities are subsumed, so that their specificity and individuality are lost, nor do they stand independent and solidly existing in their separateness. Nonduality, sometimes spoken of as "two-in-one" symbolism, or as the coincidence of opposites, is of critical importance for understanding the Vajrayana view of the proper relationship and interactions between both women and men, and between the masculine and feminine principles. Masculine and feminine form a dyadic unity, anthropomorphically symbolized by the *yab-yum* icon of a couple in sexual embrace, so familiar to those with even a passing knowledge of Tantric Buddhism. Many other symbolic pairs are also found—bell and *vajra*,[26] left and right, sun and moon, vowels and consonants, red and white, to name only a few. They are not two separate entities nor are they one entity; they are a dyadic unity, in which each mutually interpenetrates the other, is inseparable from it, and is co-necessary with it.

In this dyadic unity, the feminine principle symbolizes all-encompassing space, in which phenomena arise and in which they play. Space is emptiness, with all the connotations that term has in Mahayana Buddhism, and space is also wisdom. Thus, if there is a primordial element—but one should be very reluctant to assign priority to either element of the pair—it is space, which is "feminine."

Therefore, in many Vajrayana *sādhana*s (meditative liturgies), one finds an emphasis on the female sexual organs as awesome and sacred. The primordial source of all phenomena is the "source of dharmas,"[27] a downward pointing pyramid, which, when Tantric symbols are homologized with the human body, is located at the position of the womb. (Male practitioners also place the source of dharmas at this place in their bodies when they do *sādhana*s that call for such a visualization.) That which space accommodates is the masculine principle—form, activity, compassion. They are symbolized as the male deity in the *yab-yum* pair and in many other ways. Nevertheless, though distinctive, the masculine and feminine principles, space and form, are inseparable, for "form is emptiness but emptiness is also form."[28]

Partly to concretize these insights about femaleness and partly to offset popular Buddhist attitudes regarding women, Vajrayana practitioners are commanded to avoid the denigration of women as a root downfall. These root downfalls, systematized by Sakya Pandita in the eleventh century, are of utmost importance to Vajrayana Buddhism. The fourteenth root downfall is worth quoting in full:

If one disparages women who are of the nature of wisdom, that is the fourteenth root downfall. That is to say, women are the symbol of wisdom and Sunyata, showing both. It is therefore a root downfall to dispraise women in every possible way, saying that women are without spiritual merit and made of unclean things, not considering their good qualities. If one says a little against a woman, that can be purified. But if the woman disparaged is a Vajra sister, and one considers her as one's enemy, that is the third and heavier root downfall. If the woman is not actually a Vajra sister, to give up being friendly to her is the fourth root downfall.[29]

It is important to notice that this requirement to avoid the denigration of women would make it impossible to combine the worship of femininity with scorn for women, a combination that happens in some religious contexts.

Other aspects of the Vajrayana approach to spiritual discipline are equally "quasi-feminist." As part of the nondualistic Vajrayana approach to spirituality, which emphasizes appreciating, rather the rejecting, the world, Vajrayana Buddhism regards the body, sexuality, and emotions as key components of the spiritual quest, a revalorization for which it is justly famous. Positive feminine symbolism, not out of touch with women's realities, is essential in all three cases.

Tantric commentaries on the body are so voluminous as to defy description. But nothing could be more telling than the first reminder contemplated at length by all Vajrayana students: "precious human body, free and well-favored, difficult to obtain, easy to lose."[30] A woman meditator praises her precious human birth in the same way as does a man. Furthermore, the female organs are sometimes praised and venerated, as already demonstrated by the discussion of the uterine source of dharmas. Sexuality is impossible to avoid in the Vajrayana universe. As phenomenal experience it is appreciated and validated, and as symbol, it is routinely visualized in many *sādhanas*. By definition, sexual symbolism presupposes feminine symbolism. Finally, appreciation of emotions as the raw material of enlightenment is commonplace in Vajrayana Buddhism. The way in which the five neurotic emotions become the five enlightened wisdoms is a favored contemplative theme. In that contemplation, the emotions are not repressed but freed of their negative dimensions.[31]

In more conventional spiritual practices, which are suspicious of the body, sexuality, and the emotions, or consider them to be antispiritual, women are often identified with all three and blamed for arousing them. However, if the body, sexuality, and the emotions are seen as integral to the spiritual path, insofar as women are associated with them, then women should not be denigrated, but venerated. By itself, this would still be a highly androcentric view, but the concomitant Vajrayana emphasis on nonduality discourages projection of emotion onto the other and encourages claiming one's emotions as one's own, a point consistently stressed in Vajrayana meditation training.

Some feminists have voiced suspicions that a genuine dyadic unity is impossible. Put more abstractly, they would have to claim that genuine nondualism is impossible, that the only options are duality or monism. Whenever two elements are central in a symbolic universe, they would contend, there *will be* hierarchical ranking between the two. In their favor, many systems do retain a subtle dualism, even when they proclaim that both elements of a dyad are critical and necessary. The ambiguity attached to the *yin* element in some Chinese cosmological thinking is a good case in point.[32] Is there a similar possibility that activity and compassion, the male elements in this dyad, are given a subtly higher value? They are not, which becomes clear in the oral instructions given to the student for internalizing and utilizing the symbols for feminine and masculine principles in Tantric meditation rituals. The interplay of right and left hands, and of the *vajra* and bell, which stand for masculine and feminine, stress equality, co-necessity, and mutual interpenetration.

A more serious question would concern whether the emphasis on masculine and feminine principles reinforces, rather than undermines, gender stereotypes. Are women to be accommodating and spacelike, rather than active? Are men to be busy saving the world, but not too spacious and quiet? That humans should emulate and strive to develop only the principle that matches their physiological sex is never taught in Vajrayana Buddhism. Rather, the practitioner always strives to develop both wisdom and compassion, both spacious accommodation and effective activity. Women and men equally are given *sādhana*s in which they visualize themselves as male or as female *yidam*s, or as both together. Men and women students may begin their journey conforming to gender stereotypes, but their conformity should decrease, not increase, with practice, which, in my experience and observations, usually happens.

Toward a Feminist Reconstruction of Buddhism

When the feminist account of Buddhist history is joined with the feminist analysis of key Buddhist doctrines, a massive contradiction is apparent. This contradiction is the inspiration for the third strategy for a feminist revalorization of Buddhism—reconstruction according to postpatriarchal androgynous vision.

The most succinct way of summarizing the contradiction is to say that, in Buddhist terms, it represents an intolerable conflict between view and practice.

The "view," according to the feminist analysis of key Buddhist concepts, involves nonfixation on gender identity, the emptiness of gender, and the nonduality and mutuality of feminine and masculine principles. But the "practice" frequently excuses and condones gender hierarchy. Buddhist institutions of all types in all forms of Buddhism are more open to men than to women. Women are stereotyped as incapable of or uninterested in serious Buddhist practice. Their specific reproductive responsibilities are constructed by society to limit them from cultural expression and creativity, though men's reproductive responsibilities are not similarly construed.

To resolve that intolerable contradiction, one must alter the practice, not the view. But how? Since it is the institutions of Buddhist society, not the Buddhist worldview, that fall short, I have frequently argued that it becomes imperative to "mandate and institutionalize gender equality, to build it into the fabric of Buddhist life and institutions completely, in a thoroughgoing fashion."[33]

The reconstructive vision will be articulated in two stages. The most immediate need that comes to mind is the Buddhist parallel to the reformist wing of Christian feminism or so-called equal rights feminism in secular terminology. This kind of feminist reconstruction focuses on the contradiction between the nonsexist core of Buddhist teachings and the patriarchal overlay that has tainted it throughout its history. Reconstruction, therefore, requires only undoing undesirable accretions to uncover a pristine and adequate basis for gender equality in traditional Buddhism.

Allow women full access to Buddhist institutions and practices, the kind that men have always had, and the imbalance between male and female exemplars of the tradition will disappear. It could not be otherwise, advocates of this position would contend, for the teachings of the Buddha are equally relevant and applicable to all.

The reformers focus on the three major forms of Buddhist institutional life—lay Buddhism, Buddhist monasticism and education, and the lifestyle of yogic practitioners who are neither monastic nor lay. With proper sensitivity to the basic issue of making sure that the institutions of Buddhist life don't favor men over women, with proper encouragement and opportunity for women, we could expect a veritable flowering of accomplished women accompanying the men who have always stood out.

The issue of a lay Buddhism that fosters both women and men as Buddhist practitioners is central to Western Buddhism, since at this point, it does not appear that most Western Buddhists will become monks or nuns. Classically, Buddhism has very weak models for serious lay practice, since lay Buddhists were thought to be too busy and too easily distracted by family and profession to engage in meditation or to understand Buddhist teachings fully. Encouraged to practice the accumulation of merit through economic support of monastics, their lifestyle has received relatively little attention from Buddhist thinkers.

Therefore, reconstructing lay Buddhism in accord with feminist values is part of the project of constructing viable models of lay Buddhism for the West.

The practice of Buddhist meditation and the study of Buddhist teachings are more time-consuming and demanding than the usual program for lay involvement in a religion. Therefore, lay Buddhists need to think carefully about precisely those aspects of the householder lifestyle that earlier Buddhism saw as the liabilities that disqualified lay Buddhists from serious pursuit of the accumulation of wisdom—family and livelihood or profession. These also are major concerns that feminism has already explored in some depth, providing useful and relevant models for Buddhism.

Drawing upon the resources of both Buddhism and feminism, rather simple guidelines suggest themselves. Feminism insists that the responsibilities and opportunities for both livelihood and family should be shared equally and equitably between women and men. And since serious pursuit of Buddhism requires dedication and time, the lay Buddhist practitioner must limit both reproduction and career appropriately. Large families and workaholism are probably incompatible with serious lay Buddhist practice, because they are too time-consuming. And since both family and livelihood are, on the one hand, time-consuming and demanding and, on the other hand, rich opportunities to develop one's practice and understanding of Buddhism, those responsibilities and opportunities need to be shared by both men and women. The kind of mutual incompetence fostered by traditional sex roles is a poor and unworthy model for lay Buddhism.

Basic feminist reconstructions of monastic life would be relatively straightforward and, with few exceptions, should be relatively noncontroversial. Two reforms have the highest priority. The full ordination for nuns needs to be restored to those forms of Buddhism in which it has been lost—namely Theravada and Tibetan traditions. And the low levels of economic support for nuns and consequent lack of education for nuns also need to be corrected. Unfortunately, even these modest reforms are not acceptable in all parts of the Buddhist world, as already detailed in the beginning of this paper. Even in Buddhist groups that do not voice opposition to reinstituting the nuns' ordination, the men who hold power and authority seem to be in no rush to get on with the task.

If reinstituting nuns' ordination or supporting nuns more adequately are not immediately put into practice as valid and reasonable feminist reforms in Buddhist institutional life, then we must expect that other, more radical feminist reforms would surely be resisted. Historically, the nuns' order was under the control of the monks. The eight special rules that are attributed to the Buddha himself effectively subordinate all nuns to each and every monk, regardless of age, seniority of ordination, or level of education and attainment. According to some analyses, these rules both reflect Buddhist uneasiness with the idea of allowing women to take up the monastic option at all and are largely responsible for the decline of the nuns' order in all parts of the Buddhist world.[34] Given their poor track record and negative influence on the long-term health and well-being of the nuns' order as well as their obvious incompatibility with feminism's egalitarian vision, the eight special rules have no place in postpatriarchal Buddhism.

Among the lifestyles and options found in historical Buddhism, the lifestyle of yogic practitioners who lived unconventional lives dedicated to Buddhist practice provides the best model for contemporary feminist Buddhists. Many of the most famous, influential, and accomplished women in Buddhist history followed this lifestyle. However, frequently in Buddhist literature, these women are presented as enablers and companions of important Buddhist men, rather than as important figures in their own right. In contemporary feminist perspective, such women, who might well have male companions, would not be understood primarily as enablers, but as great teachers and role models. From their ranks will come many of the feminist Buddhist prophets who will develop the outlook of postpatriarchal Buddhism.

Some Buddhist feminists expect the story to end with feminist reforms of the lay, monastic, and yogic lifestyles. They feel that since "the dharma is neither male nor female," the presence of female teachers would not add to or change the message that has always been given. For them, it really is simply a matter of equal rights and fairness. I am in complete sympathy with the reformist feminist position vis-à-vis Buddhism. However, I no longer feel that the story is likely to end when these goals are attained, because the reformist agenda would produce the one thing Buddhism has always lacked—large numbers of thoroughly trained, well practiced, and *articulate* female Buddhist teachers who are not male identified. That is to say, for the first time, the Buddhist world would experience significant numbers of female gurus. In the nontheistic tradition of Buddhism, I feel that this new situation will have the same transformative potential as the introduction of female god-language into the patriarchal monotheisms. Minimally, in line with the reformist agenda, at least Buddhist women would have the same kind of role models that Buddhist men have always had.

But there is a much more basic question. Has everything that needs to be said about Buddhist concepts of liberation already been said by male Buddhists? Or when women finally participate in Buddhist speech, will they *add to* the sum total of Buddhist wisdom? The example of Christian feminist thought indicates that women's voices do not merely amplify what has always been said, but what they add to the message significantly. With that possibility we go beyond "equal rights" feminism, which merely wants women to be able to play the game men have previously dominated, into "transformative" feminism, which suggests that the rules of the game will change (for the better) once women really learn how to play. Such suggestions also take us beyond the current limits of Buddhist thought.

It is easy to demonstrate why the voices of truly empowered Buddhist women might take us beyond those limits. Traditional Buddhist texts often state that the enlightened state of mind is beyond gender, not obtained in a male body or a female body. If that is true, then what could women possibly say or understand that has not already been incorporated into Buddhist teachings? The dharma is not only beyond gender; it is also beyond words, which are a skillful means, the finger pointing at the moon. Currently, however, the words brought back from the wordless realm and put into dharma texts are men's words. In a society that constitutes itself by means of strong gender roles and in which only men articulate the religious experience and its vision of liberation, religious speech will grow out of male experience.

Going beyond the limits of current Buddhist thought to suggest how woman-identified Buddhist teachers might expand our verbal formulations of the dharma is unnerving and difficult. The pitfalls of such a venture are deep and the issue subtle and complex. However, I expect at least three interrelated issues to be important. These issues are interrelated in that all of them refocus the relationship between "spirituality" and "ordinary" or "mundane" existence so that they are interfused, much in the manner of Zen or Dzogchen, but incorporating women's experiences much more existentially.

The most basic of these three issues involves a deeper appreciation of the absolute centrality of sangha than has been characteristic of Buddhist thought and practice. Much of the inspiration for this perspective comes from much feminist work exploring the theme that relationship is as essential in a healthy identity as are individuation and separation. Even more important, the centrality of community and relationship to human well-being and sanity has not been recognized in patriarchal and androcentric thought. Buddhist thought, with its glorification of solitary withdrawal, could certainly benefit from this awareness. Especially since Buddhism is nontheistic and does not offer the comforting belief that an Ultimate Other cares even in a lonely universe, the refuge of sangha, of the companionship and feedback of fellow travelers on the difficult path from confusion to enlightenment, is essential.

Buddhist thought and Buddhist institutions need to become much more aware of this resource and refuge, to value it much more than has ever been characteristic in the Buddhist past, and to provide training in being a good companion on the way, just as training in Buddhist meditation and philosophy is now provided. Just as Buddhists are expected to become proficient meditators and to have some understanding of Buddhist thought, so they should be expected to know how to nurture others, to be friendly and supportive. Likewise, a Buddhist should be able to find such nurturing and emotional support readily available in her sangha. This emphasis on sangha as nurturing, supportive community is not, of course, a cop out from basic Buddhist teachings regarding suffering, a some androcentric critics have supposed, but a recognition that the matrix of enlightenment is human community. It has always been that way; that reality simply has not been articulated clearly or sufficiently in Buddhist thought to date.

Second, ordinary, everyday domestic life, which has never received much attention in formal Buddhist thought, except to be denigrated, needs to be addressed much more directly as a *Buddhist* rather than merely a lay or a secular problem. Rethinking sane economic and reproductive practices will certainly be important in this task. With reasonable guidelines for sharing and limiting both productive and reproductive activities properly in place, it will then be important to infuse these ordinary activities with a sense of sacred outlook and meditative awareness. In the same way that daily tasks, such as cooking or gardening, have been valorized as part of a meditative lifestyle when they are combined with monastic living, tasks such as cleaning or working at one's job will be considered part of one's Buddhist practice. No longer will they be considered merely distractions from more valuable pursuits, such as formal meditation practice or the study of Buddhist texts.

In this revalorization, no task needs more discussion than child care. Childrearing can no longer be delegated to women for the reason that it is regarded as being too distracting to be compatible with serious study and practice. Rather, when reproduction is properly limited and shared, child care could become an aspect of Buddhist practice. In the same way that Vajrayana Buddhism revalorized sexuality as symbol and as experience, and that Zen Buddhism revalorized ordinary labor, so, finally, postpatriarchal Buddhism may discover a middle path regarding children. This task of infusing everyday tasks with sacred outlook must be done carefully however, for without the proper foundation in meditative training and attainment, cooking, cleaning, or working at one's job will simply breed mindlessness, fixation, and lack of awareness. Even people who are well trained constantly face this problem. Desirable as it may be to experience sacred outlook in the midst of distracting or boring tasks, that attitude must be cultivated slowly and carefully. One cannot will it to happen, but must train for it and maintain a critical perspective on one's level of mindfulness and awareness in daily life.

The third question that must be dealt with in postpatriarchal Buddhism: reassess some longstanding Buddhist ideas about what is proper and adequate spiritual discipline. It must ask when such discipline actually produces gentle and balanced human beings and when it is merely a macho endurance contest. In order to do that, I believe several principles can be relied upon. The first is that there is no substitute for formal training in meditation, which will often feel "unnatural" or "against the grain." Such disciplines cannot be rejected as the products of a male or dualistic style of spirituality simply because they can be boring and difficult.

A meditation practice that grounds people more presently and fully in experience, a meditation discipline without gimmicks, hyperbole, and promises of bliss, is indispensable for dealing with the myriad stresses that a feminist woman, or anyone else, for that matter, will face. These basic formless practices of mindfulness and awareness can easily be integrated into one's ongoing life and, after some intensive experience with them, they readily inform one's life beyond formal practice. The more esoteric practices associated with Vajrayana Buddhism, which are quite time-consuming and involve visualizing an alternate reality, do produce expanded states of consciousness. But to do them seriously also requires setting aside other concerns. I am uncertain to what extent they will be integrated into postpatriarchal Buddhism that seeks balance and wholeness.

Finally, an important part of the practice of spiritual discipline should be to use it skillfully, as a tool rather than a prison, so that one is not so compulsively meditating that one misses one's life. Spiritual disciplines should not be used to deaden or distance oneself from the vibrancy of the moment.

The final important postpatriarchal question concerning spiritual discipline asks, "For what purpose?" What do we hope will result from the practice of spiritual discipline? What changes will it effect? Freedom from rebirth and communication with unseen beings, often currently the hoped for results, do not seem to be relevant. In fact, the whole orientation of practicing a spiritual discipline to be prepared for death will probably not survive into postpatriarchal Buddhism. If a spiritual discipline promotes wholeness and balance, tranquility, and deep peace, that will be sufficient. And communication with one's fellow human beings will also be sufficient. If spiritual discipline results in a sense of presence of other realms, that would be an additional bonus, but would not overshadow the desire to develop enough sensitivity to communicate with and comfort the people with whom one lives.

One can also question the relevance of exalted, euphoric states of consciousness or esoteric knowledge and understanding. They can be exhilarating, and, properly used, may deepen one's appreciation of one's life and the world, but when they are pursued instead of one's immediate connections with earth and one's fellow human beings, they are counterproductive.

Rather, the point of such discipline is basic psychological grounding, deep sanity and peace with ourselves. Out of that grows the caring for community and for each other that is so important for spiritual insight and well-being. Additionally, our sensitivity to, appreciation of, and desire to care for our earth will shine forth. Spiritual discipline will no longer encourage us to seek to leave her behind for a better world or to superimpose another purer, visualized world upon her.

The tradition speaks of becoming deities (*yidams*) and living in the palace of the deities through our spiritual discipline. For that to happen properly, we will indeed see ourselves and each other as valuable, divine beings whom we cherish and for whom we care. We will not need to leave our world behind to visualize the palace of the deities in her place. When we look out from our windows, we will see the palace of the deities. When we comfort each other, we will converse with the deities. To become sane, to live in community with each other and our earth, is to experience freedom within the world—the mutual goal of feminism and of (postpatriarchal) Buddhism.

Notes

1. See the following articles: Rita M. Gross, "Feminism and Buddhism: Toward their Mutual Transformation," *Eastern Buddhist: New Series,* vol. 19, nos. 1 and 2 (Spring and Autumn 1986), 44–59 and 62–74; "Feminism from the Perspective of Buddhist Practice," *Buddhist–Christian Studies Journal,* vol. 1 (1980), 63–72; "I Will Never Forget to Visualize That Vajrayogini is My Body and Mind," *Journal of Feminist Studies in Religion,* vol. 3, no. 1 (spring 1987), 77–90; "The Feminine Principle in Tibetan Vajrayana Buddhism: Reflections of a Buddhist Feminist," *Journal of Transpersonal Psychology in Religion,* vol. 16, no. 2 (1984), 179–92; "Yeshe Tsogyel: Enlightened Consort, Great Teacher, Female Role Model," in Janice Dean Willis, ed., *Feminine Ground: Essays on Women and Tibet (*Ithaca, New York: Snow Lion), *1989, 11–32;* "'The Dharma is Neither Male nor Female': Buddhism on Gender and Liberation," in Leonard Grob, Riffat Hassan, and Haim Gordon, eds., *Women's and Men's Liberation: Testimonies of Spirit* (New York: Greenwood Press, 1991), 105–28; and "Buddhism After Patriarchy," in Paula M. Cooey, William Eakin, and Jay B. MacDaniel, eds., *After Patriarchy: Feminist Transformations of the World's Religions* (Maryknoll, New York: Orbis Books, 1991), 65–86.

2. Chatsumarn Kabilsingh, *Buddhist Peace Fellowship Newsletter,* Summer, 1990, 24 25.

3. See Rita M. Gross, "Studying Women and Religion: Conclusions after Twenty Years," in Arvind Sharma, ed., *Today's Woman in World Religions* (Albany: SUNY Press, 1994), pp. 327–361.

4. This summary of the problem is not limited to Buddhism. All androcentric thought forms treat women as objects exterior to "mankind"—as objects to be defined, delimited, classified, and debated about by men. Women's voices are neither sought nor listened to in this process. Thus women are robbed of their role as co-creators of the human realm and are treated only as passive objects, not human subjects. Mary Daly spoke of this condition most powerfully in her famous phrase about "the power of naming" being stolen from women. For similar reason, Nancy Falk and I entitled our book, the first on women's religious lives in cross-cultural perspective, *Unspoken Worlds.*

5. Eleanor McLaughlin, "The Christian Past," *Womanspirit Rising,* ed. by Carol Christ and Judith Plaskow (San Francisco: Harper and Row, 1979), 94–95. This excellent essay is highly recommended.

6. Diana Paul, *Women in Buddhism: Images of the Feminine in Mahayana Tradition* (Berkeley: Asian Humanities Press, 1979), 236.

7. Janice Dean Willis, *The Diamond Light: An Introduction to Tibetan Buddhist Meditations* (New York: Simon and Schuster, 1973), 103.

8. Mary Daly, *Beyond God the Father: Toward a Philosophy of Women's Liberation* (Boston: Beacon Press, 1972), 69–73.

9. See especially the work of Elizabeth Schüssler Fiorenza on the New Testament. The whole question of whether "Jesus was a Feminist," to quote the title of a popular and influential article by Leonard Swidler, is quite relevant.

10. David Snellgrove, *Indo-Tibetan Buddhism: Indian Buddhists and Their Tibetan Successors* (Boston: Shambhala, 1987), 80. See also Reginald A. Ray, "Response to John Cobb," *Buddhist-Christian Studies Journal,* 8 (1988) 83–101.

11. Rahula Walpola, *What the Buddha Taught* (New York: Grove Press, 1974), 26.

12. These are the "three poisons" found at the hub of the "wheel of becoming" that occurs so frequently in Tibetan Buddhist art.

13. Rahula, 51.

14. Valerie Saiving, "The Human Situation: A Feminine Perspective," *Womanspirit Rising,* 25–42.

15. Nancy Schuster, "Changing the Female Body: Wise Women and the Bodhisattva Career in some *Mahāratnakūṭasūtras,*" *Journal of the International Association of Buddhist Studies,* 4:1 (1981) 24–69; and Diana Paul, *Women in Buddhism,* 166–243. Gross, *Buddhism after Patriarchy,* contains a feminist interpretation of the doctrine of emptiness, 173–80.

16. Chogyam Trungpa, *Shambhala: The Sacred Path of the Warrior* (Boston: Shambhala, 1995) 29–34.

17. Ann Klein, "Gain or Drain?: Buddhist and Feminist Views on Compassion," *Women and Buddhism: A Special Issue of the Spring Wind Buddhist Cultural Forum,* 6:1–3 (1986) 105–116.

18. Carol Gilligan, *In a Different Voice* (Cambridge; Harvard University Press, 1982).

19. Ann Klein, "Gain or Drain?," 108–15.

20. An enormous popular self-help literature has grown up around this theme, most notably the highly popular book *Women Who Love Too Much.*

21. See *Buddhism after Patriarchy,* especially 132–35, for a fuller discussion of the prophetic voice in Buddhist feminism.

22. Two new books on this concept add significantly to the literature. Sallie B. King, *Buddha Nature* (Albany: SUNY, 1991), and S. K. Hookham, *The Buddha Within: Tathagatagarbha Doctrine According to the Shentong Interpretation of the Ratnagotravibhaga* (Albany:SUNY, 1991).

23. See Paul Williams, *Mahayana Buddhism: The Doctrinal Foundations* (London: Routledge, 1989) 99–109, for a helpful summary of the arguments on both sides.

24. Despite the contradiction involved, such symbolic valorization of birth, combined with sociological denigration of literal birth-givers, is not uncommon in world religions. In many religious contexts, the valuable birth is one's second birth, one's ritual rebirth, which may be seen as reversing the negativities of birth from a female body. Sometimes the symbolism becomes so divorced from its basis in physical birth that many people do not even realize that rebirth is occurring.

25. Anne C. Klein, "Non-Dualism and the Great Bliss Queen: Study in Tibetan Buddhist Ontology and Symbolism," *Journal of Feminist Studies in Religion,* 1:1 (Spring 1985) 73–76.

26. Important ritual implements used in Tantric meditation rituals, they are held in left and right hands and symbolize feminine and masculine, wisdom and method, emptiness and compassion.

27. Allione, *Women of Wisdom,* 29; Chogyam Trungpa, "Sacred Outlook: The Vajrayogini Shrine and Practice," *The Silk Route and the Diamond Path: Esoteric Buddhist Art on the Trans-Himalayan Trade Routes,* ed. by Deborah E. Klimberg Salter (Los Angelos: UCLA Art Council, 1982), 236.

28. This phrase from the "Heart Sutra" sums up the entirety of Mahayana and Vajrayana Buddhism. See Trungpa, *Cutting Through Spiritual Materialism* (Berkeley: Shambhala, 1973), 187–99 for an illuminating commentary. See also Donald S. Lopez, Jr., *The Heart Sutra Explained: Indian and Tibetan Commentaries* (Albany: State University of New York Press, 1988).

29. Janice Dean Willis, *The Diamond Light: An Introduction to Tibetan Buddhist Meditations* (New York: Simon and Schuster, 1972), 103.

30. Jamgon Kongtrul (trans. Judith Hanson), *Torch of Certainty* (Boston: Shambhala, 1996) 30–33.

31. Trungpa, *Cutting through Spiritual Materialism,* 220–30.

32. *Yin,* which is feminine, should be the equal opposite of *yang,* the masculine element in Chinese cosmological thinking. In many cases, the two are seen as co-equally necessary in the scheme of things, though opposites of each other. But, in some contexts, *yin* is associated with evil, which is avoided, while *yang* is associated with good, which one attempts to increase and attract.

33. Gross, "The Dharma is Neither Male nor Female," 122.

34. Nancy Falk, "The Case of the Vanishing Nuns: The Fruits of Ambivalence in Ancient Indian Buddhism," Falk and Gross, eds., *Unspoken Worlds: Women's Religious Lives,* Belmont, CA: Wadsworth Press, 1989, 56–64.

Chapter 3

Confucianism and Feminism

Terry Woo

Asian American men have suffered deeply from racial oppression. When Asian American women seek to expose anti-female prejudices in their own ethnic community, the men are likely to feel betrayed. Yet it is also undeniable that sexism still lingers as part of the Asian legacy in Chinese America and that many American-born daughters still feel its sting. Chinese American women may be at once sympathetic and angry toward the men in their community: sensitive to the marginality of these men but resentful of their male privilege.

—Hirsch 1990, 239[1]

Introduction

Feminism and Confucianism have been involved with each other for over a hundred years. The relationship has largely been a one-sided affair: feminists criticizing the status and treatment of women determined by Confucianism. Early feminist critiques of Confucianism continue to have currency. It is therefore important to analyze their validity. How accurate are they? To what extent did the early accounts foster and reinforce, as they still do, the stereotype of an aged, changeless, decrepit, anesthetized, and barbaric China? And in turn, how have these Western images affected the notions the Chinese have about themselves?

An essay on feminism and Confucianism must therefore include a mention and an acknowledgement of the history of Western power and influence in late nineteenth- and twentieth-century China. Simone de Beauvoir serves as a potent reminder for the Western perception of the history of Chinese women. She wrote, in a footnote, that there was no need to study women in China because they had met with nothing but "long and unchanging slavery" (1952,

81). Yet it must also be said that the volume of scholarship on Chinese women has increased as have also the variety of perspectives.

Sinologists particularly have taken care to present a more balanced view. Their restraint from generalizing across place and time promises a chance for more even accounts. But first what follows is a brief look at three types of feminist critique on Confucianism: Protestant, socialist, and liberal.[2]

Feminist Critiques of Confucianism

Many feminist theorists now agree that there is no single "feminism"; but rather, that there are many feminisms. On the other hand, as Karen Offen writes, there is a common thread that runs through them: that is "the impetus to critique and improve the disadvantaged status of women relative to men within a particular cultural situation (1988, 132)." And some Western feminists have critiqued enthusiastically the presumed "universally unfavorable" conditions in which Chinese women existed.

The Protestant missionaries were prominent pioneer feminist critics in China. They attributed to Confucius the "greatly inferior position of women" and focused on "particularly the practices of foot binding and infanticide" (Varg 1958:117).

Tales were told of girls sold into slavery, and young Chinese brides married to strangers and then subjected to the rule of arbitrary mothers-in-law. The descriptions were so common in the late nineteenth and early twentieth centuries, that by and large they became symbolic of the reality for all Chinese women, in all places, for all times.[3] These gross generalizations were possible at the time because the West saw itself as progressive and China not; and that the Chinese treated their women badly was "observably" true. They did not question the veracity of the images that were encouraged by, and in turn reinforced the stereotype of the Oriental despot (ibid. 119–22).

And so it was that the plight of Chinese women, with the help of Christian feminist critique, became an outstanding standard for Chinese inferiority. In time Protestant analyses became more sophisticated and less prejudicial, especially after the missionaries read and found in the writings of Confucius the same principles of the Christian gospels. Knowledge of Chinese culture and civilization precluded the labeling of Chinese as "heathens" (Varg, 215); and eventually, aid to the Chinese for modernization replaced criticism and proseletyzing. But the torch of feminist critique had been lit. The socialists were the inheritors.

"It has been said (Curtin writes) that Confucius, whose epigrams codified the ethics of precapitalist China, had not one favorable word for women" (1975, 10). This comprehensive judgment was passed on cosmology, social custom, and philosophy. As with the Protestants, bound feet, female infanticide, loveless marriages, and the preference for breeding male children were all included; but there was also a new element. Curtin quotes Hu Shih (b. 1891), a famous Chinese writer who studied at Columbia with John Dewey, who said: "Woman had always been the greatest despot of the family and no other country could compete with China for its number of hen-pecked husbands" (ibid. 11). Chinese women had, over one generation, become both despots and victims.

Hu Shih wrote during a low point in Chinese history, in the early twentieth century when China had fallen to Japan, which had never before been a military and political force powerful enough to be reckoned with; and it had also been defeated by the "barbarian" West. He wrote before communism, the great white hope for China and Curtin's reference to the Chinese adherence to blaming traditional culture after thirty years of communist rule is to be expected. Confucianism remains the archenemy, the oppressive ideology, even as the "woman question" was understood to be a part of the larger problem of social and economic reform,

And so Andors, another socialist feminist, repeats religiously the litany of Confucianism as "hierarchical, authoritarian, and patrilineal, embodying a strict sexual and generational division of labour" (1983, 12). Thus conventional wisdom is perpetuated and antidoctrine is safeguarded by repetition: the subordination of women, through the three obediences and the four virtues, is the central feature of the traditional Chinese family system.[4]

If these Protestant and socialist feminist critics can be criticized for being unhistorical and one-sided, then liberal feminists may be seen as primarily disinterested. French writes that in this, "race divides women." White feminists:

> Write books analyzing patriarchal culture, attempting to establish feminist theory, or examining a dimension of women's condition without mentioning women of color at all—women of color are as invisible in these works as women as a sex are in the work of many men (ibid. 462–463).

Yet it is precisely the realization and admission that signal a change and begin a new chapter in the history between feminism and Confucianism.

Feminism, Sinology, and Confucianism

French describes a general tendency in feminist scholarship. Holmgren, as a sinologist, on the other hand, offers a broad and radical critique of early sinology while relating its impact specifically to the study of Chinese women. She writes in "Myth, Fantasy or Scholarship: Images of the Status of Women in Traditional China":

Nineteenth century western imagery of the brutality and cruelty of the Chinese way of life is still found relevant to the depiction of the place of women in the traditional society and our selection of view comes from a very limited slice of these early images of China. This black caricature is reinforced by the anti-Confucian bias of Chinese reformists' writings of the May Fourth era. (1981, 163)

Holmgren may be right in writing about the first interaction between feminism and Confucianism as "the most wretched of beginnings" (154). She criticizes it for narrowness: in blurring the entire dynastic tradition of women into one big amorphous whole, and for the judgments being based on a limited source of information on the upper class. Moreover, she goes on to cite how Miss Adele Fields, a Catholic missionary in Swatow in the 1880s, based her writing on anecdotal examples (158–63). Holmgren's criticisms are well taken. There is no "one tradition" for women; and likewise there is no one confluent Confucianism over the twenty-five hundred years since Confucius lived. For this reason, particular bundles of Confucianisms will be treated in historical context in this essay: Confucius and the tradition he comes from; his earlier and most influential disciples; the Han Confucians; and the Neo-Confucians.[5]

Confucius did, however, conceive of a return to "tradition": the early Chou dynasty—a hope that is akin to some feminists' reminiscence of a simpler and more peaceful time of matriarchy.[6] Confucius lived during a time of chaos. The world that was known then as China was under attack from outsiders: moreover, traditional society was disintegrating from within. Sexual mores were loose, family loyalties and obligations unstable. There were reported cases of incest and licentiousness; sons murdered fathers; vassals challenged kings at the central courts of the Chou dynasty; and ministers revolted against rulers.

Confucius's primary concern was therefore political stability and an end to suffering. To this end, it would have been incongruous for Confucius to be concerned with women, since they were neither directly involved with war nor were they active in politics, being traditionally assigned and restricted to the private sphere: the home. Men held a monopoly of military and political power. To stop war and suffering meant, essentially, to stop men. However, inferences can be made as to Confucius's attitudes toward women.

The Influences of Traditional China on Confucius

Confucius (?551–479 B.C.E.) is said to have been influenced by the following: the *I ching* or *Book of Changes;* the *Shu ching,* the *Book of History* or *Book of Documents;* the *Li chi,* the *Ritual* or *Book of Rites;* and the *Shih ching,* the *Book of Poetry* or the *Book of Odes*. I refer the reader here to Guisso's article, "Thunder over the Lake: the Five Classics and the Perception of Women in Early China," in *Women in China* (1981), for a summary of the negative attitudes toward women in these writings; and then to Kelleher (1987) for a different perspective on some of the same materials. The picture that emerges is not a consistent one. There is, on the one hand, this passage: "(The bride and groom) ate together of the same animal, and joined in sipping from the cups made of the same melon; thus showing that they now formed one body, were of equal rank, and pledged to mutual affection" (Legge, 1967, 2:429–30). On the other, there is the following, a poem from Waley's translation of the *Book of Odes* (71):

> My heart is in turmoil, I cannot sleep.
> But secret is my grief
> My heart is not a mirror, To reflect what others will . . .
> My heart is not a stone; It cannot be rolled.
> My heart is not a mat; It cannot be folded away.
> I have borne myself correctly
> In rites more than can be numbered.
>
> My sad heart is consumed, I am harassed
> By a host of (small-minded people).[7]
> I have borne vexations very many, Received insults not few.
> In the still of the night I brood upon it;
> In the waking hours I rend my breast.
> O sun, ah moon, Why have you changed and dimmed?
> Sorrow clings to me
> Like an unwashed dress.
> In the night I brood upon it,
> Long to take wing and fly away.

These two excerpts reflect simultaneously the joy and importance of marriage and family, and the unhappy and besieged life of a woman obliged to be yielding and obedient. The assignment of women to the private sphere; the three obediences and four virtues; the disparity in the garb and period of mourning for father and mother, husband and wife, all predate Confucius.[8] And these prescriptions for behavior designed to bring about harmony assume a "natural" hierarchy[9] and share as their rationale the eventually influential idea cited in the *Book of Changes:* when the women are correct and firm or virtuous, their families will gain peace and prosperity (Liu Te-han 1974, 28).

A Feminist Assessment of Confucius

The nominal subjugation of women by Confucius acquires a different light when seen through this assumption and belief that society can be harmonized through stable relationships. Feminism and Confucianism differ at the roots of their endeavors. Feminism is concerned with freedom, equality, and finally a "complete social revolution" (Cott, 15), especially from the perspective of women. Confucius, on the other hand, regards the sexes together and is concerned with order, harmony, and thus a return to peace and stability.

The paradox is this: feminism also wants peace and stability; and Confucius too, was asking for a complete social revolution from the greed, disloyalty, licentiousness, and violence of his times. But from Confucius's point of view, freedom cannot bring a peaceful society. Instead, freedom, with its complementary idea of rights, forms the antithesis of the Confucian sense of duty. In this way, Confucianism and feminism speak past each other, conveying parallel ways. For in Confucianism, all belong to one family, "within the four seas, all are brothers" (Analects 12:6): their communication is, therefore, to be guided by *jen,* benevolence or humaneness. Harmony in society depends on the web of interdependent obligations, with a special emphasis on the dictum: "Do not do to others that which you do not want done to you" (Analects 15:23; 12:2). Freedom and rights, Confucius might have argued, are precisely what cause chaos since they may too easily degenerate into license and self-centerdness.

Confucius might therefore answer positively to the accusations of the individualist feminists.[10] His philosophy and the tradition he wishes to encourage, recover, and uphold can be described as hierarchical, authoritarian, patrilineal, and embodying a strict sexual and generational division of labor. He might, however, also point out that his position is not unlike the relational feminists who support the case for women's distinctiveness and complementarity. And, he would hastily add, his conception of authority does not condone cruelty and inhumaneness in the senior partner. The senior partner in fact would have clear responsibilities and blind authority would be contrary to the spirit of *jen.* Confucius could not have supported infanticide, and bound feet would not have been accepted. Moreover, the junior partner is obliged to critique and bring to light any unjust situation. For example, a woman may, in serving her parents, repeatedly and gently remonstrate with them; but if she sees that she has not persuaded them, she should not disobey them. Instead, she should resume an attitude of respect and continue to offer herself and not complain (Analects 4:18 adapted).

This strategy of avoiding conflict is expected not only of women but of men as well and can be criticized as an integral part of the system that keeps women oppressed. But Confucius may in turn ask, using his parameters, how much closer the fight for freedom and rights has brought us to a more harmonious society. Might not the failure of feminism be measured by the continued dominance of "male" values, and the erosion and cooptation of "feminine" values and women by political and commercial establishments? Moreover, how well can a society care for its old, its young, and its disadvantaged, when there is a massive disintegration of families, evident in high divorce rates and reports of child abuse?

But these criticisms are immediately recognizable as ideologically biased. They assume family, and a particular type of family at that, to be the most important unit in a community, and harmony is valued above all else. Moreover, it attributes social problems to feminism singularly while it neglects to consider a complex weave of preexisting economic and political circumstances. Such an assessment of the "failure" of feminism is similar to particular feminist assessments of the oppression of women by Confucianism. Parts of the judgment may be right, but the whole remains a caricature of a much more involved and complicated reality.[11] After all, much of early feminism was racist in the way that many feminists now consider Confucius sexist. The prejudices are inherited.

The Philosophy of Confucius and its Implications for Women

In fact Confucius does teach equality; but his egalitarian notions are not applied socially. He applies them to the opportunity to learn: "In education there should be no discrimination in categories of persons" (Analects 15:38); and in moral progress, the development of *jen:* "When assuming *jen,* one should not yield even to one's teacher" (Analects 15:35). As to the performance of rituals, which is of central importance in traditional society, Confucius says this: "If a person is not *jen,* what would she have to do with *li,* ritual?" (Analects 3:3).

The focus is clearly on *jen. Jen* in turn can be conceived of in two parts: *chung* and *shu.* The first is an attitude of sincerity and loyalty; the second is the principle of reciprocity, using one's feelings as the basis of one's interaction with others. So far there is no clear case of misogyny or intent to malign and oppress women; Confucius is apparently not the source of sexism in China.

If, however, we accept the fact that Confucius inherited a patrilineal and authoritarian system, as has feminism, then Offen's insight can help explain the part Confucianism played in the increasing restrictions on women's lives. She comments that relational feminist arguments "seem to cut both ways; even as they support a case for women's distinctiveness and complementarity of the sexes, they can be appropriated by political adversaries and twisted . . . to endorse male privilege" (154). Perhaps Confucianism was thus twisted, by adversaries and advocates alike.

Yet it is undeniable that Confucius had no female disciples. Moreover when he was a chief magistrate, he separated the women from the men, even on the streets (Smith 1973, 56–89). But most notorious is the remark that "women and servants are difficult to keep. If you approach them, they become disrespectful; if you keep a distance from them, then they complain" (Analects 17:25). There is, however, some discussion as to which the two groups of difficult people are. In Chinese *nü tzu* can mean women in general or it could refer specifically to maid servants or concubines; likewise *hsiao jen* translates literally into "little people" and can mean servants or lower-class persons. So this again may not be a categorically negative statement against all women.

However, there is a more puzzling second statement. In citing examples that talented ministers are difficult to find, Confucius uses Emperor Wu, founder of the Chou dynasty, as an example. He notes that Wu had ten ministers, but goes on to say that there were really only nine *jen* or persons, since there was a woman among them (Analects 8:20). It is unclear what the rationale is, in differentiating between female and male ministers. It is interesting, however, to observe that Wu is considered an exemplary ruler, and that Confucius did not condemn or criticize the existence of the female minister.

More intriguing still is Confucius's attitude toward women as a source of distraction. In the Analects 18:4, a story is told of a three-day court cancellation at Lu, the home state of Confucius, because the ruler of Ch'i had sent a gift of female musicians. Confucius responded to this by leaving; no comments are recorded. Elsewhere he counsels the practice of virtue to modify one's attachment to sensual pleasures (1:7), while also making clear that it is not only the beauty of women that can deceive, but rather that men who are smooth talkers and attractive are likely also to be devoid of virtue (17:17).

Yet despite his own theories and policies, Confucius went to see Nan Tzu, the wife of the Duke of Wei, who was notorious for her lasciviousness (27:26). Later scholars have had a hard time explaining this, suggesting that Confucius had not known of her reputation. But rather simple and more plausible reasons were simply the principle of *jen* and that Confucius was a pragmatist. In his estimation, it is difficult to survive chaotic times without specious eloquence or good looks (6:14). The episode of Nan Tzu might therefore be a case of *jen* in action; an illustration of Confucius's compassion for people caught in troubled times.

But Confucius's sympathy was limited. And even if the virtues demanded of women were also demanded of men, there was one central difference: although a woman must like a man be respectful, humble, kind, righteous, benign, upright, temperate, generous, sincere, and earnest (5:15; 17:6) she must also be a helpmate to her husband in a way that would not be expected of men in their relationships to their wives (16:14). So Confucius should not perhaps be condemned as a misogynist and primary oppressor of women. But in his uncritical adherence to the traditional norms of sexual segregation and male authority, Confucius may be judged an accomplice to the continued cultural minimalization of women.

Mencius and Hsün Tzu: Two Branches of Early Confucianism

Mencius (371–289 B.C.E.), like Confucius before him, focused on the problem of politics. He emphasized the importance of a sensitive heart for compassionate government. Mencius believed that all people have this heart that is acutely affected by the suffering of others. He comments that anyone devoid of this heart is not human. This sensible heart contains four components: the heart of compassion; the heart of shame; the heart of courtesy and modesty; and the heart of right and wrong (Mencius 2:A:6). If we take this to be a central principle in Mencius's philosophy, then we must conclude that infanticide and bound feet would have been, for him as for Confucius, appalling examples of the lack of humanity.

Yet like Confucius before him, he accepted blindly the maxim in the *Book of Rites:* "A woman is one who follows or obeys." The character *ts'ung* in Chinese can mean either to follow or to obey. Mencius takes away any ambivalence in the rites dictum by stating that the correct way for a wife or concubine is compliance (3:8:2). On the other hand, he stresses the influence and importance of women. Hence, for him, the primary relationship within the five relations is the one of husband and wife (5:A:2).

The practice of these principles, however, is not so straightforward. Mencius's relationship to his mother and wife offer interesting anecdotes into the web of human relationships. First, there is the story of his mother teaching him while he was still in her womb. Then Mencius's mother, who was widowed early, is said to have moved three times in order to find a good environment for him to grow up in; she settled next to a school. In another story, he is reprimanded by his mother for unjustly complaining about his wife for being in an indecent posture when he entered her room: his mother countered that he should have announced himself rather than be lurking around. And finally, when he was offered a posting away from his mother and was perplexed as to whether he should take the position, his mother reminded him that the affairs of state must take precedence over her. It was her duty to follow him, her son, in her old age (Lieh-nü chuan 1:10–11, O'Hara 1945, 39–41).

Mencius's mother does not conform to the stereotype of an oppressed woman. She demonstrates an intelligent and active maternal devotion, which exemplifies the ethos of Confucian virtue. The source of this morality is represented in the pithy saying of the *Great Learning:* every person, from the commoner to the emperor, must take as the root of conduct, self-cultivation. It is only after one has understood oneself and nurtured one's virtue that she or he is able to bring together the family and it is only then, that one is capable of ruling the empire (1:1:4).

The accounts of Confucius and Mencius do not support extreme feminist assessments of Confucianism. Early Confucianism, at least, did not intend to "shackle" (Fu) women. On the contrary, Mencius speaks of women as wise counsellors (3:B:2) and productive members of society as silk weavers and caretakers (7:A:22). Moreover, he warns that if a man does not practice virtue, then he cannot, in turn, expect his wife and children to behave virtuously and to obey him. But an even more radical suggestion is that a great person will not observe prescribed rites and duties if the nature of the actions oppose the spirit that motivates the performance (4:B:6). This has profound implications for the binding of women's feet and the killing of babies. But the most powerful image this spirit of defiance conveys is resistance to what is unjust—which is, in this context, the oppression of women.

Mencius advocates and dares to question "tradition." He questions the principle and authencity of associating the benevolent with warfare, wary that this can easily serve as the justification for battle. So he comments that if one were to believe everything in the *Book of History,* it would have been better that the book had not been written (7:B:3). As to the conventional "truth" that men and women should not touch each other, Mencius has this to say: if a man's sister-in-law were drowning, then discretion must be used; if he did not rescue her because he holds to the rite of men and women not touching, then in Mencius's estimation, he would amount to no more than a brute, lacking in the heart of compassion (4:A:17). In the end, Mencius says, a person must seek within himself the cause for the lack of benevolence. It is only a slave who would shirk his responsibility and blame others for the want of wisdom and duty (2:A:7).

Hsün Tzu (298–239 B.C.E.), like Confucius and Mencius before him, lived during tumultuous times and was interested primarily in politics. The last era of the Eastern Chou dynasty, known as the Spring and Autumn, and the Warring States periods, lasted from 722 to 481 B.C.E. and 403 to 221 B.C.E., respectively. Confucius lived toward the end of the first period of unrest; and Mencius and Hsün Tzu lived at the end of the five hundred years of unrest, during the second period. Hsün Tzu differed in the emphasis of his solution to restore order from his predecessors; he advocated the power of *li* over the influence of *jen.* He was fully aware of the manmade quality of ritual, noting in the chapter entitled "Man's Nature is Evil," that all *li* were created consciously by the sages. And in "A Discussion on Rites," he suggests that only a sage can truly understand them and that to the *chün tzu,* the good person, they are part of worldly practices, whereas by the masses, they were believed to have supernatural efficacy.

Confucianism, in Hsün Tzu, shows the first signs of a rigid systematic definition in the "quality" of persons. Although Hsün Tzu, like both Confucius and Mencius, believed that all persons have the capacity to be sages, he stressed more than ever the value of education, because he believed human nature to be evil, so that people have to be taught to be good. At the same time, he pressed to the logical conclusion the implications of hierarchy in traditional society.

In "The Regulations of a King," he writes that heaven and earth exemplify higher and lower. If power were distributed equally, there would be great disorder and no unity in society. The notion of hierarchy is of course not new, what is new is the naked discussion of power. Previously, hierarchy and difference had been discussed and conceptualized more in terms of the exercise of *jen* and indirectly moral authority and *li*. Power and the distribution of power were not the main concerns.

But apropos to the question about women is an even more disturbing statement in the chapter entitled "Discussion of Rites": "A father can produce a child, but he cannot suckle it. A mother can suckle it, but she cannot instruct and educate it". This supports unreservedly the feminist critique that Confucianism prescribes a rigid division of labor based on gender. At the same time, it must also be noted that Hsün Tzu is at odds with Mencius on this issue. Mencius notes that the relationship between father and son, and by extension parent and child, must be one of love. It is therefore not good for them to engage in a teacher-student relationship. A teacher must at times correct a student; and if the correction has no effect, the teacher may lose his temper. If this were to happen between father and son, it would damage the love they have for each other. Therefore, Mencius recommends, fathers should not try to instruct their sons (4:A:18).

As for Hsün Tzu, if we were to consider the importance of education in Confucianism, and if we were to consider also the central role that women are to play in the home, the exclusion of women from the realm of education is contrary to the spirit of equality in education. More significantly, it seeks to lock women from any avenues of meaningful influence. This marks one point in the long and painful journey down for Chinese women. Considered "lower" and therefore deserving of less power, it became legitimate to see women as less worthwhile. This is substantively different from the strength of influence attributed to women, in the roles of mother, wife, and daughter-in-law, in the lives of the sage-emperors Wen and Wu, recorded in the *Book of Odes* (Legge 1879, 380–87). More importantly, Hsün Tzu is also different from Mencius, who acknowledges the influence and authority of women, citing as an example the wives of Hua Chou and Ch'i Liang who were able to change the practice of a whole state because they were supreme in the way they wept for their husbands (6:8:6).

The lack of homogeneity in Confucianism therefore existed from the beginning and continued into the Han dynasty. Hsün Tzu gained more prominence than Mencius during the Han and a new generation of thinkers yielded yet a new spectrum of opinions.

Tung Chung-shu: A Han Confucian

The Han dynasty lasted from 202 B.C.E. to 220 C.E. Women, during this period, were not as "bound" by tradition as is commonly assumed. Jack Dull confirms this in his article "Marriage and Divorce in Han China: A Glimpse at 'Pre-Confucian Society'" in *Chinese Family Law and Social Change in Historical and Comparative Perspective.* He writes: "In the realm of marriage, divorce, and remarriage, the picture of Han society that emerges is one that is much freer than, say, Ch'ing society." But toward the Latter Han, there were demands for a society that was more "Confucian" (23). We have seen, however, the variations on "Confucian." It would be best therefore to see what different Confucian thinkers said about the relationship between men and women: as husband and wife and as parent and child. But first a sketch of the dominant Han philosopher is in order.

Tung Chung-shu (179–104 B.C.E.) lived during the early part of the Han dynasty and was instrumental in conflating Confucianism with the Yin Yang school.[12] This Yin Yang Confucianism was also replete with necromancy, divination, and cosmological ideas borrowed from the religious Taoists (de Bary 1960: 1:191). It was adopted by Emperor Wu (140–87 B.C.E.) as a state doctrine. Unlike Confucius, Mencius, and Hsün Tzu before him, Tung wrote during a time of relative peace. The stable climate afforded a sense of leisure and order that the earlier Confucians had not experienced. This explains in part different objectives: whereas the classicists emphasize an end to chaos and the establishment of peace, Tung searches for a system to maintain peace. His focus on order is therefore like all other Confucians, but a newly unified empire would encourage and explain his "urge to organize all knowledge into a coherent whole, filling in with conjecture where necessary. Han thinkers were deeply convinced that order existed in all things, in the natural world as in society" (de Bary 1960: 1:146). And thus Tung, like his contemporaries, conceived of human beings as the microcosm of nature and believed that heaven, earth, and humans formed an intimate partnership.

The universe was seen as an organic whole. Humans, as active participants, could influence the fate of the world through the guidance of natural portents. This systematic treatment of the universe by Tung Chung-shu was rooted in his idea of the "origin" that forms the foundation to all things. If a society were to be harmonious, the people had to be educated[13] and the foundation had to be right. The principles of this foundation, this origin, was to be discovered in the *Ch'un-ch'iu* or *The Spring and Autumn Annals,* reputed to be written by Confucius about his home state of Lu. To this end, T'ung wrote the *Ch'un-ch'iu fan-lu*[14] or *Luxuriant Gems of the Spring and Autumn Annals,* an exposition on the wisdom of the *Annals.* Like other Confucian writings, the *Luxuriant Gems* contains little about women; but because it deals not only with history and politics, but with cosmology as well, *yin* or the feminine receives a more extensive treatment.

Tung's attitudes toward women are not new but he formalizes and systematizes the existing notions with unprecedented thoroughness. At the same

time, there is a familiar flexibility when he writes that the *Annals* contain two
sorts of *li:* the *li* of the classics; and the *li* of change (Tung, 59). That is, change
to the primary dictum is allowed for humane reasons, and is rooted in *i* or righteousness. He cites as examples situations found in the *Annals,* where ousting
the emperor is not considered disloyal; and disobeying one's father is not considered dishonorable. Killing one's maternal relatives is not considered unfil-
ial (73). All these are condoned under impossible circumstances.

For the most part, however, his system of natural law is predicated on
changes and differences only within a changeless natural pattern. He writes in
chapter 58, "The Simultaneous Generation of the Five Elements," that "the
ch'i, or energy, of heaven and earth come together and become one; they separate and become *yin* and *yang;* quartered they become the four seasons; mul-
tiplied they become the five elements (metal, wood, water, fire, and earth)"
(334). The alterations happen however only from *yin* to *yang;* in the changes of
seasons; and with the possible combinations of the components in the five elements. But the order in which they occur and the circular paths they take are inevitable and changeless.

The implication for this is predictable and not new. In chapter 53, "The
Principle of the Foundation," translated in part in *A History of Chinese Philosophy* by Derk Bodde, Tung elaborates on this:

> In all things there must be correlates. . . . The *yin* is the correlate of the
> *yang,* the wife of the husband, the son of the father, the subject of the
> ruler. . . . The ruler is *yang,* the subject is *yin;* the father is *yang,* the son
> *yin;* the husband is *yang,* the wife *yin.* . . . The regulations for love, right-
> eousness, and social institutions are wholly derived from Heaven.
> Heaven acts as the ruler, who shelters and confers benefits (on the sub-
> ject). Earth acts as the subject, who assists and supports (the ruler). The
> *yang* acts as the husband, who procreates (the son). The *yin* acts as the
> wife, who gives assistance (to the husband) (2: 42–43).

Tung thus affirms the "natural" foundation of hierarchy. The idea that the
husband procreates the son is an echo of Hsün Tzu; and the use of the categories
of *yin* and *yang* comes from the *I ching.* There is nothing original in Tung
Chung-shu; he was essentially a synthesizer. His primary contribution, realized
by the emperor Wu, is the institutionalization of Confucianism. From early Han
on, women had to contend not only with a loose sense of "acceptable behavior" proposed by the Confucians, symbolized by the three followings or obediences and the four virtues, but also with a much elaborated and integrated
system based on "nature"; again not a "new" idea but one present already in a
saying in the *Book of History:* just as a hen does not crow at dawn, a woman
must not rule the home, or the family will soon come to an end.

Tung's Acceptance of Feminine Influence in Politics

The idea of a woman not ruling in the home can easily be extended to the state in Tung's system and the result is obvious. First of all, there is no mention of women in the chapter "The Way of the Emperor," and in "Compliance and Opposition in the Five Elements" the establishment of a concubine in place of a wife is described as abandoning the law. Furthermore, to allow women to govern is incorrect and will cause much suffering for the masses (348). The concept of hierarchy is thus imposed on both the domestic sphere involving relations between only women, as well as the political sphere concerning relations between men and women, and the exercise of power.

Tung wrote after the rule of Empress Lu (188–180 B.C.E.), who is considered by one early historian, Ssu-ma Ch'ien, as an emperor but by a later one, Pan Ku, as a regent. Since the later part of the Latter Han, historians have treated her as a regent who had seized power wrongfully; she is also said to have treated cruelly her rival, a concubine who became the emperor's favorite.

To what degree Tung had her in mind while writing is unclear, but it is reasonable to suppose that his convictions would have been determined, in part, by her reign. Yet, in spite of his dismissal of women from the realm of power, he does support feminine influence at court. In his own conviction, a wife, as the empress, "gives assistance" to her husband. Moreover, influence can legitimately be gained from family connections through marriage. And this he reinforces by the idea of *i.*

The *Annals* established *i,* Tung writes, so that when a man assigns the title of *shih* or proper wife, the senior spouse is chosen and not the most virtuous one. Likewise, in conferring the title *fu jen* or duchess, the proper wife is chosen and not a concubine. Moreover, a righteous emperor when appointing ministers should employ those who are close to him, and not those who come from afar. These distinctions, showing a "natural" closeness and distance in relationships in turn form the rationale for another hierarchy: the internal and the external. By this measure, one's kingdom is on the "inside" and other states on the "outside." Chinese states taken together are considered to be on the "inside," and the barbarians on the "outside" (98). When this is applied to the relationship between women and men, a curious advantage accrues to women. Whereas girls do not have the same opportunities as boys, a son, in this instance, is "unequal" to a daughter in her potential to bring power and influence to the family through marriage. Because with marriage, a family can become a part of the emperor's "inside" realm.

The first incorporation of Confucianism therefore came immediately after the reign of a woman, the Empress Lu. It was in part directed at keeping women from power, but there was also a real effort to preserve a complementary sphere of influence for women. Furthermore, Tung emphasized the respect that should be accorded to wives. Confucius's comments, in the *Annals,* on the Duke of Ai, a ruler of Lu, is interpreted as prescribing respect for a wife because he left his house to welcome personally his bride. And a wife is respected primarily because she is necessary as a participant for the sacrifices to her husband's ancestors (Ch'u 1961: 102).

In Confucianism, therefore, a man alone is an incomplete man. Formal, traditional, prescribed behavior between men and women therefore remained intact in Han Confucianism. The wife serves the husband (Tung, 320) and receives her orders from him (384); a mother cannot be insincere or untrustworthy, because for a mother to be insincere or untrustworthy is like the grass and trees being rotten at the roots (430). This is therefore a curiosity of Confucianism: the woman complements the man and is sometimes perceived as "secondary" or "lower." But with a closer analysis, one finds the woman to be, like the emperor, the "root."

But despite the balance that Tung tries to strike, his cosmology dictates the unqualified subordination of women. Because he likens women and men to *yin* and *yang,* women became associated with government by law and punishment (290). Even though he concedes that there is *yin* in *yang* and *yang* in *yin,* he maintains the immovable categories of man-*yang* and woman-*yin.* The result is an uncompromising rigidity: "Even though the husband comes from a low social class, he is still *yang;* and even though the wife comes from a higher class, she is still *yin* (290)". In other words, the *yin* and *yang* of man and woman override other polarities.

The feminist critique of Confucianism does therefore apply to Tung's system. The rigidity in this form of synthesized and institutionalized Han Confucianism is one sure factor in the gradual, systematic, if unintended, oppression of Chinese women.

Han Opinions on Marriage, Divorce, and Remarriage

This cosmological straitjacket is characteristic of the New Text school only, and not the Old Text school, the less prominent of two Han Confucian schools. The New Texters believed that women and men misbehaved because the rites were deficient or that there was inadequate attention to propriety (Buxbaum 1978, 35). They argued against regulations for personal relations, saying that the emperor had no business in the bedrooms of his subjects (73).

The Old Text school, on the other hand, proposed both laws and education to straighten out and "bring to a stop the prevalent adultery and incest." One Old Texter, Wang Fu, accused the officials for neglect, for not encouraging widows to remain widows, and not forbidding women to leave their husbands for other men (72). This is the climate in which Liu Hsiang (77–6 B.C.E.)

wrote his *Lieh-nü chüan* or *Biographies of Exemplary Women,* and Pan Chao (?45/51–?114/120 C.E.) her *Nü-chieh* or *Instructions for Women.* Both writers focus exclusively on women. Liu uses as models six categories of good and virtuous women: exemplary mothers, worthy and astute women, benevolent and wise women, women of propriety, women of sexual integrity, and intellectual women; and one category of bad and wicked women (Kelleher 1987, 150).

Pan Chao writes in her introduction that her short treatise, containing sixteen hundred words, is for her daughters. It is a guide for the relationships between a young wife and the family she marries into so that her daughters and other young women, will not be afraid and worry continually, as she herself had, about what to do and how to behave so as to avoid bringing disgrace to their ancestors. Pan Chao divides her essay into an introduction and seven chapters: humility, husband and wife, respect and caution, womanly qualifications, wholehearted devotion, implicit obedience, and harmony with younger brothers and sisters-in-law. For translations and discussions of the monographs by Liu Hsiang and Pan Chao, I refer the reader to Albert O'Hara, Theresa Kelleher, and Nancy Lee Swann.

Although Pan Chao lauds and emphasizes the traditional virtues of humility, devotion, and obedience, she also has this to say about marriages that go sour: "Should actual blows be dealt, how could the matrimonial relationship be preserved? Should sharp words be spoken, how could conjugal love exist? If love and the proper relationship both be destroyed, then husband and wife will be separated" (Han shu 84:6a, Buxbaum 52). Contrary to habitual negative feminist analysis, the woman is very far from being the unconditional slave to the man. But is Pan Chao unusual in her views on the fragile nature of marriage? The answer is a clear no.

K'ung Kuang holds an opinion similar to Pan Chao's: "The Way of husband and wife is that if there is (mutual) faithfulness, then there is togetherness, but without (mutual) faithfulness there is divorce" (Hou Han shu 81: 16b–17a, ibid. 51). This view is also supported by Feng Yen, of the Latter Han dynasty, who writes: "Human nature (which is bestowed by) Heaven and Earth includes contentment and anger; the conjugal relation included the principles of separation and union" (Hou Han shu 28B:12a, ibid. 52). Far from being a minority position, it appears that the Han Confucians, New and Old Texters alike were eminently reasonable about the issue of divorce. But what about their views on remarriage?

One test case is used where the husband drowned, and his body was not recovered; the mother-in-law arranges to marry the wife—that is, her daughter-in-law—to another man four months into the three-year mourning period. As expected, there is a call for punishment. Such a marriage would be illegal, it was argued, because the husband's body had not been found and buried; and for the wife to remarry would be to commit bigamy. But this is how Tung

Chung-shu handled the argument. Citing the *Annals,* he notes that a wife was sent back to Ch'i. He interpreted this to mean that when a husband dies without a son, the principle of remarriage is appropriate. There is no reason for her not to remarry, since she has been virtuous and has not been marked by "perversity" and "licentiousness" (Buxbaum 68).

Moreover, the idea that a woman with a son should not remarry is not of Han origin. Before the Han, Ch'in-ch'ih-huang-ti or the first emperor of China, had already erected a stele that set forth prohibitions against a widow remarrying if there were sons involved. Following that was the statement that a husband who "becomes a wandering boar" could be killed with impunity. Then it goes on to note that both men and women must adhere to high moral standards (ibid. 61).

And yet, consistent with the notion of *li* of change, even the maxim that a woman with sons must not remarry can be overturned, as in the case of Ts'ai Yen, who lived during a chaotic time of rebellion at the end of the Latter Han. Ts'ai Yen was captured in 195 C.E. by the *hsiung-nu,* a non-Chinese nomadic people to the north of China. She bore the tribal chief two sons in her twelve years of captivity, but she had to leave them behind when she was finally rescued. What is unusual about her is that she was married three times in her life: once when she was very young, her husband died soon after, before she was seventeen; a second time to the *hsiung-nu;* and a third after she was rescued. She bore her third husband a daughter and her biography is in the "Biographies of Exemplary Women" in the *Hou Han shu* or *History of the Latter Han.*

Ts'ai Yen lived about seven hundred years after Confucius and three hundred years after Tung Chung-shu. The later Han years were confused and unstable like Confucius's time, and was unlike the early Han years when Tung lived, which were better organized and more stable. But the tolerance for "unvirtuous" behavior during hard times accorded by the *li* of change is understood and applied equally across time.

But even more interesting and unexpected is this remark disapproving of polygyny by a Han philosopher: "In antiquity a man had only one wife, whereas at (the present time—that is, 81 B.C.E.) some of the feudal lords have over one hundred wives and high officials have (numerous) mates" (Buxbaum 27 adapted). The disapproval of course goes both ways. Pan Ku, Pan Chao's brother, criticizes Tung Yen, who at eighteen has an affair with one of the princesses, who is fifty. The action is condemned on two counts. First, because no children can come of the union, it makes a mockery of the rites of marriage; and second, such relations harm the royal institutions. Yet, as Pan Ku notes, Tung Yen's case seemed to serve more as a model of "perverse" behavior rather than as a negative lesson object.

This, of course, contradicts the stereotypes feminism holds on relations between men and women in China. The range of attitudes and behaviors in fact appear to be very wide. If there were any slavish adherence, it would be to the idea of virtue, for both women and men. And if we should consider the Han Confucians in this light, then might they not be considered "feminist" in their concern for women through the *li* of change, as in the tolerance for exceptional situations like Ts'ai Yen? Or in their emphasis on love and fidelity between wife and husband; their focus on *i*—that is, the order to avoid and prevent—for example, the displacement of the proper wife because of a new favorite concubine; and the critique of polygyny? Do their efforts show what Offen describes as "the impetus to critique and improve the disadvantaged status of women relative to men within a particular cultural situation" (132)?

The question is extremely difficult to answer. Temma Kaplan may be right in opposing unreservedly "division of labor by sex, because roles limit freedom, and to mark distinctions is to imply superiority and inferiority" (ibid, 141). It can be argued that the sympathy and concern are corollaries to and an appeasement within a philosophy that generates hardships to begin with. Complementarity then, in Confucianism, would immediately and automatically be suspect and would disqualify the philosophy from being considered in any way "feminist," if we choose to define feminism by individualist feminists. If, on other hand, we accept that there are essential differences between male and female ways of being, and that in many ways women and men complement each other, as the relational feminists also believe, then radical and renegade Confucians may be considered feminists.

Women and their Work

One may argue that Liu Hsiang's *Biographies of Exemplary Women* and Pan Chao's *Instructions for Women* were attempts to close the education gap between men and women. One may also argue that the focus on the issues of love and fidelity, and the acceptance in principle of divorce and remarriage, were made to prevent women from being ostracized by their families and communities. Moreover, the insistence on a rigid hierarchy within a household of wife and concubines may have been an effort to stop men from abandoning their wives for young nubile concubines. And finally, the attack on polygyny must surely be seen as no less than an attack on the very foundations of the tradition. Yet, no matter how concerned the Han Confucians were about the welfare of their women, a mark remains against them because they accepted the unspoken rule that a woman cannot become an emperor, and that women cannot be appointed to the positions of teacher or public official (Ch'u 1972, 56).

On the other hand, the state sponsorship of Confucianism by Emperor Wu created a number of renowned woman scholars. One woman inherited the job of teaching the *Book of Documents* from her father, Fu Sheng (Han shu 88:10b,

Ch'u 1972. 56). Ts'ai Yen, the one who was captured by the *hsiung-nu,* wrote poetry and recited to scribes a collection of books that had been lost during a rebellion. And of course, there was Pan Chao, whose reputation for learning was so high that Emperor Ho asked that she finish the *Han shu,* which her brother, Pan Ku, and her father, Pan P'iao, had been able unable to complete. She so impressed the emperor that he then requested that she tutor the empress and other ladies at court. Talent was therefore affirmed where it was found; the emperors appreciated the women, and more importantly, there was no dissension from the Confucian ranks.

Pan Chao, Ts'ai Yen, the daughter of Fu Sheng, and the woman physician mentioned in *Han shu* (97A: 25a-b, ibid. 54) were educated, upper-class women. Commoners were generally more involved with sericulture. Sometimes the women had to manage the fields themselves when their husbands were away at war or doing corvée labor. For example, when Empress Lu was a commoner, and her husband was on duty away from home, she stayed to farm the land with her two sons. As for widows, the most famous was the widow Pa who took over the family business of cinnabar mines in present-day Szechuan and made it so successful that she was feted by the emperor himself (Han shu 91:5b, ibid.).

The examples of Empress Lu and widow Pa are drawn from Ch'in. During the Han, women and men alike became more involved in colonizing territories taken by expansionist emperors like Emperor Wu as sericulture and agriculture spread from the Yellow River region to the nomadic peoples at the frontiers (Wong, 1982, 58; Yu 1967, 4–5). Meanwhile women from poor families at home were trained in song and dance to serve as entertainers for nobles and wealthy commoners. They were not well respected and their status was extremely low (Han shu 72:12b; 97A:22–23a; 97B:11a; Ch'u 1972. 55). At the same time, Emperor Wu increased to fourteen the ranks of concubines for the inner court and organized prostitution and female infanticide, both of which started during the Han (Ch'en 1937, 59–61).

The burden of aggressive government did not fall on women alone. Men who were farmers were often overtaxed and the requirements for corvée labor were heavy. Many became bankrupt and consequently worked as tenant farmers or hired hands, others sold themselves into slavery (Wong 59). More disturbing still are skeletons excavated from Han tomb pits. Ninety-six percent are men mostly in their youth and early adulthood. Their bones show signs of wear suggesting that the men died from heavy labor and exceedingly poor working conditions. The overwhelming majority of the laborers were prisoners, most were commoners and very few were nobles or officials. They were buried in shallow graves that were turned over after only a few years to make room for the newly dead (ibid. 213).

The disadvantage of women in concubinage, prostitution, and infanticide are thus "balanced" by the disadvantage of men in corvée labor. There is symmetry here: sexual labor and death; and physical labor and death. Men and women were exploited in different ways. By extension, one might argue simplistically that they might likewise have exploited others in different ways. A man uses brute force and a woman uses sex. This is of course not true. When brute force became unacceptable, as the Confucians wanted to make it, the force of ideology, that is Confucianism, became ironically a means of exploitation.

Is Androcentrism in Confucianism Sexist?

Despite the efforts of Liu Hsiang and Pan Chao, Confucianism on the whole cannot be considered feminist, because it does not separate the problems of women from those of men. Yet, it is not right to assume that it is "sexist" in the usual sense of the word. After all Confucians do not believe that men and women are equal in the havoc they wreak. If one accepts this premise, then the feminist perspective on Confucianism must change.

Men have traditionally held most of the political and military power,[15] and so they are perceived as causing directly a lion's share of the disharmony in the world, in war and misgovernment. They are therefore the natural candidates and prime targets for conversion to peace. If we accept as historically accurate that many more young men were killed than women in ancient China, and that it was in part a surplus of women that made possible or perhaps even "customary" the widespread practices and eventual acceptance of concubinage, prostitution, and female infanticide, then would it not make sense to fight the phenomenon with at least a two-pronged approach? First, to encourage peace through self-cultivation, and virtuous behavior, and to discourage lust among men; and second, to encourage the same kind of peaceful coexistence within a household, and to preserve spheres of influence for women, and to discourage seductive behavior that might aggravate sexual promiscuity. If we therefore accept that the oppression of women resulted from political upheavals, the Confucians were merely trying to deal with the circumstances as they best knew how.

Women were clearly not the main perpetrators of widespread violence, they were often the "surviving" victims. In this, again they are different from men. Perhaps Confucius and the early Confucians had wished to emphasize *jen* or benevolent relationship as an antidote to the bullying, violence, and suffering; the stress on the responsibility of the senior partner to the junior one especially, may have been hope, albeit a naive one, in one means of alleviating some of the most immediate and personal oppression. Yet it must have also been clear that women were not totally subordinate. They in fact wielded a good deal of influence as mothers, daughters, and wives. This feminine influence, like male power, was a resource to be harnassed for harmony and the *Han shu* lists numerous examples.

One case from the *Han shu* is Yen Yen-nien who as a grand administrator was merciless and resorted to murder and severe punishments to maintain law and order. When his mother visited him from out of town, she expressed her disapproval by refusing to go to his official residence. She finally saw him when he went to see her, but even then she insisted on strict formalities to stress the distance between them. Not content to leave it at that, she further rebuked him and demanded that he be benevolent to the people. Far from the maxim that a mother should obey her son, the son here is humbled and made to obey his mother (Ch'u 1972, 53).

In another instance, the Marquis Ch'ing was forced to remarry his first wife, whom he had divorced, and who had subsequently remarried and was then widowed. The remarriage was forced by his daughter when she married the emperor and gained substantial influence (ibid. 59). A third example involves Wang Pa who became discouraged since he was unsuccessful, and gained little recognition and wealth. His children likewise achieved no great fame and fortune. Thus his wife counseled: "During your youth you cultivated pure virtue, and were not concerned with splendor and emoluments. Now how can the nobility of Tzu-po compare with your superiority? Why do you forget your old determination and become ashamed because of your children?" (294).

The wisdom and counsel of women and the concern for their well-being are integral parts of Confucianism. How is it then that the philosophy is now largely synonymous with the oppression of Chinese women?

Tung Chung-Shu, Wu Tse-T'ien and the Fear of Buddhism

Tung contributed to the oppression of women in two ways. First, he fixed the lower nature of women in a syncretic cosmological system; and second, in persuading Han Wu-ti to accept Confucianism as the state doctrine. He formulated the first complete package of national benevolent government in China. When the Han fell, Confucianism fell with it, since the two were closely identified. It continued to live in the shadows of Taoism and Buddhism until Sung Neo-Confucianism in the eleventh century, a thousand years later. It regained dominance when it was adopted as the state doctrine by the Ming dynasty.

Although Confucianism lost its dominant position, it maintained its influence in government through the bureaucracy and in the home through the emphasis on filial piety. Ching Yeh, a Confucian official, and his follower Lo Ping-wang, lived during the time of the only woman-emperor in China, Wu Tse-t'ien. Lo penned a polemic against her. It begins: "The woman Wu, who has falsely usurped the throne, is by nature obdurate and unyielding, by origin truly obscure." He continues, using Confucian concepts to oppose her and writes that "she brought disorder," "deluded the ruler," and "entrapped our ruler into an incestuous relationship" (Guisso 1979, 295).

Wu Tse-t'ien (reigned 684–705) was described in the worst possible way in Confucian terms. First she is "unyielding," which is contrary to Mencius's dictum that the correct way for a wife or a concubine is compliance (3:B:2). Second, she is a "usurper" as she did not keep the mandate of heaven: thus, she created disharmony in the husband and wife relationship by marrying Emperor T'ai-tsung first and then marrying his son, Kao-tsung. What is noteworthy in all this was that Ching and Lo were unsuccessful in their attempts to foster a rebellion. Most of the Confucian officials seemed content to accept Wu Tse-t'ien as emperor. Perhaps this was yet another case of the *li* of change.

Although there was no effective opposition against Empress Wu during her reign, the indirect effect she had on future generations of women may not have been positive. She was superstitious and used both Buddhism and Taoism to rationalize her rule, since a woman-emperor in Confucianism would be unthinkable.[16] This probably aggravated the already tenuous relations that popular Buddhism and Taoism had with Confucians. These tensions culminated in Han Yu (786–824), a Confucian official who lived a hundred years after Empress Wu. He criticized the superstitions in the two religions citing Confucius's exhortation "to respect ghosts and spirits but to keep them at a distance" (Analects 6:20). Antiforeignism against Buddhism also crept in. Han Yu wrote:

> Buddha was a man of barbarians who . . . understood neither the duties that bind sovereign and subject, nor the affections of father and son. . . . How then, when he has long been dead, could his rotten bones, the foul and unlucky remains of his body, be rightly admitted to the palace? (de Bary 1960, 373).

Han Yu was protesting against the display of a relic of the Buddha in the imperial palace. His polemic had no direct connection to the role of women in society. But his antiforeignism would form part of the foundation for Neo-Confucianism, and any elements that may be seen as contaminants to the "supreme" Chinese tradition—that is, Confucianism—had to be purified. In this way women as the "roots" and bearers of tradition came under severe scrutiny and strictures.

The Han was the first long-lasting Chinese dynasty. The second was the T'ang, but it was dominated by non-Confucian and "foreign" influences—that is, Confucianism had to share power with Taoism and Buddhism. The Sung, which followed some fifty-three years after the fall of the T'ang, struggled to maintain Chinese supremacy, but eventually fell to the Mongols who established the Yüan dynasty. It was therefore under constant threat of invasion that the Sung philosophers tried to stave off "foreign" elements and restore, resurrect, and reinstate Confucianism.

The Sung Dynasty: A Turning Point for Women

Li Yu-ning writes that the Sung dynasty was the crucial turning point for Chinese women. In the first fifty years, reformers like Fan Chung-yen (989–1052), a general who held power from 989 to 1052, far from prohibiting remarriage, advocated giving widows money to remarry. This sympathy and concern for women is continued by Wang An-shih (1021–1086), one of China's most celebrated statesmen. He proposed that a girl whose husband had killed her child be allowed to remarry, thereby circumventing the traditional divorce laws (Wolf and Witke 1975, 14). But a more practical criticism came from Yüan Tsai, a less famous contemporary of Chu Hsi's. He wrote *Shih fan* or *Precepts for Social Life.*

Yüan Tsai was most astute in his assessment of why women did not participate in extrafamilial matters. "The reason (he writes) is that worthy husbands and sons take care of everything for them, while unworthy ones can always find ways to hide their deeds from the women" (Ebrey 1981, 95). He goes on to say that families will continue to be ruined until women learn to read and do arithmetic, and until those they entrust their affairs to "have some sense of fairness and duty with regard to food, clothing, and support" (ibid. 96). In other words, things will not get better until women are educated about the practical details of life and men are educated to be better people.

Yüan is especially sympathetic to orphaned girls and suggests that they be married off and not left to live with their stepfathers. He notes too that old age is particularly difficult for women and writes also that he did not understand why daughters are considered "inferior" to sons when daughters sometimes managed the family's affairs when no capable sons were available. Moreover, Yüan says, even after the parents' deaths, "their burials and sacrifices are performed by their daughters" (95). The denigration of daughters therefore did not make sense to him, at least on a pragmatic level. But his practical advice was preempted by classicists like Ssu-ma Kuang and Chu Hsi who became dominant (Ebrey 1984, 30–37).

Cheng I and Chu Hsi

Chu Hsi included in his anthology *Chin-ssu lu* or *Reflections on Things at Hand,* Cheng I's (1033–1107) essay on "The Way to Regulate the family." More than ever before, the emphasis here is on obedience. A son must not resist or defy his mother or else "the kindness and love between mother and son will be hurt. (And) that will be great harm indeed" (Chan 1967, 171). After all "to obey is the foundation of serving parents" (ibid. 172). What a son must do if he wishes "to get into her heart and change her . . . (is to go backward), bending his will to obey . . . (which is also) the way for strong ministers to serve weak rulers" (171).

We see immediately the relevance in the portrayal of women in the family: it echoes its counterpart in government. This goes a long way in explaining the notorious comment that "people of later generations are afraid of starving to death. But to starve to death is a very small matter. To lose one's integrity, however, is a very serious matter" (177). This uncompromising statement, when understood in its political context, makes absolute sense. As Wang Fu (1692–1759), a Ming Confucian, comments, a woman who remarries is akin to the minister who surrenders to the enemy because of a fear of battle (ibid.); and the Sung Chinese were in fact under constant threat from invaders.

But theory alone does not make the total picture. Cheng I also writes: "When my cousin's own daughter also became a widow, fearing that my cousin was deeply grieved, (my father) took the widowed daughter home and gave her in marriage" (179). This obviously contradicts his own principles. And even more interesting is Chu Hsi's comment on the perpetual state of widowhood: "Generally speaking, that should be the case. But people cannot follow that absolutely" (ibid.). It is difficult to say if this is a case of the *li* of change or favoritism. Suffice it to say that this obsession with chastity had unforeseen results on the future generations of women: the straitjacket of chastity.

Yet it must be said that Cheng I, like Mencius before him, emphasized the importance of women. He cautions that people must be as careful, if not more careful, in choosing a daughter-in-law than a son-in-law. This is likely the result of the influence he experienced from his own mother, who he sees as filial, respectful, humble, obedient, humane, altruistic, liberal, and earnest. "She cared for and loved the children of my father's concubines just as she did her own. My father's cousin's son became an orphan when very young, and she regarded him as her own" (179).

Moreover, she was skilled in ruling the family. She was stern but correct, and taught that all, even the poor and humble, must be accorded respect. In teaching her children, Cheng I writes, she did not cover for them when they did something wrong, because she believed that "children become unworthy because a mother covers up their wrongdoings so the father is unaware of them" (180). Because of her instruction, Cheng I writes: "My brother and I are not particular in our food and clothing, and do not scold people in harsh language." That is, they have simple tastes and are always respectful. As to conflict in relationships, she says: "The trouble is that one cannot bend and not that one cannot stretch out!" (ibid.). In other words, children were always taught to accommodate.

But beyond accommodation, Cheng I and his brother were taught to help each other do good. Far from simply imitating each other or expecting something in return or reciprocity in their goodness, their mother emphasizes that "the trouble with our common feeling is that when our favors are not returned, we stop them. Consequently kindness cannot last very long" (181). Cheng I then finishes off the essay with his mother's education and management of the servants, to which he draws a parallel to officials serving in government. That is, officials will do well or poorly depending on "whether they can learn anything from their superiors" (182).

Cheng I's philosophy, like other Confucians', can be considered "hierarchical, authoritarian, and patrilineal, embodying a strict sexual and generational division of labor" (Andors 1983, 12). But he might be considered a relational "feminist" in his exposition on the power and influence a mother has over the family and in his emphasis on the importance of choosing well a daughter-in-law. There is, however, a big gap between a feminist and Cheng I. A feminist would expect independent judgment from a woman; not so Cheng I. In the perfect relationship, a wife always consults a husband before deciding on a matter.

Chu Hsi (1130–1200) had five daughters, nine granddaughters, and seven great-granddaughters. He was concerned foremost about marrying them off. In the *Sung shu* or the *History of Sung,* he is said to have prohibited women from becoming Buddhist and Taoist nuns. He is also said to have prevented married women from living in a nunnery together. He wanted "to stop men and women from gathering in the so-called transmission of scripture meetings in a monk's living quarters." He wanted and urged nuns to return to lay life and for their parents to arrange marriages for them. He simply did not like women and men mingling. Moreover, he believed some of these popular religious practitioners to be witches and was convinced that they were taking advantage of the people (Ch'an 1987, 151–52).

These were things he thought about and did to women. How he felt about them was also interesting. After ten years of pure living, he confessed that he was still swayed by a woman's smile. When he was dying, Chu Hsi asked all the women to leave the room. Why this was done is not clear, but women obviously represented a strong alien force to him. And it is here that the Buddhist influence is most obvious. Whereas Confucianism does not conceive woman as a symbol of lust, evil, destruction, and as a hindrance to one's enlightenment, Buddhism does have a strong tradition in this particular negative view of women. For more details I refer the reader to Chan Wing-tsit's essay, "Chu Hsi's treatment of women," in the book *Chu Hsi, New Studies* (537–47).

Lü K'un: A Confucian Feminist

Traditional accounts point to the Sung as the beginning of the decline for Chinese women. The Ch'eng-Chu school especially is thought to be responsible. Handlin, however, offers a different perspective: "Foot binding, the cults of chastity and virginity, and stricter rules against remarriage of widows . . . (might) be interpreted as reactions to the aggressive behavior of women" (Wolf-Witke 1975, 19). This suggests that urbanization, leisure, and widespread literacy resulted in what was described as the "degeneration" in women's behavior and thereby the extreme measures to counteract it. But there were alternative reactions and methods of coping. For example, literacy made it possible to close the gap between the Confucians and the commoners, and Lü K'un's *Kuei fang* or *Regulations for the Women's Quarters* was written in such a milieu. He wrote in the tradition of Liu Hsiang and Pan Chao, with the crucial difference that he was writing to the woman-on-the-street.

Lü K'un (1536–1618)[17] was the vice president of justice, his tablet was placed in the Confucian temple in 1826. He is by any definition a feminist. He proposed that men be as responsible for a good marriage as women, and posed embarrassing questions about the place of women in society, and offered radical solutions: education and independence. He asks: "How is it that women are good only for sex and beauty?" How is it that men in southern China have no *liang-hsin* or goodness of heart or conscience, and commit "female infanticide to avoid providing dowries?" Why is it that widows commit suicide senselessly? Moreover, he writes, men must be as responsible for a harmonious marriage as women. And he adds, women must be taught the legal codes, medicine, and weaving (Wolf and Witke, 34–35) if they are to survive in the world. This must surely be considered feminist.

Kuei fang was published in 1590. Lu explains that he deemed it necessary because he sees the behavior of women deteriorating: "Those born in villages hear vulgar expressions. Those living in wealthy homes are slipping into extravagance and think only of gold and pearls: although clever, they neither speak good words nor perform good deeds" (ibid. 17). He criticizes the women for exaggerated performances of *li* on the one hand, and on the other hand he criticizes them for not practicing *li*. He has in mind in the first instance women committing suicide after their fiancés die: in the latter instances he points to women walking about without covering their faces, riding in carriages and pulling aside the curtains with their faces made up "to please the eyes of crafty youths" (20).

This concern for seductiveness Lü shares with all Confucians. The preference is for an unadorned and simple appearance. He bases this on tradition, as his predecessors also did. He writes: "When the ancient kings set up restrictions in the world, only *li* were most serious, and *li* in regard to (relations between) men and women were even more serious (because the ancients) feared that that is whence disasters come" (20). We encounter again the theme that though women do not have direct political or military power, they hold tremendous sexual power and personal influence.

In fact Lü writes that the reason he has chosen to focus on women when there are so many virtuous men is because he wants to bring to light *yin chiao* or the teaching of women. Women can and should serve as models for men since it is one's moral integrity and not one's gender that determines one's worthiness. He goes on to cite Fa Mu-lan, the girl-soldier who served in the army in place of her sick father. For twelve years no one knew that she was female, and even though women and men are supposed to be separated from each other, Lü says that people should not gossip about her because the *chün tzu* has a mind of his or her own "which can be tested before the sun in heaven; and his sympathy with others (reaches the standard of) being able to mix (without blighting) his splendor with dust. Indeed, Mu-lan is my teacher" (23). This is a simple, straightforward, and unequivocal statement on the equality of men and women in moral development and education.

And beyond equality in education, we see again the function of the *li* of change and the principle of *i* as it was applied to Tsai Yen. During difficult times, the *li* of the classics can be circumvented, and in this spirit, Lü critiques cases of exemplary women and finds them wanting. Women must learn to think for themselves rather than following blindly the *li* of the classics. In the case of Wang Kuang's daughter, who killed herself after she failed to kill the barbarian who murdered her father, Lü suggests that she might have "succeeded if, instead of acting so precipitously, she had allowed the barbarian one night of pleasure and waited for him to fall asleep" (22).

He then continues with a second case in which a woman allows herself to be murdered to save her husband and father. Lü is appalled at the idea that anyone would actually encourage a daughter to endanger her own life for her father's. He notes critically that the father and husband could have fled (22) and concludes that only a total lack of imagination can cause a daughter to be sacrificed. Contrary to the implicit principle that death is more honorable than life, Lü agrees with a Sung scholar who said that "to die for something in the world is easy; to accomplish something in the world is difficult." Lü explains, "the sages value virtue, but more than that, they value virtue accompanied by talent" (21).

Lü K'un had a "conventionally successful career, rising from magistrate to governor to vice minister of justice" (15), so he understands well that if one were speaking of "allotted influence and status, then the wives of members of the gentry and of commoners should not be put together." But he continues to say that if, however, one were speaking about "the Way and righteousness, then (people) in ditches and starving to death can share the same hall with Yao and Shun. Why speak of high and low?" (25).

This loosens considerably the system formalized by Tung Chung-shu and returns Confucianism to the simplicity of Confucius. In the pursuit of *jen* one should yield to no one, not even one's teacher. This simple but radical statement of equality is hence emphasized amid the mind-numbing details of superimposed *li*.

But Lü K'un is concerned not only with extenuating circumstances. He advocates an end to the sexual division of labor. He suggests that both men and women be taught to weave cotton, then new in China. He writes: "When this is accomplished, not only will women have jobs, but will the province not enjoy the profit as well?" (26). In other words, Lü understood the problems women faced to be of an economic nature. He was not afraid to offer solutions that opposed a basic tenet such as division of labor based on gender. One might say that he applied the *li* of change to the system as his predecessors had to the personal. Lü K'un saw that the world had changed from the one that existed during the classical times.

At the same time, it is important to remember that Lü remained fundamentally Confucian when he insists on the differentiation between husband and wife, and even more so with the sexual segregation of women and men. Lü was a conservative in sexual relationships because he believes that all other relationships begin in a man and a woman living together. In this, Lü echoes Mencius in the idea that a man and woman cohabitating is the most important relationship. "It is the crossroads of life and death and (potentially) the beginning of great disorder" (34).

Conclusion

When considered in historical context, Confucianism is at once feminist, like Lü K'un, and patriarchal, like Chu Hsi. Either way, however, it is, in its core values, at odds with feminism. The ruling Confucian principle is duty and not choice; so that one does not choose to have a family or not: one is obligated to have a family. Moreover, Confucians conceive of woman and man not as individuals but as natural complements, and their relationship is regarded as the root of all others, since family begins there and family is the foundation of society. Furthermore Confucianism differs from feminism in its emphasis on self-cultivation over the fight for rights and justice.

In a world where people speak increasingly of their rights rather than their responsibilities, and where there is a bewildering spectrum of opinions, Confucianism, in its most simple adage of *jen,* seems to offer a sensible start. It stresses self-understanding and correction, then personal responsibility before the external process of admonishing and changing others. Finally, despite an apparently rigid hierarchy, Confucianism cherishes at its heart, equality in education and the *li* of change. These two principles, an equal opportunity to learning and an attitude of openness and flexibility, do not contradict feminism. Rather, this is where the two philosophies meet and where they are most able to reinforce each other.

After a hundred and fifty years of a relatively one-sided affair, and at this time when the issue of race or charge of racism is threatening the integrity of feminism, an appreciation of *jen* and a better understanding of the history of Confucianism might offer a sense of cultural recovery for Chinese feminists and a better understanding and inspiration for non-Chinese feminists. This essay and the several mentioned here hopefully mark the beginning of this new stage of development toward a less racist feminism or feminisms.

Chinese Glossary

Ch'un-chiu	Spring and Autumn Annals
Ch'un-chiu fan-lu	Luxuriant Gems of the Spring and Autumn Annals
chung	conscientiousness; loyalty
fu jen	wife; duchess
Han shu	History of the (Former) Han Dynasty
Hou Han shu	History of the Latter Han Dynasty
hsiao jen	small person or a small-minded person; inferior person; the opposite of a worthy person
i	righteousness
I ching	Book of Changes
jen	love; benevolence; human-heartedness; perfect virtue
Kuei fang t'u shuo	Regulations for the Women's Quarters
li	rites; rituals; the spirit in performance of rites
Li chi	Book of Rites
liang hsin	literally "good heart"; conscience
Lieh-nü chüan	Biographies of Exemplary Women
Nü-chieh	Instructions for Women
nü tzu	woman; concubine; servant girl
pao-t'u	treasure picture; precious impression
shih	title of proper wife
Shih ching	Book of Odes
Shih fan	Precepts for Social Life
shu	altruism; reciprocity
Shu ching	Book of Documents or Book of History
Tai-yun ching	Mahamegha Sutra; Great Cloud Sutra
ts'ung	to obey; to follow
wu hsing	five elements; five agents
yang	light; brightness; associated with maleness
yin	dark; the shady side of a mountain; associated with femaleness

Chronology of Dynasties and
Chronology of Philosophers from Chan Wing-Tsit

Table 3.1
Chronology of Philosophers

ANCIENT PERIOD

Confucianism: *Confucius   Great Learning   Mencius*, 371–289 B.C.?. . . . .
            551–449 B.C. *Doc. of the Mean   Hsün Tzu*, fl. 298–238 B.C. . . . .
Taoism: *Lao Tzu*, 6th or 4th cent. B.C.? *Chuang Tzu*, bet. 399 and 295 B.C. . . . .
Moism: . . . . *Mo Tzu*, fl. 479–438 B.C. . . . .
Logicians: . . . . *Hui Shih*, 380–305 B.C.?
                Kung-sun Lung, b. 380 B.C.?
Yin Yang: . . . . *Tsou Yen, 305–240 B.C.* . . . .
Legalism: . . . . *Han Fei*, d. 233 B.C. . . . .

MEDIEVAL PERIOD

Confucianism: *Book of*   *Tung Chung-shu* .   *Yang Hsiung*
           Changes   c. 179-c. 104 B.C.   53 B.C.-A.D. 18
           Naturalism . . . .*Wang Ch'ung*, b. A.D. 27
Taoism and Neo-Taoism: *Huai-nan Tzu*, d. 122 B.C.
                   Wang Pi, 226–249
                   Kuo Hsiang, d. 312
                   Lieh Tzu (Yang Chu)

Buddhism: *Seven Schools*, 4th cent.
        Seng-chao, 384-414
        Three-Treatise School, 4th-7th cent. . . . .
        Consciousness-Only School, 6th–9th cent. . . . .
        Tien-t'ai School, 6th cent. . . . .
        Hua-yen School, 7th cent. . . . .
        Zen School, 5th cent. . . . .
Confucian Revival: *Han Yü*, 768–824
                Li Ao, fl. 798

MODERN PERIOD

Sung Neo-Confucianism:
   Chou Tun-i (Chou lien-hsi), 1017–1073
   Shao Yung, 1011–1077
   Chang Tsai (Chang Heng-ch'ü), 1020–1077
   Ch'eng Hao (Ch'eng Ming-tao), 1032–1085
   Ch'eng I (Ch'eng I-ch'uan), 1033–1107
                Lu Hsiang-shan (Lu Chiu-yüan), 1139–1193
   School of Principle   *Chu Hsi*, 1130–1200
Ming Neo-Confucianism: School of Mind   *Wang Yang-ming*
                          Wang Shou-jen),
                          1472–1529 . . . .

Ch'ing Confucianism:
   Materialism: . . . . *Wang Fu-chih (Wang Ch'uan-shan)*, 1619–1692
   Practical Confucianism: . . . . *Yen Yiian*, 1635–1704
                                  Li Kung, 1659–1735
   Principle as Order: . . . . .Tai Chen (Tai Tung-yüan), 1723–1777

   CONTEMPORARY PERIOD
   . . . .*K'ang Yu-wei*, 1858–1927
   . . . .*T'an Ssu-t'ung*, 1865–1898
   . . . .*Chang Tung-sun*, 1886–1962
   . . . .*Fung Yu-lan*, 1890–
                                  Hsiung Shih-li, 1885–1968
                                  Communism, 1949–

For more detailed chronological charts, see Wing-tsit Chan,
Historical Charts of Chinese Philosophy, New Haven,
Far Eastern Publications, Yale University, 1955.

Table 3.2
Chronology of Dynasties

Emperor Yao	(Legendary)	3rd millennium B.C.	
Emperor Shun	(Legendary)	3rd millennium B.C.	
Hsia ⎱		2183–1752 B.C.?	
Shang ⎰ (Three Dynasties)		1751–1112 B.C. (1765–1112 B.C.)	
Chou ⎰		1111–249 B.C. (or 1027–249 B.C.)	
		Spring and Autumn	722–481 B.C.
		Warring States (480) . . .	403–222 B.C.
Ch'in . . . . (255 B.C. 221–206 B.C.			
Han . . . . B.C. 206–220 A.D.		Western (Former) Han B.C. 206–	8 A.D.
		Hsin	9– 23 A.D.
		Eastern (Later) Han. . . .	25–220 A.D.
Wei . . . . 220–265 A.D.		Three ⎱ Wei. . . .	220–265
		Kingdoms ⎰ Shu. . . .	221–263
		⎰ Wu	222–280
Chin. 265–420		Western Chin	265–317
S. and N. Dynasties. 420–589		Eastern Chin	317–420
South		North	
Liu Sung 420–479		Later (North) Wei	386–535
Southern Ch'i. 479–502		Eastern Wei	534–550
Liang 502–557		Western Wei	535–556
Ch'en 557–589		Northern Ch'i	550–577
		Northern Chou	557–581
Sui 581–618			
Tang. 618–907			

Five Dynasites 907–960	Later Liang	907–923
	Later Tang	923–936
	Later Chin	936–947
	Later Han	947–950

			Later Chou	951–960
Liao (907–)	947–1125		Later Chou	951–960
Sung		960–1279	Northern Sung	960–1126
			Southern Sung	1127–1279

Hsi-hsia	990–1227
Chin	1115–1234
Yiian (Mongol). . . . (1206–)	1271–1368
Ming	1368–1644
Ch'ing (Manchu)	1644–1912
Republic	1912–
People's Republic	1949–

Notes

1. I assume here the unity of a Chinese race/culture, and Confucianism to be its most influential and thereby "representative" worldview. Examples will be cited to disprove these assumptions later. Nevertheless, I believe the tension between American-Chinese men and women—that is, the balance between sympathy and anger—to be a common phenomenon.

2. Isaac Taylor Headland was an exception. He argued against the case of abused Chinese women. He even suggested that Chinese parents were as capable as American parents of doting on and loving their daughters (Varg, 119).

3. The three feminisms are based on Cott's categorization of liberalism, Protestantism, and socialist utopianism (1987: 16). This is similar to Offen's divisions: the egalitarian, the evangelical, and the socialist (1988, 132). Other theorists like Rosemary Radford Ruether agree to the basic position that there is no single feminism. Also of interest here are Ebrey's accounts of one man giving his younger brother away because of his family's dire financial straits; and another of the drowning of a male infant in a wine vat; and yet another, of contemplated male infanticide where a girl-baby would have been accepted into the family (1984, 106–107). Infanticide is dreadful in any circumstance, but the evidence shows that it happened not only to girls but also to boys, so that the motivation had to be at least partly economic and not wholly gender-related.

4. A woman is to obey or follow her father when young, her husband when she marries, and her son when she is old and her husband is dead. The four virtues include her obligations, her appearance, her behavior, and her speech. She must perform well her household and ritual duties; she must keep herself neat and clean, and always dress simply and not seductively; she must be gentle, kind, and compliant; and she must be soft-spoken and not quarrelsome. She must not gossip.

5. These categories are not intended to include all Confucians. Rather, they offer convenient points for the discussion here.

6. One example is Riane Eisler, *The Chalice and the Blade: Our History, Our Future.*

7. I have substituted here the translation of *hsiao jen* from "small men" to "small-minded people," or it can be read also as inferior people.

8 Liu Te-han investigates this in some detail from pages eight to eleven in his book, *Tung Chou fu nu sheng-huo or The Life of Women under Eastern Chou.* He notes that the woman often occupies a disadvantaged position. A wife has to mourn her husband for three years; but a husband is required to mourn for his wife for only a year, whereas he mourns for his eldest son for three years. Moreover, a father is mourned for three years regardless of conditions; a mother or stepmother is mourned also for three years, although the garb is different from that of the father's. But if the father were dead, then the category of mother receives only one year of mourning.

9. The five relationships are emperor and minister, father and son, older and younger brother, husband and wife and friends. Except for the class of friendship, there is an implied senior to junior relationship in the other categories.

10. Offen defines individualist feminists as those who accept the "binary logic endemic to western thought . . . and the self/other dualism" (137). These feminists insist on their birthright to self-sovereignity (136). Temma Kaplan is an example. She attacks "division of labor by sex, because roles limit freedom, and to mark distinctions is to imply superiority and inferiority" (141).

11. Offen writes that individualist feminism "blinds us to the range of effective arguments used to combat male privilege in the Western world during the past few centuries, and even to arguments put forth today by women and men in economically less-privileged countries, where women's aspirations to self-sovereignity are often subordinated to pressing short-term political and socio-economic necessities" (138). She goes on to criticize Kaplan (see note 10, above). Offen notes that Kaplan's argument is "radically individualist, very contemporary, and ultimately a very exclusionary perspective on the history of feminism" (141).

12. The Yin-yang School treats the *wu hsing* or five elements and *yin yang* as equal; occurring and relating to each other in a cycle. Tung, however, arranges them in a linear way because of an origin, which necessitates a straightline temporal sequence. "It is no wonder that loyalty and filial piety are on the forefront, for that is where the ruler and the father are to be found" (Chan 1963, 279).

13. Early Confucians emphasize self-education. Teachers and rulers are important because they are influential as virtuous models. Tung, however, believes that people are by nature "in the dark"; and in this, he continues Hsün Tzu's idea that human nature is evil. The need for a uniform education and authoritarianism are therefore justified by the people's "natural" ignorance (Chan 1963, 278).

14. I have paraphrased or translated passages directly from the Chinese text. If the reader is particularly interested in Tung Chung-shu, selected chapters and passages are available in English in: Fung Yu-lan, *A History of Chinese Philosophy,* volume two; Chan Wing-tsit, *A Source Book in Chinese Philosophy;* and also de Bary et al., *Sources of Chinese Tradition.* Tung Chung-shu deviated from mainstream Confucianism in his emphasis of the *Annals.* Nonetheless, he remained influential in his success at synthesizing different philosophies and achieving prominence for a hybrid Confucianism.

15. The following is a quote from a section in de Bary on "the historical mission of Confucianism," translated from the *Huai-nan Tzu.* It describes the emperor Chou of Shang, the dynasty previous to Chou: "Without measure were his taxes and levies, and his killing and slaughtering were without end. Drunken with lust and drowned in wine, he gathered within the palace a great multitude. He made the torture of the burning pillar. He butchered his councilors and cut open pregnant women" (186). The Confucians were also antiexpansionists and proponents for an equitable economic system. De Bary includes their arguments in a translation from *Yen-t'ieh Lun* or *The Debate on Salt and Iron:* "In the ancient times taxes and levies took from the people what they were skilled in producing and did not demand what they were poor at. Thus the farmers sent in their harvests and the weaving women their goods. Nowadays the government disregards what people have and requires of them what they have not, so that they are forced to sell their goods at a cheap price in order to meet the demands from above. . . . The farmers suffer double hardships and the weaving women are taxed twice. We have not seen that this kind of marketing is equitable'" (222). Further on, the Confucians attack the Ch'in dynasty as well as the current government: "Such worship of profit and slight of what is right, such exaltation of power and achievement, led, it is true, to expansion of land and acquisition of territory. Yet it was like pouring more water upon people who are already suffering from flood and only increasing their distress. You see how Shang Yang (prime minister of Ch'in) opened the way to imperial rule for the Ch'in, but you fail to see how he also opened for the Ch'in the road to ruin!" (223)

16. There was a minor Buddhist sutra called the *Mahamegha, Ta-yün* or *Great Cloud.* It contained a prophecy that the imminent reincarnation of Maitreya, the future Buddha, would come in female form, as a monarch of all the world. Hsüeh Huai-i, a monk, interpreted this to mean that Wu Tse-t'ien was Maitreya (Guisso 1979: 305) and he presented the sutra to her. In a separate incident, a white stone venerated as *pao-t'u* or treasure picture was found in the Lo River in 688, bearing the prophecy that a "Sage Mother shall come to Rule Mankind; and her Imperium shall bring Eternal Prosperity." Following the discovery of the white stone, Empress Wu "declared the Lo River sacred, prohibiting fishing there, and she took for herself the title, 'Sage Mother, Sovereign Divine'" (ibid. 302).

17. Lü K'un did not adhere to any one school although the Confucian tradition claims him to be one of its own. In matters of principle Lü said: "I am only me" (Lü 1962. 1). He criticized the many books of *chia li* or family regulations inspired by the Ch'eng-Chu school. He advocated a return to simplicity and criticized his contemporaries for practicing *li* that was not from the sages but the Han

Confucians. He found them excessive to the extent that they destroy *chung* and *shu.*
In other words, the practice of *li* destroys the very *jen* it was established to encourage
(ibid. 36).

Bibliography

Andors, Phyllis. 1983. *The Unfinished Liberation of Chinese Women 1949–1980.*
Bloomington: Indiana University Press.

Ayscough, Florence. 1938. *Chinese Women: Yesterday and Today.* London: Jonathan
Cape.

Black, Alison H. 1986. "Gender and Cosmology in Chinese Correlative Thinking" in
Gender and Religion, ed. Bynum, Harrell, and Richman. Boston: Beacon Press.

Bodde, Derk. 1981. "Myths of Ancient China" in *Essays on Chinese Civilization.*
Princeton: Princeton University Press.

Buxbaum, David C., ed. 1978. *Chinese Family Law and Social Change in Historical
and Comparative Perspective.* Seattle and London: University of Washington
Press.

Chafe, William H. 1977. *Women and Equality. Changing Patterns in American Culture.*
New York: Oxford University Press.

Ch'an Wing-tsit. 1987. *Chu Hsi. Life and Thought.* Hong Kong: Chinese University
Press.

———. 1989. *Chu Hsi. New Studies.* Honolulu: University of Hawaii Press.

———. trans. 1967. *Reflections on Things at Hand. The Neo-Confucian Anthology.*
New York: Columbia University Press.

———. 1963. *A Source Book in Chinese Philosophy.* Princeton: Princeton University
Press.

Ch'en, Tung-yüan. 1937. *Chung-kuo fu-nü sheng-huo shih.* Shanghai: Commercial
Press.

Ch'u, T'ung-tsu. 1972. *Han Social Structure.* Seattle and London: University of Washington Press.

Cott, Nancy F. 1987. *The Grounding of Modern Feminism.* New Haven and London:
Yale University Press.

Croll, Elizabeth. 1978. *Feminism and Socialism in China.* London: Routledge, Kegan
and Paul.

———. 1977. "The Movement to Criticize Confucius and Lin Piao: A Comment on the
Women of China" in *SIGNS 2,* no. 1:721–26.

————. 1977. "A Recent Movement to Redefine the Role and Status of Women" in *China Quarterly* no. 71 (September): 591;-97.

Curtin, Katie. 1975. *Women in China.* New York: Pathfinder.

de Bary, Theodore. 1960. *Sources of Chinese Tradition.* 2 Vols. New York: Columbia University Press.

de Beauvoir, Simone. 1952. *The Second Sex.* Trans. H. M. Parshley. New York: Knopf.

Ebrey, Patricia Buckley trans. 1984. *Family and Property in Sung China. Yuan Ts'ai's* Precepts for Social Life. Princeton: Princeton University Press.

————. ed. 1981. *Chinese Civilization and Society. A Sourcebook.* New York: Free Press.

Eisler, Riane. 1987. *The Chalice and the Blade: Our History, Our Future.* San Francisco: Harper-Row.

Ernst, Faber, 1917. "The Status of Women in China" in *The Chinese Recorder* 48, no. 9 (September): 590–602.

French, Marilyn. 1985. *Beyond Power: On Women, Men and Morals.* New York: Summit Books.

Fu, Wen. 1974. "Doctrine of Confucius and Mencius: The Shackle that Keeps Women in Bondage" in *Peking Review* no. 8 (March) 16–18.

Fung, Yu-lan. 1983. English edition of 1931 Chinese edition. Derk Bodde trans. *A History of Chinese Philosophy.* Princeton: Princeton University Press.

Guisso, R. W. L. 1979. "The Reigns of the Empress Wu, Chung-tsung and Jui-tsung (684–712)" in *Cambridge History of China* 3:290–332 ed. by Dennis Twitchett and John K. Fairbank. Cambridge: Cambridge University Press.

Guisso, R. W. L., and Johannesen, Stanley, eds. 1981. *Women in China: Current Directions in Historical Scholarship.* Youngstown: Philo Press.

Headland, Isaac Taylor. 1897. "Chinese Women from a Chinese Standpoint" in *The Chinese Recorder* no 28: 10–18. Shanghai: Presbyterian Mission Press.

Hirsch, Marianne, and Keller, Evelyn Fox. 1990. *Conflicts in Feminism.* New York and London: Routledge.

Holmgren, Jennifer. 1985. "The Economic Foundations of Virtue: Widow-remarriage in Early and Moden China" in *The Australian Journal of Asian Affairs,* no. 13 (January): 1–27.

————. 1981. "Myth, Fantasy or Scholarship: Images of the Status of Women in Traditional China" in *The Australian Journal of Asian Affairs,* no. 6: 147–70.

Kelleher, Theresa. 1987. "Confucianism" in *Women in World Religions,* ed. Sharma, Arvind. Albany: State University of New York Press.

Kuo, Li-ch'eng. 1983. *Chung-kuo fu-nü sheng-huo shih hua.* Taipei: Han-kuang wen-fa Publisher.

Legge, James, trans. 1967 reprint of 1885 ed. *Li chi, Book of Rites.* Edited by C. C. Chai and W. Chai. 2 vols. New York: University Books.

Li, Yu-ning ed. 1988. *A Collection of Essays on the History of Chinese Women.* Taipei: Commercial Press.

Liu, Hua-t'ing. 1984. *Chung-kuo wu ch'ien nien nu-hsing.* Taipei: Hsin-Kuang Publishers.

Liu, Te-han. 1974. *Tung Chou fu-nü sheng-huo.* Taipei: Hsüeh-sheng shu-chu.

Lock, Jean. 1989. "The Effect of Ideology in Gender Role Definition: China as a Case Study" in *Journal of Asian and African Studies* 24, nos. 3–4 (July-October): 228–38. Leiden: E. J. Brill.

Lü, K'un. 1962. Ed. Hou Wai-lu. *Lü K'un che hsueh hsüan chi.* Peking: Chung-hua shu-chu.

Mitchell, Juliet, and Oakley, Ann, ed. 1986. *What is Feminism.* Oxford: Basil Blackwell.

Offen, Karen. 1988. "Defining Feminism: A Comparative Historical Approach" in *SIGNS* 14: 111–57. Chicago: University of Chicago Press.

O'Hara, Albert R. 1971 reprint of 1945 ed. *The Position of Women in Early China According to the* Lieh Nü Chüan. Taipei: Mei Ya Publications.

———. 1963. "Women's Place in Early China" in *Free China Review* no. 13 (March): 31–35.

Smith, Howard. 1973. *Confucius.* New York: Charles Scribner's Sons.

Swann, Nancy Lee. 1932, *Pan Chao: Foremost Woman Scholar of China.* New York: Century Company.

Tung, Chung-shu. 1984. Ed. Yin Shu-kuan. *Ch'un ch'iu fan lu chin chu chin i.* Taipei: Commercial Press.

Varg, Paul A. 1958. *Missionaries, Chinese, and Diplomats: The American Protestant Missionary Movement in China 1890–1952.* Princeton: Princeton University Press.

Waley, Arthur, trans. 1960 reprint of 1937 ed. *The Book of Songs.* New York: Grove Press.

Wang, Fang-t'ing. 1966. *Chung-hua li-tai fu-nü.* Taipei: Commercial Press.

Williams, S. Wells. 1880. "Education of Women in China" in *The Chinese Recorder* 11: 40–53. Shanghai: American Presbyterian Press.

Wolf, Margery, and Witke, Roxane, eds. 1975. *Women in Chinese Society.* Stanford: Stanford University Press.

Wong, Zhong-shu. 1982. K. C. Chang et al. trans. *Han Civilization.* New Haven and London. Yale University Press.

Yang, Lien-sheng. 1969. "Female Rulers in Imperial China" in *Excursions in Sinology* 27–43. Princeton: Princeton University Press.

Yao, Esther S. Lee. 1983. *Chinese Women: Past and Present.* Texas: Ide House.

Yu, Ying-shih. 1967. *Trade and Expansion in Han China.* Berkeley and Los Angeles: University of California Press.

Zen, Heng-che Sophie. 1932. *The Chinese Woman.*

Chapter 4

Feminism and/in Taoism

Karen Laughlin and Eva Wong

If it is true that the "great tao" *makes no distinctions between man and woman, how is it that there are differences here? The answer: the* tao *is the same but the practice is different. It is because their natures are different and their bodies dissimilar that the practices are so very different, even though there is but one* tao *of life.—* Essentials of the Golden Elixir Method for Women, *compiled by Chi-yi Tzu. Wile 1992, 204*

For several years, the authors of this chapter led workshops together on women and Taoism. Our teacher, Master Moy Lin-shin, encouraged us to develop our understanding of how Taoist training may differ for women and men. He also invited us to reflect on how such differences figure in the individual's overall physical and spiritual development. This work led us to consider how Taoism's teachings about the feminine, individual self-cultivation, and the links between humanity and the rest of creation relate to the theory and practice of modern feminism.

The history of Taoism reveals an ongoing interaction between the age-old principles of the philosophy and the contemporary circumstances in which it is put into practice. Taoism has consistently absorbed and adapted the outlooks of other religious and philosophical systems in an ongoing project of synthesis. As a significant contemporary social movement, then, feminism is bound to have an impact on the development of Taoism today. And, we would like to suggest, Taoism also has much to say to modern feminism.

The Dialogue of Taoism and Feminism

Before developing this interaction, it is important to point out that neither feminist nor Taoist thought can be seen as unified or monolithic systems. Contemporary feminism is often described as a second or even third wave, in order to acknowledge the work of nineteenth- and early twentieth-century champions of women's rights and to affirm modern feminists' debts to their foremothers from these and earlier times. Even the most cursory survey of this moment in the history of feminism suggests a tremendous variety of outlooks and approaches.

Diversity is a key concept within feminist studies today. This refers primarily to feminists' recognition of differences among women (and men) of various races, classes, and cultures, and the impact of these differences on both theory and practice. But it also relates to the diversity characterizing feminist thought itself. While the "feminisms" sometimes exist in creative tension with one another, in other instances they stand in outright conflict even as they may share the goal of achieving a more just society.

The history of Taoism of course extends back much farther than that of feminism as an organized social movement—to a time in the history of China that some scholars have suggested may even have been prepatriarchal (see, for example, Cleary 1989, 1–2). As both a philosophy and a religion, Taoism has undergone countless transformations, adapting to the times and circumstances of those who responded to its teachings. It is said that people make Taoism, just as Taoism has guided people's actions. The Taoist canon, a still-growing collection of over sixteen hundred volumes, presents a wide variety of perspectives on the way to develop ourselves and to live in harmony with one another and with the Tao, the source of all life. How, then, can we place Taoism and feminism (or the feminisms) in dialogue with one another?

Some authors (see, for example, Chen 1974, 1989, and Reed 1987) suggest that Taoism's use of female imagery gives women and qualities associated with them a favored status within Taoism. In our opinion, although Taoism does value such qualities as softness and fluidity, which are traditionally understood as feminine, this does not mean that Taoism favors a feminine model or can be seen as a stronghold of feminism. This would be akin to saying that Taoism has a high regard for water since water shares these same qualities. In the feminist dialogue with Taoism, we need to be careful not to rely on a model of female superiority that is antithetical both to Taoism and to many modern feminisms.

Throughout the history of Taoism, both women and men have attained enlightenment or immortality. Therefore, both females and males have the potential to attain the highest levels of Taoist training. In this sense, there is sexual equality in terms of the attainment of a spiritual goal. Taoism, however, did not develop in a social or historical vacuum, and it did not escape the influences of patriarchal Confucianism, which had dominated Chinese society since the dawn of written history in China. To say that Taoism has always championed women and feminism would be to deny that historical and social conditions have an effect on the history of philosophy. It is a misrepresentation of Taoism to suggest that it exists as an abstract philosophy only. Any worthwhile discussion has to include the material, everyday conditions in which Taoism has flourished.

Given the patriarchal social conditions of China, where, then, can a dialogue between Taoism and feminism occur? In both our own practice and our research into the scriptures of the Taoist canon, we have found that Taoism, more than many other spiritual traditions, has shown a sensitivity to the needs of women in spiritual training. This is illustrated by the works of the Taoist canon that specifically address the methods of training for women, taking into account the physiological and psychological differences between women and men. In addition, there are texts in the canon that were written by women not only on the spiritual training of women but on the general principles of practicing the arts of health and longevity. It does not appear that there was any aversion to including among the Taoist scriptures texts written by women.

For us, the dialogue between Taoism and feminism begins here. Taoism emphasizes equality in the attainment of spiritual goals and recognizes that physiological and cultural differences between females and males need to be addressed to enable both women and men to train effectively within this spiritual tradition. If there is to be dialogue between Taoism and feminism, both need to meet on common ground. And, if the dialogue is to be productive, both parties' outlooks will be affected. This is what we hope to do. If both Taoism and feminism are to be living philosophical traditions that will continue to provide spiritual inspiration, then they need to use each other's perspectives to understand and critique themselves.

Rooted in the traditions of Chinese medicine, Taoist practices often seek to undo blockages on the individual level; similarly, the teachings of Taoism may suggest ways of overcoming some of the impasses that have confronted the various feminisms as they, too, have sought to heal both the individual and society. The goal of Taoist practice is to return to (or be reunited with) the Tao, the source of all creation. In order for the primordial energy that is the Tao to flow freely, work must be done to remove blockages to the circulation of that energy, within both the physical structure and the consciousness of the individual. That individual's spiritual development can then have a positive impact on society, not so much through mass social movements as through the effect of the enlightened person on those with whom he or she comes into contact.

The history of feminism, especially as it has developed in the latter half of the twentieth century, reveals an increasing tendency toward self-criticism as feminists have scrutinized the limitations or one-sidedness of their own attempts to find a place for women in contemporary culture. Insistence on female superiority and challenges to traditional feminine roles have often met with powerful resistance, both from within and without the feminist movement, and have threatened to block the development of feminist thought. From the standpoint of Taoism, the different feminist perspectives might be seen as vehicles that, while valuable at one point of development in the social history of women and men, need to be put aside once they have served their purpose. Otherwise, these perspectives become blockages to further development just as attachments to objects and ideas become blockages to enlightenment.

Without imposing on contemporary feminism an absolute chronology or a sense of "progress" (a notion that has become quite suspect within feminism since what has often been construed as progress for one social group may well have meant regression for another), we will focus on four different facets of feminist thought that have had a significant social impact in the late twentieth century: (1) the revision of history; (2) the critique of traditional female roles; (3) the question of difference and celebration of the feminine; and (4) the attempt to break down the opposition of masculinity and femininity and subvert notions of gender altogether. In each instance, we will consider how the history and teachings of Taoism intersect with these perspectives, allowing us to see both feminism and Taoism in a new light.

The Revision of History

An important feminist project has been the effort to reclaim the past for women and to make visible those women whose stories have previously disappeared from the history books. In keeping with this project, many women can be recognized for their contributions to Taoism's heritage and development. Religious and philosophical Taoism developed primarily within a strongly patriarchal Chinese culture. Many (if not most) of the figures most readily associated with Taoism—the classical philosophers Lao-tzu and Chuang-tzu; the "Yellow Emperor," Huang-ti, a key figure in the development of Chinese medicine; and Chang Tao-liang, the "Heavenly Teacher" credited with establishing Taoism as a religion—are men, often recognized as *patriarchs* of this ancient tradition. Early studies of Taoism by Western scholars often focused exclusively on male leaders or deities, overlooking the contributions of women in Chinese myth or history (see Paper 1990).

Martin Palmer's introduction to *The Eight Immortals of Taoism,* for example, reflects the impression that women Taoist immortals are rare. Discussing the Immortal Lady Ho Hsien-ku, Palmer notes, "that there is a woman at all in this group is most surprising, for there is no tradition of female ascetics in Tao chia and the number of senior female practitioners of Tao chiao can be counted on one hand" (Palmer 1991, 30).

And yet the origins of Taoism go back long before the era of state Confucianism, with its insistence on male dominance. Its roots extend to prehistory, to the time of a loosely organized, agricultural society in which both male and female shamans acted as tribal leaders. The *Li-sao,* a book of poetry and songs collected from the southern region of China (collected circa 800 B.C.E.), tells us that both female and male shamans participated equally in all ceremonial rites. In fact, the Chinese ideograph for shaman (*wu*) has in it the radical of "woman." Whether this means that the first shamans were women is impossible to verify. However, the old songs and rituals found in the *Li-sao* and the *Spring and Autumn Annals (Ch'un-chao ku-liang chuan)* contain descriptions of male shamans impersonating women.

Indeed, throughout the history of Taoism, women have played prominent roles—as teachers of other Taoist adepts or sages, as heads of monasteries, and as Taoist immortals, achieving the highest levels of enlightenment. The Yellow Emperor, one of the most respected Taoist sages, was taught by a woman, The Lady of the Nine Heavens. According to the *Lieh-hsien chuan (Biographies of the Immortals),* one of the teachers of Fei Ch'ang-fang, a highly respected Taoist magician and alchemist who lived in the first century C.E., was a woman. This same book, which recounts the folk tales of Taoist immortals, includes the biographies of a substantial number of women immortals. In his introduction to *Immortal Sisters,* Thomas Cleary also describes the lives of women who attained enlightenment and immortality.

One figure who stands out among the female Taoist immortals is Sun Pu-erh, who lived during the twelfth century. One of the seven disciples of the leader of the Complete Reality School of Taoism, she is usually represented as a woman of keen intelligence and unusual dedication to Taoist practice. Her Taoist name, Pu-erh, can be translated as "no second way," referring to her single-minded pursuit of the Tao (Wong 1990, xviii-xix).

The Chinese folk novel *Seven Taoist Masters* presents Sun Pu-erh as the wife of a wealthy landowner who sacrifices both her material comforts and her physical beauty in order to devote herself completely to her training. She achieves immortality before her six male counterparts, choosing the most rigorous path and therefore attaining the highest level of enlightenment. And it was Sun Pu-erh who advised her husband Ma Tan-yang on the matters of looking for a teacher and having the right attitude for Taoist training.

In the early fourth century, another woman, Wei H'ua-ts'un, was instrumental in founding the Sh'ang-ch'ing sect, marking one of the most important developments in Taoist history. Based on the *Yellow Court Classic (Huang-ting ching),* Sh'ang-ch'ing Taoism's mysticism and visualization techniques were to become the major influences on two later Taoist sects, the Mao-shan and Cheng-I sects. Taoist legends say that Lady Wei H'ua-ts'un appeared in a vision to Yang Hsi, Hsü Hui, and Hsü Mi (the latter a father and son), and inspired them to rewrite the Sh'ang-ch'ing scriptures and found the Mao-shan Sh'ang-ch'ing sect.

Reed (1987) cites historical evidence showing that female Taoist adepts also served as heads of monasteries and performed the same religious and educational functions in these institutions that their male counterparts did. The existence of these women attests to the fact that advanced training in the Taoist arts was available to women as well as men. The recognition they gained in their own time perhaps made it easier for other women to acknowledge and be recognized for their own spiritual development. And their stories can also be seen as role models for women and men who are similarly seeking enlightenment today.

In addition to the references to women in Chinese folk stories and other historical documents, a number of texts in the Taoist canon focus on the training of women and the methods of attaining the Tao that are particular to women. This strongly suggests that there must have been a sizable number of female individuals or communities of women who were dedicated to Taoist training. However, the number of these texts compared to the number of classics that deal with training for men is very small. The preface to Chi-yi Tzu's *Essentials of the Golden Elixir Method for Women (Nü chin-tan fa-yao)* says, "there are many texts on the cultivating the internal pill. However, they do not discuss how women should practice." Another text on women's internal alchemy, *Master Li Ni-wan's Precious Raft of Women's Dual Practice (Ni-wan Li Tsu-shih nu-tsung shuang-hsiu pao-fa)* states, "elixir classics for men come by the cartload and are piled to the rafters, but those for women could hardly fill a single volume" (Wile 1992, 206). These remarks suggest that while there was a perceived need for texts on women's internal alchemy, the climate for writing and publishing these texts was not especially favorable.

Throughout the written history of China (from 1200 B.C.E. onward), males dominated the civil service. Both the Ching-tung and Wan-li (fifteenth and sixteenth century) compilations of the Taoist canon were regulated by the Han-lin Academy. This was a department of the government staffed by Confucian scholars whose work was to compile, edit, and collect for the imperial library the written classics of all the philosophies that existed in China. Therefore, it is not surprising that the number of Taoist texts on women's spiritual practice was not large. Still, as more texts on internal alchemy for women are translated, the popular views that enlightened women are rare and that there exist no difference between the practices of women and men in internal alchemy need to be revised.

From a feminist standpoint, retelling the history of Taoism in this fashion provides valuable information that can inspire women today and pay tribute to those who are potentially forgotten. But feminist scholars of late have also pointed out the dangers of idealizing a time that can no longer be recovered (see Butler 1990, 35–36) and have suggested replacing this project of feminist myth-making with "less glorious and also more ambivalent analyses of the past"

(Gordon 1986, 21). While it has been important for women to develop a sense of their rights and place within history—in China as in the West—feminists have also recognized a need to let go of their attachments to "great women" rather than merely patterning feminist history on the history of "great men."

For rather different reasons, Taoism also warns against idealizing the heroines (or heroes) of past or present, insisting that the quest for personal fame or recognition is in fact a hindrance to true enlightenment. *Seven Taoist Masters,* for example, begins:

> Charitable deeds are not meant to be a public performance. If you display compassion in order to show others your virtue, then your actions are empty of meaning. No matter how much you give to the poor, if you are doing it only to impress others, it is not charity. (Wong 1990, 1)

Similarly, the Taoist sage is generally described as virtually invisible in society, living a simple life dedicated to self-cultivation and service to others. In the words of Lao-tzu:

> The Way floats and drifts;
> It can go left or right.
> It accomplishes its tasks and completes its affairs, and
>   yet for this it is not given a name. . . .
> Therefore the Sage's ability to accomplish the great
> Comes from his not playing the role of the great.
> Therefore he is able to accomplish the great.
> (ch. 34, Hendricks 1989, 86)

Chuang-tzu, another early Taoist classic, advises the sage to:

> climb up on the way and its Virtue and go drifting and wandering, neither praised nor damned, now a dragon, now a snake, shifting with the times, never willing to hold to one course only. Now up, now down, taking harmony for your measure, drifting and wandering with the ancestor of the ten thousand things, treating things as things but not letting them treat you as a thing. (ch. 20, Watson 1968, 209–10)

In addition to serving as a caution to those who demand recognition for women's historical achievements, the Taoist attitude toward public display points to the problems with easy assumptions about why great women are not always visible. Cleary has suggested that Taoism's respect for the unheralded sage may in fact do more to account for the relative scarcity of information about great Taoist women in China than any presumed misogyny on the part of a male-dominated power structure (Cleary 1989, 6). While examples of individual achievements may provide inspiration, this aspect of Taoist teachings also serves as a useful warning against becoming caught up in an ego-centered (and spiritually damaging) quest for recognition even as women have sought access to more prominent social roles.

Equality and the Critique of Traditional Female Roles

As the second wave of feminism took shape in the early 1970s, the feminist project of rewriting history developed alongside demands for the social equality of women and men. This call for equality was bolstered by feminist arguments that many of the roles traditionally assigned to women effectively kept them in a subservient place. Writers and activists such as Kate Millett, Germaine Greer, and Elizabeth Janeway focused on the social forces that conditioned women and men to accept roles and behaviors considered appropriate to their sex. Their work analyzed the ways this social conditioning reinforced what Millet called a "sexual politics" of male dominance. The call, then, was for women to question and even abandon the "sex roles" that bound them to the domestic sphere and kept them from full and equal participation in all aspects of society. "Femininity" itself came under fire, since traditionally feminine qualities such as passivity, softness, emotion, and dependency were seen to work to subordinate women.

One of the most extreme—and hence widely noted—advocates of this view was Shulamith Firestone, whose 1970 book, *The Dialectic of Sex,* included an argument for abolishing pregnancy as we know it. Replacing tra ditional gestation with technological reproduction (in the form of test-tube babies) would relieve women of their function as childbearers and free them to participate in a full "feminist revolution" (Firestone 1970, esp. 206ff.). But many other, less radical proposals also challenged women to reject their traditional positions as homemakers, wives, and mothers in favor of less oppressive and presumably more fulfilling alternatives. This call to equality was often played out in attempts to be like the men who held to positions of power in society—entering into the competitive business world and playing by its rules.

As feminism continued to take shape as a significant social movement, however, these critiques alienated both men who saw themselves as targets of "radical feminist" wrath and women who could not reconcile their own positions as wives and mothers with what they saw as extreme feminist rhetoric. The "Afterword" to Sylvia Ann Hewlett's 1986 best-seller, *A Lesser Life: The Myth of Women's Liberation in America* offers a good summary of this latter response:

Women can function successfully as male clones in the marketplace only if they never have children, and to demand this of most women is to thwart their deepest biological need. (This attitude also ensures that if women do have children, many of them will be doomed to poverty and exhaustion.) A movement that looks away from the central fact of most women's lives—motherhood—will never win widespread support. (Hewlett 1986, 412)

While many feminists have been quick to criticize the biological determinism implicit in Hewlett's reference to women's "deepest biological need," the call to liberate women from limiting, socially-prescribed roles did in some ways become an obstacle to the development and popular acceptance of feminism. And as women more actively began taking up key roles outside the home, many began questioning the real social impact of such changes in their position or status.

Julia Kristeva, for example, noted, "the assumption by women of executive, industrial, and cultural power has not, up to the present time, radically changed the nature of this power." For Kristeva, then, women's new social roles raise questions about "how to avoid the centralization of power, how to detach women from it, and how then to proceed . . . to render decision-making institutions more flexible" (Kristeva 1981, 452–53). What does Taoism have to say about the attempt to redefine women's social roles?

Many Taoist texts also call the adept to put aside traditional family roles and to concentrate on personal spiritual development. Chang Po-tuan's internal alchemical classic, *Understanding Reality,* for example, urges, "family and wealth cast off, they are not your own possessions." It reminds those who follow the Taoist spiritual path that "it all depends on oneself alone, apart from others" (Chang 1987, 27 and 32). This is echoed in *Cultivating Stillness:*

Many honest people have been lured into the false security of possessive love, thinking that it means having a faithful spouse and filial children. When you die, you cannot take your spouse and children with you. (Wong 1992, 115)

Similarly, the legends of Sun Pu-erh sometimes portray her as childless and as eventually leaving her husband to pursue solitary training just as her teacher, Master Wang Ch'ung-yang, abandons his family to cultivate himself before he sets off to gather his disciples and found a major school of Taoism (see Wong 1990). Yet *Cultivating Stillness* also states, "If you have the motivation, then you can cultivate immortality in the home or in the monastery. If you are training at home, then your spouse is your friend and your children are your companions" (Wong 1992, 24–25).

Contrary to the view that Taoism rejects traditional family life in favor of celibacy and monasticism, these examples illustrate the pragmatism of Taoism. If one does not have any familial attachments, or has already fulfilled one's responsibilities to the family, singular training or monasticism is the fastest way to enlightenment. However, training in the home is also viable. Under this condition, the support and understanding of the family are needed to create a conducive environment for training. At the same time, the responsibility of providing for the family is not neglected.

In Taoism, spiritual training does not and should not conflict with family values. As one develops spiritually, attitudes about family life change naturally, but it is the *view* of family life that changes, not the value of the family. If we look again at the story of Sun Pu-erh and her husband, Ma Tan-yang, we see that their understanding of family life and responsibilities changes significantly as their spiritual training progresses. According to the account in *Seven Taoist Masters,* initially, Sun Pu-erh and her husband own a large estate and appear content with their lives except for the fact that they have no children. As they approach the age of forty, Ma Tan-yang bemoans the absence of children, worrying that there will be no one to care for them in their old age, to continue their business, and to carry on the family name. Sun Pu-erh replies by reminding Ma Tan-yang of the impermanence of material possessions and the senselessness of worrying about things that may happen to them in the future. She urges him to join her in seeking a spiritual teacher so that they may spend their remaining years walking the path of immortality (Wong 1990, 20–21).

Once they find their teacher, Sun is the first to dedicate herself fully to her training, to the extent that she eventually leaves her husband to meditate in solitude in the city of Loyang. After enduring hardships and performing good deeds for the community there, she ascends to heaven. When she has made this transformation, though, she returns to the earthly realm to see how her husband is progressing in his training. Her assistance and demonstrations of the proper path help Ma to recognize that the material comforts of his life in their elegant home have distracted him from his spiritual work. Eventually he, too, leaves home and cultivates himself to the point of becoming one with the Tao.

While this story, and the passages we have quoted above, might seem to reinforce 1970s feminist critiques of traditional family roles, their message is primarily to urge us to let go of attachments. It is worth noting that in the passage from *Understanding Reality,* as in the story of Sun pu-erh and Ma Tan-yang, family and wealth seem to be equated and to be part of a lesson on the impermanence of material possessions. Note, too, that Sun Pu-erh does not fully abandon her husband, but returns to help him, in the spirit of a fellow seeker of the Tao.

The important theme underlying the story of Sun Pu-erh and Ma Tan-yang is that the change in their view of family life involved a deeper change in their view toward material possessions. Part of Taoist training involves dissolving the ego and its attachments to all things, including our spouses and children as well as the images of self and the sense of self-worth that may depend on fulfilling socially prescribed roles. Rather than condemning family life or literally urging women (or men) to abandon it, then, the Taoist texts teach the importance of cultivating an attitude of nonattachment. Moreover, their change in lifestyle after they have embraced Taoist training did not make Sun Pu-erh and Ma Tan-yang irresponsible to other members of the family. They had no children and they made sure that the servants (who were considered as part of the family in traditional China) were taken care of when they were dismissed.

Like Sun Pu-erh and Ma Tan-yang, many who practice Taoism today do so outside a monastic setting. Even in the past, many who studied in the Taoist monasteries did so for relatively short periods before returning to their homes and families. And texts of the Taoist canon such as the *T'ai-shang kan-ying p'ien (Lao Tzu's Treatise on the Response of the Tao to Human Actions),* a widely read southern Sung dynasty text outlining basic ethical values, are often addressed to people living a conventional social and professional life.

This is the lay Taoist tradition of the Action and Karma School, which emerged during the eleventh century and reached a height of its development in the sixteenth century. This school does not have a temple or monastic tradition, and its approach to Taoist training is focused on doing charitable deeds in the community and teaching others to do likewise. Together with the "fire-dwelling Taoists" (Taoist priests who live in the cities, marry, and have children), these Taoists are called *kui-shih* (referring to Taoists who live in society), not *tao-shih* (Taoists who live apart from society), and they combine a social and professional life comfortably with Taoist training.

A second, related idea that emerges from these examples is the need for single-minded devotion to one's spiritual development. Training in the Taoist arts, particularly those in the tradition of Taoist internal alchemy (which involve literal transformation of body and mind through a variety of techniques), can be very rigorous. Such training demands a high level of commitment and focus in order to develop the inner strength and wisdom that are the sources of true compassion. In a treatise on spiritual alchemy for women, Cao Zhenjie, a married woman of the nineteenth century, puts it this way:

> In the science of essence and life, men and women are the same—there is no discrimination. In sum, what is important is perfect sincerity and profound singlemindedness. An ancient document says, "Only perfect sincerity in the world is capable of ruling." A classic says, "The perfection of singlemindedness is that whereby one may heed the order of life." (Cleary 1989, 94).

This is also the meaning of Chang Po-tuan's warning that "it all depends on oneself alone, apart from others." While a supportive community can be very valuable (as seen in the way all of Seven Taoist Masters help one another), each person ultimately travels the path of the return to the origin alone.

This sincere and focused dedication is, as Cao Zhenjie's statement suggests, required of both men and women. And herein lies equality in the Taoist sense of the word. The Tao itself is said to be formless, without identity. Lao-tzu states,

> As for the Way, the Way that can be spoken of is not the constant Way;
> As for names, the name that can be named is not the constant name.
> (ch. 1, Hendricks 1989, 53)

If it is formless, then there is no division into male and female as one merges with or participates in the source.

As many postmodern feminists have also pointed out, the notions of maleness and femaleness are concepts laden with a great deal of baggage, including attachments to specific masculine and feminine qualities and roles, and to the power (or lack of power) that is traditionally associated with these roles. In Taoism, women and men are trained with the same goals in mind. These goals do not include the acquisition of power or position. On the contrary, public recognition and authority are seen as illusions or as obstacles to spiritual development.

Many of the Taoist immortals and sages are said to have turned away from active careers and ambitions to rise in the social hierarchy, much as Sun Pu-erh left behind her position as lady of the Ma household. Lao-tzu, Chuang-tzu, Lieh-tzu, and Kuan Wen-shih, sages who had helped shape the early philosophical foundations of Taoism, all left the world of ambition, authority, and social recognition to cultivate the self.

Part of Taoist training, then, involves letting go of attachments even to the forms of masculinity and femininity as well as to notions of what a man or woman can or should do. For those who are willing to follow the training to its end, there is ultimately no difference between women and men. Along the path of Taoist training, however, male-female differences do play a part.

Difference and the Celebration of the Feminine

While some feminists have insisted on the fundamental equality of the sexes by rejecting oppressive models of femininity, other have directly challenged the cultural devaluation of the feminine in an effort to overturn it. This

challenge has taken many forms. The concept of *sisterhood,* for example, became a powerful slogan for the women's movement in the 1970s as women
found strength in coming together on the basis of their common experiences.
Similarly, the emergence of women's studies as an academic field focused on
women as a specific category of analysis, united by common experiences or
perhaps just by the fact of having for so long been excluded from dominant culture. Both of these outlooks were based on assumptions about *difference,* more
specifically the differences between the lives of women and men (Eisenstein
1980, xvii-xviii).

For many feminists, a central problem with the current cultural division
into masculine and feminine is that it is inherently hierarchical, with the masculine being given the position of power and privilege. As Hélène Cixous
puts it:

> Organisation by hierarchy makes all conceptual organisation subject to
> man. Male privilege, shown in the opposition between *activity* and
> *passivity,* which he uses to sustain himself. Traditionally, the question of
> sexual difference is treated by coupling it with the opposition: activity/
> passivity. (Cixous 1986, 102)

In addition to insisting that women (and qualities associated with the
feminine) were a legitimate focus of study, then, many sought to reverse this
hierarchy, asserting the value of women's differences from men and celebrating the strengths of such feminine qualities as nurturance, caring, and cooperation. Adrienne Rich, for example, took another look at motherhood, both as
socially regulated institution and as a potentially powerful and socially transforming experience. Her 1976 book, *Of Woman Born,* argued that a feminist
revolution might free up a passionate and nurturing maternal spirit that could
counter the destructive "warrior mentality" of patriarchal culture (Rich
1976, 282).

Carol Gilligan's comparative study of male and female moral development sought to contextualize and reassess women's moral choices. Gilligan
insisted that different patterns of socialization gave rise to very different
ethics on the part of women and men. Women's moral decisions tended to be
more relational, rooted in what she called an ethic of care, connection, and
interdependence. For Gilligan, understanding and respecting these differences would not only help reverse earlier assessments of women's moral
growth but also contribute to a fuller, more productive view of human life
(Gilligan 1982, 174).

The notion of difference is a complex and multilayered one that has given
rise to substantial debate. Challenges to arguments about women's differences
from men have come from several quarters, both within and outside feminist

circles. Many feminists have pointed to the dangers of praising qualities linked with female biological functions such as childbearing. Basing our arguments in such attributes, they argue, is tantamount to acknowledging that "biology is destiny." Such "essentialism" overlooks crucial feminist insights about the inherently *social* (not biological) basis of gender distinctions.

Others critique the potentially separatist celebration of sisterhood that may accompany an insistence on difference or point out the dangers of merely inverting an oppressive system. Julia Kristeva, for example, worries that the call for a female "countersociety" becomes "a kind of inverted sexism," simply marginalizing the forces that had previously forced women to the margins (Kristeva 1981, 453). From this standpoint, the insistence on difference tends to keep feminist thinking trapped within a polarity of masculine and feminine that, some argue, we might better seek to eliminate (Eisenstein 1980, xxiii; see also de Lauretis 1987, 2).

Building on the sense of discomfort with merely inverting the masculine-feminine hierarchy, other feminists have expanded the notion of difference to acknowledge racist or elitist aspects of the feminist movement, which the early emphasis on women's solidarity tended to overlook. From this perspective, recognizing difference can lead toward even more far-reaching social change. Rather than focusing on "sexual difference" (or differences between women and men), however, it is important to look at *"the differences among women.* For there are, after all, different histories of women. There are women who masquerade and women who wear the veil; women invisible to men, in their society, but also women who are invisible to other women, in our society" (de Lauretis 1987, 136). Factors such as class, race, language, and social position also interact within each individual, creating "differences *within* women" (de Lauretis 1987, 139). Acknowledging and understanding these differences can destabilize the hierarchies and fixed categories on which many oppressive social structures and power relations are based.

Taoism and Difference

What, then, is Taoism's relationship to feminist debates about difference? Some writers have pointed out that the image of the feminine is strong in Taoist symbolism. Building on the work of Ellen Chen, Barbara Reed has argued that the Tao itself can be seen in essentially feminine terms, as a limitless potentiality symbolized by the mother's womb. The great void, in which everything has its origin and to which all seeks to return, should not therefore be seen as negation or the end of existence. Rather, it is an unchanging, creative emptiness out of which all that is in existence emerges (Reed 1987, 162–164).

This imagery of the Tao as mother and as creative potential is present in the *Tao-te ching:*

> The Way gave birth to the One;
> The One gave birth to the Two;
> The Two gave birth to the Three;
> And the three gave birth to the ten thousand things.
> (ch. 42, Hendricks 1989, 11)

> The world had a beginning,
> Which can be considered the mother of the world.
> Having attained the mother, in order to understand her
> children,
> If you return and hold on to the mother, till the end of your
> life you'll suffer no harm.
> (ch. 52, Hendricks 1989, 21)

Throughout the history of Taoism, however, the Tao has been described in many images. Water, gold, emptiness, all come to mind. The Tao has also been described as the way of heaven, as in these lines from the *Tao-te ching*, "No need to peer through your windows to know the Way of Heaven" (ch. 47, Hendricks 1989, 16); "The Way of Heaven is not to fight yet to be good at winning" (ch. 73, Hendricks 1989, 44). All of these images are attempts to characterize the qualities of the Tao, but as Lao-tzu himself aptly says, "the Way [or the Tao] that can be spoken of is not the constant Way;/ As for names, the name that can be named is not the constant name" (ch. 1, Hendricks 1989, 53). This suggests that the images of mother, heaven, water, gold, nothingness, all describe some aspects of the Tao, but not its totality. Further, to understand the round, soft, yielding, drifting, or life-giving qualities of the Tao as wholly feminine is to place limits on that which is in fact limitless.

To say that the Tao is "feminine" in nature is also to overlook the balance of *yin* and *yang* in the Tao, an idea central to the Taoist view of both the universe and the human body. Even in the *Tao-te ching*, the earliest known Taoist classic, the balance of *yin* and *yang* and the complementarity of opposites are shown to be central to Taoist philosophy. Rather than favoring either a feminine or masculine image of the Tao, the classics of Taoism—from the *Chuang-tzu*, the *Lieh-tzu*, the *Huai-nan tzu*, through the internal alchemical texts of the *Triplex Unity (Tsan tung-chi)* and the *Dragon-tiger Classic (Lung-fu ching)*, the political idealism of the *Classic of Great Peace (T'ai-ping ching)*, the talismans and liturgies of the Ling-pao scriptures, the mysticism of the Sh'ang-ch'ing texts, and the theories of cultivating mind and body in the Complete Reality (Chen-chuan) and Earlier Heaven (Hsien-t'ien) sects of Taoism—all emphasize this balance of opposites.

In Taoism, then, the image of the feminine is not independent of its opposite. Both are needed to understand the totality of the Tao. One particular statement from the *Tao-te ching* is of particular interest: "In opening and closing the gates of Heaven—can you play the part of the female?" (ch. 10, Hendricks 1989, 62). Here, "playing the part of the female" is needed to complete heaven. This is echoed in chapter 28 of the *Tao-te ching,* which begins, "When you know the male yet hold on to the female" (Hendricks 1989). These statements suggest that to attain the Tao, and enlightenment, male and female are needed to "complete" each other. Neither male nor female is favored. In recognizing the balance of male and female, Taoism values qualities that have traditionally been seen as both masculine and feminine. One can respect a value while recognizing the need for balance and diversity. This is the foundation of the respect for the feminine that is present in Taoism.

Given this underlying respect for the feminine, there is no taboo against the usage of images and symbols associated with the female in the discussion of the most advanced concepts of Taoist theory and practice. For example, in Taoist internal alchemy, pregnancy plays a central role. The seed of the refined spirit is often described as the "immortal fetus," or as a "spiritual embryo." It is formed as the culmination of a long process of gathering, purifying, circulating, and storing internal energy in the body. It is the essence of health and longevity. The Taoist adept carries and nourishes this spiritual child (also referred to as the immortal or golden pill) until it is finally born as the spirit god (*yüan-shen*).

As in many alchemical texts, Chang Po-tuan describes the formation and nurturing of the immortal fetus as a perfectly natural process, saying "fruit grows on the branches, ripe at the end of the season; how can the child in the belly be any different?" (Chang 1987, 36). Like some modern feminists, then, this language of Taoist internal alchemy gives value to nurturing and maternity. But it uses these qualities to describe a high level of spiritual development for both women and men.

Other aspects of Taoist internal alchemical training differ for men and women, however, reflecting the emphasis of this training on the physical body as the basis for spiritual work. On a practical level, Taoist masters and sages took both physiological and cultural differences between women and men into account as they developed their training techniques. The alchemical texts for the training of women outline different training techniques for women at different periods of life and development. From prepuberty, through puberty, the middle years, and old age, different methods can be employed to enhance the cultivation of body and mind. Moreover, these texts show us that while the training of women differs from that of men in the early and middle levels, once the foundations are built, methods for attaining the highest stage of alchemical transmutation, merging with the Tao and breaking the barrier between the self and the universe, become similar for women and men. A closer look at the stages of internal alchemical development should clarify the points at which this type of Taoist training may diverge and converge for women and men.

The Stages of Alchemical Development

Building the prefoundations—working with virtue and ethics. Cultivating virtue and leading an ethical life are the initial foundations of much Taoist training. When asked about how to enter the Tao, immortal Lü Tung-pin replied, "Do good deeds. Be compassionate to all things. Without knowing it, you will have entered the Tao" (Wong 1994). It is also said that without virtue, the technical methods of alchemical transformation will not take the practitioner to the highest levels of development in the return to the Tao (see Ko-hung in the *Pao-p'u Tzu*). Virtue and ethics are grounded in our actions in the everyday world. Because of inherent disposition and social upbringing, women and men may find certain virtues natural and easy to develop and others difficult to cultivate.

In the *Tai-shang kan-ying p'ien,* a Taoist book of ethics, the cultivated male exhibits respect for women and has high regard for the lives of sentient beings. In the story "Offence against a Deity," a young student is punished for making sexual overtures before a statue of the goddess of the water realm. The lord Wen-ch'ang, patron of the arts and literature, tells the youth that "any student who is guilty of being disrespectful to women will be excluded from the list of honor" (Wong 1994).

In traditional China, respect was fundamental to every woman's behavior, but this virtue was less developed in men, who valued honor over respect. During the times in which the stories of the *Tai-shang kan-ying p'ien* were written (between the twelfth and sixteenth centuries), Chinese politics and society were dominated by a patriarchal form of Confucianism. While Confucianism taught that men needed to exhibit honorable behavior in the presence of women, men saw themselves as protectors rather than equals of women. In Taoist teachings, however, respect requires that both parties regard each other as equals. The relationship of Ma Tan-yang and Sun Pu-erh of *Seven Taoist Masters* was truly one of respect for they related to each other as equals. Therefore, if men were to cultivate the underdeveloped parts of themselves, the virtue of respect needed to be developed.

In the story "Charity Rewarded," the cultivated man has a high regard for life. The governor in the story valued the lives of female infants and prevented their destruction by building public nurseries to take care of the female children who might otherwise have been killed by their parents. Again, during a time when female children were seen as liabilities more than assets to the family, Taoist ethics valued the lives of all human beings, female and male.

While some may see these stories as examples of how Taoism favors women, we think that, consistent with the philosophical approach of Taoism to personal development and with the social and historical conditions of China, these stories are better understood as teaching the basic virtues of respect and giving value to life. Men needed to cultivate these virtues not because women occupied a favored position in Taoism but because Taoism believes in the equality of all things. All sentient beings come from the Tao and there is no difference in the value of one life over another.

Building the lower foundations—working on the muscular-skeletal system. As noted in the *Queen Mother of the West's Ten Precepts on the True Path of Women's Practice (Hsi Wang Mu nü-hsiu cheng-t'u shih tse),* "The fruits of the good person alone do not qualify one for immortality" (Wile 1992, 200). Taoist internal alchemy begins with building the "external foundation," the transformation of the muscular-skeletal system. This involves strengthening the bones, making the tendons, muscles, and ligaments elastic, and developing mobility in the spinal column. This is collectively known as the *wai-chuang,* or external strengthening (see Shao t'ien-shi's *Tao-hai yüan-wei*).

With respect to external tempering, our Taoist master told us that we needed to work especially hard on strengthening the legs. We were told that in the alchemical work on the muscular-skeletal system, a woman's weakness lay in the bones and her strength lay in the mobility of the spine and the flexibility of the tendons. For men, the reverse was the case. Therefore, in the early part of our training, both of us were told to strengthen the bones in the legs and the pelvis. These instructions are consonant with a treatise on the training of women. The *Answers to Questions Concerning the Attainment of Enlightenment (Hsiu-chen p'ien-nan)* states:

> Women are yin in nature. The movement of their energy (*ch'i*) can easily be controlled. However, the "red channel" is the most harmful to cultivating the Tao. Therefore, the most important thing for women is the use of strength. Once the red channel is disconnected, the energy will flow smoothly. (our translation, 148)

The "red channel" is the passage of the woman's monthly menses. Cutting the red channel (sometimes referred to as "slaying the dragon"), is an internal transformation involving changes in the functioning of the hormonal system and the pituitary gland. But the cultivation of strength in women forms the prerequisite to the work on the transformation of the internal organs and the hormonal system. If the external structure (the muscular-skeletal system) is not strong enough, premature internal transformations may damage the body.

Traditional Taoist training for women and men took into account different patterns of socialization as well as physiological differences. *Insights on Reflections on the Mind (Kuan-hsin chai-ch'i)* says, "Just as there are yin and yang, shade and light, there are differences between men and women. In accordance with the nature of things, the work of internal alchemy for men and women is established" (our translation, 65).

Concerning this difference of internal alchemy, the *Answers to Questions* says:

> Men are yang in nature. Their energy is difficult to control. For example, if it takes men three years to control the flow the energy, the woman will accomplish it in one. If a woman with outstanding abilities receives instruction from a highly skilled teacher, and practices the cultivation of the Great Yin, within three to five years, she can attain the Tao; and with less effort than men. (our translation, 148)

This suggests that for women, the initial part of the training is difficult, but once obstacles are overcome, the subsequent stages are easy; for men, the contrary is true. The text continues:

> But women with outstanding qualities are difficult to find. The difficulty is that women need to be especially strong, motivated, and disciplined, one hundred times over that of men. Then, they will be able to accomplish the task. If women are only equal to men in strength and endurance, then they will not be able to attain anything. (our translation, 148)

Written in the nineteenth century, these comments reflect the predominant climate of a patriarchal China in their assumptions about the lack of discipline and endurance in women. However, the passage also has advice for the modern woman who aspires to Taoist training.

Social stigma is still strong against the woman who wishes to pursue Taoist internal alchemy seriously. For example, it is common for men to attend martial arts classes in the evenings or meditation retreats on weekends, but it is still less common for women to leave their spouse at home to do the same things. In order for women to receive Taoist training, which demands both time and effort, an understanding and respect must be reached between husband and wife, like that of Ma Tan-yang and Sun Pu-erh in *Seven Taoist Masters*. Moreover, the woman needs to free herself from the roles imposed on her by others and by herself. In this sense, a woman today often does need more strength and endurance than a man in pursuing Taoist training. Women may have more social obstacles to clear before they can begin any kind of serious training.

Building the higher foundations—working with the internal organs and hormonal system. According to the Taoist understanding of the body, the circuitry or energy pathways within the body are not the same for men and women. Many of the Taoist classics thus describe the techniques for purifying, circulating, and storing internal energy in different terms for women and men.

In Taoism, the internal energy itself is divided into three components, called the generative (*ching*), vital (*ch'i*), and spirit (*shen*) energies. Each is important for health and is a basic building block for physical and spiritual transformation. *Ching* is associated with that part of the energy that is responsible for procreation. *Ch'i* is related to life or breath. And *shen* is related to our consciousness. Each of these energies is further subdivided into a gross (or unpurified) and a pure form. The pure form is that with which we were originally endowed, while the gross form reflects the decay that sets in as we age and become socialized. A goal of Taoist practice, then, is to refine these energies, returning them to the pure forms that enhance health and vitality.

The unpurified form of *ching* is seen in women's menstrual blood and men's semen. When a girl reaches puberty, the earlier heaven or pure *ching* is transformed into later heaven or unpurified *ching:*

> At the age of thirteen, fourteen, or fifteen, her "original ch'i" is complete and her "true blood" full. . . . At the moment the menses descends, her "original ch'i" is broken and her "true blood" leaks. Following marriage and the birth of children, the "original ch'i" gradually is weakened and the "true blood" progressively destroyed. Although every month the menstrual flow regenerates, in reality, it every month is reinjured. (Wile 1992, 193; *Queen Mother of the West's Ten Precepts on the True Path of Women's Practice*)

The transformation of earlier heaven *ching* to later heaven *ching* marks the beginning of aging, decay, and death, since the loss of *ching* is the loss of life.

One key to women's cultivation therefore lies in the transformation of the later heaven *ching,* the blood. The *Queen Mother of the West's Ten Precepts* says that "a woman's life is bound up with her menses. If the menses is not transformed, how can her life be preserved?" (Wile 1992, 194). The works of women's internal alchemy (the *Queen Mother of the West's Ten Precepts, Answers to Questions Concerning Cultivating the Real, Methods of the Golden Elixir for Women, Correct Methods for Women's Practice, Master Li N-wan's Precious Raft of Women's Dual Practice, Cultivating Stillness for Women, The Lord of Purity's Classic for Women:* also see Cleary's translations in *Immortal Sisters*) all speak of "slaying the dragon" and "cutting the red channel." This refers to stopping the flow of menstrual blood. These texts discuss various techniques for accomplishing this. They can be divided into methods of cultivating mind and methods of cultivating body.

Methods of cultivating the mind include the taming of emotions and the dissolving of sexual desire. Women's training begins with stillness. "Ni-wan said, 'Women's practice begins with first stilling the thoughts and harmonizing the mind'" (Wile 1992, 204; *Master Li Ni-wan's Precious Raft*). Stillness is cultivated through techniques such as meditation, seeking to harmonize the mind and let it be at rest. According to *Cultivating Stillness for Women (K'un-ling miao-ching)*, women naturally tend toward inner peacefulness. This is her strength and she should use it build her foundations for further training. Her weakness, however, lies in the fluctuation of moods and being easily drawn into sexual desire, both conditions that drain generative energy (*ching*):

> If women realize the value of their health and life and do not succumb to the wishes of the opposite sex, then it will be easy for them to attain health and longevity. . . . Actually, it is really easy for women to attain the Golden Pill. They first need to sever their attachment to desire before sitting down to meditate. (our translation, 41)

The *Correct Methods for Women's Practice (Nü-kung cheng-fa)* says, "When the heart is empty and the desires purified, there naturally is a sense of peace and tranquility. With the clarity of a mirror or the transparency of water, the heart is now pure. We may now speak of understanding the foundation" (Wile 1992, 213).

When the mind is still, the effects of cultivating the body can take hold. Some of these techniques revolve around the "slaying of the dragon"—that is, the stopping of the menstrual flow. The alchemical texts are careful to clarify that stopping the flow does not mean menopause. Stopping the flow means recovering the state of adolescence while menopause is yet another sign of aging. Therefore, "those who have already experienced menses must first slay the 'red dragon' [stop the flow]; those whose menses have ceased must first cause it to resume and then 'slay' it" *(Wile 1992, 195; Queen Mother of the West's Ten Precepts)*.

The first step toward "slaying the red dragon" is the opening of the microcosmic orbit, the channel of energy that runs like a circuit from the base of the spine to the head, down through the palate, along the center of the front of the body down to the perineum and back to the base of the spine. This practice involves opening the three gates along the spine and tempering the internal energies in the three *tan-t'iens* (internal fields of energy). Various methods, including massage, exercises, and yogic body postures, are outlined in the texts. However, all emphasize that in practicing techniques that lead to the "slaying of the red dragon," it is very important for the mind to be in a state of calmness. Once the energy can flow through the microcosmic orbit without hindrance, the flow of menstrual blood will stop. In its place will be a white fluid that will first flow outward from the uterus and then be reabsorbed back into the body:

The menses turns yellow, the yellow turns to white, and the white is transformed and becomes nothing. . . . The "red channel" is a transformation of the body's postnatal [later heaven] *yin* energy. When the *yin ch'i* is excited, the impure blood flows. If one wishes to transform the blood, first train [transform] the *ch'i.* When the *ch'i* is transformed, the blood returns upward and enters the breasts where the red changes to white and circulates through the entire body. (Wile 1992, 204; *Essentials of the Golden Elixir Method for Women [Nü chin-tan fa-yao])*

With time, the circulation of internal energy becomes effortless, and the body of the woman will resemble that of a virgin before puberty. "When, through training, the breasts become like those of a virgin or a child, then a woman's body is transformed into [becomes like] a man's" (Wile 1992, 197; *Queen Mother of the West's Ten Precepts*). The later heaven *ch'ing* has now been purified and transformed into earlier heaven *ch'ing.*

Merging with the tao—dissolving the barrier between the inner and outer. Once the external and internal foundations are established, the training of women and men becomes quite similar. Now that the structural differences have been dissolved and both have strengthened their respective weaknesses, they are ready to work on development that transcends female and male qualities. *Master Li Ni-wan's Precious Raft of Women's Dual Practice* states, "Someone once asked Yüan-chün about perfect purity, and Yüan-chün answered . . . 'Is not men's practice just the same?'" (Wile 1992; 211).

When the conditions for the higher level of alchemical work are met, the methods of training for men and women are the same. Differences exist in the earlier parts of training because women and men need to use different techniques to reach these same conditions. Thus, purified *ch'ing* (manifested in a sweet saliva called "nectar") goes beyond the male or female identification of that energy. It is like the saliva of a baby, in whom the hormones work toward growth but have not yet produced the sexual differentiations that set in at puberty.

At this stage of training, the bodies of both women and men have been transformed both externally and internally to accommodate the emergence of the "immortal fetus" (*yüan-shen*). Fetal breathing, or breathing like an infant, now occurs naturally. The fetal breath is the primordial breath, or original *ch'i,* and it is connected with the Tao, which is the source of all life. To recover the original *ch'i* is to recover life. *Master Li Ni-wan's Precious Raft* describes this state: "when one's practice reaches the level that there is no going and no coming, no entering and no emerging, then far and near, inner and outer are eliminated" (Wile 1992, 208). This refers to the dissolution of the barrier between the microcosmos of the body and the macrocosmos of the universe, when the energy inside the body is the same as the energy in the universe, and both partake of the primordial vapor of the Tao. This is the state of the highest level of Taoist training, the return to the Tao, when the practitioner can "age with heaven and earth, and cultivate with the sun and moon" (Chang Po-tuan, cited in Shao T'ien-shih's *Tao-chia yang-sheng hseüh kai-yao [Essentials of the Taoist Techniques of Cultivating Health]*, our translation, 12).

It is said that the way of K'un (earth) guides a woman's training. The intrinsic nature of the woman is tranquil and still. Therefore, she should cultivate these qualities, preferably while she is an adolescent. The *Queen Mother of the West's Ten Precepts on the True Path of Women's Practice* says:

> Women's nature is like water and her substance is like flowers. In her youth she should be quiet and not wild. . . . If she is peaceful and tranquil in her life, if she can follow the rules of womanly behavior and be natural in her stillness, then this substance (generative energy) will remain close to its Earlier Heaven nature and return to its primal unity. It will not be converted into 'red pearls' and become menstruation. But unfortunately, the common girl is ignorant, childish, and attracted to action. She engages in games and wild careening. Her emotions (*ch'i*) fluctuate and her mind is unsteady. Her spirit becomes confused and her true *ch'i* (vapor) becomes unstable. Thus, this heavenly treasure is stirred up and dissipates. (our translation; see also Wile 1992, 194)

For the woman, aging and decay start at this point. The *Correct Methods for Women's Practice* also says, "Common women in the world are too deeply stained by custom . . . and are easily prey to lustful thoughts. . . . In the spring they are moved to love, but in the autumn they are wounded" (Wile 1992, 213). These two passages suggest that women build the prefoundation by cultivating their strengths (what traditional Chinese culture has seen as their intrinsic disposition toward stillness and tranquility) and working to dissolve indulgence in emotions. These texts also give advice: "Break down the barrier of the emotions and leap out of the sea of desires" (*Correct Methods for Women's Practice*"; Wile 1992, 213).

From the above discussion of women's internal alchemy, we can see that Taoism has traditionally respected and worked with difference, and that the training is oriented toward developing balance and harmony of the feminine and masculine aspects of each individual. Though some traditionally feminine qualities are valued, and, indeed, to be cultivated, they are seen as fully equal—not superior—to their masculine counterparts. Just as the refined internal energy is identified as neither male nor female, so the refined individual works to develop a rounded disposition, where neither strength nor softness dominates.

This idea of balance is also rooted in the Taoist understanding of *yin* and *yang,* the complementary forces often associated with such pairs as light and dark, strength and softness, heaven and earth, movement and stillness, and male and female. In Taoist cosmology, the initial wholeness that is the Tao (later also termed *wu-chi*) undergoes an ongoing process of differentiation as the world comes into being. Chou Tun-I, a Taoist from the Sung dynasty, describes this process in the following terms:

> From wu-chi comes t'ai-chi. When t'ai-chi moves, it creates yang. When movement reaches its extreme, stillness emerges. In stillness yin is born. Thus, movement and stillness follow each other. Yin and yang, stillness and movement form the force of creation. (*T'ai-chi t'ao-shuo* by Chou Tun-I, our translation, 210)

From this we can see how *yin* and *yang* (sometimes understood in terms of the feminine and the masculine) are both interrelated and integral to creation. These notions have countless applications in the Taoist understanding of the cosmos and of the human body, Within the body, energy pathways, organs, and even aspects of the personality are seen as either *yin* or *yang* in nature. (See the *Yellow Emperor's Book of Internal Medicine* for a discussion of the *yin* and *yang* nature of the internal organs and energy pathways of the human body.) Perfect health involves establishing a relationship of mutual support and balance between the *yin* and *yang* components. The energy pathways (the meridians and vessels) need to be open and interconnected. The organs should not be competing with each other for nutrients. And the personality should not be dominated by one or the other disposition.

"In yang there is yin and in yin there is yang." The Taoist view of *yin* and *yang* incorporates a further insight into the question of difference. In insisting on the cyclical interplay of these complementary forces, Taoism recognizes that things of this world are not wholly of one nature. If they were, there would be no flexibility; we would be caught in the rigidity that Lao-tzu condemns as inferior (chapter 76). As suggested by dots of the opposite color within the swirls of the familiar "t'ai-chi symbol," all that is *yin* already has an aspect of *yang* in it and vice versa. In terms of attitude, for example, the Taoist cultivates softness (a *yin* quality) within strength (a *yang* quality) and displays strength even while yielding. With this it is possible to respond appropriately to all circumstances, knowing when to yield and when to move forward, to act appropriately in response to circumstances and yet not be controlled by the them:

> Therefore, there is no way to get intimate with him,
> But there is also no way to shun him.

There is no way to benefit him,
But there is also no way to harm him.
There is no way to ennoble him,
But there is also no way to debase him.
For this very reason he is the noblest thing in the world.
(ch. 56, Hendricks 1989, 25)

Developing balance and harmony of *yin* and *yang* qualities or characteristics, then, is not the same as mixing the two together. The distinctions are preserved but, rather than responding according to fixed expectations (or
identities), we can respond according to conditions.

The above description of creation also illustrates the importance of this
distinction in terms of the natural cycle of growth and decline. Because each
incorporates the seed of the other, *yin* and *yang* participate in a cycle: as one
reaches its extreme, the other emerges out of it. While the two aspects are distinct, then, they exist not in tension but in a productive relation to each other,
forming "the force of creation."

This creative cycle in turn relates to the Taoist concept of return to the
origin, which, as we have seen, is also conceived as a void or emptiness full of
the potential to create. Returning to the Tao in a sense involves retracing the
steps of creation. In terms of Chou Tun-I's description, this would mean harmonizing the five elements as well as *yin* and *yang,* gradually reversing the
process of differentiation from which all creation springs. Before it is possible
to merge with the source (or to return to the Tao), the *yin* and *yang* aspects—
seen as parts of the self as well as of the universe—need once again to be in
harmony with one another. Difference, then, does have a place within Taoism.
But it is tempered by a strong sense of balance and harmony both within the individual and in society.

The Construction and Deconstruction of Gender

A key insight of feminism has been the recognition of gender as a social
construct. As we have already seen, the 1970s examinations of sexual politics
pointed to the limitations of women's traditional roles, seeking to give women
access to a full range of social positions.

But more recently, the ongoing critiques of gender have taken the argument further, suggesting that all forms of sexual identity are not biological facts
but cultural ideas. This reassessment of gender is part of a larger project of rethinking "all of the categories of human character," in order to recognize them
as social and linguistic constructions (Jehlen 264). According to this argument,
any identity can be seen as merely a role. It is a way of giving meaning to an

otherwise unstable self and actions (see Butler 145). What we have been accustomed to think of as character traits, or as given, enduring, or autonomous aspects of "human nature," should instead be seen as functions or ways of relating (Jehlen 265; Butler 16).

This argument again raises the question of difference, suggesting the need to rethink categories such as "woman" and even feminism itself insofar as they rely on a sense of stable identity. Trinh T. Minh-ha, for example, takes feminists like Judith Kegan Gardiner to task for defining female identity in terms of how it differs from a male mode (Trinh 96). Such arguments, Trinh observes, keep us trapped within the "master's logic." Women are simply being granted a bit of space in a still male dominated territory. A better strategy would be to dismantle the very idea of core identity, be it female *or* male.

This recognition in turn raises the question of how—or whether it is even possible—to step outside the rules governing gender (or sexual) identities. Can we challenge or reconceive identity, and especially gender identity in useful ways? Trinh attempts to do so by insisting on the distinction between identity and difference. The notion of difference, for her, "undermines the very idea of identity," since it suggests that even within the individual there can be multiple selves or layers. In addition, the dividing line between I and not-I, us and them, him and her is not always clear. No matter how hard we try to maintain them as distinct, "categories always leak" (94). Instead of a genuine layer of self, we are confronted with a "limitless practice of interactions and changes" (94).

In a similar vein, Judith Butler and others propose a perpetual displacement of gender patterns. Insisting that there is no fixed self in which gender is rooted, she suggests that those who wish to dismantle norms of gendered behavior act in ways that parody and play on those norms. This will help reveal gender *as* a performance and will allow individuals to take on multiple gender roles, rather than being trapped and defined in a single identity as "man" or "woman."

But Butler and others warn against assuming the position of a "transcendent subject," one who can somehow step outside culture or constructed identities. The only effective position, then, seems to be one of continual subversion of existing rules. And yet, this emphasis on multiple, constantly shifting identities or roles threatens to leave us trapped within an oppressive culture that we can challenge but cannot fundamentally transform.

Taoism shares in this challenge to rigid categories and fixed notions of identity. But rather than proposing, as Butler does, constant *action,* through a shifting parody of otherwise restrictive roles, Taoism generally upholds a principle of *nonaction (wu-wei)*. This pragmatic approach to action does not mean passivity or complete nonengagement with the affairs of the world. Rather, it means a calm, centered state of mind from which one responds appropriately to conditions as they arise. A passage from Chuang-tzu quoted earlier illustrates this. In the story, his students question Chuang-tzu about what is of value and why some things that are apparently worthless survive while others are destroyed. When asked what position to take Chuang-tzu replies:

> Halfway between worth and worthlessness, though it might seem to be a good place, really isn't—you'll never get away from trouble there. It would be very different, though, if you were to climb up on the Way and its Virtue and go drifting and wandering, neither praised nor damned, now a dragon, now a snake, shifting with the times, never willing to hold to one course only. Now up, now down, taking harmony for your measure, drifting and wandering with the ancestor of the ten thousand things, treating things as things but not letting them treat you as a thing—then how could you get into any trouble? (ch. 20, Watson 1968, 209–10)

For Chuang-tzu, distinctions exist and are sometimes of value. (We do not want to be "halfway between worth and worthlessness.") But it is best to respond to situations without fixed expectations or roles. (We are "now a dragon, now a snake.") Instead, we act according to the situation. In doing this, we are not ourselves pinned down by fixed identities or ideas of uniformly correct behavior. Instead, we see things for what they are.

According to the Taoist view of the universe, the Tao is the underlying reality of all things. This is a state of nondifferentiation and noncategorization. As the opening lines of the *Tao-te Ching* remind us, names, concepts, and constructs are impermanent phenomena that should not be confused with the unchanging essence of the Tao:

> As for the Way, the Way that can be spoken of is not the
>   constant Way;
> As for names, the name that can be named is not the
>   constant name.
> (ch. 1, Hendricks 1989, 53)

The development of constructs such as masculine and feminine or male and female, and of a gender identity rooted in these constructs, reflects a movement away from the original nondifferentiated state of existence. The Taoist path of return to the origin involves overcoming this differentiation and categorization of things. This is accomplished through the development of the intuitive, prereflective consciousness and the shrinking of the conceptualizing and analyzing mind.

Taoist theories of the mind therefore assert that the typical everyday mode of thinking involves the construction of realities. However, when the reflective or analytic part of the mind is silent, the aspect of the mind capable of intuiting the underlying reality of the Tao can emerge. These two aspects of the mind are respectively called the knowledge-god (*shih-shen*) and spirit-god (*yüan-shen*).

In most of us, it is the knowledge-god that dominates. Its activities include conceptualizing, categorizing, and naming—dividing up our experience into units it finds intelligible. Our self or ego is a product of the knowledge-god's chatter. And this chatter drains our energy as we divide things into compartments, make plans to deal with them, and worry about what might or might not happen. Most importantly, though, the knowledge-god's unfocused activity keeps us from recognizing that the underlying essence of things is the Tao, that undifferentiated energy that underlies and unites all things.

In the words of Lao-tzu:

> As soon as we start to establish a system, we have names.
> As soon as there are set names,
> Then you must *also* know that it's time to stop.
> By knowing to stop—in this way you'll come to no harm.
> The Way's presence in the world
> Is like the relationship of small valley streams to rivers and
> seas.
> (ch. 32, Hendricks 1989, 62)

From the standpoint of Taoism, this passage describes not only the problems in naming but also the way this problem can be resolved as the spirit-god begins to work through the human mind. Just as valley streams flow into rivers and seas, the Taoist adept loses her identity in the Tao, as self and Tao naturally flow together. No longer an individual with a set personality, she develops a new and wider identity as part of the universe at large (Kohn 142).

This new identity stands outside the dualities of female and male, feminine and masculine, and even self and other. The return to the origin (or the Tao) requires breaking down the barriers between self and other, subject and object. This process begins with dissolving attachments to social roles, including gender roles and identities. It continues with letting go of emotional attachments and of attachments to our ideas of reality. When it is completed, the mind is emptied of desire, thoughts, and attachments, and the body is filled with *ch'i* or the primordial vapor of the life source. Now there is no duality of self and other or of subject and object.

Even while living in the world, the Taoist sage is not trapped within the world's social or intellectual constructs. And, free of the limitations these constructs impose, the sage is able to help others overcome these limitations as well. From the Taoist standpoint, this enlightened being is rooted in society; it is said that "the great hermit is concealed in the city; what is the necessity to keeping tranquil solitude deep in the mountain?" (Chang 1987, 36). The role of the sage is not to escape society but to help other people. The sage works to relieve suffering of all kinds including that caused by oppressive social or mental constructs. This interest in transformation provides a final, significant meeting point of Taoism and feminism understood as a social movement. But the emphasis within Taoism is on changing individuals rather than social institutions. This change is brought about through a long process of individual transformation that includes letting go of selfish interests and fixed notions of identity. Enlightenment is attained through both physical changes and the development of wisdom and compassion, qualities that emerge when the barrier between self and other is broken and the ego is dissolved. The return to the origin, then, is not a form of transcendence. It is rather a way of nonaction and a mode of being, in the world. Rooted in compassion, the path or way of the Tao leads to the transformation of self and others and, therefore, of society itself.

Works Cited

General References

Belsey, Catherine and Jane Moore eds. 1989. *The Feminist Reader: Essays in Gender and the Politics of Literary Criticism.* New York: Basil Blackwell.

Butler, Judith. 1990. *Gender Trouble: Feminism and the Subversion of Identity.* New York: Routledge.

Chang, Po-tuan. 1987. *Understanding Reality: A Taoist Alchemical Classic.* Translated by Thomas Cleary. Honolulu: University of Hawaii Press.

Chen, Ellen M. 1974. "Tao as the Great Mother and the Influence of Motherly Love in the Shaping of Chinese Philosophy." *History of Religions* 14, no. 1: 51–64.

———. 1989. *The Tao Te Ching: A New Translation with Commentary.* New York: Paragon House.

Cixous, Hélène. 1986. "Sorties: Out and Out: Attacks/Ways Out/Forays," trans. Betsy Wing. In *The Newly Born Woman.* Minneapolis: University of Minnesota Press. Rpt. in *The Feminist Reader: Essays in Gender and the Politics of Literary Criticism,* ed. Catherine Belsey and Jane Moore.

Cleary, Thomas, trans. and ed. 1989. *Immortal Sisters: Secrets of Taoist Women.* Boston: Shambhala.

de Lauretis, Teresa. 1987. *Technologies of Gender.* Bloomington: Indiana University Press.

Eisenstein, Hester. 1980. "Introduction." In *The Future of Difference,* ed. Hester Eisenstein and Alice Jardine. New Brunswick, NJ: Rutgers University Press, xv-xxvii.

Firestone, Shulamith. 1970. *The Dialectic of Sex: The Case for Feminist Revolution.* New York: William Morrow.

Gilligan, Carol. 1982. *In a Different Voice: Psychological Theory and Women's Development.* Cambridge, MA: Harvard University Press.

Gordon, Linda. 1986. "What's New in Women's History?" In *Feminist Studies/Critical Studies,* ed. Teresa de Lauretis, 20–30. Bloomington: Indiana University Press.

Hendricks, Robert G., trans. 1989. *Lao-Tzu Te-Tao Ching.* New York: Ballantine.

Hewlett, Sylvia Ann. 1987. *A Lesser Life: The Myth of Women's Liberation in America.* New York: Warner Books.

Janeway, Elizabeth. 1971. *Man's World, Woman's Place: A Study in Social Mythology.* New York: Dell.

Jehlen, Myra. 1990. "Gender." In *Critical Terms for Literary Study,* ed. Frank Lentricchia and Thomas McLaughlin, 263–73. Chicago: University of Chicago Press.

Kohn, Livia. 1991. *Taoist Mystical Philosophy: The Scripture of Western Ascension.* Albany: State University of New York Press.

Kristeva, Julia. 1981. "Women's Time," trans. Alice Jardine and Harry Blake. *Signs,* 7: 13–35. Rpt. in *Feminisms: An Anthology of Literary Theory and Criticism,* ed. Robyn R. Warhol and Diane Price Herndl. New Brunswick, NJ: Rutgers University Press, 1991: 443–62.

Palmer, Martin. 1991. "Introduction." *The Eight Immortals of Taoism: Legends and Fables of Popular Taoism.* Translated and edited by Kwok Man Ho and Joanne O'Brien. New York: Meridian.

Paper, Jordan. 1990. "The Persistence of Female Deities in Patriarchal China." *Journal of Feminist Studies in Religion* 6, no. 1: 25–40.

Reed, Barbara E. 1987. "Taoism." In *Women in World Religions,* ed. Arvind Sharma, 161–81. Albany: State University of New York Press.

Rich, Adrienne. 1976. *Of Woman Born: Motherhood as Experience and Institution.* New York: Norton.

Trinh, T. Minh-ha. 1989. *Woman, Native, Other.* Bloomington: Indiana University Press.

Veith, Ilza, trans. and ed. 1966. *The Yellow Emperor's Book of Internal Medicine.* Berkeley: University of California Press.

Watson, Burton, ed. and trans. 1968. *The Complete Works of Chuang Tzu.* New York: Columbia University Press.

Wile, Douglas, ed. and trans. 1992. *Art of the Bedchanber: The Chinese Sexual Yoga Classics Including Women's Solo Meditation Texts.* Albany: State University of New York Press.

Wong, Eva, trans. 1990. *Seven Taoist Masters: A Folk Novel of China.* Boston: Shambhala.

———. trans. 1992. *Cultivating Stillness: A Taoist Manual for Transforming Body and Mind.* Boston: Shambhala.

———. trans. 1994. *Lao-tzu's Treatise on the Response of the Tao to Human Actions.* San Francisco: Harper Collins.

Sources in Chinese

Hsui-chen p'ien-nan (Answers to questions concerning women's enlightenment). By Liu I-ming. In *Tao-tsang ch'ing-h'ua,* 1 (10).

Kuan-hsin chia-ch'i (Insights on reflections on the mind). In *Tao-tsang ch'ing-h'ua,* 5 (5).

K'un-ling miao-ching (Cultivating stillness for women). In *Tao-tsang ch'ing-h'ua,* 5 (5).

Pao-p'u Tzu (The master who embraces simplicity). By Ko-hung.

T'ai-chi t'ao shuo (Treatise on the t'ai-chi). By Chou Tun-I. In *Tao-tsang ch'ing-h'ua,* 1 (6).

Tao-chia yang-sheng hseüh kai-yao (Essentials of the Taoist techniques of cultivating health). By Shao T'ien-shih. 1988. Taiwan: Chung-chou.

Tao-hai yüan-wei (On the intricacies of the Tao). 1987. By Shao t'ien-shih. Taiwan: Tzu-yao.

Chapter 5

Feminism in Judaism

Ellen M. Umansky

It wasn't all that long ago that Conservative rabbis in the United States heatedly debated whether or not to admit women into the Conservative rabbinate. Among the opponents of women's ordination were those who argued that the ordination of women represented a "watering down of tradition"[1] and a succumbing all too hastily to passing feminist demands which if ignored, might well go away. Why, some reasoned, give in to these demands now and in so doing completely change the nature of the rabbinate if two or three or ten years from now women will no longer want to be religious leaders? Why change the status quo, in other words, unless we are absolutely certain that we must?

In the fall of 1983, the opponents of women's ordination were defeated and two years later the Conservative movement followed Reform and Reconstructionism, Judaism's more liberal branches, in ordaining women as rabbis. Since then, the feminist demands to which several Conservative rabbis pointed with great alarm in the late 1970s, not only have not gone away—they have increased and slowly but steadily have begun to transform all aspects of Jewish life.

The gains that Jewish feminists have made within the last twenty years are especially impressive in light of the fact that with the possible exception of the Israel Women's Network, created in the 1980s, there is no singular, much less unified, international or national Jewish feminist movement anywhere in the world. Indeed, in the United States, where feminism has made its greatest gains, such a movement, spearheaded by the Jewish Feminist Organization (JFO), existed only briefly. Since the demise of the JFO in 1974 two years after its creation, there has not been such a movement[2] nor does there seem to be much interest in establishing one in the future.

As most if not all of us who identify ourselves as Jewish feminists have come to recognize, there is no singular "plight of the Jewish women" (a title of a paper I delivered many years ago). Nor is there any singular set of Jewish women's concerns. There is no "feminist encounter" with Judaism. Instead, there are many encounters articulated by many feminists in many different ways. This multivocality has increasingly led to a variety of definitions as to what it in fact means to be a Jewish feminist. Taken as a whole, they reveal the fact that Jewish feminists, as feminists and as Jews, do not share a common vision. For the sake of clarity, then, let me offer three very different ways in which Jewish feminists have defined themselves and continue to define themselves today.

Jewish Feminism as a Call for Increased Participation and Legal Change

To be a Jewish feminist, some argue, is to believe in and/or actively call for the greater participation of women within Jewish religious and communal life. Proponents of this definition of Jewish feminism, many of whom identify themselves either as Orthodox or as traditional Conservative, have attempted to create, facilitate, or make available public religious opportunities for girls and women from which traditionally they were exempt if not excluded.

According to the rabbis of the Talmud, those responsible for the formulation of Jewish law during the first few centuries of the common era, women and men were created with absolute dignity, equality, and worth. Yet equality, they believed, did not mean sameness. Rather, they argued, through a kind of divine economy, God created men and women as complements to one another. *By nature,* in other words, men and women were meant to occupy different societal roles so that together they might achieve wholeness. Viewing women as private persons whose natural religious domain was the home, the rabbinic sages saw as women's particular responsibility the maintaining of *kashrut* (dietary regulations) and the weekly preparation of one's homes for shabbat: cleaning, baking *challah* in a ritually prescribed way, cooking a festive meal, and kindling the Sabbath lights.

Preparations for other home-centered Jewish holidays such as *Pesach* (Passover) were also seen as women's obligations. These preparations included (and for many Jewish women still include) thoroughly cleaning one's home so as to make it free of *chametz* (leavened products), which Jews are prohibited from eating and from having in their homes for the eight days of *Pesach* (seven in Israel); making one's kitchen *pesachdik* (i.e., fit for Passover) by burning or removing all *chametz,* kashering all cooking and eating utensils (i.e., cleaning and immersing them in boiling water so as to remove all traces of *chametz;* or replacing them with utensils used only during *Pesach*), replacing the dishes eaten on during the year with those reserved for Passover use, and preparing food for the Passover *seder.*

Women were further responsible throughout the year and after giving birth for following the laws of *niddah,* biblically based rabbinic laws that regulated the times in which sexual relations between married couples were permitted. Following these laws not only necessitated separating from one's husband sexually during the menstrual period, but also, carefully counting the number of bloodfree days following one's period (or again, delivery of a child) and then, at the conclusion of a specified number of days, preparing oneself for immersion in a *mikvah*—a ritual bath often housed in a synagogue—immersing oneself, and reciting a specific blessing, after which time sexual relations between the woman and her husband could be resumed.

These laws took on great significance for Jewish women (and retain significance for Orthodox women today) not only because they were considered to be *mitzvot* (commandments) given to them by God but also because, by following these laws, it was they who came to ensure the ritual purity of their homes.

In contrast, the public sphere of religious life was seen as the natural domain of men. Included in this sphere was the study of religious texts, an obligation encumbent upon all Jewish males, and the obligation to participate in regularly scheduled public worship, including those each day in the morning, afternoon, and evening. Jewish feminists who have called for greater access by women to religious education and participation in public worship have done so, not as a means of foregoing their traditional roles, but rather as a means of expanding them.

Many of their efforts thus have focused on making available to Jewish girls and women more serious study of Hebrew and rabbinic texts and creating new ritual opportunities for women, including the celebration of *Rosh Hodesh* (the New Moon)—identified in rabbinic literature as a woman's holiday though few records exist as to ways in which it was celebrated by previous generations of Jewish women. Many have also participated in the formation of women-only prayer groups in which observant women—that is, those who view *halakhah* (Jewish law) as authoritative, are able to assume greater leadership roles than they would in mixed traditional (nonegalitarian) worship services.[3]

Many, if not most, Jewish feminists in search of greater access to Judaism's public religious life have also supported or have been actively involved in pressing rabbinic authorities for legal change. Without necessarily advocating a sweeping reform of the *halakhic* system, such feminists have called upon, and at times attempted to pressure, rabbinic authorities into reexamining those laws that have created undue hardships for women. Chief among them have been the laws of divorce and most specifically those concerning the *agunah* (literally, a woman anchored or chained to an absentee husband).

According to *halakhah,* only a husband can initiate divorce. Thus, a woman whose husband has deserted her, is insane, or is missing and presumed to be dead but whose death has not been verified by witnesses as well as a woman who is the wife of a recalcitrant husband who for various reasons refuses to give her a bill of divorcement (*get*), can never remarry (though her husband can). Throughout the centuries, rabbis have attempted to alleviate the plight of the *agunah.* Yet as Orthodox feminist Blu Greenberg has written, "problems of inequity remain, with an increasing number of women—the traditional women—paying a steep price for their adherence to Halakhah." Greenberg argues:

> In view of the fact that the unfolding Halakhah on divorce reflects an unmistakable pattern of limiting the husband's and expanding the wife's rights, the rabbis of today no longer can say they can not "work it out." To say their hands are tied, or to say they can resolve an individual problem but not find a global solution is to deny their collective responsibility. Worse, it bespeaks a lack of rabbinic will to find a halakhic way.[4]

In 1980, a group of observant Jewish feminists created an organization entitled G.E.T. whose stated aim was to apply pressure upon the Orthodox rabbinate "until women Get Equal Treatment (G.E.T.) in Jewish divorce proceedings."[5] In the fall of 1992, the International Coalition for Aguna Rights was established, with members including halakhically committed Jewish feminists in Israel and North America and representatives of major Jewish women's organizations throughout the world. Declaring 1993 the Year of the *Agunah,* it successfully staged a worldwide fast March 9, the traditional fast day of Esther preceding the celebration of Purim, to bring attention to the continuing plight of the *agunah.* It is the hope of these women, and their male supporters, that, in the words of (Orthodox) rabbi Eliezer Berkovitz: "[Orthodox rabbis] who are seriously concerned and troubled by the inadequate regard for the problems of contemporary Jewish religious life" will have the courage to speak out and "will introduce the halakhic changes that are required in recognition of the human dignity of the Jewish woman."[6]

Jewish Feminism as a Call for Equal Access

Sharing many of the same concerns as the above mentioned feminists are those pressing not only for increasing the rights and responsibilities of women within Judaism, but also for securing for women equal access to all aspects of Jewish life including those formerly reserved for men. Questioning if not rejecting traditional Judaism's insistence on gender distinctiveness as leading to the creation of gender specific roles, such feminists have sought the inclusion of women in the *minyan* (the quorum of ten necessary for public worship) and have demanded—and often gained—the right of women to receive *aliyot* (to be called up to the pulpit to recite blessings before and after the Torah reading) and to read from the Torah itself.

Unlike, in other words, more traditionally religious feminists who do not identify women's prayer groups as *minyanim* (and as such omit from their worship prayers that can only be said within the context of a *minyan*) and advocate reading from the Torah in women-only settings, "equal access feminists" have pressed, and continue to press, for women's inclusion in what formerly have been privileges or rights exclusively reserved for men.

Many such feminists, especially those within the Conservative movement, have advocated the wearing of such traditionally male garb as *kipot* (head coverings) and *Tallitot* (prayer shawls) by women. Some have even assumed for themselves such formerly male obligations as the wearing of *tefillin* (phylacteries) during morning prayer. As Conservative rabbi Susan Grossman has written, describing her own observance of this mitzvah: "Wrapping myself in tefillin . . . provides a daily rekindling of my feelings for serving God; a rededication of the actions of my hands; the desires of my heart and the intentions of my mind to God's will."[7] Many such feminists have worked to create or to participate in ceremonies paralleling those traditionally celebrated by men. These include baby naming ceremonies for girls welcoming a daughter into God's covenant with Israel (just as the ceremony of *brit milah,* ritual circumcision, welcomes a son) and adult Bat Mitzvah (paralleling Bar Mitzvah)[8] celebrated individually or with a group of women who have undertaken an intensive course of religious study together.

Calls for equal access have also included calls for women's ordination as rabbis and their investiture as cantors. Though the decision to admit women into the American Reform rabbinate predates the second wave of U.S. feminism by approximately ten years, Naamah Kelman's ordination from the Jerusalem campus of Hebrew Union College-Jewish Institute of Religion (HUC-JIR) in June 1992 clearly reflects the great impact that feminism has had on the movement since the early 1970s. At the same time, however, feminists within the Reform rabbinate continue to fight for equal access by the more than two hundred women rabbis and almost one hundred women cantors to rabbinical and cantorial positions in the U.S. and Canada, and to leadership positions within the Reform movement as a whole. Most recently, it has led to the still unsuccessful call for the addition of women to the faculty of Hebrew Union College. Housed on four different campuses—three in the U.S., one in Israel—

HUC can currently claim only two women as full-time members of its rabbinic school faculty.

From its inception as a movement in the 1930s, Reconstructionism has affirmed and worked toward achieving the equality of women in Jewish life. When the Reconstructionist Rabbinical College (RRC) first opened in Philadelphia in 1968, women were immediately accepted. As of 1993, fifty-two women have been ordained by RRC and women have long been members of both the faculty and the administration of the college. Yet despite the fact that barring the prejudices of individual congregations, women within Reconstructionism have equal access to positions of rabbinical leadership (and, in fact, a woman has already served as president of the Reconstructionist Rabbinical Association), the small size of the Reconstructionist movement in the U.S. has forced many of its rabbis, men and women, to seek positions elsewhere—either in Reform or Conservative congregations or in Jewish organizations outside the synagogue structure where the struggle for equal access to positions of lay and professional leadership very much continues.

While the relationship between feminism and the Reform and Reconstructionist acceptance of women as religious leaders may seem indirect, it was feminist agitation that directly forced the Conservative movement to reexamine its attitude toward women. In March 1972, a group of women calling themselves *Ezrat Nashim* appeared at the annual convention of the Rabbinical Assembly (the professional association of Conservative rabbis) to issue a formal call for change. Among their demands were the full participation of women in religious observance, synagogue worship, and decision-making bodies within synagogues and the general Jewish community; the recognition of women as witnesses in Jewish law (in contrast to the view held by traditional interpreters of *halakhah*); the right of women to initiate divorce (insisting, once again, that *halakhah* be reinterpreted); and the admission of women into the Jewish Theological Seminary's rabbinical and cantorial programs.

Although the group's appearance at the convention was not sanctioned by the Rabbinical Assembly, the media attention that Ezrat Nashim received helped make its members "small scale celebrities within the Conservative movement."[9] Recognizing the need for a larger, more activist organization, its members helped plan and lead a national conference in 1973 on "The Role of Women in Jewish Life."

A year later, at a second conference, the Jewish Feminist Organization (JFO) was created. It sought "nothing else than the full, direct, and equal participation of women at all levels of Jewish life." During the two years of its existence, the JFO served as an umbrella organization for numerous regional committees. Sponsoring seminars, consciousness-raising groups, bibliographical publications and other, specifically action-oriented proposals, it worked to become a force for "creative change in the [U.S.] Jewish community."[10]

Though organizational problems led to its dissolution in 1976, subregional chapters continued to function, leading to the establishment of more informal groups that reevaluated and challenged women's traditional religious roles.

Since then, a growing number of such groups have come into existence— for example, Rosh Hodesh groups, women's study groups at local synagogues, and more socially oriented women's networks that are either synagogue or community based. Also created have been more formal groups working for equal access (such as the Women's Rabbinic Network of the Reform movement) while conferences sponsored by various Jewish organizations and institutions, including Jewish community centers and college Hillel groups, are continually being organized throughout the United States. Again, the focus of most of these seems to be on securing equal access for women in terms of securing full participation and attaining roles of religious and secular leadership within the American Jewish community.

Outside North America and Israel (which at six million and almost four million respectively can claim the two largest Jewish populations in the world), Great Britain (with a population of over three hundred thousand Jews) can claim the only other Jewish community in which feminists have consistently placed the issue of equal access on the communal agenda. According to Rabbi Jonathan Magonet, principal of the Leo Baeck College in London, a rabbinical seminary jointly run by the British Reform and Liberal movements, the admission of Jacqueline Tabick into its rabbinic program in 1971 (fifteen years after the college opened) came about with "little discussion."[11] Yet essays that appeared in several Jewish publications during the late 1960s (including those published by the reform synagogues of Great Britain) indicate that both proponents and opponents of women's ordination acknowledged the difficulty of denying Jewish women this privilege in an age in which society's watchword had become 'the equality of the sexes'"[12]

Feminism, in other words, may not directly have led to the ordination of Jackie Tabick (or of the fifteen other women ordained by 1993) any more than feminism directly led to the ordination of women as Reform rabbis in the United States. Yet open discussion about women's role in society and within the Jewish community (along with more recent discussions at Leo Baeck College about ordaining as rabbis openly lesbian and gay Jews) have been fueled at least to some extent by an awareness of issues that feminism has raised in England, North America, Israel, and elsewhere in the world.

Feminism as Transformation

A third, more recent, definition of Jewish feminism, primarily given expression by feminists in the U.S. and Canada, asserts that to be a Jewish feminist is to integrate women's experiences into Jewish life, thus working toward the transformation of Judaism itself. Many such feminists, including myself, have sought to begin this transformation while continuing the struggle for equal access within existing institutions. Others have chosen to focus their energies exclusively on this transformation, working toward the creation of a "feminist Judaism" in which Judaism's three essential elements: God, Torah, and Israel (that is, the Jewish people as well as the land of Israel) are reconceptualized.

As Susannah Heschel has written, reflecting this more radical focus:

> Feminists may be misdirecting their efforts by attempting to remain within the framework of the denominations . . . [for] changes made by [Orthodoxy, Conservatism, Reconstructionism, and Reform] in response to particular feminist demands were made not by applying the central principles of each movement. [Indeed] whatever progress was made during the past decade by feminists was not because of, but in spite of, the core ideas of each of the movements. . . . Modern Judaism has built the doors of denominations, guarded by rabbis, institutions, and ideologies. But Judaism is not an edifice lying behind doors and guards, and we should not have to go through a denomination to reach it. Rather, our relations should be with the diversity and totality of Jewish tradition, unmediated by one of its modern forms.[13]

Expressing similar sentiments is theologian Judith Plaskow, who views feminism as demanding a new "understanding of Torah that begins by acknowledging the injustice of Torah and then goes on to create a Torah that is whole." Similarly, she writes:

> Feminism demands an understanding of Israel that includes the whole of Israel and thus allows women to speak and name our experience for ourselves. It demands we replace a normative male voice with a chorus of divergent voices, describing Jewish reality in different accents and tones. Feminism impels us to rethink issues of community and diversity, to explore the ways in which one people can acknowledge and celebrate the varied experiences of its members . . . [and finally,] feminism demands new ways of talking about God that reflect and grow out of the redefinition of a Jewish humanity.[14]

Focusing, for example, on questions of liturgy, such feminists have asked: If we, as Jews, believe that God is neither male nor female, then why are our traditional liturgical images of God predominately if not exclusively male?

Alternatively: if Jews believe that all of us, male and female, are created in the divine image, then why doesn't our liturgy reflect this basic theological conviction? These questions clearly move beyond those concerning equal accesses, for they recognize that equal access to rituals and liturgies created by and for men does not address their androcentric nature. Equal access alone, in other words, enables women to participate more fully in the Jewish community but, as I and other Jewish feminists have argued, it does not necessarily reflect the values and experiences of men *and women* nor view the values and experiences of both as equally central.

As Judith Plaskow, Rachel Adler, and others have written, the "otherness" of women, evident in Jewish liturgies and sacred texts, cannot be remedied simply through equal access. Neither, they have argued, can it be remedied through piecemeal *halakhic* change, for the *halakhic* system in and of itself is one that presupposes the otherness of women. Rachel Adler, in her more recent theological work, has attempted to reenvision *halakhah* from source of power to source of meaning as a way of retaining the concept of law while transforming its very nature.[15] Judith Plaskow, on the other hand, has questioned whether law, in and of itself, is in fact a male form. Thus, she has written, "How can we presume that if women add our voices to tradition, law will be our medium of expression and repair?"[16]

Recent discussions of God and liturgy among such feminists have focused on whether changing metaphorical images of God's gender is in and of itself sufficient. In this regard, many of us have concluded that it is not, for, we have come to believe, God's gender is less important than the kinds of relationships between God and humanity that the liturgy itself portrays. If, for example, we address God as king of the universe *and* queen of heaven, or for that matter, simply address God as the more gender inclusive sovereign or ruler, we may have succeeded in reinforcing the conviction that all of us are created in the image of God, yet in so doing, continue to legitimize the conviction that the human-divine relationship is one of hierarchical domination.

That is, if our only or most prevalent images of divinity are of God as ruler, with God commanding while we obey, it is all too easy to lose sight of our own responsibility in the human-divine encounter. As covenantal partners, we have argued, it is our obligation to work *with* God in repairing the world and to bear responsibility for our actions. Thus a growing number of liberal or progressive Jewish feminists, primarily identifying with the Reform, Reconstructionist, or havurah movements, the new-age fellowship, P'nai Or, or women-only communities or prayer groups specifically committed to the creation of a feminist Judaism, have begun to create new, nonhierarchical images of God that reflect the theological conviction that the Jewish notion of covenant calls for human action and human responsibility.

Major Feminist Critiques of the Tradition

Though, as I have indicated above, there is no one feminist critique of Judaism shared by all who identify themselves as Jewish feminists, most, if not all, I think, would agree, that despite rabbinic Judaism's insistence that men and women are by nature equal, there are several *halakhic* disabilities under which women traditionally have suffered. The inability of women, for example, to initiate divorce is a prime example. Their inability to serve as witnesses in a court of Jewish law is another. While some Jewish feminists do not view the notion of a sex differentiated religious tradition as in and of itself oppressive (and in fact many, more traditional Jewish feminists continue to see such sex differentiation as divinely ordained), most Jewish feminists outside orthodoxy have critiqued this sex differentiation as rendering women subordinate if not inferior.

As Paula Hyman wrote in an essay first published in the summer of 1972:

> By exempting women from time-bound positive *mitzvot* [commandments] . . . and denying them legal independence, Judaism relegated women to a second-class status. Within the family the woman may have had a necessary and noble task to fulfill. But the heart and soul of traditional Judaism remained communal prayer and study. And prayer and study were the pursuits almost exclusively of men.[17]

Emerging out of this critique is the recognition that Judaism, in both its past and present formulations, has been and for the most part continues to be androcentric, focusing on the activities and experiences of Jewish men. Though women have always been understood to be members of God's covenant with Israel, Jewish history is often presented (in religious schools and written texts) as the history of men, from the patriarchs, Abraham, Isaac, and Jacob, to Moses and Joshua to the kings, prophets, Talmudic sages, later rabbinic commentators, and so on.

As Jewish feminists have argued, women's silence if not outright exclusion from biblical stories, rabbinic discussions, and later historical descriptions of Jewish religious and communal life often makes it difficult if not impossible for women to fully feel part of the Jewish people—to feel, in other words, as if we too are normative Jews and thus part of God's covenant with Israel. As Judith Plaskow, Rachel Adler, and other Jewish feminists have pointed out, why is it that when Moses gathers the Israelites to the foot of Mt. Sinai (in Exodus 19) he says to them, "Do not go near a woman?" Are we to conclude, contrary to women's felt experience and to the presuppositions of later generations of rabbis, that women, in fact, were not there? Or, are we merely confronted with an androcentric text for which indications of women's presence or participation at Sinai are simply, in Rachel Adler's words, "non-data"?[18]

In the same vein, feminists, including me, have asked: Why does one continue to read in some historical studies of Judaism, these are the 613 commandments that Jews are obligated to perform? when traditionally only men are obligated to perform 613? What can one make of such contemporary statements as: "The study of sacred texts . . . assumes a *central* position in Judaism. Other traditions had their religious virtuosi whose virtuosity consisted in knowledge of a literary tradition; but few held, as does Judaism, that everyone must become such a virtuoso."[19] Traditionally, Judaism did *not* hold that everyone should become a literary virtuoso. Women were exempt if not excluded from the obligation to study religious texts. Thus, the "everyone" in the aforementioned sentence apparently applies only to men.

This is made even clearer when the same author writes: "The important Jew is the learned man." Or, when he writes elsewhere that according to rabbinic Judaism the study of Torah is "*the* [emphasis mine] central expression of [Jewish] piety."[20] This last sentiment has been shared by other contemporary (male) scholars. As one such scholar writes: "Jews have studied the Talmud for a great variety of reasons," "the traditional Jew studies Talmud because it communicates ultimate truth," "Jews studied Talmud because the act brought them closer to the divine," and "the pious Jew" approached the Talmud with certain questions in mind.[21] In each of these instances, the word *Jew* is clearly synonymous with "male Jew." Given this perspective, it is thus not surprising that the same author concludes: "The Talmudic tradition chronicles a people's ancient quest to find and understand its God"[22] without acknowledging that this tradition only chronicles the quest of *some* of the Jewish people.

As I and other Jewish feminists have tried to make clear, our point in raising these kinds of issues is not to denigrate either the study of religious texts or the Talmudic tradition. Rather it is to ask, if—as several (male) scholars have maintained—the study of religious texts along with participation in regularly scheduled public worship have been *the* central expressions of Jewish piety, when by and large only men studied religious texts and participated in public worship, are we to conclude that traditionally women weren't pious? Or that men were *more* pious than women because the fullest, surest paths to God were open only to them? My own research on Jewish women's spirituality reveals that Jewish women have long had, and I suspect, have always had a very rich spiritual life. Unfortunately, this life, and efforts by women in promoting this life, have often gone unrecorded.

Not coincidentally, as feminists have begun to write women back into Jewish history, so many have increasingly sought to uncover previously silenced male and female voices. These have included the voices of Sephardic and Mizrachi Jews (that is, those of non-Western or non-European descent) as well as the voices of those who are gay or lesbian. The feminist anthology, *The Tribe of Dina,* edited by Irena Klepfisz and Melanie Kaye Kantrowitz (Beacon

Press, 1989) merits particular attention as a work that highlights the experiences and contributions of both lesbian and Sephardic Jews. Faith Rogow's "Speaking the Unspeakable: Gays, Jews, and Historical Inquiry," in Christie Balka and Andy Rose's edited anthology, *Twice Blessed: On Being Lesbian, Gay, and Jewish,*[23] suggests a number of directions that one might take in attempting to incorporate lesbian and gay voices into Jewish history.

Critiques of Judaism lodged by a number of Jewish feminist theologians (writing outside Orthodoxy) have illuminated aspects of Judaism that theologically may be antithetical to a feminist perspective. Drorah Setel, for example, has maintained that traditional Judaism's objectification of women needs to be seen as part of a more general tendency to divide all human experience into dualistic categories. Thus, she argues, feminine/masculine and female/male need to be placed alongside such polarizations as material/spiritual, emotional/rational, night/day, death/life, body/soul, bad/good and passive/aggressive. Viewed from a feminist perspective, which values connectedness and relation, these dualisms, she writes, are inextricably linked with oppression. More specifically, she argues that once one affirms an essential separateness between men and women, so one inevitably is led to affirm an essential separateness among races, ethnic groups, and socio-economic classes.

While Setel acknowledges the pervasiveness of this kind of polarized thinking within the Jewish tradition, she refuses to view it as inevitable. Arguing that the feminist transformation of Judaism is not only possible but imperative, she maintains that all of us have a responsibility to fight oppression in whatever form it takes. We all have to create a Judaism, and a world, that affirms the full humanity of all people. Setel's consistency in her claims that dualisms lead to the oppression of one group over another causes her to reject Judaism's traditional understanding of separation as leading to holiness.[24] While acknowledging how deeply entrenched this view remains, she nevertheless insists that new forms of Jewish practice must be developed or old ones transformed. Those that cannot be transformed, she suggests, should be abandoned. Among them is male circumcision, which she believes theologically perpetuates the physical and spiritual separation of Jewish men from Jewish women in an all-male covenant, while at the same time hierarchically setting Jewish and non-Jewish men apart from one another.

Similarly drawing on the feminist values of connectedness and relation, other Jewish feminist theologians such as Judith Plaskow and Marcia Falk, have described the notion of chosenness (which Falk equates with "anti-Gentilism") as antithetical to a feminist Judaism. Believing, as Falk does, that the concept of divine election establishes a hierarchical understanding of Jews vis-à-vis other people (with Jews obviously, on the top, or closer to God), Plaskow further maintains that chosenness establishes internal hierarchies as well. Echoing Setel's critique of separation as leading to holiness, she argues that "since chief among these many separations is the differentiation between male and female, chosenness becomes linked to the subordination of women and other groups in the rhythms of Jewish existence." She continues:

> It is not that one can draw a direct line from the idea of chosenness to the creation of Others within the Jewish community or that the former provides an explicit model for the latter. But both are part of a cluster of important ideas that make graded differentiation a central model for understanding difference, and the two are also linked to each other both historically and psychologically.[25]

Concluding, then, that this "hierarchical understanding of difference is perhaps the most significant barrier to the feminist reconceptualization of Jewish community,"[26] Plaskow advocates replacing the concept of divine election with that of Jewish distinctness, a concept recognizing that all human communities, including the Jewish community and the subcommunities within it, are distinct and distinctive. As the term *distinctness* suggests, she writes, "the relationship between these various communities—Jewish to non-Jewish, Jewish to Jewish—should be understood not in terms of hierarchical difference but in terms of part and whole."[27]

Judaism's traditional understanding of men and women as complements to one another has also been singled out for criticism by some Jewish feminists. Rebecca Alpert, for example, in an essay entitled "Challenging Male/Female Complementarity: Jewish Lesbians and the Jewish Tradition," points out that the centrality of the notion of male/female complementarity makes it impossible for lesbians to become fully integrated into the Jewish community. Acknowledging that feminism and the gay liberation movement have also called into question the notion of male/female complementarity, she maintains that "the questions raised by lesbians both incorporate and complicate the challenges posed by" feminists and gay men.[28]

More specifically, Alpert asserts that while (heterosexual) feminists have challenged men's dominance over women, they have not challenged the tradition's assumptions concerning the centrality of male/female relationships. Similarly, although gay men have challenged this centrality, they have done so without facing exclusion from the Jewish tradition on the basis of gender. As men, in other words, their access to full participation in the community is guaranteed. The study of religious texts and participation in public worship, perhaps men's major religious activities, are not dependent upon marital status and relationships between men have always been valued. In contrast, because women's traditional religious roles (as wives and mothers) exist only in relationship to men, lesbian concerns are often rendered invisible and their participation in the community either limited or devalued.

What's more, she argues, lesbian sexuality calls into question Judaism's understanding of the fundamental purpose of marriage, namely, "species continuity," by establishing sexual pleasure and procreation as independent of one another. Lesbian feminist insistence on gender nonconformity further raises questions about the ways in which women and men define themselves in relationship to one another, while feminist efforts to image God as female have been viewed by many Jews as threatening in part, at least, because such an image conjures up "an association between women worshiping images of women and women loving women." Precisely because, in other words, women are viewed by the tradition as complements to men rather than as autonomous beings, they are never perceived as asexual. Thus, imagining God as woman threatens not only God's (metaphorical?) maleness but God's asexuality as well. Alpert concludes:

> For lesbians to be included in Jewish life in the fullest measure, the fear that female images of God are related to lesbianism must be faced directly. If lesbians, too, are made in God's image, there must be room to explore images of God that support the divinity of erotic love between women.[29]

Broadening Alpert's conclusions, I believe that complementarity can also be seen as antithetical to feminist values on another level. While certainly, as Alpert asserts, the notion of male/female complementarity presents particular problems for lesbians, it also presents a problem for anyone who believes that human companionship, while enriching one's life, does not in and of itself make one whole.

As I maintained in commenting on Alpert's essay in a panel on lesbianism and Jewish feminism at the 1990 annual meeting of the American Academy of Religion, one can value relationships and connectedness to others without asserting that outside such relationships one is not a complete human being. Indeed, I share Martin Buber's conviction that one is not capable of entering into an I-Thou relationship until one has a clear sense of who one, as a unique "I," with one's own talents, dreams, and desires, really is,. Without this, wrote Buber (emphasizing what feminists have also emphasized, namely the importance of self-actualization), it is all too easy for the "I" to lose oneself in the I-Thou relation.

The Convergence of Jewish and Feminist Values

Although, as I have indicated above, an understanding of male/female (or female/female) complementarity as source of individual wholeness is, at least in my view, antithetical to a feminist (and Buberian) understanding of relationship as source of meaning, a broader understanding of complementarity, such as that suggested by contemporary theologian, Rabbi Irving (Yitz) Greenberg, very much echoes feminist insights and concerns. According to Greenberg, it is not through individual relation that one becomes whole, but rather through the search for community. He writes:

> Judaism teaches that all human beings are part of the chain of life. The individual is not born in a vacuum. Each person's given capacities come out of the gifts and nurturing of those who precede and give us life. If we appreciate the gift, the proper response is to become part of the process that develops life further and passes it on enhanced to future generations. The goal is that some day, together, we attain the perfection of life. For humanity to attain that perfection, people must reach out and be responsible beyond themselves.[30]

The Jewish insistence that one work in community in order to achieve the goal of *tikkun olam* (repairing the world) is very much echoed in the feminist belief that "sisterhood is powerful." So too has the feminist recognition that the "personal is political" long been acknowledged within the Jewish tradition. As Drorah Setel has written: "daily observances and communal authority, which are the basis of the rabbinic concept of *halachah* . . . tie in well with feminist values of community and personal empowerment" as that which can create social change. Both perspectives, she points out, "reflect a desire to notice the extraordinary present in the mundane and to be aware of the daily choices involved in our lives, which constantly create and re-create the larger world."[31]

As many Jewish feminists have noted, *tikkun olam* holds out a vision of the human-divine relationship as one of covenantal partners. Without denying the preponderance of liturgical images that portray God as the dominating other, Jewish feminists have also acknowledged that the Jewish notion of covenant is one that envisions God and the Jewish people—both individually and in community—as having mutual responsibilities and obligations, working with one another in order to make the world whole. The Jewish vision of *tikkun olam* thus converges with feminism's future vision of a nonsexist society in which difference is honored and people of all races, classes, ethnic origin, physical abilities, and so on are accorded equal dignity and sense of worth. Though the specific content of these visions may differ, certainly the latter can be described as a feminist vision of what Jews have long understood to be the goal of human life—namely, the attaining of *tikkun ha-nefesh* (repair of the soul, of ourselves), *tikkun ha-am* (repair of the people or of our families and communities), and *tikkun olam* (repair of the world in which all of us live).

Central to both Judaism and feminism is the conviction that the healing of our selves, our communities, and the world cannot take place without the attainment of justice. As Marcia Falk has written:

> Judaism teaches a passion and commitment to justice, through a central and significant body of teachings that have been inspirational for many feminist Jews, and that have even, for some of us, parented our feminist concerns. "Justice, justice you shall pursue, so that you may live" says the biblical voice of God, words that embrace both process and ideal in an ever-renewing commitment to *tikkun olam,* repair of the fragmented world.[32]

Thus, as Drorah Setel has asserted, "in contrast to models of spirituality that emphasize detachment or otherworldliness," Jewish spirituality has long been rooted in the "interrelationship among study (in the larger sense of learning and teaching), prayer (including reflection, shared visions and communal celebration), and social work for justice."[33]

The Impact of Feminism on Jewish Denominational Life

In order to gain a better appreciation for the ways in which feminism has already had a great impact on contemporary Jewry, it is instructive to look more closely at some of the changes that have already occurred, particularly in the U.S. Jewish community—the largest Jewish community in the world and the community most deeply influenced by feminism as a movement and as a perspective. Among those changes have been those that have impacted upon the four major Jewish religious movements in the U.S.: Reform, Conservatism, Reconstructionism, and Orthodoxy.

Reform Judaism

As I have already indicated, feminism did not directly lead to the entrance of women into the Reform rabbinate. The ideology of Reform Judaism itself, which wedded Judaism to classical liberal political theory, led to a theoretical if not real commitment to women's equality as early as 1846 in Germany and soon after in the United States. It was this commitment, along with a practical need to train more rabbis to serve Reform congregations, a change in leadership at Hebrew Union College and in the decision-making process regarding ordination, and a changed social climate (marked by the growing acceptance of women religious leaders in Protestant denominations) that led to Sally Priesand's ordination in 1972.

Nonetheless, the impact of feminism on the ordination of women as Reform rabbis since the early 1970s cannot be underestimated, for feminism helped insure that once women were granted the privilege of ordination, a sufficient number of qualified women would seek to enter the Reform rabbinate despite all its personal and professional demands. In addition, since the mid-1980s, as feminism has taken deeper root in the Jewish community as a whole, and as women rabbis within the Reform movement have become more visible and more accepted, often standing on the *bima* [pulpit] along side of equally visible women cantors, feminist perceptions and expectations have slowly begun to transform the Reform rabbinate itself.

In an essay entitled "How Women are Changing the [Reform] Rabbinate," published in 1991, Rabbi Janet Marder pointed out that few women rabbis "have achieved prominent positions of leadership in the movement." To date, she notes—and the figures she gives have not significantly changed in the two years since her essay was written:

> None heads a thousand-member congregation; only three serve as senior rabbis of congregations larger than 300. But it would be wrong to conclude that women's impact on the [Reform] rabbinate has been minimal. On the contrary, one senses in conversations with women rabbis that we are witnessing the beginning of a profound transformation within the rabbinate—a change brought about by distinctive values and goals women have brought to this once exclusively male enterprise.[34]

Many women rabbis, she maintains, consciously see themselves as "agents for change," and as such, are attempting to reshape the role of the American Reform rabbi. Most, she continues, share a commitment to three fundamental values—all of which I would describe as feminist—namely—balance, intimacy, and empowerment.

While U.S. feminism of the late 1960s and early 70s focused on the struggle for women's equality as one of gaining equal pay for equal work, and did not, by and large, concern itself with the issue of balance, by the 1980s, increasing numbers of white, middle-class feminists (including Jewish feminists) began to rethink the notion of equality. If equality meant, for example, working eighty hours a week at a high pressured job, at the expense of one's health, family, and friends, perhaps the notion of equality needed to be redefined. While the goal of equal pay for equal work was not abandoned, increasing numbers of feminists began to claim that the demand for equal access did not mean that women wanted to be "just like men." Although this realization initially helped create the phenomenon of the superwoman—a woman with a high powered career, who also attempted to be a terrific wife, mother, gourmet cook and house cleaner, by the mid 1980s, as Gloria Steinem so aptly put it, increasing numbers of American middle-class women came to realize that "having it all" meant "doing it all."

Consequently, many U.S. feminists of the late 1980s and early 1990s came to replace the notion of having it all with achieving balance. While not all of the well over two hundred women ordained as Reform rabbis would identify themselves as feminists, the feminist emphasis on balance has proved to be appealing not only to the vast majority of women rabbis but also to a small, but growing, number of younger male rabbis as well. Despite the difficulties involved in seeking a balance between family and work, an increasing number of Reform rabbis, male and female, have come to ask: "How can I teach my congregants about the importance that Judaism attaches to family life and then sacrifice my own?"[35]

This question is very much related to the two other feminist values that Marder describes in her essay—namely, intimacy and empowerment. Drawing on feminist insights into the great value that women place on human relationships, Marder points to the desire among women rabbis whom she interviewed to form close relationships with their congregants. This led many to choose small congregations where it is easier to create a sense of community among members and clergy than it is in congregations that are large. While it is tempting to assert that the feminist emphasis on relatedness as an important human value has led increasing numbers of male and female rabbis to seek smaller congregations where greater intimacy is possible, there is at present, Marder continues, no data that would support this claim. Indeed, the data that are available seem to support a very different conclusion. While women on the whole do not seem to be seeking larger pulpits, most male rabbis continue to aspire to move into larger, "more prestigious" congregations.[36]

Certainly the desire for greater intimacy is not the only reason why the majority of women Reform rabbis have not aspired to larger pulpits. Nor can one conclude that men rabbis who aspire to larger congregations have a fear or a lack of interest in intimacy. But one can conclude, I think, that if feminism has influenced and helped support the decision of many women rabbis in the Reform movement *not* to seek larger, more prestigious pulpits—to seek, in other words, a different kind of rabbinate than that traditionally embodied by men—it has also meant that there are few if any women rabbis today who can be considered among the leaders of American Reform.

Some might attribute this reality both to the relatively short period of time hat women have been in the rabbinate (thus making most of the women currently ordained ineligible for serving very large congregations) and to the relative youth of women rabbis in comparison to male rabbis as a whole. Yet as long as greater prestige is attached to serving larger congregations and as long as most women rabbis for whatever reason opt out of the conventional path of "upward mobility," few women will serve on the most important committees of the Central Conference of American [Reform] Rabbis (CCAR), few will hold offices, will be invited to speak at annual CCAR conventions, or will be asked to serve as spokespersons for the Reform movement either in the United States or at international meetings or missions, be they held in Israel, Ethiopia, the former Soviet Union, or Rome.

This isn't to argue that women necessarily *should* seek "upward mobility" so that they can succeed in becoming leaders of Reform. But I am arguing that if women *do* seek a different sort of rabbinate, one that, barring the total transformation of the power structure of the Reform movement may preclude most women rabbis from gaining public recognition as the "leaders of Reform," their greatest impact upon the Reform movement in the United States may not be one "from above" but "from below." That is, while women rabbis may have relatively little impact upon current and future decisions made by the CCAR, women serving as pulpit rabbis have already exerted enormous impact upon their congregants, just as those doing Hillel work, serving as educators, or involved in other ways with Jewish youth have had a great impact upon their students and those working in communal positions have had and continue to have an impact upon those lay people with whom they come in contact in their day-to-day lives.

Not surprisingly, the third value emphasized by a significant number of women rabbis has been empowerment. Even among those who do not identify themselves as feminists, one hears a significant number speaking about replacing hierarchical structures with those in which responsibilities, privileges, and power can be shared. While some might label this "network model of leadership"[37] as female or feminine, I would label this model as feminist. It is self-consciously critical of the male models of leadership currently in existence and is one that many women rabbis, as women, have previously experienced in explicitly feminist settings (consciousness raising groups, college women's centers, feminist organizations, and so forth). Moreover, while one might argue that network leadership models are as much "feminine" as "feminist," using these models *as a means of empowering others* (without sacrificing one's self in the process), can clearly be viewed as feminist.

Empowerment has helped to create a growing core of lay leaders—men and women—within the American Reform community. Increasingly, one hears of lay committees creating new Friday night liturgies,[38] growing numbers of congregants participating in the Torah service (and an increasing number of adult women becoming B'not Mitzvah), congregants leading daily *minyanim,* parents writing baby-naming ceremonies for sons and especially for daughters,[39] and even twelve-year-old boys and girls working with their parents to help create a special service for their Bar or Bat Mitzvah. Scholar-in-residence programs have proliferated throughout the country with the weekend scholar frequently selected by a lay committee who formally invites the scholar to its congregation and often works with him/her in selecting topics on which he or she might speak.[40]

Clearly, not all these developments have been initiated by women rabbis. Growing numbers of Reform rabbis (especially younger rabbis) and growing numbers of congregants, male and female, have been influenced by feminism's understanding of empowerment as essential to self-realization and growth. Indeed, the increasing numbers of women who have assumed leadership roles within their congregations and within the Reform community as a whole in and of itself testifies to the great impact that feminism has had on the Reform movement in the United States. As early as 1970, ninety-six percent of all Reform temples in the U.S. had at some time elected a woman to its congregational board. Since then the numbers of women serving on boards has increased as has the number of women serving as officers of their congregations.

By the mid-1970s, it was no longer unusual for a woman to serve as synagogue president. Indeed, I would maintain that on the whole the question of whether women should serve as congregational presidents is no longer an issue in the Reform movement. Many congregations have already been served by at least one woman president. I believe that most if not all congregations that have not yet had a woman as president would be willing to elect one and given the growing participation of women as lay leaders within Reform congregations, undoubtedly one day will.

While much of the leadership of the Union of American Hebrew Congregations (UAHC)—the movement's congregational arm—remains male, women have increasingly assumed positions of leadership within it. Since 1973, for example, when the UAHC elected its first woman vice chairman (*sic*), several women have been elected to this position. Apparently the election of a woman as UAHC chair seems a real possibility in the not too distant future.[41]

Although the initial impact of feminism upon the movement's major women's organization, the National Federation of Temple Sisterhoods (NFTS), recently renamed as Women of Reform Judaism (WRJ), may not have been completely positive,[42] Eleanor Schwartz, former Executive Director, believes that feminism has already begun to have a positive impact upon NFTS. Always "radical in goal if not in style," NFTS, she maintains, has not surprisingly begun to attract younger, college-educated, professional women who twenty years ago might not have considered joining the sisterhood of their congregation. Yet as the participation of women in Reform congregations has increased, as more women have come to take on leadership roles in their synagogues or in the secular world, as sisterhoods have introduced programs aimed at attracting younger members and have begun to schedule meetings at times convenient for women who work outside the home and, perhaps as feminism has reasserted the importance of women's organizations and of women's forming social, professional, and spiritual bonds with one another, so, according to Schwartz, the

National Federation of Temple Sisterhoods seems to be "undergoing a renaissance."[43]

Admittedly, at present there are fewer local chapters than there were twenty years ago and not all local sisterhoods are flourishing. Indeed, some still have difficulty attracting younger members. Yet, according to Schwartz, there is great interest among new Reform congregations in establishing sisterhoods. Her prediction is that in the next few years, the number of local chapters throughout the United States will significantly rise.[44]

As in other areas, religious education within the Reform movement has not been immune to the influence of feminism. By the mid-1970s, for example, religious school textbooks "began to present female role models other than mothers and teachers."[45] As significantly, within the last ten years growing numbers of women have gained full-time positions as education directors of Reform congregations and consequently have become increasingly involved in selecting which texts are used. Not all women who are directors of Jewish education, of course, are sensitive to the kinds of issues that feminism raises. Moreover, including women as central to Jewish history and Jewish religious life does not yet seem to be a priority among the majority of those developing curricula for the religious schools under the aegis of the Reform movement.[46] Nonetheless, it is significant that in 1988, the six-hundred member National Association of [Reform] Temple Educators (NATE) elected Zena Sulkes as its first woman president and two years later elected another woman, Robin Eisenberg, to succeed her. The election of Sulkes and Eisenberg reflects not only the increasing number of women entering the field of Jewish education, but also what seems to be the growing influence of women educators within the Reform movement itself.[47]

One can also credit feminism with changes that have been made in Reform's liturgical texts. As Michael Meyer maintains, it was due to the increasing influence of the feminist movement that:

> *Gates of Prayer* [published in 1975] in its English portions, removed male language in reference to the worshipers: "all men" became "all"; "fellowship" became "friendship." One English version of the *avot* prayer [identifying God as the God of Abraham, Isaac, and Jacob] made references to the "God of our mothers" as well as our fathers. Yet although there were experimental substitutions of nongender names and pronouns also for God, the standard Reform liturgy in the 1970s continued to refer to deity as "our Father, our King" and as "He" and "Him." Moreover, the Hebrew prayers remained untouched by feminist criticism.[48]

By the late 1980s, both references to God and the words of Hebrew prayers could no longer claim such immunity. Indeed, to a large measure *because* of feminism's impact on Reform Judaism, it has become increasingly difficult to speak of a "standard Reform liturgy." Growing numbers of congregations have created their own gender-inclusive, *siddurim* as replacements for or supplements to *Gates of Prayer,* and it is not uncommon to worship in a Reform congregation in which the rabbi and congregants use *Gates of Prayer* but say "God" where the text, referring to the divine, clearly says "He."

In recognition of this growing phenomenon, and in response to increased support from members of the Reform rabbinate, cantorate, and laity for gender-inclusive language, the CCAR has recently completed a revision of three services (two for Friday evening, one for Shabbat morning) in which all English references to God are gender-inclusive and in which the mothers of Israel are mentioned in both Hebrew and English prayers. Published in 1992 as *Gates of Prayer for Shabbat,* and identified on the title page as "A Gender Sensitive Prayerbook," its intent, in the words of editor Chaim Stern, is to "reshape the language of our liturgy so . . . [as to] reflect our view [the view of the Reform movement] that masculine language and exclusively male assumptions ought to give way to broader, more inclusive expression."[49] Intended to be used as an interim prayerbook, this "gender-sensitive" liturgy is the first step toward a more thoroughgoing revision of *Gates of Prayer* to be completed by members of the CCAR liturgy committee by the year 2000.

Finally, one can credit feminism at least in part with a number of steps taken by the Reform movement in the 1980s and early 1990s. Among them was the adoption by the CCAR of the patrilineal or "nonlineal" descent resolution first brought before its members in 1980. Formally breaking with traditional Judaism's affirmation of a child's Jewishness in the case of mixed marriage only if the child's mother was Jewish (or if the child formally converted to Judaism), the resolution maintained that the child of one Jewish parent—mother or father —was "under the presumption of Jewish descent," which would then need "to be established through appropriate and timely public and formal acts of identification with the Jewish faith and people." While certainly a number of factors influenced those CCAR members who voted in favor of the proposal in 1983, among them was the recognition that given men's growing involvement in the raising of their children—clearly, a by-product of the feminist movement—"the standing of the Jewish spouses and parents in mixed marriages" should be equalized. Indeed, according to Rabbi Herman E. Schaalman in his 1987 report to the CCAR assessing the patrilineality resolution, "equalization of status between female and male . . . [was] the core of our 1983 statement."[50]

Though less explicitly, the CCAR adoption of its ad hoc committee's report on homosexuality and the rabbinate again reflects the increasing impact of feminism on American Reform. First created in 1986 in response to a resolution proposed by Rabbi Margaret Wenig and (then student rabbi) Margaret Holub, the seventeen member committee met over a period of four years. It sponsored an information session at the 1987 CCAR convention, local consultations, and a plenary session followed by small workshops at the CCAR convention in 1989. The committee's final report was presented to members of the CCAR at the 1990 convention in Seattle, Washington, and was overwhelmingly approved. Perhaps the most widely publicized piece of the report was an endorsement of the HUC-JIR newly introduced policy of viewing the sexual orientation of an applicant to the college institute's rabbinic program "only within the context of a candidate's overall suitability for the rabbinate."[51] This policy reflected a change in the HUC-JIR former policy of denying admission to openly gay or lesbian applicants, and of seeing heterosexuality as a necessary component of rabbinic suitability.

While no one on the floor of the CCAR convention in Seattle openly credited feminism with having influenced their decision, the sensitivity of many within the conference to homophobia as a continuing problem in U.S. society and in the Jewish community (including the Reform community) and the recognition that "greater education and dialogue in our congregations"[52] on this issue is essential, reflects more than a liberal commitment to pluralism.

It also reflects, I think, a growing awareness, largely brought to American consciousness through feminist writings, that religious and societal attitudes toward homosexuality, like religious and societal attitudes toward women and the construction of gender, are culturally based, reflecting the will of a given society (or at least, those invested with power in a given society) more than the will of God. Within the liberal Jewish community, including the Reform community, there also seems to be a growing acknowledgment, as feminist theologian Judith Plaskow has written, that "the creation of Jewish communities in which differences are valued as necessary parts of a greater whole is the institutional and experiential foundation for the recovery of the fullness of Torah."[53]

I do not mean to imply here that either the Reform rabbinate or laity is unanimous in its support of the ordination of gay and lesbian Jews as rabbis. Opposition continues to exist as it undoubtedly will in the future. Nor would I want to imply that those within the Reform movement who value difference agree on the kinds of differences that should be valued. Yet I *am* saying that the feminist emphasis on valuing difference and on *naming* our differences (a conviction that undoubtedly, has encouraged and continues to encourage many lesbians and gays to come out of the closet) echoes the liberal commitment to civil rights and the Reform (and Reconstructionist) commitment both to "unity in diversity" and to the basic Jewish belief that all human beings have been created with equal dignity and worth. As such, it has clarified and strengthened the belief among many Reform Jews (including the majority of Reform rabbis present at the 1990 CCAR convention) that "homosexuality can be a legitimate expression of Jewish and human personhood" and that the Reform movement should accept homosexuals "as they are and not as we [those of us who are heterosexual] would want them to be."[54]

Reconstructionism

The full acceptance of homosexuals and homosexuality is only one indication of the extent to which Reconstructionism, more so than any other contemporary Jewish movement, has been influenced by Jewish feminism. Ideologically committed to change and significantly smaller than Reform, Conservatism, and Orthodoxy (less than two percent of American Jews identify themselves as Reconstructionist, reflected in the relatively small number of Reconstructionist synagogues and *havurot* currently in existence), Reconstructionism has a leadership that is both younger than the other three movements and one comprised equally of men and women. As already noted, the Reconstructionist Rabbinical college (RRC) first opened in 1968, accepting women and men from its inception. In light of these factors, it is perhaps not surprising that the Reconstructionist movement has succeeded in affecting change in areas in which the other movements have not.

As already noted, women have long served as administrators and faculty members at the Reconstructionist Rabbinical college, courses in women's studies are regularly taught, the annual Shulamit Magnes lecture features a prominent feminist speaker, and the Jewish women's studies project at the college sponsors a variety of programs, many of which (including a 1992 retreat) are open to the entire RRC community. In 1989, the movement's prayerbook commission published a new prayerbook for Sabbath eve that is not only gender inclusive in terms of references to God and to the Jewish people, but also addresses head on some of the larger liturgical problems raised by feminists within the American Jewish community.

As David Teutsch, chair of the prayerbook commission, notes in the prayerbook's introduction, for example, the name of God is not translated as Lord both because as a masculine noun, Lord "does not work in terms of gender," and because "it is not consistent with a theology that stresses God's immanence—God made manifest through human action, through nature, and through the workings of the human heart."[55] This theology, first articulated by Rabbi Mordecai Kaplan, the movement's founder and longtime leader, is echoed in the writings of numerous Jewish feminists, many of whom, again not surprisingly, have either chosen to affiliate with Reconstructionism or because of the many similarities between feminist and Kaplanian thought, have been welcomed within the Reconstructionist movement. This welcome not only includes invitations to speak at synagogues at the Reconstructionist Rabbinical College but also to publish works in the movement's scholarly journal, *The Reconstructionist,* and in its growing number of liturgical texts.

Thus, for example, the new Friday evening prayerbook includes several new blessings by Marcia Falk that replace the male, hierarchical form of address: *Baruch Ata Adonai Eloheinu Melech haOlam* (Blessed Are You, Lord

Our God, King of the Universe) with the more inclusive, theologically immanent *N'varekh et ein ha-hayyim* (Let us bless the source of life). It also includes poems by Falk, Merle Feld, Marge Piercy, and other Jewish feminist poets, and commentaries by a number of feminists including Reconstructionist Rabbi Sheila Pelz Weinberg.

Such issues as patrilineality and the ordination of gay and lesbian Jews as rabbis have been dealt with in the Reconstructionist movement more quickly and with far less internal struggle than in the older and larger Reform movement. Its affirmation of patrilineality several years before the 1983 decision of the Reform movement came about with little fanfare and the unanimous approval by those in attendance at the 1993 annual convention of the Reconstructionist Rabbinical Association of a position paper affirming a commitment to "a full place for gay and lesbian members in the leadership of our movement organizations" (a paper passed by the lay arm of the movement, the Federation of Reconstructionist Congregations and Havurot in January 1992) signals an attitude toward sexuality that, consciously or not, is consistent with feminist values. It also, I think, signals an openness to new, and potentially more radical, leadership that has not been matched, and for the foreseeable future shows no indication of being matched, in any of Judaism's other major religious movements.

If, in the recent past, some of the leaders of the Reconstructionist movement have attempted to suppress, modify, or disown feminist activities undertaken either by Reconstructionist rabbinical students or already ordained rabbis, such actions, it seems, have been motivated less by ideological opposition than by financial concern. Without the greater financial resources of Reform, Conservatism, and Orthodoxy, the Reconstructionist movement, and in particular, the Reconstructionist Rabbinical College, continues to struggle for financial stability and support. Thus, the desire of the movement's leadership not to alienate more religiously and politically conservative benefactors is understandable in light of the very serious financial problems with which the movement consistently has been confronted.

Conservative Judaism

Having long afforded girls equality in terms of religious education and participation in the religious activities of its youth groups and summer camps, it was perhaps inevitable that Conservative Judaism would be forced to reevaluate the roles and status of women within the movement as a whole as well as within its particular rabbinic, cantorial, and lay institutions. Ezrat Nashim's "Call for Change," in 1972, to which I previously have alluded, gave greater visibility to the concerns of committed feminists within the Conservatve movement. The formal submission of their demands to the Rabbinical Assembly's law committee led them to receive serious consideration.

Early in 1973, despite some internal opposition, the committee voted to count women in the *minyan,* basing their decision on the changing "contemporary position of women in society."[56] It also brought to the movement's attention its little known 1955 decision allowing women to be called to the Torah, at least on special occasions. Though the decisions of the law committee were not binding, and in most cases, individual rabbis understood themselves to be empowered with deciding for their congregations whether or not to count women in the *minyan* and grant them *aliyot,* within the last twenty years, the number of Conservative congregations granting women these privileges has steadily, and significantly, grown.

Serious discussions concerning women's ordination as Conservative rabbis began in 1973. Though rejected by a majority vote of the law committee, the strong support for women's ordination evinced by Rabbi Gerson Cohen, chancellor of the Jewish Theological Seminary, the movement's ordaining institution, and Wolfe Kelman, executive vice-president of the rabbinical assembly, along with growing support among younger Conservative rabbis and a significant number of rabbinical students at the seminary itself, led to heated debates both in print and in public symposia throughout the 1970s. In October 1977, the majority of those present at the annual meeting of the Rabbinical Assembly voted to establish an interdisciplinary commission that would reexamine the law committee's 1973 decision not to ordain women as Conservative rabbis.

Composed of women and men, rabbis and laity, this commission subsequently attempted to determine whether Jewish law permitted women's ordination and whether ethical, psychological, sociological, educational, symbolic, and pragmatic considerations further supported or opposed the ordination of women. After a two-year period of serious study and extensive interviews with Conservative clergy and laity throughout the United States, the commission recommended to the Rabbinical Assembly that women be admitted into the rabbinical school of the Jewish Theological Seminary of America "on a basis equal to that maintained heretofore by males."[57]

Rejected by the seminary itself, whose senate of faculty and administrators continued to be divided over the issue, the question of whether or not to ordain women as Conservative rabbis subsequently was tabled indefinitely. What kept the issue alive were persistent efforts by supporters of women's ordination to have the faculty senate's decision reconsidered. Indeed, in 1980, by a vote of 156 to 115, the Rabbinical Assembly passed a resolution in favor of women's ordination.[58] Gerson Cohen announced his intention of establishing a program for women parallel to the rabbinic program for men that would enable women to serve as spiritual leaders (or "para-rabbis") of Conservative congregations. In addition, numerous women seeking to enter the rabbinical program remained a visible presence at the seminary throughout the late 1970s and early 1980s.

They took courses and in many cases studied for advanced degrees through the seminary's graduate program. Some applied for admission into the rabbinical program, forcing the admissions committee to at least acknowledge their interest if not seriously consider their application.

Equally significant was the application of Reform rabbi Beverly Magidson in the spring of 1983 for admission into the Rabbinical Assembly. Having previously accepted Reform rabbis as members, the assembly recognized that it could (and in fact narrowly did) reject Magidson's application. It would only be a matter of time before similar applications for admission from Reform and Reconstructionist women rabbis serving, or wishing to serve, Conservative congregations would be accepted. Faced with this realization, members of the Rabbinical Assembly referred the matter to the seminary faculty who, by a vote of 34 to 8, taken on October 23, 1983, agreed to accept women into its rabbinical program beginning in the fall of 1984. In the spring of 1985, Amy Eilberg, who first entered the seminary in 1976 in order to study Talmud, "both because she loved it and because, having decided to become a rabbi . . . believed ordination would eventually be possible"[59] succeeded in becoming the first woman to enter the Conservative rabbinate. As of 1993, that number has grown to over fifty.

Perhaps because the discussion of women's ordination within the Conservative movement took place in the late 1970s and early 1980s, a time in which feminist concerns were increasingly being voiced within U.S. society in general and the American Jewish community in particular, both advocates and opponents of women's ordination acknowledged the great role that feminism had played in precipitating this discussion. While some maintained that the call for women's ordination was a "gimmick" or "fad" linked to feminist concerns that if ignored, might in time fade or go away, others shared Rabbi Robert Gordis' conviction that on ethical and pragmatic grounds both the need for more rabbis to serve the growing number of Conservative congregations and "the call for equal opportunity to serve on the part of Jewish women" made women's rabbinic ordination "a highly desirable, indeed a necessary element in any program designed to advance the health of Judaism and strengthen the survival of the Jewish community."[60]

Since the acceptance of women into its rabbinical school, women have also gained full acceptance into its cantors' institute (including the privilege of investiture). After a protracted struggle, they gained admission into the Cantor's Assembly, the Conservative movement's cantorial professional association, as well. While presumably the models of leadership brought by women to the Conservative rabbinate have been similar to those offered by women in Reform and Reconstructionism, it may be too early to assess the lasting impact of women rabbis and cantors on the Conservative rabbinate and cantorate as a whole.

Certainly, however, the transformation of those Conservative synagogues in which women are counted in the *minyan,* can read from the Torah (whether on Shabbat, holidays, or for one's Bat Mitzvah) and, either as rabbis or cantors, serve as spiritual leaders, already has begun. Increasingly, one finds in Conservative synagogues, adult women engaged in serious religious study and ritual innovation (whether in the synagogue or in their homes). One finds too an increasing number of Conservative women choosing to wear *kipot* and *tallitot* in prayer.

Yet the expanding role of women in the Conservative movement has not been without emotional and institutional costs. Following the ordination of women as rabbis, a small but vocal group of Conservative rabbis and lay people opposed to the seminary's decision left the movement to form their own Union for Traditional Conservative Judaism, now identified simply as The Union for Traditional Judaism (UTJ). As Sylvia Barack Fishman has noted in her recent study of Jewish feminism in the United States:

> The founders hoped that UTJ would attract left-wing Orthodox Jews as well, who they felt had no comfortable home within the Orthodox world and would be natural allies. However, one element standing in the way of this alliance, is the fact that many left-wing Orthodox Jews are liberal on feminist issues. Thus, although the UTJ is far from a single-issue organization, and works for increased intensity of Jewish life on many levels, the issue upon which its birth was precipitated is precisely the issue upon which some potential Orthodox allies might wish the UTJ to be more flexible.[61]

Orthodox Judaism

The Orthodox movement as a whole remains resistant to the kinds of religious changes that feminists have sought to institute in North America, Israel, and elsewhere. Yet the steady growth of the "Women's *Tefillah* [prayer] Network," an informal network created in 1985 by Orthodox women already involved in women-only *tefillah* groups testifies to the impact that feminism has already had on growing numbers of Orthodox women. Created out of feelings of "consternation, disappointment, and anger"[62] over a rabbinic responsum [formal letter or pronouncement] published by five rabbis from Yeshiva University (modern Orthodoxy's rabbinic seminary) banning the formation of women's prayer groups, women involved in the *tefillah* network represent only some of those within contemporary Orthodoxy who are attempting to balance commitment to *halakhah* and to the Jewish communities in which they live with their desire to participate more fully in public worship. Directly or indirectly, this desire has been precipitated by increasing feminist awareness.

As U.S. author and lecturer Blu Greenberg has acknowledged, the encounter between feminism and tradition has not been an easy one. Yet despite what may well be the inherent tension in such an encounter, "there is no going back," she writes, "on the feminist revolution."[63] Some Orthodox rabbis agree. Rabbi Avraham Weiss, for example, has gone so far as to suggest that a course of study be created for women parallel to the rabbinic course of study for men. Without, then, ordaining women as rabbis, Orthodoxy, he suggests could nonetheless involve women in those aspects of the rabbinate, such as "the teaching of Torah and counseling—in which [halakhically] women can fully participate . . . on the same level as men." At the same time, he adds, "a new title must be created for women to serve this purpose."[64]

In Israel, traditional and religiously liberal Jewish women have been praying together at the Western Wall (the Kotel) in Jerusalem since January 1989. Known as "the Women of the Wall," these women, out of deference to the group's Orthodox members, have used traditional liturgical texts and have not considered themselves to be a *minyan*. Halakhically, at least as understood by Orthodoxy, women cannot constitute or count as members of a prayer quorum. Nonetheless, they have become the target of great opposition and occasional violence from ultra Orthodox Jews. At first this violence seems to have been motivated by the fact that these women came to the wall carrying a *sefer Torah* (a Torah scroll). Now presumably, having temporarily lost a law suit brought before the supreme court of Israel, which would have guaranteed their right to carry the Torah, Women of the Wall continue to face opposition from ultra Orthodox Jews who are against women's prayer groups in general. That this group continues to exist and that its members regularly pray at the wall together testifies to the great impact that feminism's notion of equality and Jewish feminism's insistence on women's greater participation in public religious life have had not only on the North American Jewish women who helped create Women of the Wall, but also on the Israeli women who have become ongoing members.

In the United States at least, a small but growing number of Orthodox congregations have welcomed the introduction of newly created ceremonies welcoming baby girls into the Jewish community (a clear reflection of the feminist movement). As Rela Geffen has written, "celebration of the *Bat Mitzvah*," previously "identified with non-Orthodox movements . . . [has become] incorporated into the normative fabric of modern Orthodox life." While such celebration does not include the girl's reading from the Torah, it does include her giving a speech, delivering the *dvar Torah* (sermon) at the close of the synagogue service, or participating more fully, and more publicly, in the worship service by celebrating the *Bat Mitzvah* within the context of a women's prayer group. As Geffen concludes:

The impact of the women's movement on the Orthodox synagogue is an ongoing one that should be carefully monitored. Although these changes are less sweeping than those in other movements, they are not to be taken lightly. In Orthodox synagogues where some of the changes in the context of prayer have not taken place, others outside that context have occurred. For instance, it is much more likely now than it was a decade ago to find Orthodox synagogues in which women are considered members of the congregation, can vote at synagogue meetings, and are eligible to serve on committees and be officers of the congregation.[65]

Conclusion

If one considers Jewish religious life more generally, feminism can also be held responsible for helping to create what seems to be an ever-widening gap between the Reform and Orthodox movements. At the same time, it has brought Reform and Reconstructionism closer together (as evidenced by Reconstructionism's new, formal involvement in the World Union for Progressive Judaism) and in some instances (those concerning the role of women in the synagogue) has brought Reform and Conservatism closer together, while in others (those reflecting attitudes toward conversion and patrilineal descent) has continued to underscore the very real differences between them.

Yet despite these differences, as even opponents of feminism have been force to admit, feminism has already had a significant impact upon all aspects of Jewish life. Slowly, but steadily, it has begun to transform not only the actual religious, educational, and organizational roles that women have come to assume in the Jewish community worldwide, but also women's own perception of what their roles should be. In my view, this latter transformation will lead to even greater demands for change. Despite the fact that increasing opportunities and expectations undoubtedly create new internal and external conflicts, "having tasted the fruit of the tree of knowledge, Jewish women are discovering that there is no road back to Eden."[66]

Notes

Parts of this essay are adapted from my "Feminism and the Reevaluation of Women's Roles within American Jewish Life" (in Haddad and Findly, eds., *Women, Religion, and Social Change* 1985), "Finding God: "Women in the Jewish Tradition," *Cross Currents,* Winter, 1991, "The Impact of Feminism on Reform Judaism in the United States," *The Americanization of the Jews,* eds. Robert Seizer and Norman Cohen, 1995, and "Jewish Feminist Theology,"

Choices in Modern Jewish Thought, second edition, Eugene Borowitz, ed. (1995).

1. Rabbi Gershon C. Bacon, "On the Ordination of Women," November 1979, an unpublished position paper.

2. The continuing publication of *Lilith* magazine since the 1970s has given great visibility to Jewish feminist issues, as have the many bibliographies and books on Jewish women published by Biblio Press.

3. To date, most of these have been established in North America. However, two halakhic women's prayer groups recently have been created in London, apparently following "months of debate within the Orthodox Jewish community," *The Jewish Week* (New York, March 25–April 1, 1993; taken from the *JTA/London Jewish Chronicle*).

4. Blu Greenberg, *On Women and Judaism: A View from Tradition* (Philadelphia, Jewish Publication Society, 1981), 139, 141–142.

5. Greenberg, 139.

6. Eliezer Berkovitz, *Jewish Women in Time and Torah* (Hoboken, N.J., Ktav Publishing, 1990), 134.

7. Susan Grossman, "On Tefillin," in Ellen M. Umansky and Dianne Ashton, eds., *Four Centuries of Jewish Women's Spirituality. A Sourcebook of Modern Jewish Women's Spirituality* (Boston: Beacon Press, 1992), 280.

8. It also parallels Bat Mitzvah, a ceremony created for 12- or 13-year-old Jewish girls in celebration of their achieving religious maturity. Bat Mitzvah was first introduced into the synagogue by American Rabbi Mordecai Kaplan (founder of Reconstructionism) in 1922. By the 1950s, it was introduced into a growing number of Reconstructionist and Conservative congregations in the U.S. and by the 1960s (as Bar Mitzvah made its way back into Reform Judaism), into a growing number of American Reform temples as well. Unlike adult Bat Mitzvah in which the Bat Mitzvah reads from the Torah (as does the 13-year-old Bar Mitzvah), Bat Mitzvah as celebrated by 12- or 13-year-old girls has taken on a variety of forms, from the reading of the Torah (in Reconstructionist, Reform, and most Conservative synagogues) on Shabbat morning, to the reading of the Haftarah (a selection from the prophets that accompanies the week's Torah reading) on Friday night (in some Conservative synagogues), to the recitation of special prayers, poems, or a speech that the Bat Mitzvah has written (in some Orthodox congregations). Bat Mitzvah, then, as celebrated today throughout the world—again, in contrast to the feminist introduction of adult Bat Mitzvah primarily in Canada and the United States—affords girls a religious celebration comparable but not necessarily parallel to the Bar Mitzvah, since it is the belief of many Orthodox and some Conservative rabbis that permitting a women to read from the Torah is an innovation that violates Jewish law.

9. Alan Silverstein, "The Evolution of Ezrat Nashim," *Conservative Judaism* (Fall 1975): 45.

10. From preamble to interim constitution of the Jewish Feminist Organization, quoted in Ann Lapidus Lerner, "'Who Has Not Made Me a Man,': The Movement for Equal Rights for Women in American Jewry," *American Jewish Year Book, 1977* (New York: American Jewish Committee, 1976), p. 7.

11. Rabbi Dr. Jonathan Magonet, letter to Ellen Umansky, November 16, 1992.

12. Mr. S. Rainsbury, respondent, "Would *You* Accept a Female *Rabbi?*" *The Synagogue Review* (June 1966): 216.

13. Susannah Heschel, "Introduction," *On Being a Jewish Feminist: A Reader,* ed. Susannah Heschel (New York: Schocken Books, 1983), xxv, xxiii.

14. Judith Plaskow, *Standing Again at Sinai* (San Francisco: Harper and Row, 1990), 9–10.

15. Rachel Adler, "Feminist Folktales of Justice: Robert Cover as a Resource for the Renewal of Halakhah," *Conservative Judaism* (Spring 1993).

16. Judith Plaskow, *Standing Again at Sinai: Judaism from a Feminist Perspective* (San Francisco: Harper and Row, 1990), 9.

17. Paula Hyman, "The Other Half: Women in the Jewish Tradition," reprinted in Elizabeth Koltun, ed., *The Jewish Woman: New Perspectives* (New York: Schocken Books, 1976), 106–107.

18. Rachel Adler, "'I've Had Nothing Yet So I Can't Take More,'" *Moment* 8 (September 1983) 8: 22.

19. Jacob Neusner, "Introduction," *Understanding Rabbinic Judaism: From Talmudic to Modern Times,* ed. Jacob Neusner (New York: Ktav Publishing House, 1974), 9.

20. Jacob Neusner, "Introduction," 9, 19.

21. Robert Goldenberg, "Talmud," in Barry Holtz, ed., *Back to the Sources: Reading the Classic Jewish Texts* (New York, 1984), 164, 165, 167.

22. Robert Goldenberg, "Talmud," 167.

23. Faith Rogow, "Speaking the Unspeakable: Gays, Jews, and Historical Inquiry," in Christie Balka and Andy Rose, *Twice Blessed: On Being Lesbian, Gay and Jewish* (Boston: Beacon Press, 1989), 71–82.

24. See Drorah Setel, "Feminist Reflections on Separation and Unity in Jewish Theology," *Journal of Feminist Studies in Religion* (vol. 2, no. 1): 113–18.

25. Plaskow, *Standing Again at Sinai,* 101.

26. Plaskow, *Standing Again at Sinai,* 97.

27. Plaskow, *Standing Again at Sinai,* 105.

28. Rebecca Alpert, "Challenging Male/Female Complementarity: Jewish Lesbians and the Jewish Tradition," in Howard Eilberg-Schwartz, ed., *People of the Body: Jews and Judaism from an Embodied Perspective* (Albany SUNY Press, 1992), 362–363.

29. Alpert, "Challenging Male/Female Complementarity," 370.

30. Irving Greenberg, "Community," paper included in the Tikkun Olam curriculum of CLAL (the National Jewish Center for Learning and Leadership) soon to appear in expanded, and published, form.

31. Drorah O'Donnell Setel, "Feminism in Jewish Spirituality," *Whole Earth Review* (Summer 1992): 76–77.

32. Marcia Falk, "Toward a Feminist Jewish Reconstruction of Montheism," *Tikkun,* vol. 4, no. 4, p. 54.

33. Setel, "Feminism in Jewish Spirituality," 77.

34. Janet Marder, "How Women Are Changing the Rabbinate," *Reform Judaism* (Summer 1991): 5.

35. See, for example, "Thoughts of a New Generation: Rabbis of the '90s" in *Reform Judaism* (Summer 1990): 9, in which male and female rabbinic students at HUC-JIR spoke of the importance of balancing family and work.

36. Marder, "How Women are Changing the Rabbinate," p. 7.

37. A description used by Reconstructionist Sandy Sasso in writing about women in the rabbinate, quoted in Marder, "How Women are Changing the Rabbinate," p. 8.

38. I myself served on such a committee during 1990–91 at the Jewish Community Center of White Plains, the Reform congregation to which I belong. I was the only member of the committee to have worked on liturgical change before. The process, for all of us, was an exhilarating one and we have since used the service that we created twice (with members of the committee assuming leadership roles). In deciding to undertake this task, we were encouraged by similar work already accomplished in other Reform congregations.

39. Commenting in 1984 on the recent development of parents creating covenant ceremonies for their daughters, Reform Rabbi Cary D. Kozberg wrote: "[these ceremonies] require greater legitimacy and more widespread acceptance. *Berit Mila* is a male-oriented ritual that carries with it the spiritual and emotional weight of several thousand years. Because of this tremendous weight, it has received more emphasis than the recent ceremonies for baby girls. Though I find it difficult to throw off this male emphasis, I do believe it is necessary to promote more vigorously these rites of passage for girls. Perhaps it is time to standardize them within the Jewish community. Certainly, it is time to infuse them with the 'pomp and circumstance' and emotional energy that has always accompanied circumcision for males," *Journal of Reform Judaism* (Summer 1984): 8. While these ceremonies have not been standardized, they

have for the most part been successfully promoted by Reform rabbis in congregations throughout the United States.

40. Of the many Reform congregations in which I have served as scholar-in-residence over the past few years, approximately half have had such lay committees.

41. Conversation with Eleanor Schwartz, executive director of the National Federation of Temple Sisterhoods, August 5, 1991.

42. Temple sisterhoods were first established in the late nineteenth century as social, educational, and philanthropic organizations. By the second decade of the twentieth century, they were in existence in almost every Reform congregation in the United States. In 1913 they were coordinated on a national level as the National Federation of Temple Sisterhoods.

43. Hopefully in the future studies will be undertaken to see whether feminism has had a similar effect upon the Women's League for Conservative Judaism and for such national organizations as Hadassah and the National Council of Jewish Women.

44. Conversation with Eleanor Schwartz, August 5, 1991.

45. Michael Meyer, *Response to Modernity*, p. 380.

46. Conversation with Nancy Bossov, director of education, Jewish Community Center of White Plains, White Plains, NY, August 6, 1991.

47. My thanks to Sherry Blumberg, Asst. Professor of Education at HUC-JIR in New York for providing me with this information.

48. Michael Meyer, *Response to Modernity*, p. 380.

49. Chaim Stern, "Preface," *Gates of Prayer for Shabbat* (New York: Central Conference of American Rabbis, 1992), v.

50. Herman E. Schaalman, "Patrilineal Descent: A Report and Assessment," *CCAR Yearbook 1987* (Columbus, Ohio: CCAR, 1988): 110.

51. Report of the ad hoc committee on homosexuality and the rabbinate adopted by the convention of the Central Conference of American Rabbis, June 25, 1990, *CCAR Yearbook 1990*, 111.

52. Ad hoc committee report, *CCAR 1990:* 111.

53. Judith Plaskow, *Standing Again at Sinai*, p. 106.

54. Yoel H. Kahn, "Judaism and Homosexuality," *Homosexuality, the Rabbinate, and Liberal Judaism: Papers prepared for the Ad-Hoc Committee on Homosexuality and the Rabbinate* (CCAR, 1989), p. 10, citing and affirming views originally presented to the CCAR in 1973 by Rabbi Sanford Ragins.

55. David Teutsch, "Introduction," *Kol Haneshamah: Shabbat Eve* (Philadelphia: Reconstructionist Press, 1989), xviii.

56. Cited in Sylvia Barack Fishman, *A Breath of Life: Feminism in the American Jewish Community* (New York: Free Press, 1993), 152.

57. "On the Ordination of Women," *Conservative Judaism,* 32 (summer 1979): 78.

58. Sylvia Fishman, *A Breath of Life,* 213.

59. Aviva Cantor, "Rabbi Eilberg," *Ms.* (December 1985), 46.

60. Robert Gordis, "On the Ordination of Women" (unpublished paper, 1983?).

61. Sylvia Barack Fishman, *A Breath of Life,* 59.

62. Rela Geffen [Monson], "The Impact of the Jewish Women's Movement on the American Synagogue: 1975–1985," in Susan Grossman and Rivka Haut, eds., *Daughters of the King: Women and the Synagogue* (Philadelphia: JPS, 1992), 232.

63. Blu Greenberg, *On Women and Judaism,* 159.

64. Avraham Weiss, "First woman set for Conservative ordination looks to future," *The Jewish Week* (March 1, 1985) cited in Fishman, *A Breath of Life,* 215.

65. Geffen, "Impact of Women's Movement," 233.

66. Ellen Umansky in "Feminism and the Reevaluation of Women's Roles within American Jewish Life," in Yvonne Yazbeck Haddad and Ellison Banks Findly, eds., *Women, Religion, and Social Change* (Albany: State University of New York Press, 1985), 492.

Chapter 6

Feminism in World Christianity

Rosemary Radford Ruether

In the minds of many people, feminism in Christianity is assumed to be both a modern development that began about the 1960s and a white Western middle-class movement. In this essay I wish to show that feminism has much older roots in Christianity and also that increasingly it is a multicultural global movement. Feminism, moreover, has generally been linked with other movements of emancipation, racial-ethnic, economic, and national, and these links become explicit among Christian feminists outside of privileged Western settings.

Roots of Feminism in Christianity

Christianity from its New Testament beginnings exhibited a deep tension between egalitarian and patriarchal views of women. Feminist scholars of the New Testament and early church are increasingly showing that the polemics against women's leadership found in New Testament and patristic writers can only be explained by recognizing an alternative understanding of the gospel as the "good news" of the dissolution of gender hierarchy in the new humanity in Christ that arises from the baptismal font.[1]

Patristic Christianity repressed this radical vision by spiritualizing it as equality in holiness and by pointing to its realization beyond the grave in heaven. But from the Montanists and gnostics of the second century through Medieval Christianity and the Reformation and into modern times, reform movements continued to arise in Christianity. They understood the texts of Galatians 3:28: "There is no longer male and female: for you are all one in Christ Jesus," and Acts 2:17: "In the last days it will be, God declares, that I will pour out my Spirit upon all flesh, and your sons and your daughters shall prophesy" as meaning that gender hierarchy should be dissolved also in the church, as the beginning of a redeemed society on earth.[2]

The late Middle Ages saw a renewal of radical sectarian movements that challenged the hegemony of the ruling nobility and clerical hierarchy over the interpretation of Christianity. Far from being the representatives of God, these Christian sectarians suggested that such authorities actually were the beast and the Anti-Christ of New Testament apocalyptic. They believed that theirs was the time in which God was sending forth the Spirit in anticipation of final redemption, empowering those outside these centers of power, both men and women, to prophesy.[3]

In the same period the Renaissance was bringing new tools for critical reading of the Christian tradition and widening the base of education to include lay men and women. The invention of printing allowed an emerging urban middle class to become book owners. Even though women were excluded from universities, it now became possible for fathers to choose to give daughters a high level of education through tutoring and study at home. Previously, educated women were mostly nuns, and their education focused on spiritual reading and generally excluded the new humanistic studies.

From the fifteenth through the early seventeenth century, a debate raged on the "nature" of women, mostly between men, but with some women with the new humanistic education joining the debate. Both biblical and classical texts were cited pro and contra to prove that women were essentially inferior and prone to evil or to disprove this thesis, claiming that these same texts showed greater evidence of women's equal capacity for virtue and intelligence. The literature of this *querelle des femmes* can be regarded as the first feminist literature in which women's nature and capacities were explicitly debated.[4]

One of the first humanistically educated women to join this debate was Christine de Pizan (1365–1430?). Born in Venice, Christine grew up in the court of Charles V in France, the daughter of the king's physician and astrologer. Widowed at twenty-five with three children, Christine used her education to make a living by writing, one of the first examples of a lay woman professional author. Her most well known works, *The Book of the City of the Ladies* and *The Treasure of the City of the Ladies* (both 1405) defend the equal intelligence of women with men against women's detractors, such as the author of the second part of the *roman de la rose*.[5]

In these books Christine argues for women's right to equal education. Through models of holy, virtuous, and intelligent women, picked from Christian as well as from classical literature, Christine seeks to model the full capacity of women for leadership in many walks of life. Her stress on Christian women, in contrast to the prevailing humanistic tendency to draw examples of powerful women only from pagan literature, is intended to show that women's leadership and virtue is the fulfillment of a women's relation to Christ.

In the Reformation period the *querelle des femmes* became more explicitly biblical. The detractors of women made Eve the center piece of their argument of women's proneness to sin. This meant that women's defenders began to dispute and reinterpret the view of women that had been drawn from the Bible. In numerous writings by women of this genre in late sixteenth- and seventeenth-century England, certain arguments become standard. Genesis 1:26 is used to argue for women's equal creation with man in the image of God, and her essential goodness. To claim that woman is essentially evil is an insult to the creator. The fact that woman is created last proves that she is the crown of creation, just as man is created after animals.

The defenders of women go on to claim that woman is no more guilty of the fall than man. Woman responded innocently to the serpent's appeal, but the male showed his lack of virtue in his passive acquiescence to what he knew to be against God's command. But the real sin is not eating the apple, but rather the male railing against women, exemplified by Adam's attempt to blame Eve for sin. It is this railing that is the real cause of the loss of paradise, that happy harmony between the sexes that God intended.

But God has mercy on woman by decreeing that the line of salvation that would overcome the serpent would come from the "seed of women." Old Testament heroines, as well as female disciples of Jesus, are cited to show that women have been key players in salvation history, culminating in the betrayal of Jesus by his male disciples, while his female disciples remained faithful at the cross and were the first witnesses of the resurrection. Women leaders in the Pauline epistles are also noted to show that God used women as well as men to spread the gospel in the early church.[6]

In the second half of the seventeenth century, Margaret Fell, leader of the Society of Friends, would pick up these arguments and explicitly develop them to argue for woman's right to preach and to participate in church leadership, in her tract *Woman's Speaking Justified, Proved and Allowed of by the Scriptures* (1666).[7] For Fell woman's equality with man in the image of God finds its realization in Christ. The female disciples of Jesus as the first witnesses of the resurrection are the foundation of that prophetic community upon whom God's spirit has fallen. Women are called to preach equally with men, for God's spirit has fallen upon them as much as upon men at Pentecost.

The Society of Friends in the second half of the seventeenth century produced dozens of such female writers whose tracts implicitly or explicitly laid claim to women's right to preach and teach in the Christian community.[8] Friends founded their inclusion of women in the two claims that women had an equal spiritual nature with men and that redemption in Christ has included women as much as men. Endowed with the prophetic Spirit women is not only allowed, but mandated, to speak out against those systems of evil that deny this truth.

However, the Quaker movement failed to generate a feminist movement in society in this period. Following long-standing Christian theological patterns that split church as redemptive community from the "world" as the arena of sin, Quakers claimed spiritual equality for women as prophetic truth-sayers in the church. But they did not challenge the patriarchal patterns of society, including the roles of men and women in marriage within the Society of Friends itself.

Seventeenth-century England also saw a flowering of women writers from the Anglican upper classes, continuing the Renaissance tradition of the humanistically trained woman who writes for a private circle in her home or engages in modest social endeavors under the aegis of charity for the less privileged.[9] One such woman, Mary Astell, wrote sharply in denunciation of the injustice of the marital relation for women and argued for women's right to an education.[10] Influenced by the Cambridge Platonists, Astell based her argument for women's right to cultivate their intellect on the belief that this was their means to knowledge of God in this life and beyond. But she too did not challenge the injustice of the political structures of women's subordination.[11]

A wholistic feminism no longer foundering on the split between church and world, spirituality and society, awaited the Enlightenment and liberal social theory of the late eighteenth and nineteenth centuries. Liberalism challenged the traditional Christian doctrine of the "orders of creation," that interpreted class and gender hierarchy as "natural" and divinely ordained. Basing itself on the claim that all humans have the same essential "nature," it interpreted social hierarchies as distortions of the original "natural order," giving unjust privilege to the few, while denying the many their rights to equal status before the law.

However, most male liberals made this argument on behalf of the propertied middle-class man against the old aristocracy. They had no intention of dismantling gender or class hierarchy that allowed the European middle class to rule over women and propertyless servant-class or enslaved males. Thus it fell to a new wave of feminists of the late eighteenth and nineteenth centuries to make the claim for women's inclusion in the "rights of man."

Christian Feminism in the United States

In the United States many of these liberal feminists of the 1840s rose from or joined the Quaker tradition, marrying its traditional belief in women's spiritual equality with the liberal tenets of "natural" equality. This union allowed these women to challenge women's political and legal, as well as their cultural and spiritual, subordination. Sarah and Angelina Grimké, Lucretia Mott and Susan B. Anthony represent these Quaker liberal feminists, although others, such as Antoinette Brown or Elizabeth Cady Stanton moved from mainstream Protestantism to free thought or Unitarian traditions.[12]

In these nineteenth-century American feminists we see two views of the Christian tradition that will have echoes in the 1970s–90s. One group stands solidly on the Bible, claiming that equality of women with men is the authentic meaning of God's creation of Adam, male and female, "in the image of God." The subordination of women violates God's will and the true "order of creation." This is the view taken by Quaker feminist Sarah Grimké, in her 1837 *Letters on the Equality of the Sexes and the Condition of Women.*[13]

Another group moves to the margins of the Christian tradition through free thought and even becomes explicitly anti-Christian. For Elizabeth Cady Stanton, who organized the "women's revising committee" that produced the *Women's Bible,* women's right to full humanity is brought to testify against the sexism of the Bible. Matilda Josyln Gage, in her 1893 tract, *Woman, Church and State,* indicts the whole Jewish and Christian tradition as the bearers of patriarchal oppression, over against female-centered cultures of the Mediterranean world that worshiped goddesses and honored women's power.[14]

Post-Christian or anti-Christian feminism underlies the major forms of secular feminist theory in modern Western culture. French feminism, influenced by revolutionary liberalism in the late eighteenth century and then by socialism in the nineteenth and twentieth centuries, has been predominately secular. Religion has been seen, not simply as irrelevant, but as the enemy of women's rights, and indeed the enemy of progress toward social justice generally. Olympe de Gouges, author of the 1789 tract "The Declaration of the Rights of Woman and Citizen," sought to counter the exclusion of women from the "Rights of Man and Citizen" of the male revolutionaries. She fell afoul of the power of Robespierre and was guillotined on November 3, 1793.[15]

In the 1830s the San Simonian and utopian socialist movements birthed new feminist movements that argued for women's equality, not simply in political rights, but in the rights to economic participation equally with men. For utopian socialists, this meant changing the structure of the family, as well as the public order. Only when women have the right to birth control and are no longer made the primary caretakers of children and drudges of domestic work, can there be social and economic parity of women with men.[16]

In the 1940s feminism was reborn in France with the work of Simone de Beauvoir, *The Second Sex.* Beauvoir herself moved from a primarily Marxist view of feminism as an integral part of the class struggle to an increasing recognition that gender hierarchy is distinct and entails different issues that are typically ignored by Marxist theory focused on the "worker." Sexuality and the control of women's bodies and reproductive capacity are central to male control over women.[17] Such secular feminism, however, had no interest in the feminist reconstruction of Christianity. Christianity was dismissed at the outset.

It thus has fallen to U.S. North American Christians to be the primary bearers of the option of Christian feminism in the late 1960s and 70s, although the United States also has its share of secular feminists of various types. The reason why so much feminist theology has sprung from the United States until recently seems to me to reflect both the greater diversity of Christianities in the

United States, and a lesser influence of secularity and especially of Marxism on the popular culture.

The separation of church from state at the time of the American revolution in the late eighteenth century allowed the church to become highly pluralistic, representing a great diversity of ethnic and political cultures. The lack of an established church as a foil for radical secularity has meant that progressive movements were more likely to stay within and find expression in some form of Christianity. Social views from left to right tended to be debated within the context of Christian symbols, rather than progressives aligning themselves against Christianity as the enemy of progress.

Women's ordination also won its earliest victories in the United States, with some women being ordained in the Congregationalist, Unitarian, Universalist, and Methodist Protestant traditions, already in the second half of the nineteenth century. Other Protestant denominations placated the demand of women for ordination by inventing deaconess and missionary roles, but this also meant that women began to appear as students in the institutions of higher theological education in the 1880s. It was from this first wave of theologically educated women, capable also of handling biblical languages, that Elizabeth Cady Stanton drew her "women's revising committee" for the *Women's Bible* in the 1890s.

There was a long latency period between the first victories for women's ordination in the nineteenth century and the rapid spread of ordination in mainline Protestantism from 1956 to the present. Yet once ordination was a well-established possibility in the 1970s, the numbers of women in theological education rose rapidly in the United States to one-third to one-half of seminary students. Reflecting this large presence of women students, as well as parallel movements of women's studies in colleges and universities, theological schools began to seek women professors in all fields of the curriculum. Most of these women theological educators brought with them a feminist agenda for revising the field.

This has meant that from 1968 until the present there has been an extraordinary outpouring of increasingly sophisticated feminist critique and reconstruction of all fields of theological education; scripture, church history, theology and ethics, pastoral psychology, preaching, worship, and the study of ministry. Whereas twenty years ago a feminist scholar could keep abreast of the major works on feminism across fields, today it would be difficult to read the major work simply within specialized areas of the theological curriculum.[18]

However, the secular bias of American universities means that feminist scholars in theological education are more likely to be versed in feminist studies in cognate fields of the secular curriculum than vice versa. A feminist scholar of American church history will be likely to keep up with major feminist studies in American women's history, while secular feminist historians may be much less aware of the work going on in church history. Likewise feminist theologians are likely to read secular feminist linguistic theory, while secular feminist theorists are generally oblivious to feminist theology. Thus the dialogue between secular and Christian feminism tends to be literary and one-sided, rather than a mutual meeting in the same forums of discourse. This is unfortunate.[19]

In the 1970s the élan of Christian feminist thought began to ramify in three different directions. Mary Daly, one of the pioneers of feminist critique of Christianity in her 1968 book, _The Church and the Second Sex,_ moved to the margins of Christianity in her 1973 volume, _Beyond God the Father,_ and then into increasingly militant repudiation, not only of Christianity, but even of the commonality of women with men in her 1979 _Gynecology_ and 1984 _Pure Lust._[20]

Other feminist students of religion, such as Carol Christ, followed a similar trajectory from critique to rejection. These feminist "thealogians" gave up on trying to affirm positive resources for women in the Christian tradition. Instead they sought to reclaim feminist roots from pre-Christian religions repressed by biblical faiths, or invent feminist spirituality and religion from women's contemporary experience.[21]

On the other side of the spectrum, evangelical feminists represented by books such as Letha Scanzoni and Nancy Hardesty's _All We're Meant to Be: A Biblical Approach to Women's Liberation_ and journals such as _Daughters of Sarah,_ sought to affirm the adequacy of biblical faith for women's liberation.[22] Patriarchy, for these writers, is seen primarily as a postbiblical distortion, not the authentic meaning of the scriptures. Careful exegesis will show that the true intention of the biblical writers is women's full equality with men and mutuality between the sexes.

Between these two wings of post-Christian rejectionism and evangelical feminism stands an array of intermediate positions. One important cluster of Christians feminists take what might be called a dialectical position. The Bible and the Christian tradition is seen as deeply androcentric and misogynist. This is not simply a "misinterpretation" or "later corruption," but reflects the bias of the major texts themselves, as conceived of and written by men in a patriarchal culture.

But this identification of the patriarchal content of biblical and later historical teachings does not exhaust the meaning of Christian faith. There is also a liberating experience of the faith that has continually broken through among communities of women and men, mediating an alternative experience of God and community. This liberating understanding is also enshrined within the historical texts, although overlaid with processes of patriarchal suppression and reinterpretation. It is not so much the texts themselves, but the community of liberation that is the context in which the liberating message is reclaimed and reinterpreted for today.

Various feminist liberation theologians, including Letty Russell, Rosemary Ruether, Elisabeth Schüssler Fiorenza, Mary Hunt, Beverley Harrison, and Carter Heyward, can be seen as falling into this camp of dialectical feminism.[23] It is characteristic of these feminist theologians, biblical scholars, and ethicists that they also relate themselves to other liberation movements. They identify with theologies from oppressed classes and peoples. They see the struggle of women's liberation in the context of an interstructured system of oppression of race, class, gender, and sexual orientation, both within nations and across the lines of an international system of neocolonialism.

In the 1980s there were a number of new developments in North American feminist theology. One development was to move into a deeper consideration of methodology, epistemology, and linguistic deconstruction, questioning basic concepts, such as the possibility of any universally referential language and the very concept of a "self." Dialogue with French feminism was a major impetus to this discussion of the epistemological underpinnings of any feminist thought that uses language forms that have been shaped by male consciousness.[24] Religious scholars, such as Rebecca Chopp and Katherine Keller, have raised these questions in a theological context.[25]

Another area of development has been the multicontextualization of feminist theology across ethnic and cultural lines. African-American women have long made clear that their female experience has differed significantly from that of middle-class white women. Not only were their mothers the slaves or servants of white women, but the relation of black women with black men must be placed in the context of a common liberation struggle from racism, even though the black community and church also have their problems of sexism.

Following the lead of writer Alice Walker, African-American women claimed the name "womanist"[26] for themselves to distinguish the distinct historical and cultural context in which they affirm themselves vis-à-vis both the sexism of the black community and the racist and sexist systems of white society. The patterns of the black church provide a distinct milieu that shapes the whole African-American culture. Even less than in white America is there a split between church and society for African-Americans.

A new generation of theologically trained African-American women began to speak and write, articulating this "womanist" perspective on theology and ethics. Womanist theologians look to the distinct historical experience and religious culture of African-Americans, but draw in particular on reclaimed traditions of preaching and literary writing of black women. Jacquelyn Grant spelled out the very different issues that black women bring to Christology in her *White Woman's Christ/Black*

Woman's Jesus.[27] Katie Cannon drew on the rediscovered writings of Zora Neale Hurston to shape a womanist ethics.[28]

Another ethnic community of women that began to find their distinct voice was Hispanic-Americans, a group whose origins range across Central and Latin America and the Caribbean, and whose racial roots combine white Europeans, Africans, and indigenous peoples. Even their history and political status in North American differs markedly. Hispanics from the southwest of the United States trace their ancestors back centuries before Anglos appeared in the area. Like indigenous peoples, they are the people of a conquered territory. Chicanos are their cousins from south of the border who struggle with the U.S. exploitive policies of immigration.

Most Cubans in the United States define themselves against the Castro regime in Cuba, while Puerto Ricans are American citizens, although some may relate to independence movements. Both bring with them a substantial mixture of Afro-Caribbean culture. Central Americans fleeing from oppressive regimes in Guatemala or El Salvador bring these tragedies and also struggle with immigration policies, while Hispanics from the many countries of the Southern Cone have other agendas. What defines U.S. Hispanics as a community is their colonization by North America and their common struggle to retain their language and culture in Anglo society.

Hispanic American women theologians and pastors claimed the name "mujerista" to define their distinct context, culturally and historically, in which they struggle for their personhood. Like African-American women, mujerista theologians seek to stand with their Hispanic menfolk against the common racist and cultural oppression of the Anglo context. But they also identify distinct patterns, derived from Spanish Catholic culture, of sexual and gender oppression of women, as well as valued liberatory resources that come from the blending of folk cultures in their families.[29]

Another community that began to find its distinct voice was lesbian Christian feminists. Lesbians have produced a distinct literary culture for generations. After the gay pride movement of the 70s lesbians emerged from the shadows of the gay male perspective to speak for their own experience as female identified women. Lesbians identify with the two protest movements of feminism and gay rights, and yet have often been marginalized by both movements, by feminists as lesbians and by gay males as females.

Lesbian Christians also experience a painful double jeopardy from the churches. Churches willing to open their doors to token numbers of women in ministry seek those women least likely to challenge their stereotypes of female compliance with male power. Lesbians threaten this power at its core as women who bond with other women, sexually and socially. Yet many women pastors and theologians have been willing to brave the negativity, not only to "come out" as lesbians in the church, but to do theological reflection from the lesbian context. Mary Hunt, Jeannine Grammick, Carter Heyward, and Joanne Brown are among those contributing to an emerging lesbian feminist theological literature.[30]

An emerging subtheme of feminist theory and theology in the 1980s is eco-feminism. Eco-feminism reflects on the interconnection between the subordination of women and the domination of nature in patriarchal culture; more particularly in the Christian and post-Christian West. Much eco-feminist thought has rejected Christianity altogether, accepting the view that Christianity is not only inherently antifemale, but also antinature and that these two negativities are closely intertwined. Many eco-feminists who feel that a new spirituality and consciousness is essential to the transformed relation to women and nature that is needed seek this in ancient goddess religions.[31]

Some Christian feminists, however, have sought to combine the critique of antiwoman, antinature patterns in Christianity with a positive reconstruction of an ecological feminist theology that draws on biblical and Christian resources. Among these is Rosemary Ruether in the United States, Anne Primavesi in England, and Catharina Halkes in Holland.[32] Eco-feminism brings together a new synthesis of critical reflection, drawing on history of ideas, socio-economic analysis, and cosmological and earth sciences. Feminist theology is challenged to address the patriarchalism as well as the positive resources of the scientific world picture in ways that have not been addressed by feminist theology heretofore.[33]

Spirituality, worship, and the arts represent another area of outreach of Christian feminism. As women feel pushed to the margins of the churches, but still hunger for worship and spirituality, feminist liturgical communities develop. The woman-church movement in the United States was born in 1980 and continues to grow. A multiplicity of different women prayer and worship groups that express different religious and cultural contexts have sprung up.[34] But not all feminist worship materials are addressed to independent women's groups. Many are also being adopted by progressive congregations of mainline denominations or are used by women clergy for special gatherings. Miriam Therese Winter's *Woman Prayer, Woman Song: Resources for Ritual* is one expression of this work of providing feminist resources for worship.[35]

European Feminist Theology

Although U.S. North Americans have made a major contribution to Christian feminist thought in recent decades, European Christian feminists began to network and build their own journals and organizations in the mid-1980s. In Ireland feminist theology began to appear on the curriculum of some es, but mostly found its sponsorship in special institutes and in women's discussion and liturgy groups, some claiming the name of "women-church." Led by feminist theologians Ann Louise Gilligan and Katherine Zappone, Irish feminists founded the journal *Womanspirit* to explore feminist spirituality in an Irish context.[36]

Irish feminists, mostly Roman Catholics, share the common experience of sexist oppression from the Roman Catholic Church whose influence reaches across Irish society to influence social policies on divorce, birth control, and abortion. Some Irish feminists, such as Katherine Zappone, found in grassroots work with poor women the context for reflection on a liberating spirituality that could revision the themes of God-language, conversion, and transformation of the earth.[37] Others, such as Mary Condren, moved to the margins of the Christian tradition, looking back to pre-Christian Celtic roots for inspiration in her *The Serpent and the Goddess: Women, Religion and Power in Celtic Ireland.*[38] In a land littered with the ruins, not only of medieval Christian, but also of neolithic Celtic Ireland, such explorations have a very concrete presence and meaning.

Celtic explorations and reclaimed roots also have power for English feminists, especially in Wales and Scotland. But much of English Christian feminism has been absorbed in the struggle for women's ordination in a society where the Church of England still has great symbolic social power, however small a percentage of the population actually gather in its hallowed precincts. Despite over a quarter of a century of organized effort, the Church of England moved to actually allow women priests only in 1992.

The deeply explosive tensions that the feminist challenge surfaces among traditional Anglican churchmen was highlighted in February 1991, when male seminarians and clergy, who had organized themselves against the ordination of women at the prestigious Westcott House at Cambridge University, raided the chapel, seizing the book on liturgical resources *All Desires Known,* by Anglican feminist writer Janet Morley. Carrying the book to the courtyard, the men burned it with suitable incantations.[39]

Anglican feminists founded the network of Women in Theology in the 1980s, while British Roman Catholics developed the parallel Catholic Women's Network. These networks host regular lectures and workshops on feminist issues in the church and society. In the summer of 1992 British and Irish feminists realized the establishment of a summer school on feminist theology to be held at St. David's University in Lampeter, Wales. The first summer's curriculum covered such topics as sources and traditions for feminist theology, the contribution of social sciences to feminist theology, feminist ethics, politics, and spirituality. This same network of British and Irish feminists also brought out in 1992 the first volume of their new journal, *Feminist Theology.*[40]

British feminists also are divided between those who seek to reclaim the historical tradition and those who have decided that it cannot be reclaimed, but is intrinsically hostile to women. The first position is represented by British Catholic feminist theologian Mary Grey. Her first major book, *Redeeming the Dream: Feminism, Redemption and Christian Tradition*,[41] focuses on mutuality and relatedness as the basis of rethinking both the practice of ethics and spirituality, and also the major Christian doctrines. Grey also plays a major role in European feminist theology, having been named as the successor to Dr. Catherina Halkes' chair in feminist theology at the University of Nijmegen in Holland. Grey was also president of the European Society of Women in Theological Research for its fourth meeting at Bristol University in 1991.

In Britain the major spokeswoman for the rejectionist position is Dr. Daphne Hampson, who was the first president of the European society. Daphne Hampson speaks with particular authority since she emerges from the heart of the Church of England. She did a doctorate in modern history at Oxford University and a doctorate in theology at Harvard University in Cambridge, Massachusetts. Formerly a member of the Scottish Episcopal Church, she founded the Group for the Ministry of Women in that church and for many years wrote vigorously in favor of women's ordination, refuting the theological and scriptural arguments of its opponents. Hampson wrote the theological statement in favor of women's ordination that was circulated to all members of the general synod of the Church of England before the vote on women's ordination in 1978.

However, the frustration of this struggle convinced Hampson that her effort was wrong-headed. The determined resistance of traditionalists to women's ordination reflected fixed, unchangeable limits to the Christian religion. Hampson decided that Christianity is incompatible with feminism and indeed with modern scientific truth. Christianity cannot be reformed to become compatible with feminism because its root authority must always go back to the scriptures that validate a patriarchal view of God, humanity, and the world. Christianity is not only false, it is unethical, in Hampson's view. Thus, to be intellectually and ethically consistent, a feminist must leave Christianity.

Hampson articulated her reasons for this decision in her 1990 book, *Theology and Feminism*.[42] In this book Hampson argues that the fundamental Christian view of God, Christ, and divine-human relations are built on patriarchal domination of men over women. Hampson also criticizes what she sees as the inconsistency of Christian feminists such as Rosemary Ruether, Sallie McFague, Letty Russell, Elisabeth Fiorenza, Carter Heyward, and Phyllis Trible in seeking to make an essentially patriarchal scripture and theology compatible with feminism.

Although Hampson repudiates Christianity, she does not reject belief in God or the need for spirituality independent of Christianity. In subsequent writings, she seeks to delineate her view of this non-Christian feminist theology and spirituality. Despite her stance, Hampson continues to lecture in systematic theology in the faculty of divinity of St. Mary's College, St. Andrew's University, Scotland. She has also chosen to worship with (although not join) the Quaker Meeting in Fife, Scotland. This has influenced other British women to seek out the Quakers as an option for feminists who feel no longer able to identify with the mainline Christian churches.

A few theological faculties in Britain have begun to offer the possibility of study of feminist theology. Among these are the Universities of Lancaster, Bristol, and King's College, London. The Lancaster program was developed by German-born feminist scholar Ursula King, who now heads the department at Bristol. In books such as her 1984 *Voices of Protest-Voices of Promise: Exploring Spirituality for a New Age* and her 1989 *Women and Spirituality: Voices of Protest and Promise*[43] King has sought to chart the major paradigms of feminist spirituality in Christianity, as well as in other world religions.

Feminist ethicist Grace Jantzen teaches in the philosophy of religion area at King's College. She is currently working on two major books: one feminist ethics, *Connection or Competition: Reconsidering Ethics* and one on spirituality, *Power, Gender and Christian Mysticism.*[44]

Western Europe, especially France, has had a long tradition of militant feminism, as has been indicated earlier. But Christian feminism has been weak, particularly in France, due to the inhospitable ambiance of Roman Catholicism for feminism and the choice of most French feminists of an anti-Christian position. Holland and Germany are two European countries where there has been major development of feminist theology in the last twenty-five years. Protestant women can be ordained in those countries, but the ambiance for feminist theology is one of national culture, and not simply denomination. Roman Catholics have been well represented among Dutch and German feminists, as well as in Britain (Ursula King and Mary Grey are both Roman Catholics).

Dr. Catherina Halkes, a Roman Catholic, has been a major representative of feminist theology in Holland and Europe for many years. She held the first chair of feminist theology at the University of Nijmegen. Halkes has authored a number of major books and many articles in the area of feminist revisioning of Christian anthropology and spirituality.[45] Halkes, now retired from Nijmegn, but still active in writing and lecturing, was honored for her "foremother role" by being asked to give one of the plenary speeches at the 1991 meeting of the European Society of Women for Theological Research at Bristol.

Halkes spoke on "Humanity Re-imaged: New Directions in Feminist Theological Anthropology." In this address Halkes argued against radical French feminists, such as Luce Irigaray, and in favor of an inclusive humanness, male and female. She expressed her belief that the Christian understanding of God, rightly understood, supports this inclusive "becoming" of women and men together.

Many other Dutch women are actively teaching, writing, and doing pastoral work from a feminist perspective. Among these are Riet Bons-Storm, professor of women studies, pastoral theology and psychology at the University of Groningen. Her 1992 book, *Feminist Pastoral Care: A Challenge to the Churches,* drew on a survey of work being done in pastoral care to women all over Holland.[46] Many of the women seeking such care are survivors of sexual violence and incest, and feel alienated from the churches where they feel they cannot tell their stories or receive support. For many women these experiences also raise basic questions about power, the nature of sex and love, relation to God, and redemption.

Annie Imbens-Fransen, founder and coordinator of the Foundation for Pastoral Care for Women in Holland, has also focused on the impact of incest on women's view of God and religion. She has concluded that the patriarchal character of Christianity makes women easy prey for sexual abuse in their families and also afraid to reveal their experience. The image of God is deeply affected by this abuse. Many Christian women turn away from the church because they think of God as an abusive male power. She asks how changed images of God can help women's healing process.[47]

Theologian and church historian Freda Droes was the chair of the interuniversity workgroup "Feminism and Theology." She teaches women's studies theology at the Catholic University in Amsterdam. One of her major projects is the recovery of earlier representatives of feminist theology in Holland in the first half of the twentieth century. She is also looking back to the earliest texts in Dutch in the thirteenth century up to the present to recover women's writings. Her aim is to create a tradition for Dutch women's theological work.[48]

In Germany Dorothy Sölle has been the woman theologian with the highest profile and longest publication record.[49] Yet Sölle has never received a university position in Germany and has taught part-time at Union Theological Seminary in New York for many years. Sölle's theological reflection is rooted in her deep involvement in the peace movement. Suffering and the struggle to end all forms of violence is central to her theological reflection. In the 1980s she began more explicitly to include the experience of women's suffering under patriarchy in her thought. This was expressed in her 1984 book, *The Strength of the Weak: Toward a Christian Feminist Identity.*[50]

Sölle was also recognized for her preeminence by being asked to give a plenary address at the Bristol meeting of the European Society. There she spoke on "Liberating our God-Talk: From Authoritarian Otherness to Mystical Inwardness." In this talk she confronted the patriarchal image of an authoritarian male God as a false and dangerous misrepresentation of divine transcendence. Not only does such a concept of God justify male dominance and female subordination, but it ratifies a concept of divine power based on aggressive violence.

Sölle argued that feminist theology must not only change the pronouns for God. It must change the power dynamics of the God-human relation. A God of mystical inwardness, which also calls us to vulnerable resistance to all forms of violence, is a much more authentic representation of the "otherness" of a God who is also a crucified God, than images of a nonrelational all-powerful male "outside" and "above" us. To believe in the God revealed in Jesus is to stop holding oppressive power over others, to become a woman, to become one of the weak and oppressed of the world. It means "to bear the consequences of love, to suffer with God."[51]

Germany has a growing number of feminist theological writers and universities where some women's studies in theology are taught, although not without continuing struggle. One of the actions taken at the Bristol meeting of the European Society was an official protest to Walter Kapsar, bishop of Rottenburg-Stuggart, who denied Dr. Silvia Schroer the *nihil obstat* needed for appointment to the Catholic faculty of the University of Tübingen. Schroer did her advanced degrees at the University of Fribourg in Switzerland, with particular areas of interest in feminist exegesis, and in images of the goddess and the personification of God as wisdom.[52]

German feminist scholars have taken feminist exegesis of scripture as a major concern, both for teaching and for preaching and pastoral work. In 1990 a feminist exegesis work group based in Frankfort produced the two-volume *Feministisch gelesen* aimed at providing feminist exegesis of biblical texts for preaching and for group study. The editors of this work were Eva Renate Schmidt, an ordained minister and leader in the Reformed Church, together with Mieke Korenhof and Renate Jost. Forty-five feminist exegetes contributed to the essays in these two volumes, mostly from Germany, but some scholars from other European countries and from the United States were also included.[53]

Among the German feminist theologians best known in North America is Elisabeth Moltmann-Wendel. Her 1985 *A Land Flowing with Milk and Honey*[54] surveyed a range of issues raised by feminist theology, such as images of God, relation to Jesus, and anthropology, as well as questions of a matriarchal subculture and the revival of goddess religion, a topic much discussed among German feminists. Moltmann-Wendel's work has tended to be overshadowed by her famous theologian husband, Jürgen Moltmann. They have also done work together on anthropology and God-language, such as their 1991 publication *God—His and Hers*.[55]

In Scandinavia Kari Borresen stands as one of the earliest and foremost feminist scholars in religion, having published her groundbreaking work in theological anthropology, *Subordination and Equivalence: The Nature and Role of Women in Augustine and Thomas Aquinas* in French in 1968.[56] Borresen has pursued the question of theological anthropology and the understanding of the "image of God" in patristic and medieval theology for many years, editing a major volume on this topic, *Image of God and Gender Models in the Judaeo-Christian Tradition.* It gathered together both her own work and that of other scholars, such as Danish New Testament scholar Lone Fatum, at the University of Copenhagen, Kari Vogt at the University of Oslo, and Giulia Sfameni Gasparro at the University of Messina, Italy. Phyllis Bird, at Garrett-Evangelical Seminary at Evanston, Illinois, contributed the foundational exegetical essay on the interpretation of the Genesis text.[57]

Borresen's research into concepts of anthropology, male and female, and the understanding of God has taken her into explorations of the work of medieval mystics, such as Hildegard of Bingen, Julian of Norwich, and Birgitta of Sweden. Borresen has also done major work on the theology and cosmology of Nicholas of Cusa.[58] She is a Roman Catholic, and this has made it difficult for her to obtain teaching positions either in the Catholic world (she taught for a time in Rome) or in Lutheran Norway. A lifetime grant from the royal Norwegian ministry of culture has allowed her to work as an independent scholar.

Another Norwegian feminist scholar is Dagny Kaul. Kaul has focused her work particularly on the understanding of "nature" in relation to the doctrines of human nature and of God. Kaul is concerned about feminist criteria for theology, and this has led her to an emphasis on ontological foundations for such criteria and the exploration of a renewal of the understanding of "natural law" for theology.[59] She heads the work group on eco-feminism in the European Society of Women in Theological Research.

The voices of feminist theological scholars from southern and from eastern Europe have also begun to be heard in the forums of the European Society of Women for Theological Research. Women from Italy, Spain, and Portugal have no chance of being ordained, if they are Roman Catholics, and advanced theological education is not easily accessible to them, being traditionally reserved for priests. Few women can expect to obtain teaching positions in theological faculties.

One of the exceptions to this rule is Cettina Militello who holds a doctorate in philosophy from the University of Palermo and a doctorate in theology from the Pontifical University Gregoriana in Rome. She has been professor of ecclesiology and mariology at the Facoltà Teològica de Sicilia in Palermo and also teaches at the Pontificia Facoltà Teològica Marianum in Rome. She has written several books on the subjects of women and the church, lay-clerical relations, women and theology, and the debate over women's ordination.[60]

Other southern European women, such as Carla Ricci, have been able to do theological work under other rubrics, such as philosophy or history. Ricci did her doctoral thesis on women in the gospel of Luke under the philosophy faculty at the University of Bologna. She presently teaches history of Christianity at the faculty of political science at that university. In 1991 she published a study of Mary Magdalene and other women disciples of Jesus.[61]

Marifee Ramos Gonzalez did her work in pastoral theology at the Pontifical University in Salamanca. She presently teaches religion in a state secondary
school. Since 1985 she has worked with the only association of women studying theology in Spain. This association has about twenty-five members and
meets yearly to discuss feminist research on different themes, such as problems
of women and the church. Ramos Gonzalez herself has focused her research on
problems of women and family, sexual and religious education, and addiction.

The most compelling spokesperson for Christian feminism from southern Europe to speak at the 1991 meeting of the European Society was María de
Lourdes Pintasilgo, former premier of Portugal and a member of the Grail, an
international Catholic lay women's institute. In her plenary address Pintasilgo
drew on her experience as a European woman political leader to detail the great
dangers of the Euro-American "new world order" after the collapse of Eastern
European communism.

Pintasilgo warned of the danger of a hegemonic control over global resources by the West, reducing all other nations and the poor within each nation
to permanent misery. She called for an alternative vision of a just economic order to counter this global reign of the market economy. She saw in women's
ethic of mutuality a key to this alternative vision. This women's ethic must free
itself from privatization and become effectively political.

Eastern European Christian women also made their presence felt at the
meeting of the European Society. Struggling within regimes that have just begun to emerge from communist dictatorships, and are now plagued with collapsing economies and civil war, these women spoke particularly of the pain of
their national social contexts. For these Eastern European women the very acknowledgment of themselves as believing Christians put them in bad odor with
past communist regimes. Some, like Czechoslovakian Catholic scholar Mireia
Ryskova, did their religious studies at the Charles University of Prague under
the cover of history of art, while studying theology in underground courses.

A panel of Eastern European women at the European Society from
Poland, former Eastern Germany, Czechoslovakia, and Hungary spoke of the
particular privations being experienced by women in collapsing economies and
social violence. These women have been almost entirely cut off from dialogue
with feminist theology until recently. They were anxious to bring these resources back to their Catholic and Protestant churches in Eastern Europe and
find ways to contextualize these explorations in their own situations. In response to this appeal, the European Society decided to explore the development
of an itinerant summer school of feminist theology in Eastern Europe.

Christian Feminism in the Two-Thirds World

In this section of the essay I will survey the emerging work of Christian
women religious writers and activists in those regions of the world that have

the majority of the world's populations, as well as suffering under the greatest burden of world poverty. These are the regions of the Middle East, Africa, Asia, and Latin America. Christian women in these regions speak from this context of national oppression and the struggle for justice. They place women's issues within that context.

The Middle East

Arab Christian women's voices have been triply muted, as women in the Arab world, as Christians in the Muslim world and as Arabs suffering under Western colonialisms and neocolonialism. The very existence of indigenous Christians in the Arab world is often overlooked by Western Christians, even though this was the birthplace of Christianity and has the oldest indigenous Christian communities. Yet, since the seventh century, Middle Eastern Christianity has suffered under the second class status imposed on non-Muslims by Muslim regimes and has dwindled to less than ten percent of the population of regions where Christians were once the majority.

In addition, Middle Eastern Christianity has been deeply fragmented by the historical splits of the Christian church, beginning with the division between Chalcedonian Orthodoxy, championed by Byzantine imperial Christianity in the fifth century, over against the Monophysite and Nestorian forms of Christianity that predominated among Egyptian, Syrian, and Persian, Christians. Later these indigenous churches were further divided by missions from Roman Catholicism and many forms of Protestantism. Today Middle Eastern Christians seek to overcome their disunity and defend their survival by banding together in the Middle East Council of Churches.

In no place is this plight of indigenous Christianity more poignant than in the land of Jesus' birth, life, and death. Christians who live in Bethlehem, Nazareth, and Jerusalem today feel themselves an endangered species, both in relation to the Palestinian Muslims with whom they bond as part of a common national struggle, and under the boot of Israeli occupation, which has steadily sought to oust the Palestinians from their historic homeland in order to plant a Jewish state in this region.

Yet it is precisely from the Palestinian community that there has emerged some of the major expressions of women's organizing and some of the most striking spokespersons for women. One of these is Hanan Ashrawi, a Christian Palestinian from Ramallah who holds a doctorate in English literature and teaches literature at Bir Zeit University. This university was closed for four years, from the beginning of the Palestinian *Intifada* in January 1988, and had to conduct what education it could in clandestine gatherings. Ashrawi, an accomplished poet and writer, as well as political activist galvanized the world with the clarity of her analysis of the Palestinian plight, as a leader of the Palestinian delegation to the peace negotiations in Madrid in November 1991.

Suffering under many layered oppression as Arabs, Palestinians, Christians, and women, most Palestinian Christian women choose to speak about the national struggle first, and only secondarily and with caution of women's issues within that national struggle. One such Palestinian woman who articulated this situation of woman was journalist Raymonda Tawil, in her 1983 book *My Home, My Prison.* In this book Tawil told the story of her house arrest in her Ramallah home by the Israelis in retaliation for her journalistic work. But she also made clear that, as an Arab woman, she had been brought up under another kind of "house arrest" in a culture that expected the house to be the sole legitimate sphere of women's activities.[62]

In the late 1980s Palestinian Christians began to articulate a Palestinian liberation theology, in an effort to reply to what they saw as the misuse of the Bible and the Jewish and Christian theological traditions by Zionist Jews and Christians who interpreted the Bible to justify an exclusivist and racist Jewish state. Canon Naim Ateek, an Anglican Palestinian priest, pastor of the Arab congregation of St. George's Cathedral in Jerusalem, initiated this discussion in his 1989 book, *Justice and Only Justice: A Palestinian Liberation Theology.*[63]

In March 1990 Palestinian Christians gathered at an international conference at the Tantur Ecumenical Center near Bethlehem in an effort to put Palestinian liberation theology into dialogue with the liberation theologies of Asia, Africa, Latin America, as well as Western Europe and North America. A number of Palestinian Christian women leaders spoke at this conference. Among them were Hanan Ashrawi; Samia Khoury and Cedar Duaybis, leaders in the YWCA in Jerusalem; Jean Zaru, well known in ecumenical circles for her peace work on behalf of the Palestinians and clerk of the Ramallah meeting of the Society of Friends; Nora Kort, manager of social services for Catholic relief services in Jerusalem; and Susan Younan, coordinator of Lutheran women's groups in the West Bank.[64]

These women spoke primarily of the national struggle, of women's work within the national struggle, and of their search to make their Christian faith relevant in that struggle. Yet they did not hesitate to make clear their disappointment with the official churches for their failure to support them as women. Suad Younan spoke most directly to the issues of Palestinian Christian women toward the male church leadership. As she put it:

> When we talk about justice and peace, we should always remember that charity begins at home. The question is: does the local Palestinian church practice justice when it comes to women?

A church that is unjust to its own female members cannot speak credibly of justice and peace to the larger society and world. Younan also claimed a prophetic role for Palestinian Christian women as those who speak out of this multiple injustice and oppression to "transform injustice into justice, hatred into love, and selfishness into participation."[65]

Africa

Although Christianity, the major religion in Egypt and the rest of North Africa at the end of the Roman Empire, has been dwindling since the Muslim conquest of this region, in subsaharan black Africa Christians have been growing steadily in numbers in the second half of the twentieth century. In 1990 black Africa is about two-thirds Christian, although the line between Christians and those who practice traditional African religions is hard to draw. Many African Christians quietly or openly practice a synthesis of African and Christian religions.[66]

African Christians face two major issues, one economic and another cultural. On the economic front, Africans experience devastating poverty, the fruit of neocolonialist developmental policies imposed by their former European colonizers after "liberation." This refusal to really respect an African defined economic development has also resulted in terrible political disruption and military violence, the expression to a large degree of Western interventionist funding.[67]

African liberation theologies address these issues of poverty and oppression. In South Africa this took the form of what has been called black theology, in a region that was still suffering from white minority rule.[68] But indigenous Africans, culturally colonized through Christian missionary importation of religion and education, also seek to define their cultural identity as people who can accept elements of Western religious, educational, and technological culture without losing their "Africanness."

These cultural questions have been addressed by African religious scholars who have examined the traditional religious worldviews of African peoples and sought points of commonality with the worldview of the Hebrew Bible and Christianity. John Mbiti, in his pioneering *African Religions and Philosophy*[69] and E. Bolaji Idowu, in his *African Traditional Religion,*[70] are major examples of this quest for a synthesis of Christianity and African religious worldviews.

African Christian women have begun to find their own distinctive voices within this discussion of African liberation from economic oppression and cultural repression. In critique of some African men and their Western patrons who romanticize traditional African culture and who seek to declare feminist questions out of bounds as contrary to African tradition, African feminists speak up for the liberation of their women from both traditional African, as well as Western Christian forms of patriarchy. But African women also seek to reclaim their women's culture and experience as resources for feminism. They bring these resources to the discussion of Christianity and women in Africa.

The best known of these African feminist liberation theologians is Mercy Amba Oduyoye, a Ghanaian, educated at the University of Ghana and at Cambridge University, and formerly deputy general secretary of the World Council of Churches. In her 1986 *Hearing and Knowing: Theological Reflections on Christianity in Africa,*[71] Oduyoye sought to define this double agenda of liberation from injustice and indigenization of Christianity in Africa from an African women's perspective. African Christians need to shake off Western missionary paternalism and claim the valuable cultural insights of their traditions, which did not split person from community or humans from nature, as Western religion has tended to do. But these African cultures, even those that are matrilineal, need to be transformed from male sexism to become truly committed to the full humanity of women, together with men.

Oduyoye speaks from a growing circle of African sisters, Protestant and Catholic: Elizabeth Amoah, a Ghanaian Methodist with a doctorate in religious studies who teaches at the University of Ghana, Legon; Rosemary Edet, a Roman Catholic sister from Nigeria who teaches at the University of Calabar; Bette Ekeya, a lay Catholic with a doctorate in African traditional religions teaching at the University of Nairobi, Kenya; Teresa Okure, a Nigerian Roman Catholic sister with a Ph.D. in scripture who teaches at the Catholic Institute of West Africa in Port Harcourt, Nigeria; Dorothy Ramodibe, a Roman Catholic laywoman who is administrative secretary of the South African institute of contextual theology, among others.[72]

Asia

If one can hardly do minimal justice to the work Christian feminists in Africa with a few bold strokes, this is also true for Asian Christian women. Asia, including the Pacific islands, represents more than half of the world's population, but less than three percent of it is Christian. Only one Asian country, the Philippines, is predominately Christian, having been colonized and Christianized by the Spanish in the late sixteenth century. In only one other Asian country, Korea, are Christians a substantial minority, 27 percent. As in Africa, Asian Christians face the dual problems of grinding poverty for the majority, kept in place by Western neocolonialism, and cultural indigenization of Christianity in Asian religious worldviews.

Asian Christian women experience themselves as doubly oppressed, by traditional Asian forms of patriarchy, particularly in its Hindu and Confucian forms, and also by Western Christian patriarchy. Yet Asian Christian women have also been the beneficiaries of education for women, brought by women missionaries, and political emancipation, reflecting the influence of Western liberal political thought on emerging Asian nations. Their education and fluency in English has allowed them to absorb the writings of North American feminist theology, and to search for ways to contextualize this in Asian women's culture and struggle for liberation.

It is among Asian Christian women that we find the most developed local and regional networks of feminist theology. In 1982 women theologians who were members of the Ecumenical Association of Third World Theologians (EATWOT) won approval for a women's commission. They organized national and regional gatherings on feminist theology in Asia, Africa, and Latin America. In December 1986 delegations of women met in Oaxtepec, Mexico, for an international conference of third world feminist theology. The major papers from this conference were published under the title of *With Passion and Compassion: Third World Women Doing Theology.*[73]

Asian women were well prepared for this work of the women's commission, having already begun to put in place networks of feminist theologians in various Asian countries, as well as a women's journal, *In God's Image,* that gathers its editorial board across the Asian region, including the Philippines.[74] These local networks in each country have continued to grow. Institutes, conferences, and journals have been founded in the 80s and 90s to bring together the work of Asian Christian feminists.[75] Asian women have found ways to meet across national boundaries to share their perspectives.

In December 1990 delegations of Asian feminist theologians from seven countries— India, Korea, Philippines, Hong Kong, Sri Lanka, Indonesia, and Malaysia—met in Madras, India, to share papers on feminist hermeneutical principles in their distinct historical and cultural contexts.[76] These women situated their hermeneutical work in an analysis of the history, as well as the present condition, of women in their societies. In some cases they sought resources from ancient indigenous cultures prior to the rise of Asian, as well as Western colonial, forms of patriarchy. They also sought to find their own distinctive voice in dialogue with Western feminist and Asian male liberation theologians.

The Filipina paper, "Toward an Asian Principle of Interpretation: A Filipino Women's Experience," was put together by the combined effort of Rosario Battung, Virginia Fabella, Arche Ligo, Mary John Mananzan, and Elizabeth Tapia of the women's institute of St. Scholastica College in Manila.[77] Using liberation theology methodology, the paper begins by telling the stories of six Filipino women, illustrating the manylayered oppression of women in this country.

The paper then moves to historical and social analysis, describing the present forms of oppression of women in the family, the church, and the economy. It also reaches back to indigenous Filipino traditions to claim more egalitarian social forms. The authors describe how these earlier traditions were suppressed and reshaped by Spanish and American colonizations. The second part of the paper looks at liberating traditions from Filipina history and also from biblical faith.

The authors then affirm their hermeneutical principles, based on liberating praxis, which takes as its starting point women of the poor. They sum up these principles in this way:

> From the perspective of Filipino women committed to authentic womanhood and societal transformation, we interpret and judge texts, events and realities in accordance with God's design when they (1) promote authentic personhood of women, (2) foster inclusive communities based on just relationships, (3) contribute to genuine national sovereignty and autonomy, and (4) develop caring and respectful attitudes not only among human beings but toward the rest of creation as well.

Among the tasks where further exploration is needed they list the retrieval of indigenous understandings of the sacredness of nature and the exploration of the relation between liberation and creation spiritualities in the struggle of women for full humanity.

The Korean paper, "The Critical Hermeneutical Principles for Korean Women Theologians," was put together by Yang My Gang and Kim Jeong Soo, and edited and translated by Chung Hyun Kyung and Lee-Park Sun Ai. It begins with an analysis of the manylayered forms of oppression that afflict Korean women today. This is seen in its historical context of colonization by outside empires, by Japan and the U.S.A., and the tragedies of the splitting of Korea by the allied forces after World War II and the civil war of 1950–53 in which some six million Koreans died.

The authors then describe the traditional forms of patriarchy and feudalism, and their effects on women and on the poor, and also the new legacies of dependent economic development in which women find themselves doubly exploited in factories and in the family. The history of Korean women's struggles to organize for justice is detailed, including the struggles to organize networks of Korean feminist theology and the promotion of women in the churches and in theological education.

Korean women's hermeneutical principles build on Mingung or Korean liberation theology, but contextualize this theology in terms of the oppression of poor women as the "minjung of the minjung."[78] *Han* (the collective experience of oppression) is a central concept, but takes on deeper meaning when Korean women's experiences of *han* are made explicit. Korean feminist hermeneutics claim both Korean cultural resources and Christian faith to find ways of "exorcising" this collective women's *han*.

The Indian paper, "Breaking the Silence: Indian Women in Search of Hermeneutical Principles" (written primarily by Aruna Gnanadason, then executive secretary of the national councils of churches of India, subunit on Women[79]), starts by claiming the ancient Indian female cosmic principle of *Shakti*. *Shakti* is the creative force of the cosmos found throughout nature and linked with women's generativity. Indian women, claiming their *Shakti,* can no longer be downtrodden and oppressed. United together they will also seek to overcome social oppression and heal the systems that are destroying nature as well.

In exploring the liberating alternatives in India, the authors reach behind the Aryan conquest in 1500 B.C. This conquest brought both the subordination of women and the caste system to India. The liberation of women thus must also be linked with Dalit (untouchables) liberation, the overcoming of both gender and caste oppression. The paper goes on to describe the effects of British colonization and the failure of national liberation to overcome the structures of poverty, caste oppression, and sexism.

These Indian Christian women situate their movement within the context of Indian feminism. Since the early 1970s, it has been bringing to light the patterns of violence against women, rape, wife beating, dowry burnings, and female feticide and infanticide. They see themselves as bringing together the insights of Indian male liberation theology and Western feminist theology, but contextualized in terms of Indian women's particular historical and social conditions of oppression, as well as their resources for liberation.

Although Asian Christian women speak for their distinct national, cultural, and historical contexts, they also seek solidarity with each other. They bring their quests into dialogue and seek common feminist hermeneutical principles as Asian women. One Asian feminist theologian, Chung Hyun Khung, sought to sketch this emerging Asian women's theology in her 1990 *Struggle to be the Sun Again: Introducing Asian Women's Theology*[80] (originally her doctoral dissertation at Union Seminary in New York).

Chung describes the historical emergence of Asian women's theology through three networks: the women's desk of the Christian Conference of Asia, founded in 1980; the women's commission of the Ecumenical Association of Third World Theologians, founded in 1983; and the journal *In God's Image.* These three structures have enabled Asian women to meet together, share their experiences and reflections, and also to publish the results through the journal and the Asian women's resource center for culture and theology (now based in Seoul, Korea).[81]

Chung then goes on to analyze Asian women's social and historical context as triply oppressed people: by Asian patriarchal family systems, class hierarchies, and international colonialism. Asian women's theology starts with women's *han,* their manylayered experiences of suffering. It seeks liberating resources in the understanding of Jesus as liberator, but also Mariology, the feminine coparticipant in redemption. It also seeks distinctively Asian spiritual resources. For Chung and many Korean women this means a bold affirmation of shamanism, the folk traditions that have been traditionally associated with women.

On February 8, 1991, Chung galvanized the assembly of the World Council of Churches, meeting in Canberra, Australia, by giving an address that epitomized this emerging Asian feminist theology. Chung (and a group of Korean women and men) began with a shaman dance, in which she evoked the spirits of the many communities that had been oppressed and violated around the world. She conducted a *Han-pu-ri* ceremony to liberate these oppressed spirits from their *han*. Chung then called on the Holy Spirit, linking it with these many spirits of the oppressed, to free and renew the whole creation.

The integration of women's experience of oppression with that of violated classes and races, as well as the earth itself, was made graphic as she spoke, through visual images playing on screens behind her. She summed up her talk with an image of the Buddhist female *bodhisattva,* Kuan-Yin, as her image of the Holy Spirit, the femaleness of God through which women, men, and the whole earth seeks to be freed from alienation and violence.[82]

Chung's speech evoked great controversy at the World Council, as well as back in her native Korea, where she teaches at Ewa Women's University. Western and Asian Christian traditionalists decried what they claimed was Chung's "syncretism." But Asian Christian feminists are unlikely to retreat before this criticism. They have found their distinctive voice and can only continue to expand and strengthen it.

Latin America

Latin American Christian feminism also arises in a colonized and impoverished continent groaning under five hundred years of Western European and American exploitation. But unlike Asia, this continent, conquered by the Spanish and Portuguese in the sixteenth century, is almost entirely Christian, mostly Roman Catholic, with a growing minority of Protestants. The temples and books of the indigenous religions were mostly destroyed by the colonizers. The indigenous religions survive among poor indigenous people as folk tradition, but the educated elites, mostly of European descent, have little contact with it.

When liberation theology arose in Latin America in the late 1960s, through the work of figures such as Gustavo Guitérrez,[83] it drew primarily on critical sociology to analyze Latin American economic oppression, together with a liberatory reading of the Bible and Christian theology. Class and national oppression, not race, were the primary categories. There was little reference to indigenous people or Afro-Hispanics, or any imperative to seek liberating resources from these cultural traditions.

Male liberation theologians also ignored issues of women and spoke of the "poor" and the "oppressed" as though the experience of poverty and oppression was undifferentiated by gender. When women's issues were raised, they have generally been uncomfortable with them, seeking either to rebuff these questions as irrelevant to Latin America, or else to refer to Mary and their mothers as their only clues to what might be "feminine" issues in theology.

Many nations in Latin America also have strong women's movements. These have roots in the struggle for women's education and right to vote of a century ago, and were renewed with the new élan of feminism in the 1970s. The leaders of these feminist movements are generally from the educated urban middle class, although seeking also to put their analysis at the service of the urban poor women, who labor for poor wages in factories or in the marginalized sectors of the economy. Domestic violence, rape, and denial of reproductive rights are also very much on the agenda of these feminist movements.

These Latin American feminists are generally secular in culture, having departed from whatever Christian church they may have known in childhood. Christianity is judged to be essentially patriarchal, a major part of the problem that justified women's subordination, but in no way a part of the solution.[83] This means that, like France, there has been little forum for a liberatory Christian feminism in Latin America. What forum there is has developed primarily through the efforts of a few Latin American women to bring together feminism and liberation theology, often with less than wholehearted support from male liberation theologians.

The emerging circle of feminist liberation theologians feels a need to bring their male colleagues "on board" with their struggle. In 1985–86, Elsa Tamez, a Mexican Methodist teaching scripture at the Seminário Bíblico Latinoamericano in Costa Rica, interviewed fifteen leading Latin American male liberation theologians, all of whom work from the premise of the preferential option for the poor," about their understanding of women's liberation and male machismo.[84]

In these interviews we see the difficulties of these men in taking seriously women's "oppression," starting as they do from their male view of the dependent women of their own families. We see them struggle to reach out beyond these limits to imagine a world not only outside their experience, but that they have been socialized by the culture of machismo to regard women with paternalism, lewd humor, and disdain.

A few Latin American feminist liberation theologians have managed to find positions in universities, seminaries, and special institutes, to do their theoretical work. Ana Maria Bidegain, an Uruguyan lay Catholic Church historian with doctorate from the Catholic University in Louvain, teaches at the University of the Andes, Bogotá, Colombia. She has written books on nationalism, militarism, and domination in Latin America, and also on the relation of the church to the people and political systems.[85]

Maria Clara Bingemer, a Brazilian lay Catholic theologian, teaches at the Pontifical Catholic University in Rio de Janeiro, and is the regional coordinator for the women's commission of EATWOT. She wrote, with Ivone Gebara, a study of Mariology from a feminist liberation perspective and also a study on feminist theology.[86] Ivone Gebara, a Catholic sister from Brazil, taught at the theological institute of Recife. Another Brazilian, Tereza Cavalcanti, teaches pastoral studies at the Catholic University of Rio de Janeiro and coordinates a program on women and theology.[87]

Catholic women cannot be ordained, but are engaging in ministry through base communities and pastoral institutes, developments that reflect both liberation theology's view of the church as a nonhierarchical community and also the lack of male clergy to do much of the pastoral work. Some main-line Protestant churches ordain women, but these women find it difficult to get pastorates. Latin American Protestantism is mostly conservative, culturally and politically, and its growing edge is fundamentalist.

To help support their work Elsa Tamez and other women, several based at the Seminário Bíbliico in Costa Rica, founded in 1991 the Aso-ciación de Teólogas y Pastoras de América Latina y El Caribe.[88] This associ-ation publishes a regular newsletter, gathers bibliography on feminist theology, particularly in Spanish, and organizes *Encuentros*. This network helps Latin American feminists working in teaching or pastoral work to feel less isolated, by recognizing that they are part of a growing circle of sisters in the struggle.

Conclusion

Christian feminism across ethnic and national boundaries is developing many voices and styles, as it is rethought in the distinct cultural and socio-eco-nomic realities of each context. And yet these are, in many ways, variants of a common language. This commonality is rooted in a common Christian her-itage, with all its ambiguities of positive and negative messages for women, a heritage that, for most of these women, traveled through its Western Roman Catholic or Protestant lines of development and then was exported to Latin America, Asia, and Africa in colonial, missionary forms.

Feminism around the world also shares very similar experiences of pa-triarchal oppression. Rape and wife beating is fairly similar the world over, even if the language in which the curses are hurled at women's heads may dif-fer. But social location within systems of class and race hierarchy divide women from each other, both internationally and within nations. Economic marginalization is very different for the wife of an affluent professional and for the wife of a peasant farmer or an unemployed urban migrant.

Feminist theologians in Africa, Asia, and Latin America, as well as in North America and Western Europe, are drawn primarily from middle-strata professionals. They face a common task of reaching across to the poor of their own societies, as well as linking with each other across the division of colonizer and colonized peoples. Preferential option for the oppressed women, the women at the bottom of the systems of privilege, must remain the key to a feminist theory and praxis that does not stop with inclusion of middle-class women into the class privileges of their brothers, but reaches out to a deeper transformation of the whole system.

Notes

1. Elisabeth Schüssler Fiorenza's, *In Memory of Her: A Feminist Theological Reconstruction of Christian Origens,* New York: Crossroads, 1985, is the major reconstruction of this original egalitarian, countercultural Christianity.

2. See Rosemary Radford Reuther, "Prophets and Humanists: Types of Religious Feminism in Stuart England," in *The Journal of Religion,* vol. 70, No. 1, January 1990, pp. 1–18.

3. See Norman Cohn's study of medieval radical sectarianism, *The Pursuit of the Millennium,* New York: Harper and Row, 1961; also Marjorie Reeves, *Joachim of Fiore an the Prophetic Future,* New York: Harper and Row, 1976.

4. For the history of the *querelle des femmes* in England, see Frances Utley, *The Crooked Rib: An Analytical Index to the Argument about Women in English and Scots Literature to the End of the Year 1568,* Columbus: Ohio State University, 1944.

5. See Christine de Pizan, *The Book of the City of Ladies,* Earl Jeffrey Richards, translator, New York: Persea Books, 1982, and *The Treasure of the City of the Ladies,* Sarah Lawson, introduction and translation, New York: Penguin Books, 1985.

6. See Ester Sowernam, *Ester Hath Hang'd Haman or an Answer to a Lewd Pamphlet* (1617), reprinted in Moria Ferguson, *First Feminists: British Women Writers, 1578–1799,* Bloomington: Indiana University Press, 1985, pp. 74–79. Sowernam (a pseudonym) was responding to the attack on women by Joseph Swetnam, The Arraignment of Lewd, Forward and Unconstant women (1615).

7. Margaret Fell's pamphlet was reprinted in *Women's Speaking Justified and Other Seventeenth-century Quaker Writings about Women,* London: Quaker Home Service, 1989; also reprinted in Ferguson, *First Feminists,* pp. 114–27.

8. The checklist of women's published writings of 1600–1700, in Mary Prior, *Women in English Society, 1500–1800,* London: Methuen, 1985, pp. 242–44 shows 293 authors. Examination of these writings in the British Museum and the Friend's Library in London revealed that 70 of these authors were Quakers, with a total of 171 writings. The corpus of seventeenth-century Quaker women's writings are being microfilmed by a workgroup at Earlham College. A selection was published under the title *Hidden in Plain Sight: Quaker Women's Writings, 1650–1700.* Mary Garman, et al., eds. (Wallingford, PA: Rendle Hill Publications, 1996).

9. For example, Margaret Cavendish, duchess of Newcastle, Katherine Philips, Mary Lee Lady Chudleigh, Anne Finch, countess of Winchilea, and Bathsua Makin: see Ferguson, *First Feminists.*

10. Mary Astell, *A Serious Proposal to the Ladies . . . by a Lover of her Sex* (1694), unabridged reprint of the 1701 edition, London: Source Book Press, 1970; abridged edition and other writings by Astell in Ferguson, *First Feminists,* pp. 180–200.

11. For Mary Astell's correspondence with John Norris, see Ruth Perry, *The Celebrated Mary Astell, An Early English Feminist,* Chicago: University of Chicago Press, 1986, pp., 73–97.

12. For biographies of some nineteenth-century American feminists, see Gerda Lerner, *The Grimké Sisters of North Carolina,* New York: Schocken Books, 1967; Elizabeth Cazden,m *Antoinette Brown Blackwell: A Biography,* Old Westbury, NY: Feminist Press, 1983; Lois Banner, *Elizabeth Cady Stanton: A Radical for Woman's Rights,* Boston: Little, Brown, 1980; Kathleen Barry, *Susan B. Anthony: A Biography of a Singular Feminist,* New York: New York University Press, 1988.

13. Reprint of Grimké letters: Burth Franklin, NY: 1970.

14. Elizabeth Cady Stanton, editor, *The Woman's Bible,* New York: European Publishing Company, 1895. Reprint of Gage's book by Persephone Press, Watertown, MA, 1980.

15. See Theresa L. Latour, *Princesses, Ladies and Republicaines of the Terror,* New York: Alfred Knopf, 1930, pp. 175–79.

16. See Claire Goldberg Moses, *French Feminism in the Nineteenth Century,* Albany: State University of New York Press, 1984; also Barbara Taylor, *Eve and the New Jerusalem: Socialism and Feminism in the Nineteenth Century,* New York: Pantheon Books, 1983.

17. Simon de Beauvoir, *The Second Sex* (French, 1949), New York: Alfred Knopf, 1953; also *After the Second Sex,* New York: Pantheon, 1984.

18. See Shelley Finson, ed., *Women and Religion: A Bibliographic Guide to Christian Feminist Liberation Theology,* Toronto: University of Toronto Press, 1991.

19. Major feminist journals, such as *Signs: Journal of Women in Culture and Society* and *Journal of Feminist Studies,* typically have almost no articles on religion and what little is there is usually not about Christianity or from a post-Christian perspective.

20. Daly's *The Church and the Second Sex* was published by Harper and Row; all her subsequent books have been published by Beacon Press in Boston, MA.

21. Carol Christ, *Laughter of Aphrodite: Reflections on a Journey to the Goddess,* New York: Harper and Row, 1987.

22. Nashville: Abingdon Press, 1986. *Daughters of Sarah: A Magazine for Christian Feminists,* 3801 N. Keeler, Chicago, IL, 60641.

23. For example, Letty Russell, *Human Liberation in a Feminist Perspective,* Philadelphia: Westminister Press, 1974; Rosemary Ruether, *Sexism and Godtalk: Toward a Feminist Theology,* Boston: Beacon, 1983; Carter Heyward, *Our Passion for Justice: Images of Power, Sexuality and Liberation,* New York: Pilgrim Press, 1984; Elisabeth Schüssler Fiorenza, *Claiming the Center: A Feminist Critical Theology of Liberation,* New York: Seabury Press, 1985; Mary Hunt, "Feminist Liberation on Theology: The Development of Method in Construction," Ph.D. Dissertation, Berkeley, CA, Graduate Theological Union, 1980; Beverly Harrison, *Making the Connections: Essays in Feminist Social Ethics,* Boston: Beacon Press, 1985.

24. For example, Julia Kristeva, *Revolution in Poetic Language,* New York: Columbia University Press, 1984; Luce Irigaray, *Speculum of the Other Woman,* Ithaca, NY: Cornell University Press, 1985; also *New French Feminisms: An Anthology,* ed. Elaine Marks and Isabelle de Courtivron, New York: Schocken, 1981.

25. Rebecca Chopp, *The Power to Speak: Feminism, Language and God,* New York: Crossroad, 1989; Katherine Keller, *From a Broken Web; Separation, Sexism and Self,* Boston: Beacon, 1986.

26. The term *womanist* was coined by Alice Walker; see her *Search for Our Mothers' Gardens,* San Diego, CA: Harcourt Brace Jovanovich, 1983, pp. xi–xii.

27. Atlanta, GA: Scholars Press, 1989.

28. Katie Geneva Cannon, "Resources for a Constructive Ethic for Black Women with Special Attention to the Life and Work of Zora Neale Hurston," Ph.D. Dissertation: New York: Union Theological Seminary, 1983.

29. Ada Maria Isasi-Diaz and Yolanda Tarango, *Hispanic Women: Prophetic Voice in the Church,* San Francisco, CA: Harper and Row, 1988.

30. Mary E. Hunt, *Fierce Tenderness: A Feminist Theology of Friendship,* New York: Crossroad, 1991; Jeannine Grammick, *Homosexuality in the Priesthood and in Religious Life,* New York: Crossroad, 1989; Carter Heyward, *Our Passion for Justice* (op. cit); Joanne Brown and Rebecca Parker, see their "Coming Out Rite for a Lesbian" in Rosemary R. Ruether, *Woman-church: Theology and Practice,* San Francisco: Harper and Row, 1986, pp. 173–81.

31. For example, Judith Plant, *Healing the Wounds: The Promise of Ecofeminism,* Philadelphia: New Society Publishers, 1989, and Irene Diamond and Gloria F. Orenstein, *Reweaving the World: The Emergence of Ecofeminism,* San Francisco: Sierra Club Books, 1990.

32. Rosemary R. Ruether, *Gaia and God: An Ecofeminist Theology of Earthhealing,* San Francisco: Harper/Collins, 1992; Anne Primavesi, *From Apocalypse to Genesis: Ecology, Feminism and Christianity,* Minneapolis: Fortress Press, 1991;

Catharina Halkes, *New Creation: Christian Feminism and the Renewal of the Earth* (Dutch, 1989) Louisville: Westminister/John Knox Press, 1991.

33. See the work of feminist historians of science, such as Carolyn Merchant, *The Death of Nature: Women, Ecology and the Scientific Revolution,* San Francisco: Harper and Row, 1981, and Evelyn Fox Keller, Reflections on Gender and Science, New Haven: Yale University Press, 1985.

34. Adair Lummis, Allison Stokes, and Miriam Therese Winter of Hartford Seminary are presently studying feminist spirituality groups in the USA under a Lily grant; see *Defecting in Place: Women Claiming Responsibility for Their Own Spiritual Lives* (NY: Crossroads, 1994).

35. Oak Park, IL: Meyer-Stone Books, 1987.

36. *Womenspirit: The Irish Journal of Feminist Spirituality,* c/o Rosemount Court, Bootertown, C. Dublin, Ireland.

37. Katherine Zappone, *The Hope for Wholeness: A Spirituality for Feminists,* Mystic, CT: Twenty-third Publications, 1991.

38. San Francisco: Harper and Row, 1981.

39. Janet Morley, *All Desires Known,* London: MOW/WIT publication, 1988; the incident was reported in the newsletter of the British women in theology group, winter, 1992, p. 5.

40. Information on both the summer school and the journal of the Britain and Ireland school of feminist theology, 233 Kensington Square, London W8 5HN.

41. London: SPCK, 1989.

42. Daphne Hampson, *Theology and Feminism,* Oxford: Basil Blackwell, 1990.

43. King's 1984 book was published by the Hibbert Trust, London; the 1989 book by New Amsterdam Books, London.

44. The first book forthcoming; the second published in 1995 by Cambridge University Press: Jantzen also published *God's World, God's Body,* London: Darton, Longman and Todd, 1984, and *Julian of Norwich: Mystic and Theologian,* London: SPCK, 1987.

45. Few of Halkes' books have been translated into English. Among her major books are *Gott hat nicht nur starke söhne: Grundzuge einer feminischschen Theologie,* Gutersloh: Gutersloher Verlagshaus Gerd Mohn, 1980; *Zoekend naar wat verloren ging,* Baarn: Ten Have, 1984, and *Feminisme en spiritualiteit,* Baarn: Ten Have, 1986.

46. Published in 1992.

47. With Ineke Jonker, *Christianity and Incest* (Dutch, 1985), Minneapolis: Fortress Press, 1991, and *God in der beleving van vrouwen,* 1992.

48. See her "Vrouwen gepromoveed in de theologie in Nederland" in *Proeven van Vrouwenstudies Theologie,* Deel 1, Leiden/Utrecht, 1989, pp. 53–111.

49. Sölle has published over fifteen books. Others are *Revolutionary Patience,* Maryknoll, NY: Orbis Press, 1974, and *To Work and to Love: A Theology of Creation,* Philadelphia: Fortress Press, 1984.

50. English: Philadelphia: Westminister Press, 1984.

51. In *COELI: Liaisons Internationales,* no. 60, winter, 1991–92, pp. 3–8.

52. For the report on this incident, see Margaret Hebblethwaite's article on the Bristol meeting of the European Society of Women in Theological Research, *The Tablet,* September 14, 1991. Among Schroer's publications is "Der Geist, die Weisheit und die Taube," in *Freiburger Zeitschrift für Philosophie und Theologie* 33 (1986), pp. 197–225.

53. Two volumes: Stuttgart: Kreuz Verlag, 1989.

54. English: New York: Crossroad, 1986.

55. New York: Crossroad, 1991.

56. English: Washington, D.C.: University Press of America, 1981.

57. Oslo: Solum Verlag, 1991.

58. See her "Birgitta's Godlanguage" in *Birgitta, Hendes vaerk og Hendes klostre i Norden,* Tore Nyberg, ed. Odense, 1991.

59. *Renewal of Life: A Basic Element in Feminist Ethics,* (1993) in Norwegian.

60. *Donna e Chiese,* Palermo, 1986; *Teologia al femminile,* Palermo, 1986; *Laichi-Chierici: dualismo ecclesiologico,* Palermo, 1987, and *Donna e Ministero: un dibattito ecumenico,* Rome, 1991.

61. Among her publications are "Istanze delle donne: ascolto e risposta dei vescovi statunitensi" in *Donna e Società* 87 (9188), pp. 68–78; "Esegesi del silenzio: dall'assenza delle donne nei testi alla presenza donne accanto a Gesu" in *Donna e Ministero: Un dibattito ecumenico,* Rome: Dheoniane, 1991, pp. 486–96, and "Donna soggetto ineditor nell'esegesi," in *Alleanza* 2 (1991), pp. 17–19; also her book, *Maria di Magdala e le molte altre. Donne sul cammino di Gesu?,* Naples: Editore D'Auria, 1991.

62. London: Zed, 1983.

63. Maryknoll, NY: Orbis Books, 1989.

64. Naim Ateek, Marc Ellis, and Rosemary Ruethers, eds., *Faith and the Intifada: Palestinian Christian Voices,* Maryknoll, NY: Orbis Books, 1992.

65. Ibid., p. 132.

66. Assimilation of Christianity into African cultural forms is particularly characteristic of African indigenous churches, but also is common in private lives of mainstream Christians. See E. Bolaji Idowu, *Toward an Indigenous Church,* London: Oxford, 1965.

67. See the address by Aaron Tolen, Cameroon, to the Central Committee of the World Council of Church, September 20, 1991: published in *COELI: Liaisons Internationales, no. 60, Winter, 1991–92, pp. 14–20.*

68. See, for example, Allan Boesak, Farewell to Innocence, Maryknoll, NY: Orbis Books, 1977; Manas Buthelezi, "African Theology or Black Theology," in Basil Moore, ed., *The Challenge of Black Theology in South Africa,* Atlanta: John Knox Press, 1973, pp. 29–35; Frank Chikane and M. Tsele, *Black Theology and Black Struggle,* Braamfontein: Institute for Contextual Theology, 1984, and Itumeleng Mosala and Buti Tlhagale, *The Unquestionable Right to be Free,* Maryknoll, NY: Orbis Books, 1986.

69. London: Heinemann, 1969.

70. Maryknoll, NY: Orbis Books, 1973.

71. Maryknoll, NY: Orbis Books, 1986.

72. See the section on Africa, Virginia Fabella and Mercy Amba Oduyoye, *With Passion and Compassion: Third World Women Doing Theology,* Maryknoll, NY: Orbis Books, 1988, pp. 3–68; also Mercy Amba Oduyoye and Musimbi B.A. Kanyoro, eds., *The Will to Arise: Women, Tradition and the Church in Africa,* Maryknoll, NY: Orbis Books, 1992 and Mercy Ambo Oduyoye, *Daughters of Anowa: African Women and Patriarchy* (NY: Orbis Books, 1995).

73. Ibid., *With Passion and Compassion.*

74. The address of the journal is the Asian Women's Resource Centre for Culture and Theology, 79, Lorong. Tarman Shanghai, 581000 Kuala Lumpur, Malaysia.

75. A new journal, *Lila: Asia Pacific Women's Studies Journal,* from St. Scholastica College, P.O. Box 3153, Manila, Philippines, was started in 1992.

76. These essays are in the process of being edited for publication.

77. The Filipina hermeneutical paper is available from St. Scholastica College, ibid., note 75.

78. The term *minjung* means the oppressed masses of ordinary people. See CTC: Christian Conference of Asia, *Minjung Theology: People as the Subjects of History,* Maryknoll, NY: Orbis Books, 1981.

79. Gnanadason is presently head of the women's desk, World Council of Churches, 150, Route de Fernay, Geneva, Switzerland; the Indian women's paper is available in unedited form from her.

80. Maryknoll, NY: Orbis Books, 1990.

81. Op. cit., note 74.

82. The video of Chung Hyun Kyung's presentation, "Come Holy Spirit: Renew the Whole Creation," at the Seventh Assembly of the World Council of Churches in Canberra, Australia in 1991 is available from Lou Niznik, 15726 Ashland Drive, Laurel, MD, 20707.

83. Gustavo Gutierrez's foundation book is *Liberation Theology;* see the 15th anniversary edition (Maryknoll, NY: Orbis Books, 1988).

84. Elsa Tamez, ed., *Against Machismo* (Oak Park, IL: Meyer's Books, 1987).

85. See Ana María Bidegain, "Women and the Theology of Libertion," in *Through Her Eyes: Women's Theology from Latin America,* Elsa Tamez, ed. (Maryknoll, NY: Orbis Books, 1989), pp. 15–36.

86. Ivone Gebara and María Clara Bingemer, *Mary: Mother of God, Mother of the Poor* (Maryknoll, NY: Orbis Books, 1989). A more recent book by Ivone Gebara is *Theologia a Ritmo de Mujer* (Madrid: San Pablo, 1995).

87. See the article by Tereza Cavalcanti, "The Prophetic Ministry of Women in the Hebrew Bible," in *Through Her Eyes,* pp. 118–139.

88. The Association of Women Pastors and Theologians is located at the Seminario Biblico (now Biblical University) of Latin America, Apdo. 901–1000, 001 San José, Costa Rica.

Chapter 7

Feminism in Islam

Riffat Hassan

Islam: Sources of the Tradition

Before engaging in any meaningful discussion of feminism in Islam, it is useful to refer to the sources of the Islamic tradition, since much confusion surrounds the use of the term "Islam." The Islamic tradition—like other major religious traditions—does not consist of, or derive from, a single source. If questioned about its sources many Muslims are likely to refer to more than one of the following: The Qur'an (the book of revelation believed by Muslims to be God's Word), Sunnah (the practical traditions of the prophet Muhammad), *hadith* (the sayings attributed to the prophet Muhammad), *fiqh* (jurisprudence) or *madahib* (schools of law), and the *Sharī'ah* (the code of life that regulates all aspects of Muslim life).

While all of these "sources" have contributed to what is cumulatively referred to as "the Islamic tradition," it is important to note that they do not form a coherent or consistent body of teachings or precepts from which a universally agreed upon set of Islamic "norms" can be derived. Examples can be cited of inconsistency between various sources of the Islamic tradition, e.g., the Qur'an and the *hadith* as also of inner inconsistency within some, e.g., the *hadith* literature.

In view of this fact, it is inappropriate, particularly in a scholarly context, to speak of "the Islamic tradition" as if it were unitary or monolithic. Before one can make any generalization on behalf of this tradition, it is necessary, therefore, to identify its different sources and examine each of them separately as well as with reference to the other sources.

Theoretically, the two most important sources are the Qur'an and the *hadith*. Of these two, undoubtedly, the Qur'an is the more important. However, since the early days of Islam, the *hadith* literature has been the lens through which the words of the Qur'an have been seen and interpreted.

Important as the *hadith* literature is to the Islamic tradition, it is necessary to point out that every aspect of this literature is surrounded by controversies. In particular, the question of the authenticity or otherwise of individual *ahadith* (plural of *hadith*) as well as of the *hadith* literature as a whole, has occupied the attention of many scholars of Islam since the time of Ash-Shafi'i (died in A.D. 809). As stated by Fazlur Rahman in his book *Islam*, "a very large proportion of the Hadiths were judged to be spurious and forged by classical Muslim scholars themselves."[1] This fact has generated much skepticism regarding the *hadith* literature in general among a number of Muslims. Though few of them are willing to go as far as Ghulam Ahmad Parwez (founder of the Tulu'-e-Islam or the Dawn of Islam group in Pakistan) who rejects the *hadith* literature virtually in toto, many Muslims are likely to be in agreement with the following observations of Moulvi Cheragh Ali, an important Indian Muslim scholar who wrote in the nineteenth century:

> The vast flood of tradition soon formed a chaotic sea. Truth, error, fact and fable mingled together in an undistinguishable confusion. Every religious, social, and political system was defended when necessary, to please a Khalif or an Ameer to serve his purpose to support all manner of lies and absurdities or to satisfy the passion, caprice, or arbitrary will of the despots, leaving out of consideration the creation of any standards of test. . . . I am seldom inclined to quote traditions having little or no belief in their genuineness, as generally they are inauthentic, unsupported and one-sided.[2]

Though valid grounds exist for regarding the *hadith* literature with caution, if not skepticism, Fazlur Rahman is right in saying that "if the Hadith literature *as a whole* is cast away, the basis for the historicity of the Qur'an is removed with one stroke."[3] Furthermore, a pointed out by Alfred Guillaume in his book, *The Traditions of Islam:*

> The Hadith literature as we now have it provides us with apostolic precept and example covering the whole duty of man: it is *the basis* of that developed system of law, theology, and custom which is Islam. . . .[4] However skeptical we are with regard to the ultimate historical value of the traditions, it is hard to overrate their importance in formation of the life of the Islamic races throughout the centuries. If we cannot accept them at their face value, they are of inestimable value as a mirror of the events which preceded the consolidation of Islam into a system.[5]

Not only does the *hadith* literature have its own autonomous character in point of law and even of doctrine,[6] it also has an emotive aspect whose importance is hard to overstate. It relates to the conscious as well as to the subconscious patterns of thought and feeling of Muslims individually and collectively. H. A. R. Gibb has observed perceptively:

> It would be difficult to exaggerate the strength and the effects of the Muslim attitude toward Muhammad. Veneration for the Prophet was a natural and inevitable feeling, both in his own day and later, but this is more than veneration. The personal relationships of admiration and love which he inspired in his associates have echoed down the centuries, thanks to the instruments which the community created in order to evoke them afresh in each generation. The earliest of these instruments was the narration of hadith. So much has been written about the legal and theological functions of the hadith that its more personal and religious aspects have been almost overlooked. It is true, to be sure, that the necessity of finding an authoritative source which would supplement the legal and ethical prescriptions contained in the Qur'an led to a search for examples set by Muhammad in his daily life and practice. One could be certain that if he said this or that, had done this or that, approved this or that action, one had an absolutely reliable guide to the right course to adopt in any similar situation. And it is equally true that this search went far beyond the limits of credibility or simple rectitude, and that it was in due course theologically rationalized by the doctrine of implicit inspiration.[7]

Normative Islam: Interpretation of Text and Tradition

Having underscored the significance of the Qur'an and the *hadith* as primary sources of the Islamic tradition, it is important to point out that through the centuries of Muslim history, these sources have been interpreted only by Muslim men who have arrogated to themselves the task of defining the ontological, theological, sociological, and eschatalogical status of Muslim women. While it is encouraging to know that women such as Khadija and 'A'isha (wives of the prophet Muhammad) and Rabi'a al-Basri (the outstanding women Sufi) figure significantly in early Islam, the fact remains that until the present time, the Islamic tradition and Muslim culture remain overwhelmingly patriarchal, inhibiting the growth of scholarship among women particularly in the realm of religious thought.

Given this state of affairs, it is hardly surprising that until recent times, the vast majority of Muslim women have remained wholly or largely unaware of their "Islamic" (in an ideal sense) rights. Male-centered and male-dominated Muslim societies have continued to assert, glibly and tirelessly, that Islam has given women more rights than any other religion, while keeping women in physical, mental, and emotional confinement and depriving them of the opportunity to actualize their human potential. Here, it is pertinent to mention that

while the rate of literacy is low in many Muslim countries, the rate of literacy
in the rural areas where most of the population lives, is among the lowest in the
world especially for Muslim women.

Contemporary Muslim Women and the Process of "Islamization"

Since the nineteen-seventies, largely due to the pressure of antiwomen
laws which have been promulgated under the guise of "Islamization" in a number of Muslim countries, women with some degree of education and awareness
have begun to realize that religion is being used as an instrument of oppression
rather than as a means of liberation from unjust social structures and systems
of thought and conduct. This realization has stemmed from the fact that women
have been the primary targets of the "Islamization" process.

In order to understand the motivation underlying this process, it is useful
to bear in mind that of all the challenges confronting the contemporary Muslim
world, the greatest appears to be that of modernity. The caretakers of Muslim
traditionalism are aware of the fact that viability in the modern technological
age requires the adoption of the scientific or rational outlook, which inevitably
brings about major changes in modes of thinking and behavior. Women, both
educated and uneducated, who are participating in the national workforce and
contributing toward national development, think and behave differently from
women who have no sense of their individual identity or autonomy as active
agents in a history-making process. They regard themselves merely as instruments designed to minister to, and reinforce, a patriarchal system that they believe to be divinely instituted.

Unable to come to grips with modernity as a whole, many contemporary
Muslim societies make a sharp distinction between two aspects of it. The first—
generally referred to as "modernization" and largely approved—is identified
with science, technology, and a better standard of life. The second—generally
referred to as "Westernization" and largely disapproved—is identified with em-
blems of "mass" Western culture such as promiscuity, break-up of family and
community, latch-key kids, and drug and alcohol abuse. Many Muslims see
"emancipated" women, not as symbols of "modernization" but as symbols of
"Westernization." The latter is linked in Muslim minds not only with the colonization of Muslim people by Western powers in the not-too-distant past, but
also with the continuing onslaught on "the integrity of the Islamic way of life"
by Westerners and Westernized Muslims who uphold the West as a model for
intellectual and social transformation of Muslim communities.

Many traditional societies—including the Muslim—divide the world
into "private" space (the home, which is the domain of women) and "public"

space (the rest of the world, which is the domain of men) Muslims, in general, tend to believe that it is best to keep men and women segregated—in their separate, designated spaces. The intrusion of women into men's space is seen as leading to the disruption, if not the destruction, of the fundamental order of things. If some exigency makes it necessary for women to enter into men's space, they must make themselves "faceless," or at least as inconspicuous as possible. This is achieved through "veiling," which is, thus, an extension of the idea of the segregation of the sexes.

Women-related issues pertaining to various aspects of personal, as well as social, life lie at the heart of much of the ferment or unrest that characterizes the Muslim world in general. Many of the issues are not new issues but the manner in which they are being debated today is something new. Much of this ongoing debate has been generated by the enactment of manifestly antiwomen laws in a number of Muslim countries. For instance, since the "Islamization" process was initiated in Pakistan by General Muhammad Zia-ul-Haq in the nineteen-seventies, many Pakistani women have been jolted out of their "dogmatic slumber" by the enactment of laws such as the Hudood Ordinance (1979), the Law of Evidence (1984), and the Qisas and Diyat ordinance (1990), which discriminate against women in a blatant manner. These laws which pertain to women's testimony in cases of their own rape or in financial and other matters, and to "blood-money" for women's murder, aimed at reducing the value and status of women systematically, virtually mathematically, to less than that of men. The emergence of women's protest groups in Pakistan was very largely a response to the realization that forces of religious conservatism (aided by the power of the military government) were determined to cut women down to less than a fully human status (stating that in many matters two women were regarded as being equal to one man), and that this attitude stemmed from a deep-rooted desire to keep women *in their place,* which is understood as being secondary, subordinate, and inferior to that of men.

Though women's groups have put up serious resistance to the erosion of women's status and rights in Pakistan and other Muslim countries, it is still not clearly and fully understood by many Muslim women activists that the negative ideas and attitudes pertaining to women that prevail in Muslim societies generally are rooted in theology. Unless, or until, the theological foundations of the misogynistic and androcentric tendencies that have become incorporated in Muslim culture are demolished, Muslim women will continue to be brutalized and discriminated against despite improvement in statistics relating to women's education, employment, social and political rights, and so on.

No matter how many socio-political rights are granted to women by patriarchal Muslim countries, as long as these women are conditioned to accept the myths and arguments used by religious heirarchs to shackle their bodies, hearts, minds, and souls, they will never become fully developed or whole human beings, free of guilt and fear, able to stand equal to men in the sight of God.

The importance of developing a theology of women in the context of the Islamic tradition—as the West has developed "feminist theology" in the context of the Jewish and Christian traditions—is paramount today with a view to liberating not only Muslim women, but also Muslim men, from unjust social structures and laws that make a peer relationship between men and women impossible.

While it is good to know that there have been significant Muslim men, such as Qasim Amin in Egypt and Mumtaz 'Ali in India, who used their scholarship in staunch support of women's rights, it is disheartening to also know that even in the age characterized by an explosion of knowledge, all but a handful of Muslim women lack any knowledge of Islamic theology.

In the contemporary world there is an urgent need for Muslim women to engage in a scholarly study of Islam's primary sources in order to become effective voices in the theological deliberations and discussions on women-related issues that are taking place in much of the contemporary Muslim world. Though political activism is necessary in order to combat the onslaught of anti-women laws and acts of brutality toward women in a number of present-day Muslim societies, it is not sufficient by itself to overturn what has been imposed in the name of Islam.

Legislation legitimized by reference to a religious argument can be superseded or set aside, in most contemporary Muslim societies, only by reference to a better religious argument. A profound tragedy of Muslims, as pointed out by Fazlur Rahman, is that those who understand Islam do not know modernity and those who understand modernity, do not know Islam. However, through study, reflection, and interaction among human and women's rights activists, it is possible to equip "modernist" Muslims—both women and men—to understand Islamic ideals as well as Muslim realities and be able to counter the retrogressive arguments being used to deny women their God-given rights by means of better theological arguments. This is essential if the Qur'anic vision of what a Muslim society should be is to become actualized in any Muslim society or community.

Women and Normative Islam: Three Fundamental Theological Assumptions

Much of what has happened to Muslim women through the ages becomes comprehensible if one keeps one fact in mind: Muslims, in general, consider it self-evident that women are not equal to men who are "above" women or have a "degree of advantage" over them. There is hardly anything in a Muslim woman's life that is not affected by this belief. Hence it is vitally important, not only for theological reasons but also for pragmatic ones, to subject it to rigorous scholarly scrutiny and attempt to identify its roots.

The roots of the belief that men are superior to women lie, in my judgment, in three theological assumptions: (a) that God's primary creation is man, not woman, since woman is believed to have been created from man's rib and is, therefore, derivative and secondary ontologically: (b) that woman, not man, was the primary agent of what is customarily described as "man's fall" or expulsion from the Garden of Eden, and hence "all daughters of Eve" are to be regarded with hatred, suspicion, and contempt; and (c) that woman was created not only *from* man but also *for* man, which makes her existence merely instrumental and not of fundamental importance.

The three theological questions to which the above assumptions may appropriately be regarded as answers are: (1) How was woman created? (2) Was woman responsible for the fall of man? and (3) Why was woman created? While all three questions have had profound significance in the history of ideas and attitudes pertaining to women in the Islamic, Christian, and Jewish traditions, I consider the first one that relates to the issue of woman's creation, more basic and important, philosophically and theologically, than any other in the context of gender-equality. This is so because if man and woman have been created equal by God who is the ultimate arbiter of value, then they cannot become unequal *essentially* at a subsequent time. On the other hand, if man and woman have been created unequal by God, then they cannot become equal *essentially* at a subsequent time.

How was Woman Created?: The Issue of Woman's Creation

The ordinary Muslim believes, as seriously as the ordinary Jew or Christian, that Adam was God's primary creation and that Eve was made from Adam's rib. While this myth has obvious rootage in the Yahwist's account of creation in Genesis 2:18–24, it has no basis whatever in the Qur'an, which in the context of human creation speaks always in completely egalitarian terms. In none of the thirty or so passages that describe the creation of humanity (designated by generic terms such as *an-nas, al-insan,* and *bashar*) by God in a variety of ways is there any statement that could be interpreted as asserting or suggesting that man was created prior to woman or that woman was created from man. The Qur'an notwithstanding, Muslims believe that *Hawwa'* (the Hebrew/Arabic counterpart of Eve), who incidentally is never mentioned in the Qur'an, was created from the "crooked" rib of *Adam*, who is believed to be the first human being created by God.

Here it needs to be mentioned that the term Adam is not an Arabic term but a Hebrew one meaning "of the soil" (from *adamah*, "the soil"). The Hebrew term *Adam* functions generally as a collective noun referring to the human (species) rather than to a male human being. In the Qur'an also the term *Adam* refers, in twenty-one cases out of twenty-five, to humanity. Here it is of interest to note that though the term *Adam* mostly does not refer to a particular human being, it does refer to human beings in a particular way. As pointed out by Muhammad Iqbal:

> Indeed, in the verses which deal with the origin of man as a living being, the Qur'an uses the words "Bashar" or "Insan," not "Adam," which it reserves for man in his capacity of God's vicegerent on earth. The purpose of the Qur'an is further secured by the omission of proper names mentioned in the Biblical narration—Adam and Eve. The term "Adam" is retained and used more as a concept than as a name of a concrete human individual. The word is not without authority in the Qur'an itself.[8]

Qu'ran - humanity created, not man then women

An analysis of the Qur'anic descriptions of human creation shows how the Qur'an evenhandedly uses both feminine and masculine terms and imagery to describe the creation of humanity from a single source. That God's original creation was undifferentiated humanity and not either man or woman (who appeared simultaneously at a subsequent time) is implicit in a number of Qur'anic passages. If the Qur'an makes no distinction between the creation of man and woman—as it clearly does not—why do Muslims believe that Hawwa' was created from the rib of Adam?

Although the Genesis 2 account of woman's creation is accepted by virtually all Muslims, it is difficult to believe that it entered the Islamic tradition directly, for very few Muslims ever read the Bible. It is much more likely that it became a part of Muslim heritage through its assimilation in the *hadith* literature. That the Genesis 2 idea of woman being created from Adam's rib did, in fact, become incorporated in the *hadith* literature is evident from a number of *ahadith*. Of these, six are particularly important since they appear to have had a formative impact on how Muslims have perceived woman's being and sexuality (as differentiated from man's). The *matn* (content) of these six *ahadith*—three from *Sahih Al-Bukhari* and three from *Sahih Muslim*, and all ascribed to the companion known as Abu Huraira—is given below:

1. Treat women nicely, for a woman is created from a rib, and the most curved portion of the rib is its upper portion. So if you would try to straighten it, it will break, but if you leave it as it is, it will remain crooked. So treat women nicely.[9]

2. The woman is like a rib; if you try to straighten her, she will break. So if you want to get benefit from her, do so while she still has some crookedness.[10]

Hadith - sayings attributed to the prophet Mohammad

3. Whoever believes in Allah and the Last Day should not hurt (trouble) his neighbor. And I advise you to take care of the women, for they are created from a rib and the most crooked part of the rib is its upper part; if you try to straighten it, it will break; and if you leave it, it will remain crooked; so I urge you to take care of woman.[11]

4. Woman is like a rib. When you attempt to straighten it, you would break it. And if you leave her alone, you would benefit by her, and crookedness will remain in her.[12]

5. Woman has been created from a rib and will in no way be straightened for you; so benefit by her while crookedness remains in her. And if you attempt to straighten her, you will break her, and breaking her is divorcing her.[13]

6. He who believes in Allah and the Hereafter, if he witnesses any matter he should talk in good terms about it or keep quiet. Act kindly toward women, for woman is created from a rib, and the most crooked part of the rib is its top. If you attempt to straighten it, you will break it, and if you leave it, the crookedness will remain there so act kindly toward women.[14]

I have examined these *ahadith* elsewhere and have shown them to be flawed both with regard to their formal *isnad* as well as their material *matn* aspects. The theology of woman implicit in these *ahadith* is based upon generalizations about her ontology, biology, and psychology contrary to the letter and spirit of the Qur'an. These *ahadith* ought, therefore, to have been rejected— since Muslim scholars agree on the principle that any *hadith* that is inconsistent with the Qur'an cannot be accepted. However, despite the fact that the *ahadith* in question contradict the teachings of the Qur'an, they have continued to be an important part of the ongoing Islamic tradition.

Undoubtedly one of the major reasons for this is that these *ahadith* come from the two most highly venerated *hadith* collections by Muhammad ibn Isma'il al-Bukhari (810–70) and Muslim bin al-Hallaj (817–75). These two collections known collectively as *Sahihan* (from *sahih,* meaning sound or authentic) "form an almost unassailable authority, subject indeed to criticism in details, yet deriving an indestructible influence from the *ijma* of general consent of the community in custom and belief, which it is their function to authenticate."[15]

While being included in the *Sahihan* gives the *ahadith* in question much weight among Muslims who know about the science of *hadith,* their continuing popularity among Muslims in general indicates that they articulate something deeply embedded in Muslim culture—namely, the belief that women are derivative creatures who can never be considered equal to men.

Theologically, the history of women's subjection in the Islamic (as well as the Jewish and Christian) tradition began with the story of Hawwa's creation. In my view, unless Muslim women return to the point of origin and challenge the authenticity of the *ahadith* that makes all representatives of their sex ontologically inferior and irremediably crooked, male-centered and male-controlled Muslim societies are not at all likely to acknowledge the egalitarianism evident in the Qur'anic statements about human creation.

Was Woman Responsible for Man's Expulsion from Paradise: The Issue of Woman's "Guilt" in the "Fall" Episode

Many Muslims, like many Jews and Christians, would answer this question in the affirmative, though nothing in the Qur'anic descriptions of the so-called "fall" episode would warrant such an answer. Here it may be noted that whereas in Genesis 3:6, the dialogue preceding the eating of the forbidden fruit by the human pair in the Garden of Eden is between the serpent and Eve (though Adam's presence is also indicated, as contended by feminist theologians) and this has provided the basis for the popular casting of Eve into the role of tempter, deceiver, and seducer of Adam, in the Qur'an, the "Shaitan" (Satan) has no exclusive dialogue with Adam's *zauj* (mate).

In two of the three passages that refer to this episode—namely Surah 2: Al-Baqarah: 35–39 and Surah 7: Al-A'raf: 19–25—the Shaitan is stated to have led both Adam and *zauj* astray, though in the former (verse 36) no actual conversation is reported. In the remaining passage—namely, Surah 20: Ta-Ha: 115–124—it is Adam who is charged with forgetting his covenant with God (verse 115), who is tempted by the Shaitan (verse 120), and who disobeys God and allows himself to be seduced (verse 121).

However, if one looks at all the three passages as well as the way in which the term *Adam* functions generally in the Qur'an, it becomes clear that the Qur'an regards the act of disobedience by the human pair in *al-jannah* (the Garden) as a collective rather than an individual act for which an exclusive, or even primary, responsibility is not assigned to either man or woman. Even in the last passage in which "Adam" appears to be held responsible for forgetting the covenant and for allowing himself to be beguiled by the Shaitan, the act of disobedience—the eating from "the tree"—is committed jointly by Adam and *zauj* and not by Adam alone or in the first place.

Having said that, it is extremely important to stress the point that the Qur'an provides no basis whatever for asserting, suggesting, or implying that Hawwa', having been tempted and deceived by the Shaitan, in turn tempted and deceived Adam and led to his expulsion from *al-jannah*. This fact notwithstanding, many Muslim commentators have ascribed the primary responsibility for man's "fall" to woman, as may be seen from the following extract:

> In al-Tabiri's *Tarikh* (1:108) the very words Satan use to tempt Eve are then used by her to tempt Adam: "Look at this tree, how sweet is its smell, how delicious is its fruit, how beautiful is its colour!" This passage is

concluded by God's specifically accusing Eve of deceiving Adam. Later in the narrative (1:111-;112) al-Tabari mentions a report that is also cited by other commentators, the gist of which is to say that Adam while in his full reasoning faculties, did not eat of the tree, but only succumbed to the temptation after Eve had given him wine to drink. Al-Tha'labi in citing the same report also stresses the loss of Adam's rationality through the imbibing of wine, and al-Razi (*Tafsir* 3:13) says that such a story, which he has seen in several *tafsirs,* is not at all far-fetched. Implicit in this specific act, of course, is both Eve's culpability and Adam's inherent rationality. Lest any should miss the point that Eve is actively and not just innocently involved in Adam's temptation, Ibn Kathir asserts that God surely knows best, it was Eve who ate of the tree before Adam and urged him to eat. He then quotes a saying attributed to the Prophet, "But for Banu Isra'il meat would not have spoiled (because they used to keep it for the next day), and but for Hawwa' no female would be a traitor to her husband!" (*Bidaya* 1:84).[16]

There is hardly any doubt that Muslim women have been as victimized as Jewish and Christian women by the way in which the Jewish, Christian, and Islamic traditions have generally interpreted the "fall" episode. However, it needs to be pointed out that the Qur'anic account of the episode differs significantly from the Biblical account, and that the "fall" does not mean in the Islamic tradition what it means in the Jewish, and particularly in the Christian, tradition.

To begin with, whereas in *Genesis 3* no explanation is given as to why the serpent tempts either Eve alone or both Adam and Eve, in the Qur'an the reason why the Shaitan or ("Iblis") sets out to beguile the human pair in *al-jannah* is stated clearly in a number of passages.[17] The refusal of the Shaitan to obey God's command to bow in submission to Adam follows from his belief that being a creature of fire he is elementally superior to Adam who is a creature of clay. When condemned for his arrogance by God and ordered to depart in a state of abject disgrace, the Shaitan throws a challenge to the Almighty: he will prove to God that Adam and Adam's progeny are unworthy of the honor and favor bestowed on them by God, being—in general—ungrateful, weak, and easily lured away from "the straight path" by worldly temptations.

Not attempting to hide his intentions to "come upon" human beings from all sides, the Shaitan asks for—and is granted—a reprieve until "the day of the appointed time." Not only is the reprieve granted, but God also tells the Shaitan to use all his wiles and forces to "assault" human beings and see if they would follow him. A cosmic drama now begins, involving the eternal opposition between the principles of right and wrong or good and evil, which is lived out as human beings, exercising their moral autonomy, must now choose between "the straight path" and "the crooked path."

- God allow's satan to
go and tempt

In terms of the Qur'anic narrative, what happens to the human pair in *al-jannah* is a sequel to the interchange between God and the Shaitan. In the sequel we learn that Adam and *zauj* have been commanded not to go near "the tree" lest they become *zalimin.* Seduced by the Shaitan, they disobey God. However, in Surah 7: Al-A'raf :23 they acknowledge before God that they have done *zulm* to themselves and earnestly seek God's forgiveness and mercy. They are told by God to "go forth" or "descend" from *al-jannah,* but in addressing them the Qur'an uses the dual form of address (referring exclusively to Adam and *zauj*) only once (in Surah 18: Ta-Ha: 123); for the rest, the plural form is used, which necessarily refers to more than two persons and is generally understood as referring to humanity a whole.

In the framework of Qur'anic theology, the order to "go forth" from *al-jannah* given to Adam or the children of Adam cannot be considered a punishment, because Adam was always meant to be God's vicegerent on earth, as stated clearly in Surah 2: Al-Baqarah: 30. The earth is not a place of banishment but is declared by the Qur'an to be humanity's dwelling place and a source of profit to it.[18] The *al-jannah* mentioned in the fall story is not—as pointed out by Muhammad Iqbal—"the supersensual paradise from which man is supposed to have fallen on this earth."

There is, strictly speaking, no "fall" in the Qur'an. What the Qur'anic narration focuses upon is the moral choice that humanity is required to make when confronted by the alternatives presented to them by God and the Shaitan. This becomes clear if one reflects on the text of Surah 2: Al-Baqarah: 35 and Surah 7: Al-A'raf: 19, in which it is stated: "You (dual) go not near this tree, lest you (dual) become of the *zalimin.*" In other words, the human pair is being told that if they go near the tree, then they will be counted among those who perpetrate *zulm.* Commenting on the root ZLM, Toshihiko Izutsu says:

> The primary meaning of ZLM is, in the opinion of many of the authoritative lexicologists, that of "putting in a wrong place." In the moral sphere it seems to mean primarily "to act in such a way as to transgress the proper limit and encroach upon the right of some other person." Briefly and generally speaking *zulm* is to do injustice in the sense of going beyond one's bounds and doing what one has no right to.[19]

By transgressing the limits set by God, the human pair becomes guilty of *zulm* toward themselves. This *zulm* consists in their taking on the responsibility for choosing between good and evil. Here it is important to note:

> (The) Qur'anic legend of the "Fall" has nothing to do with the first appearance of man on this planet. Its purpose is rather to indicate man's rise from a primitive state of instinctive appetite to the conscious possession

of a free self, capable of doubt and disobedience. The "Fall" does not mean any moral depravity, it is man's transition from simple consciousness, to the first flash of self-consciousness, a kind of waking from the dream of nature with a throb of personal causality in one's own being. Nor does the Qur'an regard the earth as a torture hall where an elementally wicked humanity is imprisoned for an original act of sin. Man's first act of disobedience was also his first act of free choice; and that is why, according to the Qur'anic narration, Adam's first transgression was forgiven. . . . A being whose movements are wholly determined like a machine cannot produce goodness. Freedom is thus a condition of goodness. But to permit the emergence of a finite ego who has the power to choose after considering the relative values of several courses of action open to him, is really to take a great risk: for the freedom to choose good involves also the freedom to choose what is the opposite of good. That God has taken this risk shows his immense faith in man; it is now for man to justify this faith.[20]

Since there is no "fall" in the Qur'an, there is no original sin. Human beings are not born sinful into this world, hence do not need to be "redeemed" or "saved." This is generally accepted in the Islamic tradition. However, the association of the "fall" with sexuality, which has played such a massive role in perpetuating the myth of feminine evil in the Christian tradition, also exists in the minds of many Muslims and causes untold damage to Muslim women.

It is remarkable to see that though there is no reference to sexual activity on the part of man or woman even in their postlapsarian state of partial or complete nakedness in either Genesis 3 or the Qur'an, many Muslim scholars have jumped to the conclusion that exposure of their *sau'at* ("the external portion of the organs of generation of a man and of a woman and the anus"),[21] generally translated as "shameful parts," necessarily led the human pair to sexual activity that was "shameful" not only by virtue of being linked with their "shameful parts" but also because it was instigated by Shaitan. The following explanation by A. A. Maududi—one of contemporary Islam's most influential scholars—represents the thinking of many, if not most, Muslims on this point:

The sex instinct is the greatest weakness of the human race. That is why Satan selected this weak spot for his attack on the adversary and devised the scheme to strike at their modesty. Therefore the first step he took in this direction was to expose their nakedness to them so as to open the door of indecency before them and beguile them into sexuality. Even to this day, Satan and his disciples are adopting the same scheme of depriving the woman of the feelings of modesty and shyness and they cannot think of any scheme of "progress" unless they expose and exhibit the woman to all and sundry.[22]

The initial statement leaves no doubt about Maududi's negative view of "the sex-instinct," which he describes as "the greatest weakness of the human race." Associating sexuality with Shaitan's "attack on the adversary." Maududi assumes that on discovering their state of physical exposure, the human pair resorted irresistibly to an act of "indecency"—sexual intercourse. However, there is nothing in the text that warrants this assumption. In fact, according to the text, the human pair's first act on discovering their exposed state was one of "decency"—namely, that of covering themselves with leaves.

That Maududi—like many other Muslims, Jews, and Christians—sees women as the primary agents of sexuality (regarded as the Shaitan's chief instrument for defeating God's plan for humanity) is clear from the way in which he shifts attention from the human pair to the woman, in the above passage. In turning his eyes away from the "nakedness" of the sons of Adam to focus on the "nakedness" of the daughters of Hawwa', he is typical of Muslim culture.

Though the branding of women as "the devil's gateway" is not at all the intent of the Qur'anic narration of the "fall" story—as the foregoing account has shown—Muslims, no less than Jews and Christians, have used the story to vent their misogynistic feelings. This is clear from the continuing popularity of *ahadith* such as the following:

> Narrated Usama bin Zaid: The Prophet said, "After me I have not left any affliction more harmful to men than women."[23]
>
> Ibn Abbas reported that Allah's Messenger said: "I had a chance to look into Paradise and I found that the majority of the people were poor and I looked into the Fire and there I found the majority constituted by women."[24]
>
> Abu Sa'id Khudri reported that Allah's Messenger said: "The world is sweet and green (alluring) and verily Allah is going to install you as vicegerent in it in order to see how you act. So avoid the allurement of women: verily, the first trial for the people of Isra'il was caused by women."[25]

Why was Woman Created?" The Issue of the Purpose of Woman's Existence

The Qur'an, which does not discriminate against women in the context of the "fall" episode, does not support the view—held by many Muslims, Christians, and Jews—that woman was created not only from man but also for man. That God's creation as a whole is "for just ends" (Surah 15: Al-Hijr: 85) and not "for idle sport" (Surah 21: Al-Anbiya': 16) is one of the major themes of the Qur'an. Humanity, fashioned "in the best of molds: (Surah 95: At-Tin: 4) has been created in order to serve God (Surah 51: Adh-Dhariyat: 56). God cannot be separated from service to humankind, or—in Islamic

Believers in God must honour rights of God and rights of creatures [handwritten margin note]

terms—believers in God must honor both *Haquq Allah* (rights of God) and *Haquq al-ʻibad* (rights of creatures).

Fulfillment of one's duties to God and humankind constitutes the essence of righteousness. That men and women are equally called upon by God to be righteous is stated unambiguously in a number of Qur'anic passages such as the following:

> The Believers, men
> And women, are protectors,
> One of another; they enjoin
> What is just, and forbid
> What is evil: they observe
> Regular prayers, practise
> Regular charity, and obey
> God and His Apostle.
> On them will God pour
> His mercy: for God
> Is exalted in power, Wise,
> God hath promised to Believers,
> Men and women, Gardens
> Under which rivers flow,
> To dwell therein,
> And beautiful mansions
> In gardens of everlasting Bliss
> But the greatest bliss
> Is the God Pleasure of God:
> That is the supreme felicity.[26]

Members and protectors of each other [handwritten margin note]

Not only does the Qur'an make it clear that man and woman stand absolutely equal in the sight of God, but also that they are "members" and "protectors" of each other. In other words, the Qur'an does not create a hierarchy in which men are placed above women, nor does it pit men against women in an adversary relationship. They are created as equal creatures of a universal, just, and merciful Creator whose pleasure it is that they live—in harmony and in righteousness—together.

In spite of the Qur'anic affirmation of man-woman equality, Muslim societies in general have never regarded men and women as equal, particularly in the context of marriage. Fatima Mernissi's observations on the position of a Muslim woman in relation to her family in modern Morocco apply, more or less, to Muslim culture generally:

> One of the distinctive characteristics of Muslim sexuality is its territoriality, which reflects a specific division of labour and a specific concep-

tion of society and of power. The territoriality of Muslim sexuality sets ranks, tasks, and authority patterns. Spatially confined, the woman was taken care of materially by the man who possessed her in return for her total obedience and her sexual and reproductive services. The whole system was organized so that the Muslim "ummah" was actually a society of male citizens who possessed among other things a female half of the population. Muslim men have always had more rights and privileges than Muslim women, including even the right to kill their women. . . . The man imposed on the woman an artificially narrow existence, both physically and spiritually.[27]

Underlying the rejection in Muslim societies of the idea of man-woman equality is the deeply rooted belief that women who are inferior in creation (having been made from a crooked rib) and in righteousness (having helped the Shaitan in defeating God's plan for Adam) have been created mainly to be of use to men who are superior to them.

The alleged superiority of men to women, which permeates the Islamic (as also the Jewish and Christian) tradition, is grounded not only in hadith literature but also in popular interpretations of some Qur'anic passages. Two Qur'anic passages—Surah 4: An-Nisa': 34 and Surah 2: Al Bagarah: 228—in particular, are generally cited to support the contention that men have "a degree of advantage" over women. Of these, the first reads as follows in A. A. Maududi's translation of the Arabic text:

> Men are the managers of the affairs of women because Allah has made the one superior to the other and because men spend of their wealth on women. Virtuous women are, therefore, obedient: they guard their rights carefully in their absence under the care and watch of Allah. As for those women whose defiance you have cause to fear, admonish them and keep them apart from your beds and beat them. Then, if they submit to you, do not look for excuses to punish them: note it well that there is Allah above you, Who is Supreme and Great.[29]

It is difficult to overstate the impact of the general Muslim understanding of Surah 4: An-Nisa': 34, which is embodied in Maududi's translation. As soon as the issue of woman's equality with man is raised by liberal Muslims, the immediate response by traditional Muslims is, "But don't you know that God says in the Qur'an that men are *qawwamun* in relation to women and have the right to rule over them and even to beat them?" In fact, the mere statement, *ar-rijal-o qawwamun-a 'ala an-nisa* (literally, the men are *qawwamun* in relation to women) signifies the end of any attempt to discuss the issue of woman's equality with man in the Islamic *ummah*.

It is assumed by almost all who read Surah 4, An-Nisa': verse 34, that it is addressed to husbands. The first point to be noted is that it is addressed to *ar-rijal* (the men) and the *an-nisa* (the women). In other words, it is addressed to all men and women of the Islamic community. This is further indicated by the fact that in relation to all the actions that are required to be taken, the plural and not the dual form (used when reference is made to two persons) is found. Such usage makes clear that the prescriptions contained in this verse were not addressed to a husband or wife but to the Islamic *ummah* in general.

The key word in the first sentence of this verse is *qawwamun*. This word has been translated variously as "protectors and maintainers (of women)," "in charge (of women)," "having preeminence (above women)," and "sovereigns or masters (over women)." Linguistically, the word *qawwamun* means "breadwinners" or "those who provide a means of support or livelihood." A point of logic that must be made here is that the first sentence is not a descriptive one stating that all men as a matter of fact are providing for women. What the sentence is stating, rather, is that men ought to have the capability to provide (since "ought" implies "can"). In other words, this statement, which popular Muslim culture and tradition have regarded as an actual description of all men, is, in fact, a normative statement pertaining to the Islamic concept of division of labor in an ideal family or community structure. The fact that men are *qawwamun* does not mean that women cannot or should not provide for themselves, but simply that in view of the heavy burden that most women shoulder in childbearing and rearing, they should not have the additional obligation of providing the means of living at the same time.

Continuing with analysis of the passage, we come next to the idea that God has given the one more "strength" than the other. Most translations make it appear that the one who has more strength, excellence, or superiority is the man. However, the Qur'anic text does not accord superiority to men. Using an idiomatic expression which literally means "some in relation to some," the Qur'anic statement could mean either that some men are superior to some others (men or women) and that some women are superior to some others (men or women). The interpretation that seems to me to be the most appropriate contextually is that some men are more blessed with the means to be better providers than are other men.

The next part of the passage begins with a "therefore," which indicates that this part is conditional upon the first: in other words, if men fulfill their assigned function of being providers, women must fulfill their corresponding duties. Most translations describe this duty in terms of the wife being "obedient" to the husband. The word *salihat,* which is translated as "righteously obedient," is related to the word *salahiat,* which means "capability" or "potentiality." A woman's special capability is to bear children, and she carries and protects the fetus (which is hidden from the eye) in her womb until it can be safely delivered.

What is outlined in the first part of this passage is a functional division of labor necessary for maintaining balance in any society. Men who do not have to fulfill the responsibility of childbearing are assigned the functions of being breadwinners. Women are exempted from the responsibility of being bread-winners in order that they may fulfill their function as childbearers. The two functions are separate but complementary, and neither is higher or lower than the other.

The three injunctions in the second part of the verse were given to the Islamic *ummah* in order to meet a rather extraordinary possibility: a mass rebellion on the part of women against their role as childbearers—a function assigned to them by God. If all or most of the women in a Muslim society refused to bear children without just cause as a sign of organized defiance or revolt, this would mean the end of the Muslim *ummah*. This situation must, therefore, be dealt with decisively. The first step to be taken is to find out the reasons for this act of defiance and to offer counseling. If this step is unsuccessful, the second step to be taken is isolation of the rebellious women from others. (It is to be noted here that the prescription is to leave the women in solitary confinement. By translating this line, "Keep them apart from your beds," Maududi is suggesting, if not stating, that the judging party is the husband and not the Islamic community—an assumption not warranted by the text.)[28] If the second step is also not successful, then the step of confining the women for a longer period of time may be taken by the Islamic community or its representatives. Here it is important to point out that the Arabic word *daraba* that is generally translated as "beating" has numerous meanings. When used in a legal context as it is here, it means "holding in confinement," according to the authorative lexicon *Taj-ul-'Arus*.[29] (In Surah 4: An-Nisa': 15, women who are proven to be guilty of immorality are also given the punishment of being confined to their homes.)

While Muslims, through the centuries, have interpreted Surah 4: An-Nisa': 34 as giving them unequivocal mastery over women, a linguistically and philosophically/theologically accurate interpretation of this passage would lead to radically different conclusions. In simple words, what this passage is saying is that since only women can bear children (which is not to say either that all women should bear children or that women's sole function is to bear children)—a function whose importance in the survival of any community cannot be questioned—they should not have the additional obligation of being bread-winners while they perform this function. Thus, during the period of a woman's childbearing, the function of breadwinning must be performed by men (not just husbands) in the Muslim *ummah*.

Reflection on this Qur'anic passage shows that the division of functions mandated here is designed to ensure justice in the community as a whole. There are millions of women all over the world who are designated inaccurately as "single" parents (when, in fact, they are "double" parents) who bear and raise children singlehandedly, generally without much support from the community. This surely does not constitute a just situation. If children are the wealth and future of the *ummah,* the importance of protecting the function of childbearing and childraising becomes self-evident. Statistics from all over the world show that women and children left without the care and custodianship of men suffer from economic, social, psychological, and other ills.

What Surah An-Nisa': 34 is ensuring is that this does not happen. It enjoins men in general to assume responsibility for women in general when they are performing the vitally important function of childbearing (other passages in the Qur'an extend this also to childrearing). Thus the intent of this passage, which has traditionally been used to subordinate women to men, is in fact to guarantee women the material (as well as moral) security needed by them during the period of pregnancy when breadwinning can become difficult or even impossible for them.

The second passage that mentions the so-called "degree of advantage" that men have over women is Surah 2: Al-Baqarah: 228, which reads:

> Divorced women
> Shall wait concerning
> For three monthly periods.
> Nor is it lawful for them
> To hide what God
> Hath created in their wombs,
> If they have faith
> In God and the last Day
> And their husbands
> Have the better right
> To take them back
> in that period, if
> They wish for reconciliation.
> *And women shall have rights*
> *Similar to the rights*
> *Against them, according*
> *To what is equitable*
> *But men have a degree*
> *(of advantage) over them,*
> And God is Exalted in Power, Wise[30]

As can be seen, the above cited passage pertains to the subject of divorce. The "advantage" that men have over women in this context is that women must observe a three-month period called *iddat* before remarriage, but men are exempted from this requirement. The main reason why women are subjected to this restriction is because at the time of divorce a woman may be pregnant and this fact may not become known for some time. As men cannot become pregnant they are allowed to remarry without a waiting period.

In my judgment, the Qur'anic passages—in particular the two discussed above—on which the edifice of male superiority over women largely rests, have been misread or misinterpreted, intentionally or unintentionally, by most Muslim societies and men. A "correct" reading of these passages would not, however, make a radical or substantial difference to the existing pattern of male-female relationships in Muslim societies unless attention was also drawn to those *ahadith* that have been used to make man not only superior to woman, but virtually her god. The following *hadith* is particularly important:

> A man came in with his daughter and said, "This my daughter refuses to get married," The Prophet said, "Obey your father." She said, "By the name of Him Who sent you in truth, I will not marry until you inform me what is the right of the husband over his wife." He said . . . "if it were permitted for one human being to bow down (*sajada*) to another I would have ordered the woman to bow down to her husband when he enters into her, because of God's grace on her." (The daughter) answered, "By the name of Him Who sent you, with truth, I would never marry!"[31]

A faith as rigidly monotheistic as Islam cannot conceivably permit any human being to worship anyone but God, therefore the hypothetical statement "If it were permitted . . . " in the above cited *hadith*, is, ipso facto, an impossibility. But the way this *hadith* is related makes it appear that if not God's, at least it was the Prophet's will or wish, to make the wife prostrate herself before her husband. Each word, act, or exhortation attributed to the Prophet is held to be sacred by most of the Muslims in the world and so this *hadith* (which, in my judgment seeks to legitimate *shirk*: associating anyone with God—an unforgivable sin according to the Qur'an) becomes binding on the Muslim woman. Muslims frequently criticize a religion such as Hinduism where the wife is required to worship the husband (*patipuja*) but in practice what is expected from most Muslim wives is not very different from *patipuja*. In India and Pakistan, for example, a Muslim woman learns almost as an article of faith that her husband is her *majazi khuda* ("god in earthly form"). This description, undoubtedly, constitutes *shirk*.

Most *ahadith* dealing with the subject of married women describe a virtuous woman as one who pleases and obeys her husband at all times. Pleasing the husband can, in fact, become more important than pleasing God. Putting it differently, one can say that most Muslims believe that a woman cannot please God except through pleasing her husband. Some *ahadith* are cited to illustrate this point:

> The wife of Sufwan B. Mu'attal went to the Prophet when we were with him and said, "O Messenger of God, my husband . . . beats me when I perform my devotions, and makes me eat when I fast . . . " (The Prophet) asked Sufwan about what she had said and he replied, "O Messenger of God . . . she fasts and I am a young man and have not patience." The Messenger of God said, "From now on let a woman not fast except by permission of her husband" (Ibn Hanbal).[32]
>
> A woman whose husband is pleased with her at the time of her death goes straight to Paradise (Tirmidhi).[33] There are three (persons) whose prayer is not accepted nor their virtues taken above: the fugitive slave till he returns to his masters and places his hand in their hands; the woman on whom her husband remains displeased; and the drunkard, till he becomes sober (Baihaqi).[34]
>
> Hadrat Anas reported that the Holy Prophet had said: "For a woman her husband is Paradise as well as hell: (Ahmad and Nasa'i).[35]
>
> Hadrat Ibn Abi Aufi reported that the Holy Prophet has said: "By Allah in whose hand is my life, the woman who does not discharge her duties to her husband is disobedient to Allah, and the discharge of duties toward Allah depends on the discharge of duties towards the husband" (Ibn Majah).[36]

Man and woman, created equal by God and standing equal in the sight of God, have become very unequal in Muslim societies. The Qur'anic description of man and woman in marriage: "They are your garments/And you are their garments"[37] implies closeness, mutuality, and equality. However, Muslim culture has reduced many, if not most, women to the position of puppets on a string, to slavelike creatures whose only purpose in life is to cater to the needs and pleasures of men. Not only this, it has also had the audacity and the arrogance to deny women direct access to God.

Islam rejects the idea of redemption, of any intermediary between a believer and the creator. It is one of Islam's cardinal beliefs that each person—man and woman—is responsible and accountable for his or her individual actions. How, then, can the husband become the wife's gateway to heaven or hell? How, then, can he become the arbiter not only of what happens to her in this world but also her ultimate destiny? Surely such questions must arise in the minds of thoughtful Muslim men, but Muslim women are afraid to ask questions whose answers are bound to threaten the existing balance of power in the domain of family relationships in most Muslim societies.

Qur'anic Islam versus Islam in History and Issues of Women's Sexuality

The foregoing account provides much evidence to show that the Qur'an does not discriminate against women whose sexuality is affirmed both generally and in the context of marriage. Furthermore, while making it clear that righteousness is identical in the case of man or woman, the Qur'an also provides particular safeguards for protecting women's special sexual/biological functions such as carrying, delivering, suckling, and rearing, offspring.

Underlying much of the Qu'ran's legislation on women-related issues is the recognition that women have been disadvantaged persons in history to whom justice needs to be done by the Islamic *ummah*. Unfortunately, however, the cumulative (Jewish, Christian, Hellenistic, Bedouin, and other) biases that existed in the Arab-Islamic culture of the early centuries of Islam infiltrated the Islamic tradition, largely through the *hadith* literature. It undermined the intent of the Qur'an to liberate women from the status of chattels or inferior creatures, and make them free and equal to men.

A review of Muslim history and culture brings to light many areas in which—Qur'anic teachings notwithstanding—women continued to be subjected to diverse forms of oppression and injustice, not infrequently in the name of Islam. However, there are also areas in which the message of the Qur'an has been heeded. For instance, in response to the Qur'an's condemnation of female infanticide which was not uncommon among pre-Islamic Arabs, Muslim Arabs abolished the practice of burying their daughters alive. This means that when Muslims say with pride that Islam gave women the right to live, they are, indeed, correct.

However, it needs to be added here that though Muslims do not kill their baby daughters, they do not, in general, treat them equally with boys. Generally speaking, the birth of a daughter is met with resignation and even sadness. A woman who only gives birth to daughters is likely to be the target of harsh and abusive behavior and threatened with divorce. It will be interesting to see what change, if any, takes place in Muslim culture when the fact becomes widely known that it is not the mother but the father who determines the sex of the child!

Underlying the gruesome practice of female infanticide was the notion, prevalent among Bedouin Arabs, that the birth of a daughter meant not only additional drainage of extremely scarce means of survival, but also—and more importantly—a real hazard to their "honor." The concepts of "honor" and "shame," which have a profound significance in Bedouin culture (as also in Mediterranean societies), are linked with the idea of women's chastity or sexual behavior. Pre-Islamic nomadic Arabs who lived in a state of constant

Bedouin

warfare with the environment and with other tribes, had a separate word for the honor of women— '*ird*. B. Fares observes:

> '*Ird* from its etymology seems to be a partition which separates its possessor from the rest of mankind. . . . This partition is certainly fragile since it was easily destroyed. . . . (In the pre-Islamic *jahiliyya* period) '*ird* was intense and of momentous importance; besides it was the guiding motive in the acts and deeds of all the Arabs except those of the Yemen . . . on account of its sacred nature, it was entitled to take the place of religion; the Arabs put it in the highest place and defended it arms in hand.[38]

So fearful were pre-Islamic Arabs of the possibility of having their '*ird* compromised by their daughters' voluntary or involuntary loss of chastity, that they were willing to kill them. Obviously, to them their honor mattered more than the lives of their daughters. It is important to note that the "honor" killings still go in a number of Muslim societies in which a woman is killed on the slightest suspicion of what is perceived as sexual misconduct. There are also many instances of women being killed for other reasons and the murder being camouflaged as an "honor" killing in order to make it appear less heinous a crime.

The term '*ird* does not appear in the Qur'an. However, just as in the case of Bedouin Arabs, most Muslim men's concept of "honor" revolves around the orbit of women's sexuality, which is seen as a male possession. Commenting on how men's honor is intertwined with women's virginity (which symbolizes their chastity) in patriarchal Muslim culture, Fatima Mernissi observes:

> Virginity is a matter between men, in which women merely play the role of silent intermediaries. Like honor, virginity is the manifestation of a purely male preoccupation in societies where inequality, scarcity, and the degrading subjection of some people to others deprive the community as a whole of the only true human strength: self-confidence. The concepts of honor and virginity locate the prestige of a man between the legs of a woman. It is not by subjugating nature or by conquering mountains and rivers that a man secures his status, but by controlling the movements of women related to him by the blood or by marriage, and by forbidding them any contact with male strangers.[39]

Since women's sexuality is so vitally related to men's honor and self-image in Muslim culture, it becomes vitally important in Muslim societies to subject women's bodies to external social controls. On way in which some Muslim societies (for example, in North Africa) have sought to do so is by means of female circumcision, which ranges from cutting off the tip of the clitoris to virtual removal of the clitoris and the sealing of the mouth of the vagina except for a small passage.

The extent of physical, emotional, or psychological damage done to women by the practice of female circumcision depends, among other things, upon the nature of the "operation" and how it was performed. Having heard personal testimonies from Muslim women who have experienced the horror of radical circumcision, I have no doubt at all that this practice constitutes an extreme form of cruelty toward women, which must not be tolerated. Here it needs to be pointed out that though the Islamic tradition (following the Jewish tradition) requires male circumcision, it does not require female circumcision. Female circumcision practiced in countries such as Egypt, Sudan, and Somalia, is thus, rooted in the culture of those regions and not in religion.

Another way in which Muslim societies seek to control women's bodies is by denying women access to means of birth control. Here it may be noted that though there are Qur'anic statements referring to the killing of one's living children, there are no Qur'anic statements that may be interpreted as prohibiting birth control. While the Qur'an does not address the issue of family planning specifically, or directly, its teachings shed a good deal of light on how this issue—and other contemporary issues—may be understood, or dealt with, within the ethical framework of normative Islam.

The Qur'an puts great emphasis on the preservation of what we commonly refer to as "fundamental human rights" such as (a) the right to be respected for one's humanity[40]; (b) the right to be treated with justice and equity[41]; (c) the right to be free of traditionalism, authoritarianism (religious, intellectual, political, economic), tribalism, classism, or caste-system, sexism and slavery[42]; (d) the right to privacy and protection from slander, backbiting, and ridicule[43]; (e) the right to acquire knowledge[44]; (f) the right to work, to earn, to own property[45]; (g) the right to have a secure place of residence in an environment in which one's possessions and covenants are protected and in which one can move freely[46]; (h) the right to leave one's place of origin under oppressive conditions[47]; (i) the right to develop one's esthetic sensibilities and enjoy the bounties created by God[48]; and (j) the right not only to life but to "the good life," which is possible—according to Qur'anic perspective—only in a just society because justice in a prerequisite for peace and peace is a prerequisite for self-actualization[49].

For Muslims, the Qur'an, being God's Word, is the primary and most authoritative source of Islam. As mentioned above, the Qur'an strongly affirms and upholds fundamental human rights. It follows, therefore, that these rights must be acknowledged and protected in all Muslim societies and communities. Given the unhappy socio-cultural, economic, and political conditions of much of the present-day Muslim world where the increase in the birth rate is among the highest in the world, the need for family planning may be regarded as self-evident. The right to use contraceptives, especially by disadvantaged masses whose lives are scarred by grinding poverty and massive illiteracy, should be seen—in the light of the Qur'anic vision of what an Islamic society should be—as a fundamental human right. This is particularly applicable to Muslim women who, though over five hundred million in number, are among the most unrepresented or voiceless and powerless "minorities" in the world.

One Qur'anic passage commonly cited by opponents of birth control in Muslim societies is Surah 2: Al-Baqarah: 223, which states:

> Your wives are
> As a tilth unto you
> So approach your tilth
> When or how you will;
> But do some good beforehand,
> And fear God,
> And know that you arc
> To meet Him (in the hereafter),
> And give (these) good tidings
> To those who believe.[50]

The likening of a wife to life-containing soil has profound meaning, but the average Muslim is not sensitive to the subtleties of the comparison or to the implications of the Qur'an's reminder to the husband that he should act righteously. Since wives are described as a "tilth" and permission has been given to the husbands to approach them "when or how you will," the average Muslim man believes not only that husbands have the right to have sexual intercourse with their wives whenever they choose, but also the right to impregnate them at will in order that they might yield a "harvest."

Numerous *ahadith* attributed to the Prophet insist that a wife must never refuse to have sexual relations with her husband. For instance, Imam Muslim reports that the following *ahadith* on the authority of Abu Huraira:

> Allah's Apostle said: "When a woman spends the night from the bed of her husband the angels curse her until morning."
> . . . Allah's Messenger said: "By Him in whose hand is my life, when a man calls his wife to his bed and she does not respond, the one who is in the heaven is displeased with her until he (her husband) is pleased with her."[51]

In view of this insistence that the husband's sexual needs be instantaneously satisfied (unless the wife is menstruating, fasting, or in some other exceptional circumstances) it is rather ironic to note that a large number of Muslim women suffer from "frigidity." Like the earth, all-too-often they are "cultivated" without love or proper care, and never discover the wonder or joy of their own womanhood.

Undoubtedly the threat of unlimited pregnancies and childbirths with little or no health care available have made many Muslim women afraid of sex. But the manner is which Muslim societies have legislated that regardless of her own wishes a woman must always meet her husband's sexual demands as duty, has also lead to sexual intercourse becoming a mechanical performance, which leaves both the man and the woman sexually unsatisfied.

A number of studies[52] conducted by social scientists indicate that Muslim societies put a high premium on female fertility. Among the reasons why this should be so is the belief, however unfounded, that birth control and abortion are morally "wrong." A second reason is a hankering for a son and then more sons. A third and more traditional reason is the desire to keep women tied to the homestead and in a state of perpetual dependency upon men.

It has been assumed by conservative Muslim scholars (who form the majority of scholars in the Muslim world) that birth control is demonic in origin and its primary purpose is to facilitate immorality. A. A. Maududi's views cited below are typical of this viewpoint:

> Co-education, employment of women in offices, mixed social gatherings, immodest female dresses, beauty parades, are now a common feature of our social life. Legal hindrances have been placed in the way of marriage and on having more than one wife, but no bar against keeping mistresses and having illicit relationships prior to the age of marriage. In such a society perhaps the last obstacle that may keep a woman from surrendering to a man's advances is fear of an illegitimate conception. Remove this obstacle too and provide to women with weak character assurance that they can safely surrender to their male friends and you will see that the society will be plagued by the tide of moral licentiousness.[53]

In this day and age it hardly needs to be argued that a woman who has no control over her own body or who is compelled by social and religious pressures to play the part of a reproductive machine becomes less than a fully autonomous human being. Furthermore, there is a definite connection between the status of women and their ability to control or determine the number and spacing of children they will have, as a number of studies have shown.[54]

While the issue of birth control is of great urgency and importance to many Muslim women, the issue of segregation and veiling seems to me to affect an even larger proportion of women in Muslim culture. In recent times, the heated, ongoing discussion in a number of Muslim societies (Egyptian,

Iranian, Pakistani, Malaysian, Sudanese) as well as among Muslim minority groups (in West Europe or North America) on whether Muslim women are required to veil themselves totally or partially, shows that the issue of veiling is at the heart of the greatest dilemma confronting contemporary Muslims—namely, their ambivalence toward modernity.

While it is beyond the scope of this paper to analyze all the Qur'anic statements that have a bearing upon the institution of *purdah* (segregation and veiling), a few observations need to be made. The Qur'an does not confine women to "private" space. In fact, in Surah 4: An-Nisa': 15, confinement to the home is prescribed as a punishment for unchaste women! The Qur'anic law of modesty[55]—addressed to men as well as to women—does indeed discourage exhibitionism in dress or conduct. Its underlying message—addressed particularly to women who have, since time immemorial, been reduced to sex objects by androcentric cultures—is: if you do not wish to be treated like a sex object, do not dress or act like sex objects. The purpose of the Qur'anic legislation pertaining to women's attire or behavior is not to confine them, spatially of psychologically, but to enable them to move around in "public" space without the fear of being molested.[56] Its larger aim is to transform women into persons who are secure and self-respecting and who do not feel that their survival depends on their ability to attract, entertain, or cajole those men who are not interested in their personhood but only in their sexuality.

In evaluating the impact on Muslim women of veiling, it is necessary to clarify two points. The first is that "veiling" can be understood in a variety of ways, ranging from the wearing of a head scarf to a total covering of the body from head to foot. The second is that, in recent time, the veil has functioned not as a symbol of women's oppression but as an emblem of their political, economic, and cultural emancipation and as a means of asserting their multifaceted identities. The "veiled revolution" which has taken place in Iran and Egypt in the 1980s illustrate this well.

The wearing of a head scarf by a Muslim woman, especially if she has worn the head scarf as an act of free choice, does not restrict her autonomy as a person. However, total veiling of the body, especially if it is imposed externally, certainly constitutes a serious deterrent to the full and healthy development of Muslim women. While the Qur'an has given the Muslim woman the right to work, to earn,[57] to go about her daily business without fear of sexual harassment, Muslim societies, in general, have imprisoned and entombed many Muslim women in oppressive veils and put them behind locked doors.

Nothing illustrates the obsession of Muslim men with women's sexuality and the desire to control it more than the constant effort made by many of them to ensure that not a single hair on the head of any women related to them is visible to a man who is not related to them! Not satisfied with "the outer garment"[58] prescribed for Muslim women in a specific cultural context, conservative Muslims seek the help of a weak *hadith*[59] to compel women to cover themselves from head to foot, leaving only the face and hands uncovered. Ultraconservative Muslims have gone even further, requiring that a woman also cover her face.[60] Certainly there are no Qur'anic statements which justify the rigid restrictions regarding segregation and veiling which have been imposed on Muslim women in the name of Islam. If, for instance, the Qur'an had intended for women to be completely veiled, why would it have required Muslim men to lower their gaze when looking at them?[61]

Conclusion

Within the Islamic tradition both negative and positive attitudes are found toward women and women's issues. However, the Qur'an, which *is* the primary source on which Islam is founded, consistently affirms women's equality with men and their fundamental right to actualize the human potential that they possess equally with men. Seen through a nonpatriarchal lens, the Qur'an shows no sign of discrimination against women. If anything, it exhibits particular solicitude for women, much as it does for other disadvantaged persons.

In conclusion, it is of importance to note that there is more Qur'anic legislation pertaining to the establishment of justice in the context of family relationships than on any other subject. This points to the assumption implicit in much Qur'anic legislation, namely, that if human beings can learn to order their homes justly so that the human rights of all within its jurisdiction—children, women, and men—are safeguarded, then they can also order their society and the world at large, justly. In other words, the Qur'an regards the home as a microcosm of the *ummah* and the world community. It emphasizes the importance of making it "the abode of peace" through just living.

Notes

1. Fazlur Rahman, *Islam* (Garden City, New York: Doubleday, 1968), 70.

2. Quoted in Alfred Guillaume, *The Traditions of Islam* (Beirut: Khayats, 1966), 97.

3. *Islam*, 73.

4. *Traditions of Islam*, 15.

5. Ibid., 12-;13.

6. Marshall Hodgson, *The Classical Age of Islam*, volume 1, of *The Venture of Islam: Conscience and History in a World Civilization* (Chicago: University of Chicago Press, 1974), 232.

7. Hamilton Gibb, *Studies on the Civilization of Islam*, edited by Stanford J. Shaw and William R. Polk (Boston, Beacon Press,: 1962), 194.

8. Muhammad Iqbal, *The Reconstruction of Religious Thought in Islam* (Lahore: Shaikh Muhammad Ashraf, 1962), 83.

9. M. M. Khan, translation of *Sahih Al-Bukhari* (Lahore: Kazi Publications, 1971), 346.

10. Ibid., 80.

11. Ibid., 81.

12. A. H. Siddiqui, translation of *Sahih Muslim*, volume 2 (Lahore: Shaikh Muhammad Ashraf, 1972), 752.

13. Ibid.

14. Ibid., 752–53.

15. *Traditions of Islam*, 32.

16. Jane I. Smith and Yvonne Y. Haddad, "Eve: Islamic Image of Women," *Women and Islam*, edited by Azizah Al-Hibri, Pergamon Press, 1982, 139.

17. See Surah 15: *Al-Hijr:* 26–43; Surah 17: *Bani Isra'il:* 61–64; Surah 18: *Al-Kahf:* 50, and Surah 38: *Sad:* 71–85.

18. *The Reconstruction of Religious Thought in Islam*, 84.

19. Toshihiko Izutsu, *The Structure of the Ethical Terms in the Koran*, Keio Institute of Philosophical Studies, Mita, Siba, Minatoku, Tokyo, 1959. 152–53.

20. *The Reconstruction of Religious Thought in Islam*, 85.

21. E. W. Lane, *Arabic-English Lexicon* (London: Williams and Norgate, 1863), book 2, part 4, 1458.

22. A. A. Maududi, *The Meaning of the Qur'an* (Islamic Publications, 1976), volume 4, 16, footnote 13(2).

23. *Sahih Al-Bukhari*, volume 7, 32.

24. *Sahih Muslim*, volume 4, 1431.

25. Ibid.

26. Surah 9: *At-Tawbah:* 71–72, translation by 'Abdullah Yusuf 'Ali, *The Holy Qur'an* (Brentwood, Maryland: Amana Corporation, 1989), 459.

27. Fatima Mernissi, *Beyond the Veil* (Cambridge: Schenkman Publishing Company, 1975), 103.

28. *The Meaning of the Qur'an*, volume 2, 1971, 321.

29. Rafiullah Shehab, *Rights of Women in Islamic Shariah* (Lahore: Indus Publishing House, 1986), 117.

30. *The Holy Qur'an,* 92 (emphasis is mine).

31. Sadiq Hasan Khan, *Husn al-Uswa,* 281.

32. Ibn Hanbal, Al-Hadith, volume 3, 80.

33. Muhammad Imran, *Ideal Women in Islam* (Lahore, 1979), 50.

34. Ibid., 51.

35. Ibid.

36. Ibid.

37. Surah 2: *Al-Bagarah:* 187.

38. Article on *Ird* in supplement to the *Encyclopedia of Islam* (Leiden: E. J. Brill, 1938), 96–97.

39: "Virginity and Patriarchy," in *Women and Islam* (Oxford: B. Blackwell, 1991), 183.

40. For instance, see Surah 17: *Al-Isra':* 70.

41. For instance, see Surah 4: *An-Nisa':* 135, 136; Surah 5: *Al-Ma'idah:* 8.

42. for instance, see Surah 2: *Al-Baqarah:* 177, 256, 282; Surah 3: *Al-'Imran:* 79, 159; Surah 4: *An-Nisa':* 36, 92, 135, 136; Surah *Al-Ma'idah:* 89; Surah 6: *Al-An'am:* 107, 108; Surah 9: *At-Tawbah:* 60; Surah 10: *Yunus:* 99; Surah 12: *Yusuf:* 40; Surah 16: *An-Nahl:* 82; Surah 18: *Al Kahf:* 29; Surah 24: *An-Nur:* 33; Surah 42: *Ash-Shuru:* 21, 38, 48; Surah 47: *Muhammad:* 4; Surah 58: *Al-Mujadalah:* 3.

43. For instance, see Surah 4: *An-Nisa':* 148–49; Surah 24: *An-Nur:* 16–19, 27–28, 58; Surah 33: *Al-Ahzab:* 53; Surah 49: *Al-Hujurat:* 11, 12

44. For instance, see Surah 9: *At-Tawbah:* 122; Surah 20: *Ta-Ha:* 114; Surah 39: *Az-Zumar:* 9; Surah 96: *Al-Alaq:* 1–5

45. For instance, see Surah 4: *An-Nisa':* 11–12, 31.

46. For instance, see Surah 2: *Al-Baqarah:* 229; Surah 3: 17, 77; Surah 5: *Al-Ma'idah:* 1; Surah 17: *Al-Isra':* 34; Surah 67: *Al-Mulk:* 15.

47. For, instance, see Surah 4: *An-Nisa':* 97–100

48. For instance, see Surah 7: *Al-A'raf:* 32; Surah 57: *Al-Hadid:* 27.

49. For a detailed account of human rights affirmed by the Qur'an, see my paper entitled "On Human Rights and the Qur'anic Perspective" published in *Journal of Ecumenical Studies,* volume 19, no. 3, Summer 1982, pp. 51–65; reprinted in *Human*

Rights in Religious Traditions, edited by Arlene Swidler, Pilgrim Press, New York, 1982, pp. 51–65; also in *Muslims in Dialogue: The Evolution of a Dialogue,* edited by Leonard Swidler, Edwin Mellen Press, Lewiston, 1992, pp. 463–95.

50. *The Holy Qur'an,* 90.

51. *Sahih Muslim* volume 2, 723.

52. For example, A. Aitken and J. Stoekel, "Muslim-Hindu Differentials in Family Planning Knowledge and Attitudes in Rural East Pakistan," in *Journal of Comparative Family Studies,* spring 1971.

53. *Birth Control* (Islamic Publications, 1976) 176.

54. For instance, *Status of Women and Family Planning* (New York: United Nations, 1975), 4.

55. See Surah 24: *An-Nur:* 30 and 31.

56. See Surah 33: *Al-Ahzab:* 59.

57. See Surah 4: *An-Nisa':* 32.

58. Reference here is to Surah 33: *Al-Ahzab:* 59.

59. In this *hadith,* 'A' isha reports that the prophet Muhammed told Asma, her sister, when she appeared before him wearing thin clothes, "O Asma, when woman attains her puberty, it is not proper that any part of her body should be seen except this" and he pointed to his face and hands (*Rights of Women in Islamic Shariah,* 4).

60. In this context, See A. A. Maududi, *Purdah and the Status of Woman in Islam* (Lahore: Islamic Publications, 1975).

61. Reference here is to Surah 24: *An-Nur:* 30.

Postscript

Katherine K. Young

Insiders to the world religions have made important contributions to discussions of religion. But some feminists claim that *only* insiders can legitimately discuss their own groups.This exclusivity, I suggest, creates problems. These involve the nature of epistemology and scholarship; the politics of identity; the proper sphere for feminism; the tension between revolution and reform; and the polarization between men and women. These problems will be addressed here in two sections: (1) academia, and (2) the larger world.[1]

Academia

The nature of both scholarship and the university itself are now under debate. After examining these topics, I will return to the distinction between feminism and women's studies. I will argue that scholarship is the proper domain of women's studies alone, and that it is distinct from feminist advocacy. The latter often draws on the former, but scholarship is not its primary purpose.

In the following pages, I will explore the following tensions: (1) emotion versus reason; (2) relativism versus critical assessment; (3) advocacy versus scholarship; and (4) dialogue versus scholarship.

Emotion versus Reason

The notion of an insider epistemology raises questions about emotion and reason as well as identity and knowledge. Is the insider's perspective always necessary, as feminists have claimed? If so, how does it make a difference? These questions have broad implications for understanding not only the teaching of religion in universities and the nature of scholarship itself but also the possibility of understanding other cultures. Can it really be claimed that insiders are always correct?

Feminists have argued that only a woman can describe adequately the experience of being a woman. Only a Hindu woman, to take an example from the context of this book, can describe adequately the experience of being a Hindu woman. The corollary is that men are always outsiders when it comes to the experience of women. Even though Hindu men are not total outsiders (as Hindus) to women as Hindus, to use the same example, they remain outsiders (as men) to Hindu women. The same applies to male anthropologists, male scholars in the field of religious studies, and so on. What defines insider status for women, like racial but unlike religious or national groups, is *biology*. For women in the field of religious studies, though, the criterion by which to identify insiders involves something additional. Insiders are defined in terms of culture as well. They must be both women *and* Hindus, for instance, or both women *and* Christians. Those who lack insider credentials, presumably, are qualified neither for research nor for teaching.

As if foreseeing the great epistemological shifts toward the end of the century, Wilfred Cantwell Smith wrote in 1959 that "even the secular rationalist is coming to be seen as a person like another: not a god, not a superior impersonal intellect, monarch of all it surveys, but a man with a particular point of view."[2] If the word "man" were emphasized, of course, feminists would have no trouble with this quotation. Smith wrote precisely what they have been saying: *men* have often had a particular point of view when speaking about religion, for at the very least they have generally spoken as *men* with a gendered perspective. Just as the Frankfurt school (and Romanticism) paved the way for the idea of engaged scholarship, so did Smith. He noted that the investigator could be transformed from "the detached academic intellect, surveying its material impersonally, almost majestically, and reporting on it objectively"[3] to one who was personally involved in the search for God or truth. Because Islam, Hinduism, and Buddhism acknowledge no strict distinction between the religious and secular realms, authors form these traditions, according to Smith, can write about them on a more personal basis. "This much at least can be conceded," observed Smith, "that along with the academic tradition of detached and secular study of religion, [there are now studies of religion] . . . carried out by religious people for religious people".[4]

There is an overlap between the position of Smith and that of feminists. In the following quotation from his work, I have changed the pronouns and inserted references to women to show that Smith, in his concern for including insiders (Muslims here) in more general discussions of religion, paved the way for women to be taken seriously as religious insiders. "By 'religion' here I include . . . the faith in women's hearts. On the external data about women and religion, of course, an outsider, i.e. a man, can by diligent scholarship discover things that an insider woman does not know and may not be willing to accept. But about the meaning that the system has for those women of faith, an outsider man cannot in the nature of the case go beyond the believing woman; for their piety is also the faith, and if women cannot recognize his portrayal, then it is not their faith that he is portraying."[5] The same quote could be rewritten as a reference to the faith of Muslim or Taoist women.

Insiders often complain that they are misrepresented by outsiders. It surely makes sense for scholars to find out if Hindus or Muslims or African Christians *feel* misrepresented. In the past, that problem was often ignored, although Jews complained about it for centuries, so it can hardly be argued that the problem was unknown until modern times—let alone that it was discovered by feminists.[6] Muslims in North America often complain that they are misrepresented by journalists.[7] Women complain that they have been misrepresented by (male) historians.

Muslims might *feel* misrepresented in Western media. But are they? That is a legitimate question for scholars. To find out, the evidence must be examined. Are Muslim men routinely portrayed as devilish fiends? Are Muslim women who choose to wear the *hijab* portrayed as ignorant and subservient? Are they portrayed that way in some media but not others? In some Western countries but not others? By some journalists but not others? The same scholarly processes should be applied to religion. Feelings might or might not be the result of sound arguments. It is one thing to say that human beings should never be *reduced* to rationality; it is an entirely different thing to say—that is, to imply—that we should *abandon* rationality. This would amount to arguing that because democracy is not perfect (and never can be perfect)], we should abandon it.[8] Even Smith, who contributed in no small way to the shift to the believer's perspective, recognized accountability to the facts and logic, and *modified* his belief "that no statement about a religion is valid unless it can be acknowledged by that religion's believers."[9] He noted that "the reverse is certainly not true. Not every statement about Islam that is acceptable to Muslims is *ipso facto* true: one can flatter or beguile."[10]

Feminists, trying to protect the integrity of believing women, are not always so generous to male scholars. They seldom play down the distortions of male colleagues as "unintentional" or "not unfriendly." But the theoretical point, accountability to facts and logic, remains. At the very least, feminists argue, women should be involved in the study of women (and, in this case, world religions). Unfortunately, some feminists *would* deny that women must be held accountable to the facts, to sould arguments, to ethical bottom lines.

It could be argued that feeling is a problem in connection only with contemporary phenomena, because our knowledge of the past is limited to whatever archeological, textual, or inscriptional evidence we happen to find. But contemporary scholars can try nevertheless to account for the way living communities interpret their own histories and how interpretations shape their identities, even when these interpretations conflict with the information collected by scholars.

Scholarly interpretations are seldom neutral, when it comes to their effects. They can have political repercussions, for example. At the very least, they can perpetuate the personal, cultural, religious, or political biases of investigators. For all these reasons, insider interpretations can offer useful correctives.

Even so, the subjective approach can present problems. Not everyone, by any means, supports it. T. Patrick Burke, for instance, argues that there are so many varieties of Christianity—which consists not merely of three main branches but many thousands of separate churches based on sectarian doctrines, ethnic origins, and so on—that members of one community can be diametrically opposed to those of another on questions of doctrine, practice, or even historical claims. How can *all* be considered correct interpretations of Christianity? Moreover, not all members of these communities are equally knowledgeable. Many—especially in this modern and secular age—know little or nothing about their scriptures, rituals, or doctrines. The fact is, moreover, that outsiders can experience virtually every aspect of a foreign religion except the act of believing in its truth, which would convert them, as it were, to insiders. In any case, Burke argues, good phenomenological description is not altered by whether something actually exists or not. Nor is the description of a belief altered by whether it is true or false.[11] This approach does not oppose that of Smith, by the way. The latter does not conflate the beliefs of religious people and the rightness or wrongness of those beliefs as determined by scholars. Nor does he ignore the rich variety that is part of all traditions.

The Cartesian assumption that *to know* is *to prove* has diminished the subjective in Western scholarship. Elaine Pagels argues, moreover, that "English is unusual within its language group in having only one verb ('to know') to express different kinds of knowing. (Modern European languages use one word to characterize intellectual knowledge and another for the knowledge of personal relationships: French, for example, distinguishes between *savoir* and *connaître*.[12]) This has made it easier to ignore the relational and emotional aspects of knowledge. By the *very same logic,* of course, it would be easy to ignore the *cognitive* aspect of knowledge. In fact, our focus on the cognitive might have come about precisely *because* scholars recognized the dangers of ignoring it. In any case, it is true that there is more to human existence than reason. Emotion, too, is an important feature of human existence. Scholars in the humanities and social sciences have by now taken this into account. They know that no individual can have direct access to the feelings of another individual. The same is true at the collective level. There are some things that only insiders can know from personal experience. Feminists have found this insight very useful, arguing that no man—no male scholar— can ever know what it feels like to be a woman. If knowledge of women is going to be gathered, according to many feminists, women themselves must do it. It makes sense, therefore, to account for emotion in any study of human subjects.

Subjective epistemologies can create the impression that anything goes. In the case of scholarship, this would leave no room for accountability; everything could be reduced to personal emotion, personal identity, the need for self-esteem, and so on. One author in this book unquestioningly accepts an insider's attribution of the subordination of women in India and the origin of the caste system to the "Aryan conquest" around 1500 B.C.E. But this statement is considered highly questionable today. Scholars now doubt that there was any invasion and conquest at all.[13] The origin of the caste system is generally thought to have developed within India itself, moreover, as tribal and then lineage society was transformed by the process of state formation into a more hierarchical structure. Because the author is not a specialist on Indian prehistory (nor, presumably, was the informant), she cannot be expected to know this. Another one of our authors assigns the occasional Buddhist view that only men can attain to the higher stages of the spiritual path to the Hindu concept of karma. But this has never been the main interpretation within Hinduism. Karmic change has usually been assigned to caste (*varna*), not sex. In fact, assigning it to a sex was more common in Buddhism than in Hinduism.[14] Once again, the author cannot not be expected to know this; Hinduism is not her field of expertise. Even when an author is an insider, she (or he) may not present all sides on any given topic, some of which have generated considerable controversy within the tradition itself.

One author gives special attention to Palestinian Christians, calling them "the indigenous Christians in the land of Jesus, who have lost their homeland." But Nathanson[15] points out that the Palestinians never "lost" their homeland; many of them are still living where their ancestors had lived for generations. Nor have the Palestinians "lost" their state, in any meaningful sense, because there had not been a Christian state in this region since the High Middle Ages. And even then, it was not ruled by Palestinians; the Kingdom of Jerusalem was ruled by European Christians. It is true, of course, that the Palestinians *lack* a state (although it could be argued that Jordan has, in effect, become a Palestinian state). Christian autonomy in what is now Israel was last destroyed, in fact, by Muslims (not Jews) when they reconquered territories that had been reconquered, in turn, by Christians (that is, the Crusaders).

Another author, continues Nathanson, laments the fact that Jewish women do not wear ritual "garments" that Jewish men are expected to wear. But things are not quite as simple as they seem. It is true that only men are expected to attend public worship wearing either the *tallit* or *tefillin*. Whether women *may* wear them, however, is another matter. Some Orthodox women have noted that the *halakhah* (Jewish law) does not actually prohibit women from doing either, although it does not require them to do so. And it cannot be argued that this is due merely to the fact that very few women until recently have ever expressed any desire to wear these things; not only was this topic discussed in the medieval period, but some rabbis actually approved of women wearing ritual regalia. As for women not being expected to wear the *kipah* (a small cap that, in modernizing communities, has replaced the hat worn in more traditional ones), the fact is that both men *and women* in traditional communities are expected to cover their heads—and not only in the synagogue but at all times;[16] it is only in Conservative synagogues that women sometimes do not bother to cover their heads. And it is only in Reform synagogues that neither women *nor men* do so;[17] in some Reform synagogues, men are explicitly instructed *not* to cover their heads. A more important problem for Jewish women is the fact that only men are allowed by the *halakhah* to initiate divorces. It must not be assumed, however, that the rabbis have lacked concern for the plight of unhappily married women. Their problem in this case and many others, has been how to satisfy human needs *without* undermining the Torah's authority, and thus that of the entire tradition. The Torah itself allows only husbands to initiate divorce. The characteristic rabbinic solution is not to deny the legitimacy of scripture but to work around it. For example, a husband who fails to fulfill halakhically defined obligations to his wife—including the satisfaction of her sexual desires[18]—can be strongly "encouraged"[19] by the religious court to grant her a divorce. Then, too, marriage contracts have long been compulsory. These are intended primarily to ensure that divorced *women* are financially secure.

The point is that there should be some academic forum for *testing* statements made in the name of feminism. That would at least keep debates informed and honest. This reminds me of the ancient Indian tradition of debating philosophical and religious topics. There was always supposed to be an umpire (*madhyastha*) who could ensure that all information was correct and that any analysis accounted for the complexity of its topic. When thinkers reported these debates as part of their intellectual deliberations, they included the umpire's remarks.

To avoid the problems of factual error, it could by argued, insiders have an absolute moral right to speak as insiders. But this does not necessarily mean that they are correct.[20] The first point is jurisdictional and epistemological, the second factual. By analogy, physicists have the general qualifications to write about energy fields or optical illusions, but this does not mean that what they write is correct. There is a difference, moreover, between the natural and human sciences. The former can be approached with greater objectivity; the latter must take into consideration the human element. Any adequate epistemology must be not only personalistic (accounting for the subjective aspect of human existence) but *also* objective (accounting for the context in which we live to the degree that this is possible given the information and methods at our disposal).

Then, too, critics have pointed out that an exclusive focus on the individual or group means that men and women will always be limited to the experiences of their particular sexes, cultures, religions, and so forth. Taken to its extreme, male novelists could not adequately (or even legitimately) describe female characters. Nor, of course, could female novelists describe male ones. Secular women could not write about religious women (or men). Nor could religious women write about secular women (or men). Christian women could not teach about Taoist women (or men). Nor could Taoist women teach about Christian women (or men). Because the experience of each person is ultimately unique, in fact, we could describe only our own personal experiences. The result would be solipsism: only the individual self would be considered real. That, in turn, would undermine the notion of relationality—which would be ironic in view of the fact that many feminists (including many of those who advocate the subjective approach) consider relationality a defining feature of femaleness. Moreover, the belief that only the self is real leads to a highly inflated notion of autonomy. Taken beyond the level of freedom within the limits of democracy, the notion of autonomy leads directly to communal fragmentation. No community could exist without some sense of common experience.

Outsiders, according to Burke, often notice facts that are unknown, unacknowledged, or unappreciated by insiders. They might be more willing than insiders to recognize historical change. They might be more willing than insiders to discuss what the latter consider undesirable features of their traditions. Then, too, outsiders might be more likely to come up with theories. At the very least, outsiders are in a good position to translate traditional terms into those more accessible to other outsiders. So outsiders need not simply accept whatever insiders happen to say. It is true that insiders, too, can be scholars; they can have the same training as outsiders, the same ability to become aware of their own biases, the same broad knowledge on which to build theories. But just as insiders must make an effort to detach themselves from their own traditions, especially when communal loyalties are challenged, outsiders must make an effort to feel empathy for alien traditions. The point here is simply that both outsiders *and* insiders might have blind spots that can be corrected by multiple perspectives.

Relativism versus Critical Assessment

Charles Taylor, a noted Canadian political scientist and philosopher, suggests that we begin with a presumption, a provisional hypothesis, that "all human cultures that have animated whole societies over some considerable stretch of time have something important to say to all human beings."[21] Taylor thinks that we become serious students of other cultures by moving into their particularities and fusing our horizon with theirs—a concept introduced by Hans Gadamer and not unlike phenomenological *epoché* and empathy. That

could mean transforming our standards. The point is to underscore the importance of both sound method and reliable facts when studying people. But Taylor suggests in addition that critical assessment can come into play
subsequently:

> A favorable judgment on demand is nonsense, unless some such theo-
> ries are valid. Moreover, the giving of such a judgment on demand is
> an act of breathtaking condescension. No one can really mean it as a
> genuine act of respect. It is more in the nature of a pretend act of respect
> given on the insistence of its supposed beneficiary. Objectively, such an
> act involves contempt for the latter's intelligence. To be an object of
> such an act of respect demeans. The proponents of neo-Nietzschean
> theories hope to escape this whole nexus of hypocrisy by turning the
> entire issue into one of power and counterpower. Then the question is
> no more one of respect, but of taking sides, of solidarity. But this is
> hardly a satisfactory solution, because in taking sides they miss the dri-
> ving force of this kind of politics, which is precisely the search for
> recognition and respect. Moreover, even if one could demand it of
> them, the last thing one wants at this stage from eurocentered intellec-
> tuals is positive judgments of the worth of cultures that they have not
> intensively studied. For real judgments of worth suppose a fused hori-
> zon of standards . . . they suppose that we have been transformed by the
> study of the other, so that we are not simply judging by our original fa-
> miliar standards. A favorable judgment made prematurely would be not
> only condescending but ethnocentric. It would praise the other for being
> like us.[22]
>   There is perhaps after all a moral issue here. We only need a sense
> of our own limited part in the whole human story to accept the presump-
> tion. It is only arrogance, or some analogous moral failing, that can de-
> prive us of this. But what the presumption requires of us is not preemptory
> and unauthentic judgments of equal value, but a willingness to be open to
> comparative cultural study of the kind that must displace our horizons in
> the resulting fusions. What it requires above all is an admission that we
> are very far away from that ultimate horizon from which the relative worth
> of [aspects of] . . . different cultures might be evident. This would mean
> breaking with an illusion that still holds many "multiculturalists"—as
> well as their most bitter opponents—in its grip.[23]

Taylor draws attention in this passage to what can happen when problems
are assessed in subjective terms, when entitlement is based on identity rather
than merit according to external criteria. He worries about relativism. If there
can be no right and wrong, judged according to some objective criteria, no one

can pass judgment on anyone else's experience *or behavior.* Relativism makes growth impossible, moreover, because growth requires at least a provisional standard for comparison and inspiration.

Taylor warns us of what can happen when the foundation of right and wrong shifts from external criteria or sources (God or the Good) to "the voice within" and one's moral intuitions and then to feelings. This has led to the pervasive subjectivity of contemporary Western society.[24] Subjectivism makes inevitable the loss of value and judgment. And that, in turn, makes inevitable the demand for uniform treatment on the basis of identity alone. This implies a much broader range of demands than ever before (when it was enough to insist on intrinsic human worth and to demand a few inalienable rights).

If postmodernists and deconstructionists had their way, there would be as many feminisms as there are women. That would make consensus for social action impossible. Forced to acknowledge the two major problems posed by post-modernism and deconstruction—the instability of all perspectives; the collapse into relativism and social inaction—some feminists argue expediently for using deconstruction only when it serves their own political purposes. Others argue for the heuristic value of truth claims and the usefulness of provisional generalizations.[25] Still others argue for a bottom line to feminism: political activism to extend and protect women's interests as a class. Marsha Hewitt, for instance, has suggested that it is important to recognize woman as a "stable subject." This would provide "the basis for the formulation of the notion of *universal patriarchy* that is the source and sustainer of women's oppression. The notion of *woman* as the stable subject of feminine gender constructions functions as an underlying unity of all cultural, racial, class, and linguistic differences between women, which in turn provides a basis for solidarity by virtue of the universal commonality of being female."[26] As if in defiance of the postmodernists, Hewitt gives what amounts to an affirmation of "essentialism": "Further, the presumption of a stable subject," she writes, "allows for the designation of a set of characteristics or attributes that are sex-specific as well as possessing a corresponding ethics."[27] Not incidentally, Hewitt can be classified as an exponent of the Frankfurt school, although she modifies critical theory to suit her own brand of feminism. In short, some feminists part company with postmodernists and deconstructionsists for the following reasons: being ahistorical; being irresponsible by ignoring problems caused by class; and being too preoccupied with the instability of knowledge and other abstract problems. Even Derrida is now put down, occasionally, as a male thinker who reduces reality to nothing more than a bunch of "discourses." If women follow Derrida's advice, warns Linda Kintz, women will not be able "to speak at all as women in a system of deconstruction"[28] and will not be able to move beyond the old dualisms.

Advocacy Versus Scholarship

Feminism, by its own admission, is all about politics (or power). It is often distinguished by feminists themselves from women's studies, which is the scholarly arm of the women's movement—a distinction carefully noted in the definitions at the beginning of the introduction to this book. Despite the distinction, these two are often blurred. Curiously, this occurs in the classroom itself.

In his report on the state of religious and theological studies in American universities,[29] Ray Hart observes that there is a growing ferment, thanks to the new pluralism (intent on "decentering occidental [religious studies] . . . from its Eurocentric Christianist hegemony"[30] along with "engaged scholarship," even advocacy, in the name of women, gay people, minority students, environmentalists, and others. He describes the demands of women, who have developed a new kind of scholarship that involves "a reexamination of relations between 'evidence,' modes of discourse, forms of apprehension and transmission, and *power:* the *standing* of those who speak in relation to what is spoken about."[31] Speaking of the future, he argues that "pluralism" and "contextualization" will undermine the notion of a canon along with the status and authority of scriptures. This, he believes, will lead to a new classification of religious topics–"sacred scriptures," for instance, instead of "biblical studies." Moreover, "the field is said now and for the future to be focused upon the 'neglected,' the 'marginalized,' and the 'overlooked' in the study of religion."[32] Hart goes on to observe that feminism in departments of religious studies has been closely linked to all of these things.

Some of these proposals are hardly new. Anthropologists have often studied the religions of marginal communities. And historians of religions have certainly specialized in the sacred scriptures of religions other than their own, an approach well-represented in many departments. Every topic is worthy of academic study, especially those that have so far been neglected. If the motivation for study is scholarly, as understood by Taylor, this is clearly a good thing. But if the motivation is primarily political and the approach is advocacy, the result is highly problematic.

Taylor analyzes a massive change occurring—not only in Canada but in many other Western countries as well. According to him, personal identity is now shaped by recognition, absence of recognition, or misrepresentation by others. Therefore "a person or group of people can suffer real damage, real distortion, if the people or society around them mirror back to them a confining or demeaning or contemptible picture of themselves."[33] Of course, it is extremely important for societies to strive to eliminate any negative representations and to be inclusive. The problem arises when groups turn the issue of representation solely into a politics of difference—that is, *group* differences—instead of working to correct problems of representation. The politics of difference is supposed to ensure the recognition of not only difference (which offers protection against assimilation into the larger society) but equality (which offers entry into the larger society). But once equality is "inside difference" (because everyone has a unique identity and each is equal by virtue of that fact alone), according to Taylor, "its demands are hard to assimilate to that politics. For it asks that we give acknowledgement and status to something that is not universally shared. Or, otherwise put, we give due acknowledgement only to what is universally present—everyone has an identity—through recognizing what is peculiar to each. The universal demand powers an acknowledgement of specificity."[34]

The politics of difference can cause serious damage to departments of religious studies. There are signs even now that their very existence in public universities has become questionable.[35] This is partly because all of the humanities are vulnerable as universities and governments, faced with economic crises, look for places to cut budgets. Why support studies that do not foster the skills needed for business and industry? But religious studies is more vulnerable than other fields within the humanities. For one thing, it gained academic status relatively recently. Then, too, the study of religion is bound to be contentious in any public university due to the separation of church and state. When religious studies departments were first established at public universities, they were supposed to be different from theology departments. They were supposed to teach "objectively" about the many religions of our world. Now, thanks largely to advocacy in the classroom,[36] things are different. Teachers see themselves, more often than not, as "engaged scholars," or advocates of this or that worldview. And senior administrators, who decide where the money goes, are often secular; they have little use for religion of any kind. No wonder some religion departments, and even humanities departments, have closed or been threatened with closure.[37]

If only individuals can know and express their own experiences, moreover, religion departments would have no obvious reason or excuse to exist. Seminaries might be permissible as schools for the systematic study of religion from the perspective of insiders. But even these would be highly problematic. If only women could describe their own experiences, we would need sexually segregated seminaries. And, given fragmentation along sectarian lines, we would need doctrinally segregated seminaries as well. The end result would be solipsism. Smith warns, however, that "the student of comparative religion begins with the postulate that it is possible to understand a religion other than one's own. . . . if this postulate be false, then the whole study must of course be called off. Admittedly, one would be left with . . . the factual data of the *Encyclopedia*, but with the added proclamation now that one does not and cannot understand what the data signify."[38] This, he opines, hardly warrants religion departments financed by the public purse.

Why should feminism be an illegitimate topic in the university, though, and not theology? This question can be rephrased: If theology is legitimate in the university, why not feminism? Both, obviously, are expressions of world-views. It is generally conceded that there is a difference between the *study* of theology and the *proselytization* of it. The former has generally been allowed in universities, even the state-supported ones, and the latter confined to seminaries (universities or colleges operated by religious groups). The meaning of proselytization is very close to advocacy, the latter being a secular version of the former. Therefore, just as the general theology of Christianity (not to mention that of a particular denomination) should not be proselytized in the classroom, so too, I would argue, the general worldview of feminism (not to mention that of a particular school) should not be advocated there. It would be perfectly appropriate, of course, for teachers to espouse their beliefs in another context (political, say, or religious). Women may wear different hats, as it were, depending on the context.

Dialogue Versus Scholarship

Some people argue that the classroom is a suitable context for "dialogue." I will have much more to say about this below. For the time being, I will discuss this approach as understood in connection with "engaged scholarship" as explained by Smith. Observing that scholarship in religion should be "engaged," he agues that "when both the writer and that about which he or she writes becomes personal, so does the relationship between them. [There is] an encounter. When persons or human communities meet, there arises a need to communicate. What had been a description is therefore in process of becoming a dialogue."[39] According to Smith, "the personalization of our studies with which we began eventuates in their attaining fully human status, overcoming the local or particularist. . . . Even a face-to-face dialogue gives way to a side-by-side conversation, where scholars of different faiths no longer confront each other but collaborate in jointly confronting the universe, and consider together the problems in which all of them are involved."[40]

Not everyone in the field of religious studies would agree that the university is an appropriate venue for "dialogue." For one thing, this approach has been used mainly in ecumenical religious circles, not academic ones. Like phenomenology, it begins with mutual respect and the acknowledgement of two different perspectives. And like those who do phenomenology, those who engage in dialogue assume that both participants, or groups of participants, are motivated at least partly by their own personal commitments. But phenomemologists, as I have noted, are trained to become as self-conscious as possible about their presuppositions and to bracket them *out* in order to approach others with respect; this is not the case in dialogue. Dialogue, phenomenology—and activism—are very different.

The field of religious studies has something important to offer anyone interested in the problem of critical assessment. Because of its long-standing involvement in cross-cultural studies and in-depth knowledge of specific religions, it can offer proper *preparation* for dialogue. Although dialogue itself does not belong in the classroom, I would argue, academic preparation for it does.

One way to avoid conflict between identity and empathy is to adopt a team approach to religion and gender. These teams should include female and minority scholars—or male scholars, I might add, in fields now dominated by women. Those on the team should be chosen on the basis of academic merit, moreover, not "equity." The whole idea would be to encourage mutual respect, not domination by any particular group—not even one that was once ignored.

Having said this, I would add that the boundaries between insiders and outsiders are becoming increasingly blurred. Insiders identified with both feminism and women's studies seldom hesitate to use outsider scholarship even as they attack it for racism or sexism. Woo, for instance, bases her own attack here in this volume on that of a Western female Sinologist named Jennifer Holmgren; the latter had criticized early Sinologists for their simplistic criticisms of Chinese culture.[41] (The case of Holmgren indicates also that contemporary Western female Sinologists are critically aware of nineteenth-century excesses, have absorbed the critique of Orientalism, and have benefited from it.)

Then, too, some insiders are converts or initiates (as are some authors of this book). They carry at least some, and often many, outsider presuppositions into their new contexts. Some insiders are diaspora scholars, moreover, and greatly influenced by their host cultures—especially if they were brought up there.

The ambiguity involved in defining insiders and outsiders is easily illustrated, observes Nathanson,[42] by the case of Judaism. According to the *halakhah,* it should be easy to distinguish between insiders and outsiders: anyone born of a Jewish mother is a Jew—except, of course, for someone who converts to another religion.[43] But halakhic status as a Jew does *not* necessarily result in being an "insider." From the Orthodox point of view, non-Orthodox Jews born of Jewish mothers are Jews in the sense of belonging to the Jewish *people;* they are *not,* however, followers of the Jewish *religion.* The Jewish religion is defined by acceptance of the *halakhah*'s authority. (Orthodox Jews realize that no one can attain the halakhic ideal, of course, but they define religious Jews as those who accept that ideal.) Given that definition of Judaism, the Orthodox are merely pointing out the obvious: non-Orthodox Jews do *not* accept the *halakhah*'s authority, although some of them acknowledge it as a "guide" to proper living. Hasidic Jews present another problem. They are considered religiously Jewish by the Orthodox, because their way of life is based firmly on the *halakhah* (although it took a while for the Orthodox to realize this). But neither the non-Orthodox *nor* the Orthodox are insiders in Hasidic communities. Each Hasidic community, with its own ethos and its own charismatic leader, is socially and emotionally closed to outsiders—including Jewish ones. In a statement considered highly controversial by the Jewish world at large (including some members of the Orthodox world), one American Orthodox rabbinical association has declared that all non-Orthodox Jews—including all members of the Reform, Conservative, and Reconstructionist movements—are followers of "another religion." Even though non-Orthodox leaders would never say that Orthodox Jews are members of "another religion," the fact remains that Orthodox Jews would not exactly be insiders in these communities. The truth is that non-Orthodox Jews can be just as hostile to Orthodox Jews as the other way around. This problem has become extremely urgent, Nathanson continues, in view of recent developments in Israel.

The Chief Rabbinate of Israel is Orthodox. Non-Orthodox forms of Judaism are allowed in Israel, but they do not have the authority to determine personal status. In most cases, until recently, this has not made much difference to non-Orthodox Jews living there. A massive influx of Jewish refugees from Russia has changed things, though, because many of these people—children of Jewish fathers but gentile mothers—do not qualify as Jews in the halakhic sense. The Orthodox rabbinate has not denied that these people are Jewish citizens under the Law of Return, but it has denied that they are Jewish religiously. Apart from anything else, this means that they may not intermarry unless they undergo Orthodox conversion with those who are. Given the outrage in non-Orthodox communities, especially in America on which Israel depends, the Orthodox and non-Orthodox in Israel have considered several attempts to negotiate a compromise such as allowing non-Orthodox rabbis to participate in Orthodox conversion ceremonies.[44]

Even *within* religious communities, in short, the status of insider does not mean the same thing to all people. When people call themselves insiders, therefore, other scholars must still ask precisely *what* that means and to *whom*. Relevant to this discussion is the fact that the distinction between insider and outsider is in some ways more characteristic of Western perceptions than those of other civilizations. Although exclusive communities can be found in most complex societies, they are few in some. Take the case of Hindu identity. People are born Hindus and, traditionally, into specific castes and subcastes. But to these identities, Hindus add others. Some are associated with sects. Others are associated with gurus. Boundaries are so fluid that Hindus make pilgrimages to the holy places of non-Hindus (Buddhists, Jains, Muslims, or Sikhs). All of these phenomena tend to blur the boundaries separating religions. Even today, visitors to India are struck by the variety of images on the dashboards of Hindu-owned motor rickshaws—usually Śiva, Viṣṇu, Gaṇeśa, or Lakṣmī, but sometimes Jesus, Mary, or Buddha. Mahatma Gandhi, Mother Teresa, or even a Muslim sheikh might be included. The list could go on. A similar point could be made about traditional Chinese religion. As a famous saying goes, "a Confucian by day, a Taoist by night." In Japan, people commonly identify themselves as followers of both Buddhism and Shinto. Multiple identities are acknowledged but without exclusive boundaries.

I think it is important to maintain boundaries in some contexts. Boundaries distinguish study and teaching, for example, from other functions of the university. Academic boundaries defend the university as a place of research, of independent thinking, and teaching. That is the proper domain of women's studies: the biological nature of women, the interaction between culture and female biology, the problems of women, and proposed solutions to them. Because the university is a large and complex institution, though, many of its activities have little or nothing to do with scholarship itself. This is the realm, outside of scholarship and teaching, in which political activities might be appropriate. I do not mean that feminists should refrain from drawing on women's studies (or any other branch of scholarship); on the contrary, I believe that political analysis should always be based on good scholarship.

The Larger World

The topics under discussion here are of interest not only to academics. Feminists have influenced other institutions in society—political, legal, and economic ones. Next to their influence on the university, however, their influence on religious institutions, at least in North America, is probably the greatest (though this is by no means uniform). I have noticed a push for uniformity on the topic of women and religion, a kind of feminist orthodoxy, despite feminist talk of diversity. In addition, I have noticed some important blind spots that could cause problems for feminism in the future. To explore these topics, I will examine two tensions: (1) revolution versus reform and (2) debate versus dialogue.

Revolution versus Reform

Where does all this leave feminism and world religions? Feminism is avowedly political. For purposes of this discussion, its aim is to improve the status and solve the particular problems of women in religious communities. The question is not whether politics should be eliminated but what the proper sphere of politics is and what kind of politics is most appropriate—that is, both practical and ethical. From what has been said so far about the need for equality in practice no less than in theory, it should be clear that women should be politically aware and organized. But women must be aware of historical, ethical, and cultural complexities.

The most difficult problem of all is how to resolve the debate between feminists demanding religious reform and feminists demanding religious revolution. Throughout the history of religions, at least in complex societies, there have been those who advocated reforms of one kind or another. Sometimes, the resulting changes have been profound (the transition from biblical to rabbinic Judaism, for example, or from vedic religion to bhakti Hinduism). Sometimes, reformers are either pushed out or "encouraged" to leave on their own (the early Christian departure from Judaism). The fact is that the reforms demanded are often of such magnitude that they cannot be assimilated. This is what happened when Hindus found it necessary to call some groups *āstikas* (Hindus) and other *nāstikas* (non-Hindus) depending on whether the Vedas were accepted as scripture or not. Groups that leave become sects. After a while, of course, sects can become large or influential enough to be considered distinct religions on their own. The same criteria can be applied to feminist demands for change.

When feminist beliefs and practices conflict sharply with the prevailing ones, some people conclude that change threatens collective religious identity. Results can include everything from confusion and mild consternation to formal heresy trials or excommunication. Sometimes, traditionalists succeed in ousting feminist reformers. Mary Ann Lundy, for instance, was fired by the Presbyterian Church (U.S.A.) after she helped lead a "Re-Imagining Conference."[45] At other times, feminist reformers decide on their own to leave; the most obvious example of this would be Mary Daly, who left the Roman Catholic Church. At the moment, some feminists are trying to establish indirect worship of "the Goddess" *within* Judaism and Christianity. After so many Jewish and Christian, ethos-building centuries, it surely makes sense to expect goddess-oriented "reformers" with any integrity to establish their own religious communities.

In the West today, many Protestant groups have made major reforms to improve the status of women. Although at least partly because major social changes never happen overnight, women who seek leadership positions often complain that changes have not been radical enough. Some Catholic feminists believe that their own church has not—and probably will not—go far enough. Several solutions are possible: to forget about religion altogether; to try and force the church to adopt their point of view; or to do what Christian dissenters have always done: form their own churches. Religious affiliation is no longer dictated by the state. People are free to choose not only other forms of the Christian religion, moreover, but other religions. This can be very difficult because of family ties, childhood attachments, and community loyalties. But Christians who no longer approve of their own churches have always had the courage and integrity to make choices of this kind. And this is true not only of Christians.

At this point, several questions must be raised. Is there any reason to assume that all religions should handle gender in the same way? Must all religions believe in a supreme goddess? Must all encourage women to become priestesses? And what might be the long term advantages or disadvantages? Men might become so totally alienated from a religion dominated by women that they either abandon religion entirely or quietly form their own secret religions (which partially explains the dramatic rise of fraternal "lodges" in nineteenth-century North America).

If we support "biodiversity," it could be argued, we should support "religiodiversity" as well. There are some feminists, in fact, who call for exactly that: a diversity of new visions. For them, however, the only acceptable diversity is one that represents *new* ways of thinking about religion or even new religions. One strategy for achieving this is to foster syncretism. Syncretism is the result of cultural collisions.[46] It is often used to bring about harmony between two or more cultures.[47] On the other hand—and this should be noted carefully—it is often exploited to assert the dominance of one culture over its rivals.

In the introduction to this book, I discussed the relation of Marxism and the Frankfurt school of critical theory to feminism. Both called for revolution. For Marx that would take place in the streets; for the critical theorists, it would take place in the universities. A case could certainly be made that the latter is occurring today under the leadership of some feminists (and their allies). Because Marxism was well-known for hiding and shielding its political activities behind respectable "fronts" (the religious community founded by the African-American Father Divine in the United States being a classic example[48]), we can hardly rule out the possibility that reformist rhetoric is used as a "front" for revolutionary goals. Historians of religion, therefore, might consider the possibility that some new religious movements are actually secular ideologies masquerading as religions.

This call for respecting religiodiversity might seem dangerously close to the idea of maintaining the status quo. My idea here, though, is quite different. It requires the members of religious communities to examine carefully the scope for reform in the name of justice for women (and men, as I will argue). Justice presupposes, however, a much deeper understanding than commonly found so far of the *complexity* and *ambiguity* involved in any study of gender (including both biological and cultural asymmetries). We must learn to view the world through both the "female eye," as it were, *and* the "male eye." When this is done, seeing from both points of view together, we begin to see *stereoscopically.* Only on this basis, I think, can we develop a worthy gender ethic for the future. This ocular analogy can be extended, of course, to all groups in relation to their counterparts.

Even when the need for religiodiversity is appreciated, one question remains: Is there an ethical bottom line? This question might make religious communities wary. The last thing they want is interference from outsiders (or those who are insiders by birth but outsiders by conviction). But does that dissolve them from the ethical responsibility for seeking justice? I think they should at least examine the merits of change in light not only of their own traditions but also of scholarship based on science, cross-cultural studies, or whatever else might be academically relevant. With these things in mind, the need for change could be reassessed from within. If the demand for change has merit, insiders would have to determine what kinds of change could be instituted without destroying their tradition's identity. This is not a new problem. Hindus, for instance, have developed many hermeneutical strategies for reinterpreting their scriptures, especially in the nineteenth century, a period of many reforms. Sometimes, they have argued that, because a passage is not found in *śruti* (the supreme revelation), it is an accretion and should be removed. At other times, they have argued that, because some practice is not accepted by good people today, it should be removed. At still other times, they have argued that, because of changing social conditions, a practice is no longer permitted in the present age (the *kaliyuga*). So, too, according to Nathanson,[49] Jews have found scope for change. The entire rabbinic tradition, in fact, is a commentary on scripture intended to expand its application to everyday life, although the rabbis have always insisted that, far from inventing new interpretations of their own, they have merely rediscovered the original ones revealed as the "Oral Torah" to Moses on Mount Sinai.

At the end of the day, any community might decide, even if the ethical merit of change is clear, that the degree of change required could not be incorporated; as in all ethical dilemmas, choices must be made. Some people might leave the community, seeking justice elsewhere. Others might reaffirm the priority of group solidarity. In some extreme situations, of course, the state might intervene with its own bottom line and force all communities to comply with the law. A legal bottom line would therefore replace an ethical one. In general, though, it is best to protect the separation of church and state. First, this safeguards religious freedom. Second, voluntary associations are important checks on state power. Legal interference by the secular state into the internal affairs of religious groups should never occur unless there are *compelling* reasons such as eliminating human sacrifice.

Politics is a universal feature of human existence, but political activity has ethical limits. This reminds me of the Hindu belief that life has four goals: (*puruṣārthas*)—*dharma, artha, kāma, and mokṣa. Dharma* (righteousness and justice) is first on the list for two reasons. First, it must set the limits, the ethical bottom line, for politics (*artha*) and love, or pleasure (*kāma*). Second, it is the foundation of liberation (*mokṣa*). Even though Hinduism once marginalized women, lower castes, and outcastes in this big picture, the general idea is still useful.

Debate versus Dialogue

There is an important role for dialogue in connection with problems created by gender (although, as I have said, it should not take place in the classroom). The following section has emerged from my collaboration over ten years with Paul Nathanson on a larger but closely related topic: a historical and cross-cultural examination of relations between men and women—one that concludes with a suggestion that, surprisingly enough, has not yet been tried. The latter is identified in the subtitle of our manuscript: *Beyond the Fall of Man: From Feminist Ideology to Intersexual Dialogue.*[50]

Of greatest interest here is the fact that Nathanson and I have not only collaborated on research and analysis, we have also engaged in dialogue. Together, we have seen just how complex and ambiguous it can be to call ourselves insiders and outsiders. In some ways, for example, Nathanson is an insider. He was brought up in a Jewish home, but not an Orthodox one. Nevertheless, he was sent to an Orthodox day school. Judaism was his first love. Nevertheless, he was deeply moved by the story of Jesus, a man who sacrificed himself out of compassion. But there was no room for Jesus in the synagogue. As an adult, therefore, he explored Christianity. Eventually, he joined the Anglican Church and studied theology with ordination to the priesthood in mind even though his theology, like that of most other ordinands, was so liberal that it precluded belief in the divinity of Jesus and most other clauses in the traditional creeds. No matter what curious or hostile Jews said, Nathanson maintained that he had never stopped being religiously Jewish, and he never claimed that either he or other Jews could "fulfill" themselves as Jews by becoming Christians. It was with all this in mind that he led a Jewish-Christian dialogue group. Nathanson left the church a few years later. By that time, he had come to realize that the church was so secular, despite a thin veneer of traditional rhetoric, that remaining made no sense. He now considers himself, as always, a Jew (although he appreciates Christianity far more than he would have otherwise). As a Jew no less than as a Christian, therefore, Nathanson has been both an insider and an outsider. And the same thing applies to his status as a man. Being gay, he is both an insider and an outsider to the world of men (not to mention Jewish men). Given the purpose of our research, his experience of religious and sexual ambiguity has been extremely useful.

I have had a similar experience. I was brought up in a Protestant church. As an adult, though, I joined an orthodox Hindu community, although that sojourn did not last long in the sense of maintaining an orthodox Hindu way of life. Then, too, my former husband was an African-American (who was part Cherokee). I was called affectionately "the Sister" by my many sisters-in-laws. In these three ways, I have been an insider. But I have been an outsider, too. I no longer belong formally to a Protestant church. I am an outsider in the Hindu world. For one thing, I was brought up in the West. And I was trained there as a scholar of Hinduism. Moreover, my African-American sisters-in-law never forgot that I was white and thus an outsider to their community and its culture. We all had to live with the fact that the history of the interaction of our two communities had been, and was still, very troubled.

Although our contributions have surely overlapped, and although our attitudes have come together over the years (interaction taking place on a line-by-line basis), we have both come to the project with our own distinctive interests. In connection with our project, Nathanson's primary interests and areas of academic expertise are Western art history, Western ethics and religions (including interreligious dialogue), the experience and identity of men in contemporary Western societies, and the ways in which men have been represented or misrepresented by contemporary Western popular culture. Even though I have contributed fundamentally to the research and analysis on Western traditions—including the cultural history of men, the phenomenon of witches, modern intellectual trends, and the new goddess religions—my areas of academic expertise have been Eastern religions, especially Hinduism, comparative studies of the world religions, and the anthropology of religion—all of which have contributed to the formulation of general theories.

My point here is that Nathanason and I have made good use of our divergent backgrounds and experiences—male and female, Jewish and Christian, gay and straight. Collaboration on this project has enabled us to achieve far more than either of us would ever have been able to achieve alone—which underscores the fact that no one can write adequately about either men or women without referring to the other. In fact, our collaboration has helped us define the whole idea of "intersexual dialogue." Speaking for myself, I am amazed at how my consciousness has been raised. Over and over again, Nathanson has forced me to rethink my own presuppositions about both men and women—including many inspired by feminism. For the first time, I have been forced to question conventional wisdom (defined by feminists) about male biology, men's cultures, and—not the least—men's problems. And Nathanson has said that he, too, was forced to rethink much of what he had assumed about both men and women. Most of what follows in this section is based on the results of both our research and our experiment in intersexual dialogue.

As Nathanson and I demonstrate, there is one striking omission in most Western feminist discussions of religion. There is virtually no opening to *men* (although there are occasional token references to the existence of at least some honorable men). The underlying assumption is that the task of feminism, its raison d'être, is to improve the status of *women as a class* in relation to *men as a class.* Because every problem of women as a class is blamed on men as a class, and because these problems have never been completely solved, some feminists assume that they must continue to undermine men as a class in every conceivable way. A presupposition of dialogue, however, is *respect* for the "other." In this case, that would mean truly listening to men, taking them seriously as people rather than adversaries (even collective as distinct from individual adversaries), being sincerely open to their interpretations of their own experiences, which might contradict feminist interpretations of them, not assuming that women know men better than men know themselves even "for their own good", and so on. Given their long-standing critical stance toward men, some feminists might find the possibility of genuine dialogue with men (as district form politically motivated debate) dangerous. In fact, they might dismiss the whole idea as "fraternizing with the enemy." or they might argue that until people are equals, dialogue is fundamentally flawed.[51] The goal of dialogue, however, is reconciliation (being able to live in harmony despite real differences) or at least tolerance (enduring, if not respecting the differences of others), not conquest or conversion.

For many feminists—and many men, for that matter, because they are still two or three generations behind women when it comes to assessing their own personal needs and thinking about their own problems—dialogue is undesirable, at least for the time being. But there are some reasons for them to rethink that position. First, there are epistemological ones. Male scholars could make important contributions to our knowledge of women. The insights of men would be particularly valuable in two contexts. Men obviously do not experience women as women experience themselves. That alone means that the insights of men could correct or at least raise questions about those of women just as the insights of women can correct those of men. Then, too, it is obviously impossible to write about women without writing also about men. This raises a serious problem for those feminists who believe in epistemological exclusivity. The insights of men are valuable, then, at least to the extent that some feminists distort the history of *men's* particularity into gross generalization and stereotypes, to the extent that they *silence* men just as men once silenced women. By the same logic, of course, women's insights about men can help men to understand themselves. Their criticisms are important when *women's* particularity is ignored or when women are silenced, or when they are in need of an outsider's possibly more objective view. Our point, though, is that some women can be accused of gynocentrism just as some men can be accused of androcentrism. Our hope is that scholars will break new ground by bringing women's studies and men's studies together in ways that do justice to the experience of *both* sexes.

Unless we can end the polarization between men and women, which is now rampant in North America—several problems will have to be faced. For one thing, any sustained attack eventually loses its ability to arouse indignation. Sensibilities are deadened. By now, most men have come to realize that women deserve more respect and recognition, but men have also come to reject the stained attack on their identity, both cultural and biological. And with good reason. Then, too, any sustained attack on a specific group can easily be used to foster hatred. Whether deliberately or not, some feminists have demonized men as a class and most, in the name of solidarity, have *not* launched an ethical critique in the public square against this. Do women really want to claim, or be in silent solidarity with the claim, that men are either inherently evil because of culture or innately evil (even though that is an oxymoron) because of nature itself? Some do.[52] It could be argued, and often is, that women have been exposed to similar treatment from men. It was once thought by many people, for instance, that women were stupid by nature because of their reproductive organs. But two wrongs do not make a right. If it is wrong to use biology (or sociobiology) for the purpose of diminishing the status of women, it is surely wrong to use it for the purpose of diminishing that of men.

Possibly even worse, as we point out in *Beyond the Fall of Man,* the negativity of sustained attacks can be internalized by the targets. Women have discovered this for themselves. So have men. There is evidence to suggest that many men have internalized the notion that they are inherently inadequate, immoral, or evil. One result is resentment. That is fairly obvious. Another response, however, is not so obvious: loss of identity accompanied by neurotic self-hatred. This negativity could be projected either inwards in acts of self-destruction or outwards as acts of violence against society in general or women in particular.

Also, sustained attacks on any group often end up in disrepute of those who launch them. Feminists sometimes rely on dubious statistics—or at least on the assumption that few people will check statistics and question either the figures or the methodological problems associated with them. When the facts do come out, of course, the cause is tarnished. Men get the idea that women have no serious case for change when they find out that statistics are either inflated (as a result of using extremely broad definitions of rape or harassment, for example, when conducting surveys) or even *invented* (as in the case of a report that violence against women increases dramatically just after Superbowl Sunday).[53] It is up to feminists to acknowledge these problems. It is up feminists, moreover, to acknowledge positive changes, which might encourage men, instead of preserving the sense that women are always victims and must continue the struggle against men.

Finally, political expediency and intellectual opportunism foster a general environment of cynicism. At least some people have noticed that many feminists apply deconstruction to the "texts" of those defined as their enemies but never to their own. Why should men agree to create a new social order based on truth and justice when their potential partners resort to dubious methods?

The danger for women is that advances can always be rolled back (though this is much easier in some countries than others, especially those in which reforms have been legalized). Women do need to be vigilant. But do women and men need to polarize society as well? Must we stand by passively while relations between men and women deteriorate even more than they already have? Must it be, as a diplomat once said, that nations act wisely only when they have exhausted all other alternatives? Polarization, after all, can lead all too easily to cycles of revenge and counter-revenge.

In this context, I would like to discuss one analogy that comes out of my study of India. I refer to another prolonged struggle for social and political transformation: the Indian struggle against Britain. My goal here is to use this analogy in connection with relations between men and women.

It took two centuries for Indians to achieve independence, the culmination of a long struggle for political self-assertion to eliminate colonial rule. They had to fight against people with whom they had daily contact and a complex set of relations. Although they could have tried to throw the British out physically (because not many British people lived in the subcontinent, and most of those who did had not developed a strong sense of Indian identity), this would have involved violence and possibly led to a cycle of violence and revenge. From a Hindu perspective (that of most Indians), even if they could have accomplished their goal of throwing out the British without violence, they would still have been left with the Muslims. And the identity of Muslims really had become deeply rooted there.

Something similar could be said about women and their conflicts with men. Women sometimes oppose men with whom they have daily contact and a complex set of relations. The situation is inherently ambiguous, moreover, because their relations with men sometimes involve cooperation (just as trade unions oppose capitalists but live on wages earned from them). It was impossible for Hindus to create a world without Muslims, which necessitated cooperation. So, too, women cannot create a world without men. Even in a world ruled by women, there would still be men. Like the Indians, women must motivate those currently defined as their adversaries to create a more just society. But the analogy can be taken still further. Most Hindus preferred a nonviolent solution and acknowledged the need for an inclusive society. As a result, of course, total victory was impossible. Is this not true for women as well?

In his leadership of the Indian independence movement, Mahatma Gandhi was well aware that any change of the status quo would cause not only resentment but also injustice to many individuals and groups. Gandhi constantly warned his supporters to blame the system, not individuals or groups. In addition, he explained that their actions would liberate not only India from Britain but also Britain from the moral burden of imperialism. The struggle was to be waged with integrity. It was to be conducted with good will and even cordiality toward the British. And it was to involve no violence toward individual Britons. Because Gandhi tried to practice what he preached, many Britons acknowledged the merits of his cause even though it was not in their own interest to do so. When he visited England, for example, Gandhi was feted by the very people who had lost their jobs in India due to his boycott of British goods. Many feminists, too, focus on the systemic problems created by sexism. They, at any rate, do not think of their project as an attack on individual men.

Gandhi did not allow his followers to think about the British even as an evil *class* that profited from imperial power at the expense of Indians. The British, he believed, should be understood not as "others" but as "brothers" or "sisters." Moreover, Gandhi encouraged people to aim for a change of heart in those perceived as oppressors. This idea was rooted deeply in his understanding of nonviolence. *Ahiṁsā* was not just nonviolence in deed. It was nonviolence in thought, too. It involved looking on transgressors without hostility[54] even while opposing them. This presupposed the need for a deep understanding of etiquette.[55] In other words, the struggle was against the systemic problems created by the Raj, not against the British either as individuals *or* as a class.

Western feminism, as Nathanson and I point out in our manuscript, is a critique of men—that is, those who have profited from power *as a class,* though whether they still do in every country and to what degree can be questioned. It is true that some feminists focus attention on systemic problems resulting from the power of men, not on men themselves. But because their critical theory is rooted in the notion of *class,* it runs a much greater risk of vilifying men—both individually and collectively—than it would if the focus were on the problems themselves (as advocated by Gandhi). This approach has resulted, for instance, in a gynocentric version of the Christian concept of the Fall: men are condemned as a class for introducing evil and suffering into the world (replacing the Goddess with their God) and ending Paradise (conquering matrifocal cultures).[56]

Class analysis is common to all forms of feminism, but it is particularly strong in gynocentric—and thus, as Nathanson and I point out, dualistic[57]— ones. They not only define women as a class (characterized by every positive quality) but also demonize men as a class (characterized by every negative quality). What might have begun as a moral critique of men, in short, quickly becomes an ontological denunciation. It becomes increasingly easy to argue that men are evil not because they are ignorant or foolish or abuse power but because they are, well, male. Whether the hostility of feminists toward men as a class is mild or intense, the fact remains that feminism has encouraged women to think of men as the primary "others." A worldview based on conflict between "us" and "them" is a worldview founded on dualism. This state of affairs is ironic, to say the least, in view of the fact that feminists themselves have noticed this way of thinking when applied by men to women, repeatedly warned women of its disastrous results, and even claimed (turning logic on its head) that only men are infected by the virus of dualism. What goes around, as they say, comes around.

Feminists who identify themselves with socialism or liberation theology, I would add, do not identify with this dualism. They argue that men and women of the proletarian class or the poor of any society should act in solidarity to end their oppression by destroying the hegemony of the dominant class, which they often identity as the rule of the "Great Fathers" (custodians of patriarchy). But even here, it could be argued, a distinction is rarely made between the negative qualities ascribed to the "Great Fathers" and those ascribed to all men. In the interest of solidarity, feminists have often refused to acknowledge publicly how easy it is to slip from one proposition to the other. In the interest of carrying on the struggle for revolution, moreover, feminists are often reluctant to acknowledge historic improvements.

Ontological dualism is based on biological determinism of the very kind that women rightly rejected when it was said (first by Freudians) that "anatomy is destiny."[58] Although biological determinism as applied to men might seem at first glance like just retribution, Gandhi would have pointed out that there is no such thing as just retribution, that two wrongs do not make a right. (The same would be said by the leaders of many other religious communities—some Christians, for example, would point out that the ideal is "turning the other cheek" and that taking revenge has no moral legitimacy under any circumstance.) Far from seeing the British as moral cretins, Gandhi respected them as people with moral sensibilities that would eventually support Indian independence. And he was correct.

Some authors of this book have taken a position not unlike that of Gandhi. When relationality rather than autonomy is the starting point, says Woo, men are a necessary part of the analysis. They are no longer just conspirators against women. They themselves have faced serious historical problems—being exploited through slavery, corvée labour, tenant farming, overtaxation, and bankruptcy. Excavations of Han tombs show that 96 per cent of the skeletons are male, for example, and that most of them are young men whose bones reveal abuse form heavy labor. Woo concludes that "the disadvantage of women in concubinage, prostitution, and infanticide are thus 'balanced' by the disadvantage of men in corvée labour. There is a symmetry here: sexual labor and death; and physical labor and death. Men and women were exploited in different ways." Narayanan also points out that the "opportunities for men and women were curtailed by their class, community, and caste, and women were not singled out for various forms of discrimination. Men, for example, have not been given the opportunity to stay home and take care of children. In fact, men have seldom had the opportunity to choose their own careers.[59]" Laughlin and Wong, writing of Taoism, note that although some authors have interpreted Taoism's feminine imagery as a sign of favored status for women, "in the feminist dialogue with Taoism, we need to be careful not to rely on a model of female superiority that is antithetical both to Taoism and to many modern feminisms."

They go on to point out that both men and women are believed to have the potential for enlightenment, and that both have attained immortality. (The same could be said of Western religions.)

Returning now to my analogy with the Indian independence movement. Gandhi realized, in any case, that the problem was much deeper than British rule. No worthy society could be created in India without solving age-old problems, not the least of which was mistreatment by upper caste Hindus of untouchables. Gandhi did more than ask upper-caste Hindus to have a change of heart and atone for this historic injustice. Once again, he set the example himself by performing a traditional occupation of the untouchables (cleaning the latrines) and encouraged other upper-caste Hindus to do the same. Because change would inevitably involve suffering or loss of some kind, Gandhi appealed directly to the notion of self-sacrifice as a moral ideal (as distinct from a legal requirement). By analogy, individual men and women in other societies should act in their own lives to ensure that they themselves are not perpetuating other kinds of discrimination.

But what about their taking responsibility for wrongs that occurred in the past? Many white men in the United States today argue that they must not be blamed for the racism of their ancestors or of other white people. They do not own slaves. Most of them, by far, do not even have ancestors who owned slaves either because their ancestors were too poor or because they had not yet migrated to America. These men argue, similarly, that they must not be blamed for the misogyny of their ancestors or of other men. They themselves have not prevented women from going to college or taking up careers. They have not raped or injured women. This argument really does make moral sense. Individuals must be held morally accountable for their *own* behavior.

But, as Nathanson and I argue in *Beyond the Fall,* to the extent that people cannot make moral choices (for ancestors or even for other people in the present), they cannot be considered moral agents at all. Morality is meaningless, in short, if guilt can somehow be collective, inherited, or vicarious. Moral claims are meaningless, moreover, if they are motivated by nothing but political opportunism or expediency. Like women, men are people, not the hostages of history or statistics to be used by reform-minded social scientists and bureaucrats. At the same time, those who make these arguments must avoid using them to absolve themselves of responsibility for the present and the future. (Because the British were still *in* India, for example, they could still *choose* to leave and at least try to repair the damage that they themselves had done.) It is true that some men still benefit form what their ancestors did. That, too, must enter the moral equation. On the other hand, women have always had their own forms of power. And they have not always used these wisely or benignly. Like men, therefore, women must acknowledge the past but take responsibility for the present and future. This, at any rate, is the implication of what Gandhi said. So much for the individual. What about the state? Democratic states act on behalf of their citizens. It makes sense to argue that the state should undo or compensate for specific wrongs committed in the name of its citizens. These would include wrongs such as forced sterilization, testing nuclear weapons in populated areas, and so forth.

Failure to acknowledge the past feeds the sense of exploitation, and, as I have already noted, feelings are important to insiders. Gandhi would have suggested that in this case, men should acknowledge both the past (claiming advantages over women) and the present (continuing to reap some benefits). In addition, though, he would probably observe that where major changes are occurring men individually and collectively are paying the price of change economically, politically, psychologically, and so on just as the British paid the price of change individually and collectively, both in India and England. In countries where substantial changes have occurred, moreover, those *women* who are reaping the benefits of a changing system (no matter how slow and imperfect), should *empathize* with those men who have lost jobs and opportunities as a result of the demographic shift created by the move of women into the workplace. It seems to me that women have a moral responsibility to minimize disruption and loss for men in their struggle for equality. (Of course, men in positions of power also have a responsibility to eliminate the "glass-cciling" and relieve the clustering of women in poorly paid, part-time work at the bottom of the industrial ladder). The difference between the Indians and the British can be summed up by an exchange that occurred when Indira Gandhi was having dinner with Churchill after independence. Churchill said "you must have hated us." She replied, "we never hated you. We hated British rule." Churchill then replied, "But I did [hate you Indians]."[60]

Striving for internal transformation and eventual reconciliation means avoiding triumphalism. Indians were usually wise enough not to claim that they threw the British out. For one thing, the event was not that decisive. Then, too, it could always be argued that the British decided to go of their own accord. The satisfaction of triumphalism, or revenge, is *emotional.* But it is neither moral nor practical. For one thing, it can create resentment, which leads in turn to revenge. Even if women were to defeat men, it would be a hollow victory unless men emerged with enough dignity to want cooperation with them.

Freud is famous for asking the following: "The great question that has never been answered and which I have not yet been able to answer, despite my thirty years of research into the feminine soul, is 'What does a woman want?'"[61] Well, what do we women want? Do we want victory and revenge? Or do we want justice and tolerance, if not reconciliation?

Notes

1. It should be recognized that what follows is in the form of an essay. It develops my own views, which might not be those of my colleagues. I would like to thank my co-editor, Arvind Sharma, for discussion on Gandhi's political and moral strategies. One section of this chapter draws extensively from my joint manuscript with Paul Nathanson called *Beyond the Fall of Man: from Feminist Ideology to Intersexual Dialogue,* which is nearing completion. I thank him for permission to present some major ideas from this text.

2. Wilfred Cantwell Smith, "Comparative Religion: Whither—and Why? in *The History of Religions: Essays in Methodology,* ed. Mircea Eliade and Joseph M. Kitagawa (Chicago: The University of Chicago Press, 1959), 46.

3. Smith, 44.

4. Smith, 45-46. Reat, following Smith, has argued that what distinguishes religious studies from the humanities is precisely the personal engagement of its scholars with some form of ultimate or at least overriding concern that gives meaning and direction to life. He declares that even secular scholars must acknowledge that they stand for something. Moreover, they should respect others, face them directly, and be open to the possibility that the encounter might change their own views of the purpose and meaning of life [N. Ross Reat, "Insiders and Outsiders in the Study of Religious Traditions," *Journal of the American Academy of Religion,* 51.3 (1983): 466. This places Reat in the tradition of dialogue.

5. This is my altered version of the quote by Smith 1959, 42.

6. I thank Paul Nathanson for this observation.

7. See Edward W. Said, *Covering Islam: How the Media and the Experts Determine How We see the Rest of the World* (New York: Pantheon Books, 1981).

8. This was drawn to my attention by Paul Nathanson.

9. Smith, 43.

10. Smith, 43.

11. See T. Patrick Burke, "Must the Description of a Religion Be Acceptable to a Believer?" *Religious Studies,* 20.1 (1984): 631-636. See also Arvind Sharma, "Playing Hardball," *The Council of Studies in Religion Bulletin* 15.1 (February 1984) 1-4.

12. Elaine Pagels, *The Origin of Satan* (New York: Random House, 1995) 167.

13. That scenario is being replaced by three others: (1) several waves of migration and a long period of interaction between Indo-European and indigenous peoples; (2) a linguistic transfer (of Sanskrit) from a small group of migrants to the majority (local inhabitants) whose culture remains influential if not dominant; or (3) a denial of either invasion or migration because the homeland of the Indo-Europeans is, in fact, India

itself (according to its much larger ancient territory). See Klaus K. Klostermaier, *A Survey of Hinduism* (Albany: State University of New York Press, 1994) 38 and George Erdosy, "Language, Material Culture, and Ethnicity: Theoretical Perspectives," in *The Indo-Aryans of Ancient South Asia: Language, Material Culture and Ethnicity,* ed. George Erdosy (Berlin: Walter de Gruyter, 1995) 1-31.

14. In making karmic connections between action and results, Manu never mentions rebirth as a woman as a negative result of bad karma but mentions birth in a low caste twice (see *Manusmṛti* 12:1-82, especially 12:43).

15. I thank Paul Nathanson for the following discussions of Judaism.

16. The use of headgear for religious purposes dates back to "time immemorial." It originated in the ancient Semitic world, presumably to express humility in the presence of God, but was not expressly commanded by the Torah (possibly because there was no need to do so). The status of this requirement is custom, therefore, rather than *halakhah* (although custom is backed by strong emotion). Orthodox men now cover their heads at all times, but they have not done so always and everywhere. Even now, moreover, Orthodox men may refrain from wearing *kippot* or hats when doing so might have a negative effect on earning a living (as it could for lawyers in court) or compromise safety (as it could in a hostile environment). In the case of women, there is an additional factor to consider: the erotic associations of hair. As a result, it has long been customary among the Orthodox for married women to cover their hair in public (that is, outside the bedroom); they have used kerchiefs, hats, or wigs (although the latter are sometimes so elaborate and attractive that they defeat the original purpose). As in the case of men, though, women have not done so always and everywhere. At the moment, in a larger society that no longer associates women's hair with eroticism, some Orthodox authorities are questioning the need to worry about all this.

17. Reform rabbis and cantors, however, do wear ritual regalia. They do so, implicitly, as "professional Jews."

18. There are other reasons for granting women divorces. One of them, for example, is a husband's undesirable occupation; wives are not expected to tolerate what they find physically repugnant.

19. This can amount to intimidation. The religious court can persuade recalcitrant husbands by shaming them or even by threatening to prevent them from receiving public honors such as being asked to read the Torah in synagogue. It did not always work, but rabbis did often try to help women. This is not necessarily the case with another problem, however. Orthodox feminists have rightly claimed that the rabbis could be more "creative" in finding a halakhic solution to the problem of *agunot* (literally, "anchored women"). The husbands of these women are missing. They could be dead, but they might not be. Unless the husbands are pronounced dead, however, their wives may not remarry. The problem is most likely to occur in connection with war, as in modern Israel.

20. I owe this formulation to Arvind Sharma.

21. Charles Taylor, *Multiculturalism and 'The Politics of Recognition'* (Princeton: Princeton University Press, 1992) 66.

22. Taylor, 70.

23. Taylor, 73.

24. Taylor, 28-29.

25. Morny Joy, "And What If Truth Were A Woman?" in *Gender, Genre and Religion: Feminist Reflections,* ed. Morny Joy and Eva Neumaier-Dargyay (Waterloo, Ont.: Wilfrid Laurier University Press, 1995) 284 ff.

26. Hewitt, 264.

27. Hewitt, 264.

28. Linda Kintz, "In-different Criticism: The Deconstructive Parole," in J. Allen and I. Marion Young, eds. *The Thinking Muse* (Bloomington: Indiana University Press, 1989) 130.

29. Ray L. Hart, "Religious and Theological Studies in American Higher Education—A Pilot Study," *Journal of the American Academy of Religion,* 59.4 (1991): 715-793.

30. Hart, 767.

31. Hart, 769.

32. Hart, 769.

33. Taylor, 25.

34. Taylor, 39. And that, in turn, leads to demands for universal rights, entitlements, immunities, and economic benefits (but ignores universal duties and responsibilities because of the focus on the individual rather than the family, community, or society). In theory, at least, this avoids the problem of "first-class" and "second-class" citizenship (Taylor, 37-39).

35. Hart reports that different types of departments in different types of school perceive the issue of vulnerability quite differently, those in public universities with small and emerging departments being most pessimistic (Hart 744-56).

36. See the approach of Tina Pippin, "Border Pedagogy: Activism in a Wymyn and Religion Classroom," *Council of Societies for the Study of Religion Bulletin,* 24.1 (February 1995): 3-5.

37. These include San Diego State University, the University of Tampa, and the University of Pennsylvania. See Edith Shurer Whyschogrod, "President's Report to the AAR Board of Directors, November 1993," *Religious Studies News* 9.1 (February 1994): 6; Warren G. Frisina, "Three Departments of Religion under Threat of Dissolu-

tion," *Religious Studies News* 8.4 (November 1993): 9; "University of Pennsylvania Reverses Position—Department of Religious Studies to be Retained," *Religious Studies News* 9.3 (September 1994): 1; and Warren G. Frisina, "University of Tampa Eliminates Religion Courses," *Religious Studies News* 10.1 (February 1995): 14.

38. Smith, 54-55.

39. Smith, 47.

40. Smith, 55.

41. Jennifer Holmgren, "Myth, Fantasy or Scholarship: Images of the Status of Women in Traditional China," *Australian Journal of Asian Affairs,* 6 (1981): 147-170.

42. This discussion on *halakhah* has been furnished by Paul Nathanson.

43. Even then, however, the new status is problematic from a Jewish point of view. This is partly because Jews have no reason to acknowledge the legitimacy of alien rituals in the first place; converts who change their minds, in any case, are welcomed back without formality as *ba'alei teshuvah* (literally, "those who have mastered repentance.")

44. See the statement by the Union of Orthodox Rabbis of the United States and Canada and subsequent discussions (*New York Times,* 1 April 1997, B, 2:1); and the discussion of a bill in the Israeli parliament to ensure that Orthodox rabbis have the sole authority to perform conversions (*New York Times,* 2 April 1997, A, 6:4).

45. Mary Ann W. Lundy, "Department under Fire," in *Re-Membering and Re-Imagining,* ed. Nancy J. Berneking and Pamela Carter Joern (Cleveland: Pilgrim Press, 1995) 121.

46. Although syncretism is often criticized as the contamination of "pure" religion by traditionalists, it is usually seen in a more positive light by historians of religions. Michael Pye, for instance, has said "syncretism is the coherent yet somewhat uneasy coexistence of elements drawn from diverse religious contexts. Even when a smooth cohesion has been achieved the various elements often seem to maintain their potential for conveying independent meanings" [Michel Pye, *Comparative Religion* (New York: Harper and Row, 1972) 146].

47. For a good illustration of this see Tazim R. Kassam "Syncretism on the Model of the Figure-Ground: A Study of Pir Shams' *Brahma Prakāśa*" in *Hermeneutical Paths to the Sacred Worlds of India,* ed. Katherine K. Young (Atlanta: Scholars Press, 1994).

48. Father Divine (born George Baker) was active in Harlem in 1932, at the time of the Great Depression. In the following decades, he developed an extensive cooperative system for members of his community. This provided food, clothing, and homes as well as hotels where they could vacation [See Gayraud S. Wilmore, *Religion and Black Radicalism* (Garden City: Doubleday & Co.,1972) 215-16]. Because of its cooperative ventures and philosophy of holding everything in common, the movement seemed at

first to be the perfect front for Marxists, who were then trying to infiltrate the African-American community and realized that the black churches would be suitable. Marxists used to join with Divine in his parades down Fifth Avenue in New York City. Eventually, however, they abandoned this front, finding Father Divine's eccentricities, his love of many Rolls Royces, and his private plane detrimental to Marxism's image of working for the proletariat.

49. I thank Paul Nathanson for this observation.

50. Paul Nathanson and Katherine K. Young, *Beyond the Fall of Man: from Feminist Ideology to Intersexual Dialogue* (forthcoming).

51. Gregory Baum has argued that "dialogue demands equality. Honest conversation is not possible between partners [who] have an unequal access to power. For the powerful modifies his speech so that his superior position remains protected; and the powerless is too vulnerable to be perfectly honest. Inequality of economic, political and cultural power is the great barrier that keeps humanity divided and cannot be overcome by dialogue. . . . Liberation is the precondition of dialogue and mutual understanding. . . . Some situations demand conflict." See Gregory Baum, "Religious Pluralism and Common Values," *Journal of Religious Pluralism*, 4 (1994): 13. He says that there can be no real dialogue until we reach utopia or something close to it (because the precondition for that is equality). Some feminists argue likewise. But dialogue could awaken those with power to the need for change. Or it could help those without power to refine their arguments for it. At the very minimum, it could discourage extreme polarization; only that situation, they believe, can generate revolution. Of course, it could just as easily generate totalitarianism, fragmentation, or anomie. My point here is not to deny the need for women to have their say—which is precisely what dialogue should allow—but to warn against making the preconditions of dialogue unrealistic (such as *absolute* equality of participants) or defining it too narrowly (not accounting for different *kinds* of power—some of which are wielded primarily by women. That would, for all intents and purposes, mean putting it off indefinitely).

52. For example, it is sometimes said that men are evil because of "testosterone poisoning." See Paul Nathanson and Katherine K. Young, "Biology is Destiny," *Ecumenism* 27. 2:29-32. The creation of this negative predisposition toward men as a class can occur at the symbolic level. In her review of Elizabeth A. Johnson's *She Who Is: The Mystery of God in Feminist Theological Discourse,* Mary Aquin O'Neill observes that "male images of God, when alluded to, are almost universally cast as negative. "Patriarchal" becomes the code word for an image of God that is unfeeling, controlling, distant" [*Religious Studies Review* 21.1 (January 1995) 21].

53. Christina Hoff Sommers, *Who Stole Feminism? How Women Betrayed Women* (New York: Touchstone, 1994) 188-192.

54. The word *ahiṁsā* literally means no-injury or killing (from the negative prefix *a* and the noun *hiṁsā*). Accordingly, it conveys the notion of non-maleficence. But this Sanskrit compound conveys in addition the positive sense of benevolence, because

a compound conveys more than the sum of its parts. *A-dvaita,* for instance, literally means not-two. But it connotes oneness.

55. Dialogue could facilitate healthy change and prevent polarization between groups however they might be defined. But dialogue even with the best intentions can break down. That is the time for more formal ways of resolving conflict, such as binding arbitration, which must be part of due process in all institutions. Before we arrive at an impasse, though, we might make use of another technique in addition to dialogue: etiquette. As Nathanson and I have argued, etiquette is often the object of suspicion [Katherine K. Young and Paul Nathanson, "Interfaith Etiquette in a Multireligious Society," in *Towards a Code of Etiquette: Interfaith Dimensions of Canadian Multiculturalism,* ed. Adjul Lodhi, Tom Parkhill, and Melynda Jarratt (Fredericton, N.B.: Atlantic Human Rights Centre, St. Thomas University, 1990) 89-118]. This is due partly to the Christian (especially Protestant) tradition of antinomianism; even when translated into secular terms, etiquette can be consciously or unconsciously associated with the Jewish covenant of "law" in contrast to the Christian covenant of "love." For Marxists, etiquette can be associated with bourgeois rules imposed on proletarians to make them orderly and thus suitable for work in factories. For existentialists, etiquette can represent the veneer of civility, which destroys authenticity. For feminists, it can represent the chivalry of patriarchy. Anthropologists, however, remind us that etiquette is a symbolic and ritualistic way of facilitating social harmony and is necessary for all communal life.

Because etiquette is concerned with form, not content, it can facilitate interaction among people with radically different views. Abbé Dubois, a French missionary to India, observed at the end of the eighteenth century that Indians differed greatly according to language, dress, and religion and yet were capable of creating a comparatively tolerant society. The only intrusion of conformity came in the form of etiquette, a minimal set of rules to govern public behavior [Abbé Dubois, *Hindu Manners, Customs, and Ceremonies,* 3rd ed. (Oxford: Clarendon Press, 1906) 11]. By analogy an academic conference has a set of minimal rules, such as "don't disrupt the speaker," to facilitate exchange between scholars with radically different perspectives, some of which might be charged with emotion. Women, too, might want to adopt a new form of etiquette to replace the "shock" and "anger" tactics of recent years. In fact, etiquette might be useful among women themselves now that feminist disunity has become evident to everyone. It might be useful in addition to men who blame women for snatching away jobs and other opportunities or subjecting their identity as men to a relentless attack. Anger is understandable in these circumstances, just as it was for women when they realized how patriarchal culture had subordinated them in the public world. But once again: although anger is understandable, it is not ethical—especially if it takes the form of hatred or revenge.

56. Katherine K. Young, "Goddesses, Feminists, and Scholars" in *The Annual Review of Women in World Religions,* eds. Arvind Sharma and Kathrine K. Young, vol. 1 (Albany: State University of New York Press, 1991) 105-179.

57. Nathanson and Young (forthcoming).

58. Nathanson and Young 1989.

59. Male aristocrats in feudal Europe had a choice, I would add, but only between the "chalice" and the "sword." Male peasants, of course, had not choice at all.

60. This account was narrated to me by Arvind Sharma.

61. Sigmund Freud; quoted in Ernest Jones, *Sigmund Freud: Life and Work,* vol.2 (London: Hogarth Press, 1956) 421.

Notes on Contributors

Arvind Sharma (B.A. Allahabad 1958; M.A. Syracuse 1970; M.T.S. Harvard Divinity School 1974; Ph.D. Harvard University 1978) lectured at the University of Sydney, Australia before moving to Montreal, Canada where he is a Professor of Comparative Religion at McGill University. He has published several papers and monographs dealing with the position of women in Indian Religions, some of which are incorporated in *Sati: Historical and Phenomenological Essays* (1988). He is the editor of a trilogy on women and religion: *Women in World Religions* (1987), *Religion and Women* (1993) and *Today's Woman in World Religions* (1994).

Katherine K. Young is Professor, History of Religions, McGill University. She publishes in the areas of South Indian religions, gender and religion, and comparative ethics. She has co-authored, with H. C. Coward and Julius J. Lipner, *Hindu Ethics: Purity, Abortion, and Euthanasia* (State University of New York Press) and has edited *Hermeneutical Paths to the Sacred Worlds of India* (Scholar's Press). She has a forthcoming book entitled *New Perspectives on Women in Hinduism*. Along with being the general editor of a series with State University of New York Press called McGill Studies in the History of Religions: A Series devoted to International Scholarship, she is one of the editors of *The Annual Review of Women in World Religions* (State University of New York Press) and *Gender in World Religions* (McGill).

Vasudha Narayanan is Professor of Comparative Religion at the University of Florida. Her books include *The Way and the Goal* (1987) and *The Vernacular Veda* (1994). She is the co-author of *The Tamil Veda* (1989) and a co-editor of *Monastic Life in Christian and Hindu Traditions* (1990). Her forthcoming books include: *The Hindu Tradition: An Introduction* (Prentice Hall) and *The Hindu Tradition in the United States* (Columbia University Press). She was awarded a John S. Guggenheim Fellowship in 1991 and an NEH Fellowship in 1998–1999. Her more recent research has focused on feminism in the Hindu tradition.

Rita M. Gross received her Ph.D. in the History of Religions from the University of Chicago for the first dissertation on women studies in religion, *Exclusion and Participation: The Role of Women in Aboriginal Australian Religion.* In 1990, she received the annual Award for Excellence in Scholarship from the University of Wisconsin-Eau Claire. She has been a leader in feminist studies in religion for twenty years. A founder of the women and Religion section of the American Academy of Religion, she served as its program chair for five years. She has written many articles and essays on a wide variety of topics pertaining to women and religion. Her book *Unspoken Worlds: Women's Religious Lives* (edited with Nancy Auer Falk) is widely used in courses on women and world religions. *Buddhism After Patriarchy: A Feminist History; Analysis, and Reconstruction of Buddhism,* was published by SUNY Press in 1993 and *Feminism and Religion: An Introduction* was published by Beacon Press in 1996. In addition to her work in feminist scholarship in religious studies, Rita Gross has played a leading role in Buddhist-Christian dialogue in North America. A member of the Buddhist-Christian Theological Encounter (the Cobb-Abe group), she is a past president of the Society for Buddhist-Christian Studies and served as program chair for its 1992 International Conference. Her articles and essays have been translated into Dutch, German, French, Spanish, and Japanese.

Terry Woo is currently finishing her dissertation on *Women during the Reign of T'ang Ming-huang* 712–756 C.E. She is interested in two general issues: First, the dissonance between the importance and position accorded to women and the feminine ideal in philosophy, in contrast to the secondary place they frequently occupy socially; and second, the interpenetration that happens amidst the continued distinctiveness of the primary Chinese religions—Confucianism, Taoism, Buddhism and folk practices.

Karen Laughlin is Associate Professor of English at Florida State University, where she teaches classes in modern and American drama, film, humanities, and women's studies. A native of Westfield, New York, she received her Ph.D. in Comparative Literature from the University of Toronto. She is the co-editor of *Theatre and Feminist Aesthetics* (Fairleigh Dickinson, 1996) and has also published numerous articles and book chapters on dramatic literature and theory. Since 1976, she has been studying the Taoist arts with Master Moy Lin-Shin. She serves as President of the Taoist Tai Chi Society of the United States of America and a Director of the International Taoist Tai Chi Society. As a member of the Translation Committee of the Fung Loy Kok Institute of Taoism, she has also been active in editing English translations of Taoist texts and scriptures.

Eva Wong Ph.D., was born and raised in Hong Kong where she began studying the Chinese classics and Taoist texts at the age of fourteen. She continued to study and practice Taoist arts after settling in the United States and is the author of over eight books on Taoism, including *The Shambhala Guide to Taoism, Fegshui: The Ancient Wisdom of Harmonious Living for Modern Times, A Course in Traditional Chinese Fengshui,* and translations of *Seven Taoist Masters, Cultivating Stillness, Lao-tzu's Treatise on the Response of the Tao, Lieh-tzu, Harmonizing Yin and Yang, Cultivating the Energy of Life,* and *Teachings of the Tao,* a collection of selected texts from the Taoist Canon.

Ellen M. Umansky is the Carl and Dorothy Bennett Professor of Judaic Studies at Fairfield University in Fairfield, Connecticut. Her recent publications include the co-edited volume: *Four Centuries of Jewish Women's Spirituality: A Sourcebook* (Boston: Beacon Press, 1992).

Rosemary Radford Ruether is the Georgia Harkness Professor of Applied Theology at the Garrett-Evangelical Theological Seminary and a member of the graduate faculty of the joint program in theological and religious studies of Northwestern University in Evanston, Illinois. She is the author or editor of twenty-seven books and numerous articles on the subject of Christian theological history and social justice. She has written on such topics as sexism and racism, economic exploitation, and war and peace. Among her recent books is *Sexism and Godtalk: Toward a Feminist Theology* (Beacon Press), a three vol ume documentary history entitled *Women and Religion in America* (Harper and Row), *Gaia and God: An Ecofeminist Theology of Earth Healing* (Harper San Francisco) and *Women and Redemption* (Fortress Press). Dr. Ruether holds the Ph.D. degree in classics and patristics from the Claremont Graduate School in Claremont, California. She is a frequent lecturer on University campuses and church conventions, and has been actively involved in movements for social justice for over twenty years. She is married and is the mother of three children.

Riffat Hassan teaches in the Religious Studies Program at the University of Louisville. She was born in Pakistan and received her Ph.D. in Arts from the University of Durham in England. She is the author of several articles, and of two books on Sir Muhammad Iqbal: *An Iqbal Primer: An Introduction to Iqbal's Philosophy* (1979) and *The Sword and the Sceptre: A Collection for Writings on Iqbal, Dealing Mainly with his Life and Poetical Works* (1977). The position of women in Islam is an abiding focus of her work.

Name Index

A

Adam, 257, 258, 259
Adler, Rachel, 187, 188
Adorno, Theodore, 15
Ahmad, 268
Ai, Duke of, 124
Ā'ishah, 18, 250
Akbar, 54
Ali, Moulvi Cheragh, 249
Ali, Mumtaz, 253
Alpert, Rebecca, 191–192
Amin, Qasim, 253
Ammaiyar, Karaikkal, 38, 39
Amoah, Elizabeth, 234
Amritanandamayi Ma, 64, 65, 67, 68
Anandamayi Ma, 64, 65, 67, 68
Anandi Ma, 63
Andal-Goda, 33, 38, 39, 42, 43, 44, 45,
    46, 47, 52, 67
Andors, Phyllis, 112
Annamacharya, 47
*Answers to Questions Concerning the
    Attainment of Enlightenment, (Hsiu-
    chen p'ien-nan)*, 165, 166
Anthony, Susan B., 217
Ardhanārīśvara, 66
Amritanandamayi Ma, 64, 65
Arundale, Rukmini Devi, 54

Arundati, 68
Ashravi, Hanan, 231, 232
Asoka, King, 27
Astell, Mary, 217
Ateek, Canon Naim, 232
Aurobindo, 29

B

Baihaqi, 268
Baiju, Bavra, 54
Balka, Christie, 190
Basava Tatva Darshana, 46
Basri, Rabi'a al-, 250
Battung, Rosario, 235
Beauvoir, Simone de, 13, 110, 218
Berkovitz, Eliezer, 182,
Besant, Annie, 54
Bhagavad Gita, 37
Bharata Nātya Śāstra, 50
Bharati, Guru Ma Jyotishanand,
    63–64, 68
Bhattar, Parasara, 45
Bidegain, Ana Maria, 239
Bingen, Hildegard of, 229
Biographies of Exemplary Women,
    126, 127
Bodde, Derk, 122

Bons-Storm, Riet, 227
Book of History (Book of Documents),
    113, 119
Book of Poetry (Book of Odes), 114
Borresen, Kari, 228, 229
Brown, Joanne, 223
Brown, Antoinette, 217
Buber, Martin, 192
Buddha, Gautam, 30
Bukhari, Muhammad ibn
    Isma'il al-, 256
Bumiller, Elisabeth, 33
Burke, T. Patrick, 282, 285
Butler, Judith, 173

C

Cannon, Katie, 222
Cao Zhenjie, 158, 159
Carmichael, Amy, 33
Cavalcanti, Tereza, 240
Chan Wing-tsit, 134
Chandralekha, 56
Chang Po-tuan, 156, 159, 162, 170
Chang Tao-liang, 151
Chen, Ellen, 161
Cheng I, 133, 134
Ch'ing, Marquis, 130
Ching Yeh, 130, 131
Ching-tung, 153
Chinniah, 53
Chin-ssu lu (Reflections on Things at
    Hand), 132
Chi-yi Tzu, 153
Chopp, Rebecca, 221
Chou Tun-I, 171, 172
Chu Hsi, 132, 133, 134, 137
Chuang-tzu, 151, 154, 159,
    162, 173
Ch'un-ch'iu (The Spring and Autumn
    Annals), 121–22, 125, 152
Chung Hyun Khung, 236–38
Churchill, 305
Citrarekha, 52
Cixous, Hélène, 16, 160

Classic of Great Peace (T'ai-ping
    ching), 162
Cleary, Thomas, 152
Cohen, Gerson, 204,
Condren, Mary, 224
Confucius, 4, 13, 113–19, 111, 124,
    126, 129
Correct Methods for Women's
    Practice, 167
Cultivating Stillness, 156, 167
Curtin, Katie, 111, 112
Cusa, Nicholas of, 229

D

Daly, Mary, 220, 294
Dasyai, Tirukkoneri, 62
Derrida, Jacques, 10–11, 12,
    15–16, 287
Devi, Shantala, 48, 49, 50
Devi, Swarnakumari, 58
Devi, Tara, 67, 68
Devraj, Lala, 29
Dewey, John, 112
Dikshitar, Muthuswami, 40, 47
Divine, Father, 295
Dragon-tiger Classic
    (Lung-fu ching), 162
Droes, Freda, 227
Duaybis, Cedar, 232
Dull, Jack, 120–21
Dumas, Alexandre, 2, 25
Durga, 66, 67

E

Ecumenical Association of Third World
    Theologians (EATWOT), 235
Edet, Rosemary, 234
Eisenberg, Robin, 199
Ekeya, Bette, 234
Eliade, Mircea, 8
Eliberg, Amy, 205,
Elizabeth I, Queen, 34

Emperumanar Ramanuja, 44, *See also*
  Ramanuja
Erndl, Kathleen, 65
Essentials of the Golden Elixir Method
  for Women (*Nu chin-tan fa-yao*),
  153, 167
Eve, 254, 257
Ezrat Nashim, 184

F

Fa Mu-lan, 136
Fabella, Virginia, 235
Falk, Nancy, 29, 32, 190, 194, 202, 203
Fan Chung-yen, 132
Fares, B., 270
Fatum, Lone, 229
Fei Ch'ang-fang, 152
Feld, Merle, 203
Fell, Margaret, 216
Felton, Monica, 59
Feng Yen, 125
Fields, Adele, 113
Fiorenza, Elisabeth Schüssler, 221, 225
Firestone, Shulamith, 155
Fishman, Sylvia Barack, 206
Foucault, Michel, 11, 17
Freud, 305
Friedan, Betty, 14
Fu Sheng, 127, 128

G

Gadamer, Hans, 285
Gage, Matilda Joslyn, 218
Gandhi, Indira, 305
Gandhi, Mahatma, 60, 301–05
Gardiner, Judith Kegan, 173
Gargi, 33
Gasparro, Giulia Sfameni, 229
Gibb, H. A. R., 250
Geffen, Rela, 207–08
Gebara, Ivone, 239–40
Gilligan, Ann Louise, 224

Gilligan, Carol, 92, 160
Gnanadason, Aruna, 236
Goda Mandali, 44, 45
Gordis, Robert, 205,
Gouges, Olympe de, 218
Gowri, Mylapore, 54
Grant, Jacquelyn, 221
Greenberg, Blu, 182, 207
Greenberg, Irving (Yitz), 193,
Greer, Germaine, 155
Grey, Mary, 225, 226
Grammick, Jeannine, 223
Grimké, Angelina, 217
Grimké, Sarah, 217, 218
Gross, Rita, ix, 4, 18, 19, 20, 21, 32
Grossman, Susan, 183
Guitiérrez, Gustavo, 238

H

Halkes, Catherina, 223, 225
Hallaj, Muslim bin al-, 256
Hampson, Daphne, 225
Han Wu-ti, 130
Han Yu, 131
Hancock, Mary, 65
Hardesty, Nancy, 220
Haridas, Svami, 54
Harrison, Beverley, 221
Hart, Ray, 288
Hassan, Riffat, ix, 6, 18, 21
Hawwa', 257, 258, 261
Hegel, 15
Heschel, Susannah, 186
Hewitt, Marsha, 15, 287
Hewlett, Sylvia Ann, 155
Heyward, Carter, 221, 223, 225
Ho Hsien-ku, 151
Holmgren, Jennifer, 112, 113, 291
Holub, Margaret, 200
Horkheimer, Max, 15
Hou Han shu (*History of the Latter*
  Han), 126
Hsiung-nu, 126, 127
Hsü Hui, 152

Hsü Mi, 152
Hsün Tzu, 119–20, 121, 122,
Hu Shih, 112
Huai-nan tzu, 162
Huang-ti, 151
Hunt, Mary, 223
Huraira, Abu, 255, 272
Hurston, Zora Neale, 222
Husserl, Edmund, 8
Hyman, Paula, 188

I

Ibn Majah, 268
I ching (Book of Changes), 113,
    122, 138
Imbens-Fransen, Annie, 227
Instructions for Women, 127
Iqbal, Muhammad, 255, 259
Irigaray, Luce, 16, 226
Islam, 249
Iyer, Subramania, 58
Izutsu, Toshihiko, 259

J

Jagadguru, 46
Jaganmata Akka Mahdevi Ashrama, 46
Janabai, 40
Janeway, Elizabeth, 155
Jantzen, Grace, 226
Jesus Christ, 30, 214, 231, 237
Jewish Feminist Organization (JFO),
    179, 184
Joshi, Anandibai, 61
Jost, Renate, 228
Joy, Morny, 16

K

Kali, Goddess, 64, 66, 67
Kao-tsung, 131
Kaplan, Mordecai, 202,

Kaplan, Temma, 127
Kapsar, Walter, 228
Karve, Anandibai, 60
Karumariamman, Goddess, 65–66, 69
Kaul, Dagny, 229
Kaye Kantrowitz, Melanie, 189
Kelleher, Theresa, 114, 125
Keller, Katherine, 221
Kelman, Naamah, 183
Khadijah, 18, 250
Khoury, Samia, 232
Khurana, Shanno, 56
Kim Jeong Soo, 236
King, Ursula, 226
Kintz, Linda, 287
Klepfisz, Irena, 189
Korenhof, Mieke, 228
Kort, Nora, 232
Kothai Venkatachapathy, 44
Krishna, Lord, 39, 45, 47, 52
Krishna, Ambujam, 47
Kishwar, Madhu, 28, 30, 37, 38
Kristeva, Julia, 16, 156, 161
Kuan Wen-shih, 159
Kuan-Yin, 238
Kuang K'ung, 125
*Kuei fang (Regulations for the Women's
    Quarters)*, 135

L

Lakshmi, Goddess, 39, 41, 44, 66, 67
Lalla, 39, 47
Lao-tzu, 151, 154, 159, 161, 175
Laughlin, Karen, ix, 2, 5, 13, 15, 19, 303
Lee-Park Sun Ai, 236
Li chi, 138
Li Yu-ning, 132
*Lieh-hsien chuan (Biographies of the
    Immortals)*, 152
Lieh-nü chüan, 138
Lieh-tzu, 159, 162
Ligo, Arche, 235
Li-sao, 152
Liu Hsiang, 124, 125, 127, 129, 135

Lo Ping-wang, 130, 131
Lord of Purity's Classic for Women,
    The, 167
Lu, Empress, 123, 128
Lu K'un, 135, 136, 137
Lü Tung-pin, 164
Lundy, Mary Ann, 294
Luxuriant Gems, 121

M

Ma Tan-yang, 152, 157–58, 164, 166
Magidson, Beverly, 205
Magonet, Jonathan, 185
Mahabharata, 68
Mahadevi, Akka, 38, 39, 40, 41, 45, 46,
    47, 68
Mahadevi, Mate, 41, 45, 46, 67
Mahadevi, Queen Sembiyan, 33, 48,
    49, 57
Mandali, Goda, 68
Mananzan, Mary John, 235
Mānava Dharma Śāstra, 35
Mansih Tomar, Raja of Gwalior, 54
Manu, 38, 42, 43
Manushi, 33, 38
Manu Smriti, 35
Marder, Janet, 195, 196,
Marcuse, Herbert, 15
Master Li-wan's Precious Raft of
    Women's Dual Practice (Ni-wan Li-
    Tsu-shih nu-tsung shuang-hsiu pao-
    fa), 153, 167
Marx, Karl, 9–10, 295
Mary Magdalene, 229
Maududi, A. A., 260, 261, 263, 265, 273
Mbiti, John, 233
McFague, Sallie, 225
Mencius, 118–19, 120, 121, 131,
    133, 137
Mernissi, Fatima, 262, 270
Meyer, Michael, 199
Millett, Kate, 155
Militello, Cettina, 229
Minakshi, 40

Mirabai, 30, 39, 40, 43, 47
Misra, Mandana, 37
Moltmann, Jürgen, 228
Mott, Lucrecia, 217
Moy Lin-shin, 148
Muddupalani, 52
Muhammad, 250
Mukherjee, Sharbari, 54
Muktananda, Swami, 29
Muslim, Imam, 272

N

Nācciyār Tirumoḻi, 38, 43
Nagaratnammal, Bangalore, 52, 53
Nammalvar, 39, 44
Nan Tzu, 117
Nārada Smriti, 35
Narayanan, Vasudha, ix, 2, 3, 15,
    17, 303
Nathanson, Paul, 7, 8, 283, 291, 296,
    297, 298, 302–04
National Federation of Temple Sister-
    hoods (NFTS), 198
Nasa'i, 268
Nashim, Ezrat, 184, 203
Norwich, Julian of, 229
Nü-chieh, 138

O

Oduyoye, Mercy Amba, 234
Offen, Karen, 111
O'Hara, Albert, 125
Okure, Teresa, 234

P

Pa, widow, 128
Pagels, Elaine, 282
Palmer, Martin, 151
Pan Chao, 125, 128, 129, 135
Pan Ku, 123, 126, 128

Parvati, 40, 66
Parwez, Ghulam Ahmad, 249
Piercy, Marge, 203
Pintasilgo, María de Lourdes, 230
Pizan, Christine de, 215
Plaskow, Judith, 186, 187, 188, 190,
    191, 201
Ponniah, 53
Prajavani Daily, 46
Pratapasimha, Nayaka King, 52
Priesand, Sally, 194
Primavesi, Anne, 223
Purandara, 47
Pure Lust, 220

Reddy, Muthulaksmi, 61, 62
Reed, Barbara, 153, 161
Ricci, Carla, 229
Rich, Adrienne, 160
Ricoeur, Paul, 10, 11, 15
Rogow, Faith, 190
Roman de la rose, 215
Rose, Andy, 190
Roy, Ram Mohun, 29, 35
Ruether, Rosemary R., ix, 6, 17, 221,
    223, 225
Rushdie, Salman, 19
Russell, Letty, 221, 225
Ryskova, Mireia, 230

Q

*Queen Mother of the West's Ten Pre-
    cepts on the True Path of Women's
    Practice (Hsi Wang Mu nu-hsiu
    cheng-t'u shih tse),* 165, 167, 170

R

Rabi'ah al-Basri, 250
Radhika Santwanam, 52
Raghunāthanāyakabhyudayamu, 52
Rahman, Fazlur, 249, 253
Rama, 44, 52, 56
Ramabai, 58, 61
Ramabai, Pandita, *See* Ramabai
Ramabai Ranade, *See* Ramabai
Ramabhadramba, 52
Ramakrishna, 29
Ramamurthy, Nallamuthu, 60
Ramanuja, 44
Rāmāyana epic, 56
Ramodibe, Dorothy, 234
Ramos Gonzales, Marifee, 230
Rangarajan, Srinidhi, 44
Ratnamma, *See* Mahadevi, Mate
Ravana, 56
Reat, Ross N., 7

S

Sagarwali, Asghari Begum, 55, 57
Sahih Al-Bukhari, 255
Sahih Muslim, 255
Said, Edward, 11, 12, 17
Saiving, Valerie, 89
Sakya, Pandita, 98
Samavai, Queen, 48
Samyukta Karnatak, 46
Santhakumari, P., 55–56
Saptapadalu, 52
Sarabhai, Mallika, 56, 57
Sarada, *See* Sarasvati, Goddess
Sarasvati, Goddess, 50, 59
Sarasvati, Jagatguru Shankaracharya
    Kapileswaranand, 62
Sarma, Acharya Visvanath Dev, 63
Sartre, Jean-Paul, 13
Sastry, Shyama, 47
Savitri, 68
Scanzoni, Letha, 220
Schaalman, Herman E., 200
Schmidt, Eva Renate, 228
Schroer, Silvia, 228
Schwartz, Eleanor, 198–99
Seetha of Basavangudi, 47–48
Sen, Keshub Chunder, 29
Setel, Drorah, 190, 193, 194

Seven Taoist Masters, 152, 154, 157,
    164, 166
Shakti: The Power of Women, 56
Shakti, Ma Yoga, 63
Sharma, Arvind, x, 1, 17
Shih ching, 138
Shih fan, 138
Shu ching, 138
Shiva, Lord, 39, 40, 45, 66
Singer, Milton, 43–44
Sita, 56
Sivananda, 29
Sivanandam, 53
Smith, Wilfred Cantwell, 9, 13, 280,
    281, 289, 290
Sölle, Dorothy, 227–28
Sri Ma, 63
Śrīmālādevī, Queen, 96
Srinivasan, Parvati, *See* Sundaraja
Sri Vaishnava, 41
Ssu-ma Ch'ien, 123
Ssu-ma Kuang, 132
Stanton, Elizabeth Cady, 217, 218, 219
Steinem, Gloria, 195
Stern, Chaim, 200
Subbalakshmi, 58–61
Sukanya, 68
Sulkes, Zena, 199
Sun Pu-erh, 152, 156–58, 164, 166
Sundaraja, 47
Sunithi, 67, 68, 69
Swamiji, Lingananda, 46
Swann, Nancy Lee, 125
Sweden, Brigitta of, 229

T

Tabick, Jacqueline, 185
Tagore, Rabindranath, 49, 54
T'ai-shang kan-ying p'ien (Lao Tzu's
    Treatise on the Response of the Tao
    to Human Actions), 158, 164
T'ai-tsung, Emperor, 131
Tamaz, Elza, 239, 240

Tanjore Quartette, 53
Tansen, 54
Tao-chia yang-sheng hseuh kai-yao
    (Essentials of the Taoist Techniques
    of Cultivating Health), 170
Tao-te ching, 162, 163
Tapia, Elizabeth, 235
Tawil, Raymonda, 232
Taylor, Charles, 285, 286, 287, 288
Teutsch, David, 202
Tirmidhi, 268
Tiruppāvai, 43, 44, 45, 52
Tiruvāymoḻi, 62
Tribe of Diana, The, 189
Trible, Phyllis, 225
Trinh T. Minh-ha, 173
Triplex Unity (Tsan tung-chi), 162
Tsai Yen, 126, 128
Tung Yen, 126
Tung Chung-shu, 121–24, 125, 130, 136
Tyagaraja, 47, 53

U

Umansky, Ellen, ix, 5, 6, 17
Understanding Reality, 156
Upanishads, The, 66, 67
Upasani Baba, 29, 63

V

Veereshalingam, 52
Venkatanarasu, 52
Venkateswaran, 43
Vijayaraghava, 52
Vishnu, Lord, 39, 41, 42, 45, 56, 66
Vogt, Kari, 229

W

Wales, Prince of, 60
Walker, Alice, 17, 221

Wan-li, 153
Wang An-shih, 132
Wang, Ch'ung-yang, 156
Wang Fu, 124, 133
Wang Pa, 130
Wei, Duke of, 117
Wei H'ua-ts'un, 152
Weinberg, Sheila Pelz, 203,
Weiss, Avraham, 207,
Wen-ch'ang, 164
Wenig, Margaret, 200,
Willingdon, Lady, 60
Winter, Miriam Therese, 223
Wong, Eva, ix, 2, 5, 13, 15, 19, 303
Woo, Terry, ix, 2, 4, 14, 15, 17, 20,
    21, 303
Wu, Emperor, 117, 121, 128, 131
Wu Tse't'ien, 130, 131
Wu-ti, Han, 130

Y

Yang Hsi, 152
Yang My Gang, 236
Yellow Court Classic (*Huang-ting
    ching*), 152
Yen Yen-nien, 130
Yogananda, 29
Yoga Shakti, Ma, 63
Younan, Susan, 232
Yüan Tsai, 132
Yüan-chün, 169

Z

Zappone, Katherine, 224
Zaru, Jean, 232
Zia-ul-Haq, Muhammad, 252

Terms Index

Adam, 254, 255, 257
Adamah, 254
Adhyāpakas, 45
Agape, 7
Agunah, 182
Ahadith, 255, 256, 261, 267, 268, 272
Ahiṁsā, 302
Al-insan, 254
Aliyot, 5, 183, 204
Al-jannah, 257, 259
Ammans, 66
An-nas, 254
An-nisa', 264
Araiyar sevai, 43, 55
Araiyars, 45
Arrijal, 264
Artja, 296
Āstikas, 294

Bar mitzvah, 5, 207
Bashar, 254
Bat mitzvah, 5, 207
Bawari, 40
Bhavas, 50, 51
Bhajana, 43
Bhakti, 25, 37, 38, 40, 47, 50, 64, 65, 66, 67, 68, 69
Bima, 195

Bodhicitta, 92
Brahmins, 35
Brit milah, 183

Challah, 5, 180
Chametz, 180, 181
Ch'i, 122, 167, 169
Ch'ing, 169
Ching, 167
Ch'un-chiu, 138
Ch'un-chiu fan-lu, 138
Chung, 116, 138
Chün tzu, 119, 136
Connaître, 282

Daraba, 265
Dasi attam, 53
Deconstruction, 10, 15
Devadasi, 51, 53, 59, 61, 62
Dhamar, 54
Dharma, 32, 40, 79, 296
Dharma shastra, 34, 37, 40, 43, 50
Dharmic, 41
Dhrupad, 54, 55
Dhruva prabandha, 54
Difference, 160

Epoché, 8, 13, 285

Fiqh, 248
Fu jen, 123, 138

Garbha, 51, 95
Get, 182

Hadith, 248, 255, 256, 263, 267,
    269, 275
Halakhah, 6, 181, 184, 187, 206, 283,
    284, 291
Han-pu ri, 238
Han shu, 128, 130, 138
Haquq Allah, 262
Haquq al-'ibad 262
Havurot, 202
Hijab, 281
Hsiao jen, 117, 138

I, 138
Iddat, 266
Ijma, 256
Intifada, 231
Ird, 7, 270
Isnad, 256

Jagadguru, 46
Jen, 20, 115, 116, 117, 119, 120, 136,
    137, 138

Kaliyuga, 296
Kāma, 296
Karma, 85
Kashrut, 5, 180
Kipah, 284
Kippot, 5, 183, 206
Kuei fang t'u shuo, 138
Kui-shih, 158

Li, 116, 119, 120, 122, 126, 127, 131,
    135, 136, 137, 138
Liang-hsin, 135, 138

Madahib, 248
Madhyastha, 284
Mahasiddhas, 82
Majazi khuda, 7, 267
Mandali, 43
Mangalam, 44
Matas, 66
Matn, 255
Minyan, 5, 183, 204, 206, 207
Minyanim, 197
Mitzvot, 181, 188
Moksa, 69, 296
Moksha, 3, 32, 40, 41, 42, 51, *See
    also* Moksa
Mridangam, 55

Namaskar, 60
Namaste, 27
Nāstikas, 294
Nautch, 55
Niddah, 5, 181
Nirguṇa, 66
Nü tzu, 117, 138

Pao-t'u, 138
Parampara, 52
Patipuja, 267
Pesach, 180
Pesachdik, 180
Prabandha, 54
Pratityasamutpāda, 88
Puranas, 66
Purdah, 274
Purusarthas, 296
Purusha, 66

Qawwamun, 263, 264
Querelle des femmes, 215, 216

Raga, 48, 43
Rshikas, 62
Rosh Hodesh, 181

Sādhanas, 98, 99, 100
Sahih, 256
Sajada, 267
Śakti, 64, 65
Samsāra, 87, 90
Sangha, 91
Sannyasa, 63
Sannyasi, 63, 64
Sati, 35
Sau'at, 260
Savoir, 282
Seder, 181
Shakti, 25, 56, 64, 65, 67, 68, 69, 236, 237, *See also* Śakti
Sharī'ah, 248
Shastras, 35
Shen, 167
Shih, 123, 138
Shih-shen, 175
Shirk, 7, 267
Siddurim, 200
Smarta, 65
Śruti, 296
Sthala mahatmayam, 42
Śūdra, 35
Śūnyatā, 83, 87, 95

Tabla, 55
Tallit, 283
Tallitot, 5, 183, 206
Tan-t'iens, 168
Tao-shih, 158
Tathāgatagarbha, 95, 96, 97
Tefillah, 206
Tefillin, 5, 183, 283
Thavil, 55
Tikkun ha-am, 193

Tikkun ha-nefesh, 193
Tikkun olam, 6, 193, 194
Torah, 207
Ts'ung, 118, 138

Ummah, 263, 264, 265, 266, 269, 275
Ustad, 55

Vachanas, 46
Vaggeyakara, 40
Vajra, 98, 100
Varna, 26, 283
Veena, 59
Vidushis, 56
Vratas, 39

Womanism, 30
Wu, 152
Wu-chi, 171
Wu hsing, 138
Wu-wei, 173

Yab-yum, 4, 98
Yang, 138
Yajna, 63
Yidams, 100, 106
Yin, 121, 138
Yin and yang, 122, 124, 171, 172
Yuan-shen, 163, 169, 175

Zalimin, 259
Zauj, 257, 259
Zulm, 259

Subject Index

African-Americans, 221–22
Analytical method, 87
Androcentrism, 79–83, 93, 129–30, 188, 220, 252
An-Nisa, 265, 266, 274
Anthropology, 19
Art: Means to salvation, 36, 37, 49; Means of reform, 56

Biological Determinism, 156, 161
Birth Control, 224, 271–73
Black Power movement, 14
Bombay Legislature of 1934, 62
Buddhism: Bodhisattva path, 92, 94; Bodhisattva vow, 94–95; Buddhist, 78, 105; Community importance, 104; Compassion, 93–94; Dyadic unity, 98, 100; Egalitarian, 78; Egolessness, 87–89, 94, 95; Emptiness, 91–92, 94, 98; Equal potential for enlightenment, 96–97; Feminist values and reforms 81, 91, 92, 94, 102; Gender and ego, 89–91; Gender roles, 85, 87; Gender stereotypes, 90; Hierarchy, 81, 85–87; Ideological bias, 116; Impermanence, 87; Interconnectedness, 92; Institutionalized oppression, 97, 101; Karma, 85; Lay

Buddhism, 101; Lower expectations of women, 97; Mahayana , 87, 91, 93, 97, 98; Nonsexist core, 91, 97, 101; Nun subjugation, 95, 102–03; Nyingma, 86; Ordination of women, 21, 102; Patriarchy, 91; Peace and prosperity through obedience, 114; Postpatriarchal Buddhism, 106–107; Reform in, 4; Sexism in, 4, 18, 82–84, 95; Six realms of sentient beings, 80; Social ethic, 94–95; Symbol system revalorization, 80–81; Tantric symbols, 98; Tantric commentaries on the body, 99; Tibetan, 79, 86, 102; Theravada, 102; Teachings vs practice, 84, 90, 93, 100–01; Universal liberation, 94; Vajrayana, 97, 99, 100; Woman as outsider, 78; Women entertainers, 128; Women's responsibilities, 79
Buddahood, 95–96

Caste: Oppression, 237; Reform, 61
Celibacy, 68
Chastity and/vs devotion, 40, 68
Ch'eng-Chu school, 134
Child brides, 47, 57
Childrearing, 105

328

China: Chou dynasty, 113, 119; Ming
dynasty, 130; Nineteenth century
views on women, 166; Patriarchal
social conditions, 150; Respect vs
honor, 164; Subordination of
women, 112; Sung dynasty, 132; Traditional family system, 112; Traditional family systems, disintegration
of 113; Warring States periods, 119
Christianity: Africa, 233–34; Asia,
234–38; Bible as justification for
racism, 232; Biblical texts and gender equality, 215; Biblical teachings
vs Christian faith, 220; Biblical reinterpretation, 216, 217; and Buddhism, 84–85, 89; Control over
women's bodies, 218; Diversity,
218–19, 220, 282; God as male
power, 227; Incompatible with feminism, 225; India, 58, 60; Interpretation conflicts, 215, 228; Education of
Women, 215, 217, 234; Feminist
roots in, 214; Feminist theology vs
feminist studies, 219; Feminist
"thealogians", 220; Feminism in the
Two-Thirds World, 230–40; Gender
equality, 216, 220; Gender hierarchy,
214, 217; Gender roles, 217; Liberation Theology, 238; Matriarchal subculture, 228; Middle Ages, 215, 224;
Middle East, 231–33; Ordination of
women, 219, 224, 225–26, 229, 240;
Patristic Christianity origins, 214;
Quaker movement, 216–17, 226; Reformation Period, 216; Religious
synthesis, 233, 238; Renaissance,
215, 217; Revival of Goddess religion, 228; Sectarian movements,
215; Women disciples, 216; Women
missionaries, 219; Women's prayer
groups, 223; World Council of
Churches, 238
Choice, 33
Civil Rights movement, 14
Class analysis, 302
Colonization 61, 236, 238

Compassion, 94
Concubines, 127, 128
Confucianism, 4–5, 13–14, 110–44;
Antiforeignism, 131; Categories of
good women, 125; Chastity, 133,
135; Cultural minimization of
women, 117; Diversity in, 120; Education, 116, 120, 132, 134–35; Fall
of, 130; Family relationships, 133;
and Feminism, 110–44; Feminist and
patriarchal, 137; Filial piety, 130;
Gender complementarity, 124, 127,
137; Gender equality, 114; Gender
roles, 120, 122–23, 127, 137; Han
Confucianism, 113, 124, 125; Hierarchy in traditional society, 119, 123;
Hierarchy's foundations, 122; Honor
of the ancestors, 125; Liberal feminist critique of, 111; Literacy 135;
Lu's critique of accepted female
ideal, 136; Neo-Confucianism, 113,
131; Protestant feminist critique of,
111; Rights vs responsibilities, 137;
Sensitive heart, 118; Sexual segregation, 116, 134; Socialist feminist critique of, 112; Social gender roles,
114, 116, 118; Superstition, 131;
Witches, 134; Women's distinctiveness and complementarity, 116;
Women in the private sphere, 114;
women's influence , 120, 129–30,
134; Women's oppression, 123; denounced 132; Women and political
power, 123; Women as symbol of
lust, 134, 135; Yin Yang Confucianism, 121
Confucius: Political stability, 113; Traditional China, 113
Conversion to Christianity, 58
Critical theory, 12
Cultural construction of gender, 201
Custom, 34

Dancing as celebration of body, 50
Debate vs dialogue, 297–305

Deconstruction, 10–11, 12, 15, 172
Deification of women, 64–65, 67
Devotee, 66
Dharma, 26, 84
Diversity, 22
Divinizing women poets, 41–42,
Divorce, 125, 132, 182, 184, 224,
   266–67
Dowry, 135

Earth Goddess, 42
Ecological work by women, 57
Ecumenism, 8, 13–14
Ego: Buddhist, 87–91; Western, 90
Emotion: Contribution to feministm,
   93; Imitation and appropriation of,
   45; Political importance of, 8; Tam-
   ing of, 168; vs Reason, 279–85
Epistemology, 279, 280, 283

Feminism: Balance, 195–96; Christian,
   81, 103, 214–41; Contemporary,
   151; Contemporary Buddhist, 103;
   Definition, 2, 79–80; Demonization
   of men, 302; Desire for intimacy,
   196; Dialectical, 221; Diversity
   within, 17, 149; Eco-feminism, 223;
   Evangelical, 217; French, 16, 218,
   226; History, 17, 150; Hinduism,
   15–69; Inclusion of men, 298–302;
   Lesbian Christian 222; Ontological
   foundations of, 229; Racist, 20, 21,
   112, 116, 138, 161; Taoism, 13,
   148–76; Western European, 226;
   World religions, 3; Radical, 13, 102,
   155; Reformist agenda, 103; Rejection of term, 30; Revision of history,
   151; Transformative, 103; United
   States, 26, 195, 217–23;
   Wholistic, 217
Feminist myth-making, 153
Foot binding, 112, 115, 118, 119, 134
Frankfurt School, 9–10, 15
Freedom: Within realm of love, 42

Gender equality as normative
   position, 97
Gender polarization, 299, 302
Get Equal Treatment (G.E.T.), 182
Girl-soldiers, 136
Goddesses, 64–65, 67

Hair, 65
Hermeneutics, 10, 15
Hindu feminist agenda, 57
Hindu tradition/Hinduism: Caste hierarchy, 28, 54, 57; Chastity and honor,
   56; Child marraige, 57; Courtesans,
   50–52; Education of women, 53, 55,
   58, 60; Education of widows, 47–62;
   Female ideal, 35–36; Gender equality, 25, 26, 38, 55, 64, 69; Hierarchy
   and equality, 26–28; Important
   women, 33, 40; Matrilineage, 28; Reform movements, 60; Renegotiation
   of power in, 3; Salvation through art,
   36, 37, 49; Temple girls, 61–62;
   Women and sacred texts (Vedas) 34,
   35, 37, 62, 63; Women creating opportunities for women, 29–30, 36, 37–48,
   53, 59; Women gurus, 63–69; Women
   and performing arts, 49–57; Women's
   roles, 3, 29; Women's sectarian
   groups, 43; Writings on sex, 52
Hindu Succession Act of 1956, 26
Hispanic-Americans, 222
History of Chinese Philosophy, 122
History of women: Feminist, 83;
   Reevaluation, 82, 151; Bias against
   women, 83
Homosexuality, 185, 189, 191–92,
   203, 222
Hudhood Ordinance of 1979, 252

India: British rule, 35; Colonial times,
   55; Medieval traditions, 51; Social
   reformers, 58
Infanticide (female) 116, 118, 128, 135,
   164, 269, 270

Insiders/outsiders 18, 279–85, 297; Ambiguity in defining, 291; Credibility, 3, 9; Influence on perspective of, 6; Interpretation, 81, 281; Within one community, 292

International Coalition for Aguna Rights, 182

Islam: Adam representing all humanity, 255, 257, 259; Creation of humanity, 255; Female circumcision, 271; Feminism in 248–78; Freedom of choice, 260; Gender discrimination, 7, 21, 254, 256, 262, 269, 274; Gender equality, 254, 255, 262, 269, 275; Gender roles, 263–65, 268; Gender segregation, 252, 273, 274; Genesis, 257, 258; Human Rights, 271; Individual accountability to God, 268; Legalized oppression, 252; Literacy, 251; Male honor, 270; Men's support of women's rights, 253; Modernity, 251; Normative, 250–51; Original sin, 260; Personal relationships with the Prophet, 250; Qur'an historicity, 249; Qur'an interpretation, 250; Qur'an as tool for oppression, 263; Reform in, 6; Sexual duties, 272; Sexual instinct as negative, 261; Social ideal of a woman, 263; Veiling, 273–75; Virginity, 270; Westernization, 251; Women as agents of sexuality, 261; Women and Normative Islam, 253–68; Women's obedience to men, 264, 267; Women as possessions, 263; Women's rights, 18, 250; Women's sexuality, 273, 274

Israel Women's Network, 179

Judaism, 6, 179–213; Circumcision, 190; Chosenness 190; Conservative, 203–06; Family life, 196; Feminism's influence on, 198; Gender essential equality, 180; Gender complementarity, 180, 191, 192; Gender separatedness, 190; Human-divine relationship, 187; Images of God's gender, 187; Justice, 194; Equal access, 182–85; Feminist Conservative movement, 183; Halakhic changes, 182; Nongender names in liturgy, 199, 202; Nonhierarchical images of God, 187; Opportunities for women, 181; Ordination of lesbians and gays, 185, 203; Ordination of women, 179, 183–85, 194–96, 204–06; Orthodox feminism, 182; Reconstructionism, 184, 202; Religious hierarchy, 190; Revising of school curricula, 199; Self-knowledge, 192; Theory vs practice, 188; Women's leadership roles, 198; Women-only prayer groups, 181, 206, 207; Women's oppression, 190; Women roles in, 6, 180, 181, 183; Women taking part in religious ceremonies, 183, 188–89, 204, 207; Writing women into Jewish history, 189

Knowledge: social construction of, 12

Law of Evidence (1984), 252
Logocentrism, 11

Madras legislature of 1929, 62
Mahila Samta Sainik Dal, 31
Male dominance vs misogyny, 83
Marriage: Hinduism, 38, 68; to God, 41, 43; Renunciation of, 63
Marxism, 9, 10, 14, 218
Mencius' heart of compassion, 118
Menopause, 169
Menstruation, 5, 63; and energy (ch'i), 165–70; and purity, 64, 66, 68, 69, 169; and religious participation, 68–69; Stopping the flow of, 168; as unpurified form of ching 167, 169
Missionaries: in China, 111
Monism, 66–67

Name identity, 58, 175
Neocolonialism, 221, 231, 233–34
Nondualism, 66

Oppression of women: Hinduism,
  31, 34
Ordination of women: Buddhism 21,
  102; Hinduism, 63; Judaism, 179,
  183–85, 194–96
Orientalism, 11–12, 19–20

Patriarchy: as oppression, 14; Bud-
  dhism, 91; changing, 40; China, 150;
  Western Canon written by, 15
Phenomenology, 8, 12–13, 290
Politics and ethics, 296
Polygyny, 126, 127
Polytheism, 66–67
Postmodernism, 10
Power, 13, 22, 288; in Hindu tradition,
  25, 27; through devotion, 66;
  through submission, 25, 68; vs
  equality, 32
Pregnancy, 96, 155, 156, 163, 266, 267
Prostitution, 61, 128
Psychoanalysis, Postmodern, 11, 17
Public realm: Women in Hindu tradi-
  tion, 36

Qisas and Diyat ordinance, 252

Reform, 14
Reinterpretation of the fall story, 216,
  258–59
Relativism vs. critical assessment,
  285–90
Religion: as means of exploitation, 129;
  sanctioning gender inequality, 57
Remarriage, 28, 61, 125–26, 132, 133,
  135, 266–67
Repressive female ideals, 42
Revolution vs. reform, 293–96

Romanticism, 7, 12; and Christian
  Love, 7; and science, 8; Feminist critique, 12

Scholarship: Contemporary Buddhist,
  82; Western, 19, 82, 151; on Chinese
  women, 111; vs. Advocacy, 288–90;
  vs. Dialogue, 290–93
Self as concept, 221
Self-realization, 25, 48
Semen as unpurified form of _ching,_ 167
Sexuality: Revalorization, 105
Shamanism, 238
Silence, 299
Sinology, 4, 111–12, 291
Sisterhood, 160, 193, 198, 199
Socialism: Western, 15
Spiritual discipline, 106
Stereotypes, 20, 97; Chinese, 20; Chi-
  nese women, 111–12
Superwoman phenomena, 195

Taoism, 5, 18–19, 148–76; Canon,
  149; Celibacy vs family life, 157;
  Construction and deconstruction of
  gender, 172–76; Family values,
  157–58; Feminist diversity in, 149;
  Gender complementarity, 163, 171;
  Gender equality 149, 158–59; Gender equality in religious participation, 152–53; Gender inequality,
  160; Individual transformation, 176;
  Material possessions, 157; Monasticism, 157; Motherhood 156, 160;
  Notable female figures, 152; Origins
  of, 150; Prepatriarchal, 149;
  Recognition of women's historical
  achievements, 154–55; Redefinition
  of social roles, 155–56; Scriptures,
  150; Sexual desire, 168; Spiritual
  goal, 149; Tao, 159, 161–63, 164;
  Traditional female qualities, 155;
  Women's internal alchemy, 153;
  Women's moral decisions, 160;

Women writers, 150; *Yin and Yang* complementarity, 171–72
Theism, 66
Theological model, 41
Tokenism, 82

Union with God, 39, 42–43

Veiling, 68

Western: Canon, 16; colonialism, 231; control of global resources, 230; influence/sense of superiority, 11, 111; misrepresentation of others, 281; romantization of African culture, 233; subjectivity, 110, 233, 281, 287; stereotypes of China, 110
Widowhood: Christianity, 215; Confucianism, 124–26, 132, 133; Hindu tradition, 28, 36, 57–61
Widow's Home, 59

Womanism, 17, 30, 221
Women: Ascetics, 46, 151; Agents of oppression, 31, 34; As their own agents, 40, 47; Financial 48; Women as witnesses in Jewish law, 184; Composers, 47–48, 63; Diversity, 161; Empowering women, 29–30, 32, 34; Feminizing men/society, 93; In Chinese folk stories, 153; In public/private realm, 2, 5, 20, 62; Unnurtured nurturers, 93; Patrons, 48–49; Performing arts, 49; Physicians, 61, 128; Refusal of traditional roles, 38; Scholars, 127, 150; Stereotypes, 28; Theological models, 41; Venerating God, 38–42
Women of Reform Judaism (WRJ), 198
Women's Studies, 2
Women's rights: activism in India, 15
World Council of Churches, 9
World religions, 1, 2
Writing the female self, 16